D0025171

THE MODERN CORPORATION
AND PRIVATE PROPERTY

2249 0666\ 6509140　　HD
2795
.B47
1991

THE MODERN CORPORATION
AND PRIVATE PROPERTY

Adolf A. Berle and Gardiner C. Means

With a New Introduction by
Murray L. Weidenbaum and Mark Jensen

DISCARDED

Transaction Publishers
New Brunswick (U.S.A.) and London (U.K.)

JAN 1 5 2008

NORMANDALE COMMUNITY COLLEGE
LIBRARY
9700 FRANCE AVENUE SOUTH
BLOOMINGTON, MN 55431-4399

Ninth printing 2007

New material this edition copyright © 1991 by Transaction Publishers, New Brunswick, New Jersey. Originally published in 1932 by Harcourt, Brace & World, Inc. Copyright © 1968 by Adolf A. Berle.

All rights reserved under International and Pan-American Copyright Conventions. No part of this book may be reproduced or transmitted in any form or by any means, electronic or mechanical, including photocopy, recording, or any information storage and retrieval system, without prior permission in writing from the publisher. All inquiries should be addressed to Transaction Publishers, Rutgers—The State University, 35 Berrue Circle, Piscataway, New Jersey 08854-8042.

This book is printed on acid-free paper that meets the American National Standard for Permanence of Paper for Printed Library Materials.

Library of Congress Catalog Number: 90-48752
ISBN: 0-88738-887-6
ISBN: 978-0-88738-887-3
Printed in the United States of America

Library of Congress Cataloging-in-Publication Data

Berle, Adolf Augustus, 1895-1971.
    The modern corporation and private property / Adolf A. Berle and Gardiner C. Means; with a new introduction by Murray L. Weidenbaum and Mark Jensen.
        p. cm.
    "Originally published in 1968."
    Includes index.
    ISBN 0-88738-887-6
    1. Corporations—United States. 2. Corporation law—United States.
3. Corporate governance—United States. I. Means, Gardiner Coit, 1896-.
II. Title

HD2795.B53   1991
338.7'4'0973—dc20   90-48752
                                                                        CIP

CONTENTS

Tables and Charts, vii
Introduction to the Transaction Edition, ix
Property, Production and Revolution
　A Preface to the Revised Edition
　by Adolf A. Berle, xix
Implications of the Corporate
Revolution in Economic Theory
　by Gardiner C. Means, xli
Preface (1932), li

BOOK I *Property in Flux: Separation of the attributes*
of ownership under the corporate system

I:	PROPERTY IN TRANSITION	3
II:	THE APPEARANCE OF THE CORPORATE SYSTEM	11
III:	THE CONCENTRATION OF ECONOMIC POWER	18
IV:	THE DISPERSION OF STOCK OWNERSHIP	47
V:	THE EVOLUTION OF CONTROL	66
VI:	THE DIVERGENCE OF INTEREST BETWEEN OWNERSHIP AND CONTROL	112

BOOK II *Regrouping of Rights: Relative legal*
position of ownership and "control"

I:	EVOLUTION OF THE MODERN CORPORATE STRUCTURE	119
II:	POWER OVER PARTICIPATIONS ACCRUING TO SHARES OF STOCK	141
III:	POWERS OVER THE ROUTING OF EARNINGS AS BETWEEN SHARES OF STOCK	171
IV:	POWER TO ALTER THE ORIGINAL CONTRACT RIGHTS OF SECURITY HOLDERS	186

v

V: THE LEGAL POSITION OF MANAGEMENT   *196*

VI: THE LEGAL POSITION OF "CONTROL"   *207*

VII: CORPORATE POWERS AS POWERS IN TRUST   *219*

VIII: THE RESULTANT POSITION OF THE STOCKHOLDER   *244*

BOOK III   *Property in the Stock Markets: Security exchanges as appraisers and liquidators*

I: THE FUNCTION OF THE PUBLIC MARKET   *255*

II: FLOTATION AND BANKERS' DISCLOSURE   *264*

III: DISCLOSURE BY THE CORPORATION TO THE MARKET   *278*

IV: MANAGEMENT IN THE MARKET   *286*

BOOK IV   *Reorientation of Enterprise: Effects of the corporate system on fundamental economic concepts*

I: THE TRADITIONAL LOGIC OF PROPERTY   *293*

II: THE TRADITIONAL LOGIC OF PROFITS   *299*

III: THE INADEQUACY OF TRADITIONAL THEORY   *303*

IV: THE NEW CONCEPT OF THE CORPORATION   *309*

Appendixes, 317
Statistical Appendix to Revised Edition
    by Gardiner C. Means, 343
Table of Cases, 363
Table of Companies, 367
Index, 375

TABLES AND CHARTS

TABLE I: *The 200 Largest Non-banking Corporations in the United States, Jan. 1, 1930*   *20*

TABLE II: *Gross Assets of 150 Identical Corporations Common to Both 1919 and 1928 List of 200 Largest American Corporations*   *35*

TABLE III: *Comparison of Growth of Large Corporations with Growth of All Corporations*   *36*

TABLE IV: *Growth of Large Corporations as Indicated by Relation of Their Statutory Net Income to That of All Corporations*   *39*

TABLE V: *144 Out of 200 Largest Companies Distributed According to Number of Stockholders*   *49*

TABLE VI: *Stockholdings by Management*   *50*

TABLE VII: *Stockholders of the Three Largest American Corporations*   *52*

TABLE VIII: *Estimated Number of Book Stockholders of American Corporations (1900–1928)*   *56*

TABLE IX: *Estimate of the Number of Book Stockholders of American Corporations in 1922 by Industries*   *57*

TABLE X: *20 Largest Stockholders of the Pennsylvania Railroad Co. (as of Dec. 31, 1929)*   *79*

TABLE XI: *United States Steel Corporation, Stockholdings of Board of Directors*   *81*

TABLE XII: *Control of the 200 Largest Corporations*   *86*

TABLE XIII: *Summary According to Type of Ultimate Control of 200 Largest Corporations*   *106*

TABLE XIV: *Summary According to Type of Immediate Control of the 200 Largest Corporations*   *107*

CHART I: *Rate of Growth in Number of Book Stockholders*   *55*

CHART II: *Distribution in Ownership of Corporate Stocks*   *61*

CHART III: *Major Elements in the Control of the Van Sweringen System of Railroads*   *70*

Statistical Appendix

TABLE I: *The 100 Largest Manufacturing Corporations in 1962 Measured by Size of Assets*   *347*

TABLE II: *Adjusted Assets of the 100 Largest Manufacturing Corporations in 1962 and the Assets of All Manufacturing Corporations*   *351*

TABLE III: *Manufacturing Concentration in 1929*   *353*

TABLE IV: *Comparison of Total Assets Held by the 100 Largest Manufacturing Corporations with Assets Held by All Manufacturing Corporations and All Manufacturing Enterprise*   *354*

TABLE V: *Change in Concentration 1950–1965 Derived from Statistics of Income*   *356*

TABLE VI: *The 200 Largest Non-financial Corporations Classified by Type of Ultimate Control, 1929 and 1963*   *358*

CHART I: *Share of Value Added by Manufacture Accounted for by 200 Largest Manufacturing Companies, 1947–1963*   *354*

INTRODUCTION TO THE
TRANSACTION EDITION

Berle and Means' monumental work on the corporation has become one of those enduring classics that many cite but few read. As would be expected, a current rereading reveals that much of the book has become a period piece. In part, its success has been its undoing. The initial reaction to its publication led a generation of researchers to answer questions raised in the book. Consequently, much of the field of study focusing on the corporate system has moved beyond the point at which lawyer Adolf Berle and economist Gardiner Means wrote about it.

Also, the economy has evolved. Who, writing in the depth of the Great Depression of the 1930s, would have anticipated the double-digit inflation of the late 1970s? Nevertheless, this classic raises many of the fundamental questions that still beset those concerned both with the role of business in society and the governing power of the large corporation. In fact, the book is so rich with insights and thought-provoking analysis that, in this introductory essay, we can do little more than whet the reader's appetite, while simultaneously warning about the host of legal and statistical detail which is now mainly of historical interest.

The role of the corporation

The most enduring theme of *The Modern Corporation and Private Property* is the divorce of ownership from the control of the modern corporation. It is the view of the authors that, as a practical matter, stockholders have traded their legal position of private ownership for the role of recipient of capital returns (Book I, Chapter I). In addition, a close parallel is drawn between workers who surrender the direction over their labor and shareholders who become merely recipients of "the wages of capital."

Without using the term, Berle and Means show a keen awareness of the concern of modern "agency" theory: the interests of the directors and managers can diverge from those of the owners of the firm, and they often do so. This separation between ownership and control of a corporation through expanded ownership of the company creates what Berle and Means call the quasi-public corporation. The characteristics found in a quasi-public corporation are its tremendous size and its reliance on the public market for capital.

In Book I, Chapter II, Berle and Means predict, on the basis of historical experience, that "practically all" economic activity will be carried on under this quasi-public corporate form. That forecast has suffered from the rapid rise of the service sector of the economy. There, individual proprietorships and partnerships remain widely used methods of organizing business activity, and dependence on organized capital markets is far less than in the case of the large corporation.

Nevertheless, Berle and Means are closer to the mark than the more recent and widely circulated projection in the late 1970s by Michael Jensen and William Meckling, that "The corporate form of organization is likely to disappear completely . . . . the larger corporations as we know them are destined to be destroyed."

Given the effective separation of ownership from management, Berle and Means noted the likely characteristic increase in the size of the modern corporation and the concentration of the economy. However, two more recent developments should be kept in mind. As the authors properly perceived in Book I, Chapter III, mergers and acquisitions are an important method of increasing corporate size. However, changes in corporate control can also lead to reducing the size of the company. An example during the 1980s was the split up of Beatrice Foods into a variety of smaller companies, which occurred in connection with that $12 billion giant corporation going "private."

Table 1

Mergers and Acquisitions Over $1 Billion, 1982-1989

Year	Number of Deals	Value ($ millions)
1982	10	$19,440.3
1983	6	9,110.5
1984	19	55,178.5
1985	26	61,458.6
1986	31	67,932.4
1987	30	62,175.9
1988	42	96,399.4
1989	35	117,477.4

Source: Computed from *Mergers and Acquisitions*, various issues.

A more basic criticism of the Berle and Means approach is that mergers among existing firms do not necessarily mean that the economy is becoming more "concentrated." In the dynamic industrial society that characterizes the

United States, the rise of new companies overshadows the decline of the old. Thus, Berle and Means could accurately bemoan the demise of forty-nine of the largest 200 corporations within one decade. Yet, we can celebrate the fortunes of many of today's giants that are not on their list–IBM, Philip Morris, Boeing, United Technologies, Dow Chemical, Xerox, Pepsico, Digital Equipment, Hewlett Packard, Sara Lee, Conagra, Unisys, Lockheed, Motorola, Monsanto, TRW, and Textron. Even Berle and Means would have to admit that this is an impressive array of "newcomers."

Mergers and acquisitions continue to be an important force in maintaining a dynamic economy. In 1989 alone, thirty-five giant mergers occurred with an aggregate value of over $117 billion (see Table 1). At times, changes in control, or even threats of hostile takeovers, may serve to increase the efficiency and profitability of individual firms.

The management of the corporation

Berle and Means made a fundamental contribution in their analysis of the extent to which management of the modern corporation has been separated from its ownership. But they may have gone overboard in stating that the power and control has shifted away from the common stockholders (Book I, Chapter IV). Berle and Means state that this separation has totally eliminated the checks and balances that owners once exercised over management. With this undaunted power, management supposedly pursues its own interest, oblivious to the welfare of the owners. A contrary view has been developed in more recent years. According to Harold Demsetz, "In a world in which self-interest plays a significant role in economic behavior, it is foolish to believe that owners of valuable resources systematically relinquish control to managers who are not guided to serve their interest."

As the reader might suspect, neither polar alternative accurately describes the complex reality of the world of corporate decision making. Top managements do possess significant discretion over the use of corporate resources. Merely consider the ability of the CEO of a major company to satisfy his whim in terms of the selection of charities and pet causes that the organization will support. However, shareholders are not left powerless. Ample evidence is furnished by the proxy fights and takeover battles between different groups of owners grappling for control that, on occasion, brighten the financial pages of the daily newspapers. Clearly, the power of management is far from the absolute position that Berle and Means forecast.

A fundamental development not foretold in *The Modern Corporation and Private Property* is the use by institutional investors of the latent powers they possess. Although Berle and Means were aware of the role of pension funds and insurance companies, they did not foresee either the growing importance of these investors or their desire to participate in corporate decision making.

According to a Columbia Law School Institutional Investor Project, the top twenty pension funds in 1989 owned 10.6 percent of General Motors common stock and 9.1 percent of IBM. In addition, institutions owned at least one-half of the stock of twenty-seven of the top fifty U.S. corporations and at least one-third of forty-seven of the top fifty.

Peter Drucker has referred to this phenomenon as "pension fund socialism." The term may have been more prescient than he anticipated. The most activist role has been those of government pension funds. Thirteen of the top twenty pension funds are controlled by state or local governments. The top five state pension funds–three from New York and two from California–control $202 billion, or roughly 8 percent of total pension fund assets of $2.5 trillion.

By forming a Council of Institutional Investors, a group of managers of large state pension funds have created a mechanism whereby a small number of large shareholders (or rather their agents) can work together. In a few recent cases, some of the largest institutional investors, notably state government employee pension funds, have entered into specific takeover battles. In the case of the attempt in 1990 to take over Lockheed, several large institutional investors supported the management slate after gaining assurance that in the future they could name three members of the board of directors.

In a broader sense, the increased activism of institutional investors is a response to the authors' concern about the euthanasia of the shareholder.

The "control" of the corporation

Berle and Means vaguely define the concept of "the control" of the corporation. They refer to a subgroup of the stockholders who have the actual power of selecting the board of directors through any of the following ways: (1) complete ownership of common stock, (2) majority control, (3) legal devices, (4) minority control, and (5) management control. The authors note in Book I, Chapters V and VI, that the interests of those in "control" differ from the profit–maximizing desires of the other owners and, as these interests move further apart, "the control" will ultimately lie in the hands of the management. Berle and Means provide an early and earthy statement of the agency problem: those who control the corporation, even if they own a large block of stock, "can serve their own pockets better by profiting at the expense of the company than by making profits for it." This raises a serious question about the incentives for managers of the modern corporation to conduct business in accordance with the welfare of the owners.

Boards of directors have responded to these concerns in a variety of ways. Granting key executives options to purchase the stock at some fixed price above the current market value provides them with a powerful incentive to maximize share performance. Bonuses in the form of stock ensure that the recipients, at least to some degree, will start to think like shareholders. Predictably, however, corporate activists (corporate critics would be a more accurate phrase) oppose these methods of compensation whenever the issue is presented at a corporate annual meeting. Yet, shareholder approval is overwhelming in virtually all cases.

Nevertheless, many serious analysts of the corporation contend that the normal incentives previously described are not sufficient. They write favorably about "leveraged buyouts" and "going private," methods of increasing the ownership position of management by an order of magnitude. If these types of responses to the fundamental issues raised by Berle and Means became more widespread, they would make the corporation a less attractive place for many private investors who have no interest in "controlling" the affairs of the company whose stock–or bonds–they buy.

The position of the shareholder

Berle and means bemoan the changed, more passive, role of the shareholder of the modern corporation. They note the extent to which the bondholder is superior, being guaranteed a fixed return on the funds invested in the corporation. In contrast, the stockholder is in a less desirable position, not knowing whether there will be any return at all on the investment (Book II, Chapters VI-VIII).

This portion of the book may have weathered least well. At the present time, we hear so often of the bondholders who have suffered an erosion of the market value of the principal because the managers have so highly leveraged the firm. Typically, this has been done by issuing high yielding but very risky "junk bonds."

Even in more stable corporate relationships, stockholders can receive benefits not available to bondholders, notably participating in the growth of the firm. Writing in the Great Depression, Berle and Means could not envision the rapid inflation of the post-World War II period, when stocks became a major hedge against the erosion of real value. At the same time, bondholders often experienced serious declines in the market value of their portfolios, even when the nominal value of their assets and income streams remained unimpaired.

Stock exchanges and stock markets

Berle and Means considered the listing of corporate shares on a stock exchange and the resultant open market for these securities as essential to, and as a product of, the rise of the modern corporation. In their view, dispensed shareholders have exchanged control for liquidity.

The authors discuss the many possible mechanisms that the directors possess in affecting the asset value of the stock or the distribution of company earnings (Book II, Chapters II and III). Based on the imperfections of normal judicial protection of shareholder rights, *The Modern Corporation and Private Property* presents the case for substantial regulation of security markets (Book II).

As we have seen in the more than half century since its publication, such protection can be exercised by both private sector and public sector institutions. Thus, the private New York Stock Exchange (NYSE) determines many "rules of the game," and, according to the authors, makes "slow but steady progress" in ensuring the availability of securities at their market value to all potential investors. Furthermore, it is the NYSE that requires all listed companies to set up audit committees staffed entirely by outside directors. Simultaneously, the U.S. Securities and Exchange Commission plays the role of "cop on the beat," to ensure an adequate flow of information to the prospective purchasers and current owners of corporate shares.

The prescience of the authors is especially evident in Book III, Chapter III, where they describe the problem of insider information. They state that the legal system can only choose randomly of the many unethical acts committed in securities markets and occasionally settle on one special case on which to act upon. However, Berle and Means reach a conclusion more optimistic than experience to date can justify: "As the standards of disclosure of corporate affairs become more exacting, the problem of the directors and managers in the market will become increasingly less important."

Without defending the unethical practices of such slick operators as Ivan Boesky, the fact is that in 1990 no legal definition of insider trading exists to guide the honest market participant who wants to obey the law. Instead, legal advisers can only provide examples of the kinds of behavior that have resulted in government prosecution and those that have not.

Corporation responsibility

For whose benefit does the corporation operate? Book IV, Chapter I, raises this fundamental issue. The traditional legal answer is that the corporation is conducted for the benefit of the owners. Berle and Means view corporate responsibility to shareholders in the sense of "equitable control" where managers, having obtained power from the dispersed group of stockholders, act in the best interest of the owners of the firm. The authors then question this by analyzing the profit incentive to the executives. According to the authors, executives have such an "insignificant" fraction of traditional property rights that the incentive of profits is not strong enough to insure that they will make effective use of corporate property.

The large degree of managerial discretion over corporate resources is borne out by a variety of case studies. Researchers at the Harvard Business School reported that none of the top executives of twelve successful American companies was very concerned about the market value of the company's stock. One chief executive stated this position very forcefully:

> The highest priority with me is perpetuation of the enterprise. I'd like to leave this joint in better shape than when someone passed me the baton. I have to take care of the shareholders in this, but I don't sweat the shareholders too much.

Over the years, a far broader definition of the responsibility, some call it the social responsibility of the corporation, has developed. In an influential and widely cited report on the subject, the Committee for Economic Development (CED) describes the professional manager as a "trustee" balancing the interests of many diverse participants and constituents in the enterprise, including customers, employees, suppliers, and the community. Shareholders are listed only as one among those worthy groups–and they are listed last.

It turns out that the CED statement is not too different from the description provided in *The Modern Corporation and Private Property*: "New responsibilities towards the owners, the workers, the consumers, and the State thus rests upon the shoulders of those in control."

Berle and Means contended that the divorce of ownership from management destroyed the traditional belief that profit maximization will drive the corporation to most efficiently use its assets (Book IV, Chapter II). In good measure, the wave of hostile takeovers in the late 1980s was a response to managers who paid insufficient attention to the concerns of the shareholders. Too many chief executives focused on the theater and opera as the epitome of a corporation's responsibility to society. They seemed to forget that a business is an economic institution, designed to provide goods and services for consumers in order to benefit the stockholders.

Berle and Means forecast that, as the size of the corporation and the number of holders of its stock grew, a point would be reached where "the control" would be held by a self-perpetuating board of directors. Since the judicial process (along with the authors' understanding) is unable to deal with intricacies and vagaries of corporate "control," the authors saw no way that laws would be established to prevent such situations from occurring.

Hence, the fiduciary role of the corporate board of directors (Book II, Chapter V) deserves continuous attention and needs to be updated from the rather simple view held by Berle and Means.

Both in legal theory and business practice, the board is the link between the shareholders who own the enterprise and the executives who manage it. Until the past decade or two, the senior executives of the enterprise often comprised the majority of the typical corporate board, with the firm's attorneys and bankers (commercial and investment) serving as outside directors, together with important customers and political figures in the locality in which the company maintained its headquarters.

In recent years, however, most of the boards of the larger companies consist primarily of outside (non-management) directors, most of whom at least nominally are independent of the management. However, the chief executive (CEO) usually serves as chairman of the board, setting the agenda for meetings and presiding over the deliberations.

Currently, the boards of directors of about 60 percent of the larger corporations have set up nominating committees to propose both candidates for the board and senior officers of the company. These committees usually have a strong majority of outside directors, typically four out of five. However, these statistics do little to illuminate the continuing powerful role of the chief executive in initiating or approving committee selections. In practice, approximately 80 percent of outside directors are chosen by the chairman–chief executive, who usually exercises an effective veto over the other selections.

Under the circumstances, many critics charge that the typical director acts as a rubber stamp, quickly approving the recommendation of the chairman–CEO. Although this charge does not lack substance, reality is far more complicated. Virtually all modern authorities on corporate governance agree that in times of crisis the board, led by the outside directors, exercises its powers, usually to the acclaim of impartial observers. However, short of emergencies, the board is reluctant–and finds it difficult–to override the recommendations of the management.

In their 1989 study of corporate boards, Jay W. Lorsch and Elizabeth MacIver report a widely held view of directions:" . . . to advise the management . . . he can't do much more than that." There are many reasons for that situation, several altogether sensible. The management knows more about the details of the company's operations than the outside directors and there is a natural tendency to defer to the inside directors. More fundamentally, a committee can set policy but it cannot run an organization, only one leader can. Hence, a wise board does not attempt to compete with the chairman–CEO, but views its role as primarily providing advice and counsel.

All that is correct. Nevertheless, there are occasions when the board should turn down the proposals by the management because the interests of the shareholders dictate such action. Examples include a recommended acquisition that would unduly dilute the value of the stockholders' investment, or a request by a strong division chief for a capital investment that would not likely yield a return adequate to cover the cost of capital.

Sadly to report, it is the rare board that, under those circumstances, can say "no." On the positive side, wise CEOs informally review controversial proposals with key outside directors prior to formal presentation to the board. Thus, they avoid situations where they force their boards to turn them down on important matters. Too frequently, however, the CEO–chairman simply dominates the board's decision making, even though independent outside directors constitute a clear majority.

In Book IV, Chapter III, the authors return to analyzing the role of and the motivating influence on the professional manager. In more recent years, clear evidence has been developed on the motivations that comprise the driving force of modern corporations. Corporate managers are not fundamentally different from other individuals nor do they differ from those of the past. Self-interest does and should be expected to dominate their decision making.

The same factors that encourage managers to be generous to themselves in allocating corporate resources can also be the driving force behind corporate acquisitions. After all, acquisitions do increase the amount of corporate resources in the winning management's span of control. Studies by the Conference Board confirm with telling statistics what most people instinctively know: top executives in larger companies are paid more than their counterparts in smaller firms. Size of firm is the most compelling factor.

To be sure, profitability and other factors help to determine management pay and fringe benefits. But, on average, the chief executive of a $10 billion company gets paid much more than the head of a firm whose yearly sales are only $5 billion. In plain English, the bigger the company, the larger the rewards to top management. The intangible management benefits from controlling large enterprise also are substantial. Being on the cover of *Fortune* or *Business* Week is a heady experience.

The future of the corporation

Berle and Means wrote that the corporation as an institution may become not only an equal to the state, but even supersede it as the dominant social organization (Book IV, Chapter IV). From an economic viewpoint, they are correct. The privately owned corporation is the prevailing form of organizing the production and distribution of goods and services in the

United States, and in other capitalist nations as well. The corporation is likely to continue playing this role for the indefinite future because, as the late Neil Jacoby stated, "There is simply no promising alternative way of organizing and carrying out most of the tasks of production."

Moreover, the rise of political action committees with large budgets for political contributions has given many corporations direct access to powerful governmental decision makers. Also, the lack of geographic limits to the exercise of corporate power, a characteristic noted in passing by Berle and Means, has given rise to the multinational enterprise. Yet the contrast between government and business powers remains striking. The largest company cannot tax us; the smallest unit of government can. The most profitable corporation cannot throw us in jail; the smallest municipality can.

A half century later, what can we say about Berle and Means' *The Modern Corporation and Private Property?* Despite its many specific shortcomings, the book remains a useful introduction to the internal organization of the corporation in modern society. The analysis by this unique combination of lawyer and economist is still relevant to exploring the relationships between the owners of the firm and its managers.

To extend an old phrase, many of the answers provided by this book have been superseded by more recent events, but the questions raised continue to be worthy of the attention of scholar and practitioner alike.

Murray L. Weidenbaum
Mark Jensen

PROPERTY, PRODUCTION AND

REVOLUTION

A Preface to the Revised Edition

THIRTY-SIX YEARS after its first publication, there is here presented a revised edition of *The Modern Corporation and Private Property*. Because it was causative both in development of legal and economic theory and in policies and measures of the United States government, including laws creating the Securities and Exchange Commission, the original text is reproduced. It is a document in the history of the past generation.

To it is added my preface reviewing some of the developments forecast in the first edition; also added is Dr. Means' summary of contrast of corporate concentration as it appeared when we first plotted it, and as it appears in 1968. I am indebted to the *Columbia Law Review* for permission to reprint in my own prefatory statement material first appearing in that review.

No attempt is here made to describe the development of economic theory, or list the great number of books and articles based on or carrying forward the conceptions set out in the first edition. Enough to say that their impetus is far from spent. Institutions such as the modern corporation have not only affected economic life; their study has demanded place in (if they have not recast) a good deal of economic and political theory.

More than thirty years ago, in the preface of this book, I wrote:

The translation of perhaps two-thirds of the industrial wealth of the country from individual ownership to ownership by the large, publicly financed corporations vitally changes the lives of property owners, the lives of workers, and the methods of property tenure. The divorce of ownership from control consequent on that process almost necessarily involves a new form of economic organization of society.

Dr. Means and I had pointed out that the two attributes of ownership—risking collective wealth in profit-seeking enterprise and ultimate management of responsibility for that enterprise—had become divorced. Accordingly we raised the questions:

> Must we not, therefore, recognize that we are no longer dealing with property in the old sense? Does the traditional logic of property still apply? Because an owner who also exercises control over his wealth is protected in the full receipt of the advantages derived from it, must it *necessarily* follow that an owner who has surrendered control of his wealth should likewise be protected to the full? May not this surrender have so essentially changed his relation to his wealth as to have changed the logic applicable to his interest in that wealth? An answer to this question cannot be found in the law itself. It must be sought in the economic and social background of law.

We based these questions on the growing dominance of the corporate form, the increasing decision-making power of corporate management, the increasingly passive position of shareholders, and the increasing inapplicability of the ethical and economic justifications given (rightly enough at the time) by classic economics.

The object of this preface to the revised edition is to review some aspects of this conception in the light of a generation of experience and consequent developments.

I. The continuing current of change to "Collective Capitalism"

Factually, the trend toward dominance of that collective capitalism we call the "corporate system" has continued unabated. Evolution of the corporation has made stock-and-security ownership the dominant form by which individuals own wealth representing property devoted to production (as contrasted with property devoted to consumption). The last great bastion of individually owned productive property—agriculture—has been dramatically declining in proportion to the total production of the United States, and even in agriculture, corporations have been steadily making inroads. Outside of agriculture, well over 90 per cent of all the production in the country is carried on by more than a million corporations. In all of them, management is theoretically distinct from ownership. The directors of the corporation are not the "owners"; they are not agents of the stockholders and are not obliged to follow their instructions. This in itself is not determinative. Numerically most of the million corporations are "close"—the stockholders are also the directors or are so related to them that the decision-making power rests with the stockholders. Quantitatively, however, a thousand or so very large corporations whose stockholders' lists run from 10,000 up to 3,200,000, as in the case of American Telephone and Telegraph, account for an overwhelmingly large percentage both of asset-holders and of operations. *Fortune* Magazine tabulated the 500 largest United States industrial corporations and found their combined sales were 245 billion dollars in 1963 or about 62 per cent of all industrial sales. The factor of concentration is, of course, higher in the public-service industries: communications, transportation and public utilities. It is not unfair to suggest that if these industries were included (they are not in the *Fortune* tabulation), 600 or 700 large corporations, whose control nominally is in the hands of their "public" stockholders (actually, of their managers), account for 70 per cent of commercial operation of the country—agriculture aside. There has been a slow but continuing trend toward corporate concentration reckoned by the percentage of industry thus controlled. Actually the total trend is more marked because, in contrast to total economic growth, the proportion of American economic activity represented by individually controlled agriculture has been relatively declining. American economics at present is dominantly, perhaps overwhelmingly, industrial.

The effect of this change upon the property system of the United States has been dramatic. Individually owned wealth has enormously increased. It is today reckoned at more than 1,800 billion dollars. Of more importance is the distribution of that figure. Relatively little of it is "productive" property—land or things employed by its owners in production or commerce—though figures are hazy at the edges. The largest item of individually owned wealth, exclusive of productive assets, is described as "owner-occupied homes" (approximately 520 billion dollars). These, of course, are primarily for consumption, though a fraction of them are probably farmsteads. The next largest item—consumer durables—accounts for 210 billion dollars more; these are chiefly automobiles and home equipment, again chiefly used for personal convenience and not for capital or productive purposes.

The property system as applied to productive assets breaks down (as of the end of 1963) as follows: 525 billion dollars of shares of corporate stock; 210 billion dollars in fixed income financial assets (federal, state and local government securities, corporate and foreign bonds, life insurance values, etc.); and 360 billion dollars in liquid assets, chiefly cash in banks. These figures mean that, far and away, the largest item of personally owned "property" representing productive assets and enterprise is in the form of stock of corporations. In addition, a substantial amount of other assets held by individuals consists of claims against intermediate financial institutions—banks, insurance companies and the like, whose holdings include large amounts of corporation stocks, bonds and securities. "Individually owned" enterprise is thus steadily disappearing. Increasingly, the American owns his home, his car, and his household appliances; these are for his consumption. Simultaneously, he increasingly owns stocks, life insurance, and rights in pension funds, social security funds and similar arrangements. And he has a job, paying him a wage, salary or commission.

Comparable figures do not run back to 1932; no one prior to Franklin D. Roosevelt had been vividly interested in developing a first-rate system of social statistics. My own crude figures, worked out in 1934 at the Columbia Law School in a little-noted volume, *Liquid Claims and National Wealth,* showed that the total of all domestic stocks and bonds reached a peak of 100.7 billion dollars in 1929—to which must be added 54 billion dollars of net liquid claims (chiefly bank balances), and 12.6 billion dollars of life insurance values; but there was no division between individually owned and corporate-owned wealth at that time. My co-author, V. E. Pederson, and I estimated that in a single decade (1922–1932) more than one-sixth of the entire national wealth had shifted from individual hands into managerial—that is, corporate—hands, and we suggested that at that rate forty years would see the wealth of the entire country split, most of it being operated by corporate management, though its "ownership" would be represented by individual "holdings" of stocks, bonds, and other liquid claims.

Based on the figures to date, that development has gone far toward accomplishment. In crude summation, most "owners" own stock, insurance savings and pension claims and the like, and do not manage; most managers (corporate administrators) do not own. The corporate collective holds legal title to the tangible productive wealth of the country—for the benefit of others.

The word "revolutionary" has been justifiably applied to less fundamental change. The United States is no longer anticipating a development. It is digesting a fact.

II. *The emerging conception of property*

Lawyers are accustomed to conceive of property in terms of ancient classification. If tangible, it was "real"—that is, land or rights derived from land; or it was "personal"—mobile, capable of being used, taken away, moved, transferred and so forth by its owners. If intangible, it was a "chose in action"—a claim on or against other individuals or entities capable of being enforced or protected in the courts. Some of this was "negotiable," passing under the law-merchant or adaptations thereof. The *proprietas* (the relation of the individual or owner to this property—real, personal or claims) was assumed to be fixed.

There is no occasion to change these classic definitions. They do quite well for the purposes of defining rights, methods of transfer, handling intervening claims, and the myriad minor problems of transmission and adjustment. What has changed is the conception of *proprietas*. I here suggest that a new classification has been superimposed on the old theory.

My thesis is that "property" is now divided into two categories: (a) consumption property on the one hand and (b) productive property on the other—property devoted to production, manufacture, service or commerce, and designed to offer, for a price, goods or services to the public from which a holder expects to derive a return.

In respect of productive property, the *proprietas* has now been made subject to an over-all, political determination as to the kind of civilization the American state in its democratic processes has decided it wants. This is an on-going process, not yet complete.

As a corollary, productive property has been divided into two layers: (1) that fraction which, though not managed by active owners, is administered to yield a return by way of interest, dividends or distribution of profit, and (2) that layer dominated and controlled by the representatives or delegates of the passive owners, whose decisions are now subject to the political process just noted. In this category, social development is at present intense and likely to continue.

This essay does not deal with forces present and emerging that now bear on or will later affect consumptive property. Unquestionably these exist. As population, urbanization and congestion steadily increase, one man's consumptive use may become another man's privation. Enjoyment of consumptive property may depend upon facilities as well as regulations provided by the state. Thus automobiles require both roads and traffic rules; suburban homes can become untenantable unless land-use control is provided by the community; and the right to sell or transfer may be restricted by antidiscrimination laws.

In general, however, the impact of modern and economic evolution seems to be an expansion of a very old common-law maxim: Use your own property so as not to injure others. The essential aim is to preserve the greatest available degree of consumption and choice as empty land fills up, roads become congested, and the capacity to invade others' lives by esthetic horrors is enlarged by technique. American law and law schools have, happily, developed a growing number of scholars and experts in this field. Let us confine (the word is scarcely apt) ourselves to the impact of economic and social evolution on *productive* property in its two aspects: (1) managerial-productive (management) and (2) passive-receptive (stock and security ownership).

III. The changing content of property °

We must note an enormous expansion of the scope of the term "property" in this connection. Not only is it divorced from the decision-making power of its supposedly beneficial holders (stockholders and their various removes), but it has come to encompass a set of conceptions superimposed upon the central reality of domination over tangible things. Businessmen describe an enterprise, great or small, as "the property." They do not mean merely the physical plant. They include access to all the facilities necessary to produce, transport, distribute and sell. They mean an entire organization of personnel without which the physical plant would be junk; they mean a hierarchy of executives, technical experts, sales managers and men; as well as the dealer organization and the labor-relations habits. These relationships are increasingly protected, not merely by the law of contract, but by an increasing body of law imposing upon individuals a measure of loyalty to the central enterprise. For example, they may not acquire and sell to others, as part of their personal capacity or equipment, confidential technical information, data on sales, or customer good will. Underlying this extension of the property concept to management relationships is recognition of the fact that the "capital" has been projected far into the realm of intangibles. The central enterprise is spending good money—often in immense amounts—building this organization,

---

° The rapid increase in technical development necessarily downgrades the position of physical or tangible things and upgrades the factors of organization and technical knowledge. Organization is not reducible to a formula. Technical knowledge is rarely if ever assignable to any single individual, group of individuals or corporation. It is part of the heritage of the country and of the race. In neither case do the traditional formulae applicable to common-law property fit the current fact.

this technical information, these relationships; it is entitled to be protected against their appropriation by individuals.

A counterforce registers the impact of this extension. Literally enormous quantities of technical information have been accumulated by government and thrust into fields of non-statist enterprise. Resources of nuclear energy and nuclear physics are the most dramatic—but by no means the only or even perhaps the most significant—of these intrusions. Nearly two-thirds of all technical research is now financed by the federal government. Through a great number of modern industries—one thinks at once of electronics, of aviation, and of space-satellite communication—this government-financed technique enters the process of corporate explosion. By no stretch of imagination can it be described as property primarily created by private enterprise. Like it or not, these assets are social and statist in origin. Complete turnover of these assets to "private" (that is, non-statist) ownership seems wholly unlikely. Illustration of the impact—and of a compromise —is found in the Communications Satellite Act authorizing creation of ComSat, a corporation owned one-half by the federal government and one-half by private investors. The proportion of investment by current communications enterprises such as A.T.&T. was severely limited, despite the fact that the primary function of the new facilities to be provided in outer space was to offer A.T.&T. and like corporations new avenues of communication.

Earlier discovery that electromagnetic energy could be used for radio and later television resulted in an odd and undetermined new form of property. It took the form of short-term exclusive licenses, granted by the Federal Communications Commission, to use specific wave lengths. These were granted to private companies but rapidly ripened into an uncodified but thoroughly recognized expectancy (if not right) that the licensee companies, through renewal of their licenses, would continue to enjoy the wave-length frequencies assigned them. Temporary licenses, plus expectancy of their renewal, became the basis for dollar-value markets for radio and TV stations, big and little. The statist right thus became engulfed in a "private property" institution. The ComSat debate and the resulting statute sufficiently indicate resistance to this process, and the compromises reached between the state and the non-statist users of the assets developed by the state.

"Property" when used in connection with and as adjunct to legal (that is, corporate) ownership is thus changing its import—not because the old rules relating to ownership of a plant have changed, but because of the addition of an enormous proportion of new content differing both in kind and in origin from the old. The Research Institute of America * in a private report observed:

> A third industrial revolution is in the making, as dramatic as those which followed the harnessing of steam power and the proliferation of electricity. This one will be sired by the release of nuclear and thermonuclear energy, the electronic conversion of energy to work, and the use of cybernetics and computers to free human energy from routine decision-making. By 1980, the industrial world will be as different from today's as today is different from the 19th century.

To project this discussion would take us into the realm of science fiction far beyond the competence of this writer. One observation nevertheless appears warranted. Whatever the fantasy of the science-fiction writers, it will probably be outstripped in both scope and speed by the fact. In the light of what has already been achieved, the Jules Vernes and the H. G. Wellses of yesterday seem like children. Can the science-fiction writers of today expect a better fate?

As technology and its organization for production and use evolve, so will property. The "private," and, still more, individualized, aspects will become increasingly attenuated. Elisha Gray, having developed the embryonic idea of telecommmunication, organized a private company to put it to productive use and asked private investors to join him and risk their capital in the venture. Today's Elisha Gray or Alexander Graham Bell would be a team, working in a great research center, more often than not financed by the federal government. Such techniques as they emerge are "property" of a government that does not need the private investor to supply risk capital—although as a gesture toward old times, it may offer participation, as was done in the ComSat legislation. Plainly we are moving toward a new phase fundamentally more alien to the tradition of profit even than that forecast in *The Modern Corporation and Private Property.*

A shift in attitude toward corporate property arises in part from the changed origin of finance capital. The property of corporations is dedicated to production, not to personal consumption; but, even more significant, that property is no longer the result of individual effort or choice. This change has come silently. Its implications even yet are not understood.

Corporations were originally groups of investors pooling their individual contributions of risk capital to organize and carry on an

* Research Institute of America, *Your Business in the Next 15 Years,* June 30, 1964.

enterprise. Since they had saved their earnings or gains and had risked them in the undertaking, they were assimilated to the owner of land, who cleared and cultivated it, and sold its products. As the economics of the time went, this was justifiable. They had sacrificed, risked and, to some extent, worked at the development of the product. Presumably they had done something useful for the community, since it was prepared to pay for the product.

A mature corporation typically does not call for investor-supplied capital. It charges a price for its products from which it can pay taxation, costs, depreciation allowances, and can realize a profit over and above all these expenses. Of this profit item, approximately half goes as income taxes to the federal government, and 60 per cent of the remaining half is distributed to its shareholders. It accumulates for capital purposes the undistributed 40 per cent and its depreciation charges. This is a phenomenon not of "investment," but of market power. Since corporations legally have perpetual life, this process can continue indefinitely. The result has been that more than 60 per cent of capital entering a particular industry is "internally generated" or, more accurately, "price-generated" because it is collected from the customers. Another 20 per cent of the capital the corporation uses is borrowed from banks chiefly in anticipation of this accumulative process. The corporations in aggregate do indeed tap individual "savings," but for only a little less than 20 per cent of their capital, and mainly through the issuance of bonds to intermediate savings-collecting institutions (life insurance companies, trust funds, pension trusts and savings banks).

The corporation becomes the legal "owner" of the capital thus collected and has complete decision-making power over it; the corporation runs on its own economic steam. On the other hand, its stockholders, by now grandsons or great-grandsons of the original "investors" or (far more often) transferees of their transferees at thousands of removes, have and expect to have through their stock the "beneficial ownership" of the assets and profits thus accumulated and realized, after taxes, by the corporate enterprise. Management thus becomes, in an odd sort of way, the uncontrolled administrator of a kind of trust having the privilege of perpetual accumulation. The stockholder is the passive beneficiary, not only of the original "trust," but of the compounded annual accretions to it.

Not surprisingly, therefore, we discover a body of law building up to protect and deal with this remarkable phenomenon. To that fact itself perhaps is due a continuing tendency: subjection of property devoted to *production*—that is, chiefly in managerial hands—to legal rules requiring a use of it, more or less corresponding to the evolving expectations of American civilization.

IV. Development of property law

Inevitably, the common-law legal system moves to normalize the new areas thus comprehended within the general head of "productive property." Two major lines are observed. The first (primarily outside the scope of this essay) proceeds through taxation. The principle has been established that the federal government—and, in lesser measure, state governments—both may and should take a portion of the profits of corporations through the device of direct corporate income tax. Under the recent tax reduction, the federal government presently taxes corporate profits above $25,000 at the rate of about 50 per cent. This virtually makes the state an equal partner as far as profits are concerned. Factually, though silently, the process recognizes a fundamental and entirely demonstrable economic premise. Corporations derive their profits partly indeed from their own operations, but partly also from their market position and increasingly from techniques resulting from state expenditures of taxpayers' money. In this sense, the American state is an investor in practically every substantial enterprise; without its activity, the enterprise, if it could exist at all, would be or would have been compelled to spend money and effort to create position, maintain access to market, and build technical development it currently takes for granted. Under these circumstances, there is little reason or justification for assuming that *all* profits should automatically accrue to stockholders. Put differently, stockholders—not having created the entire enterprise—are no longer the sole residuary legatees (after production costs and depreciation) of all the profits of an industrial progress, much of which is derived from state outlay.

A second line of development impinges directly on management operation. It arises from an evolving social concept of what American civilization should look like. It began with the minimum-wage legislation and the Wagner Act, later revised by the Taft-Hartley Act and modified by the Landrum-Griffin Act. These statutes, and the growing body of case and administrative law under them, limit the decision-making power of corporate managements with respect to wages and labor relations. Of interest is the fact that these laws in the main (though not universally) are applied to general enterprise for profit-making operations in production or commerce. Slowly a distinction began to develop between both expenditures and activities for personal consumption, and enterprises directed toward the offer of goods or services to the public from whose purchase or payment a profit is expected.

The latter, it increasingly appears, are subject to the imposition of rules derived essentially from the Bill of Rights. These rules are designed to assure that the market power of enterprise shall not be used so as to create or perpetuate conditions which the state itself is forbidden to create or maintain. In 1952, the writer drew attention to this tendency, noting:

> [T]here is being generated a quiet translation of constitutional law from the field of political to the field of economic rights. The main outlines of this new body of law are only scarcely discernible now; yet its future history is certain to be important. . . . The emerging principle appears to be that the corporation, itself a creation of the state, is as subject to constitutional limitations which limit action as is the state itself. If this doctrine, now coming into view, is carried to full effect, a corporation having economic and supposedly juridical power to take property, to refuse to give equal service, to discriminate between man and man, group and group, race and race, to an extent denying "the equal protection of the laws," or otherwise to violate constitutional limitations, is subject to direct legal action.

The doctrine had been applied to municipal corporations by the Supreme Court and extended to a private corporation performing the equivalent of public functions through the operation of a company town. It has been gradually expanded in a number of directions.

Dramatically, the recently enacted Civil Rights Act has forthrightly moved into this field. It provides among other things that certain enterprises offering goods and services or accommodations to the public may not discriminate against any member of the public because of racial origin. Gone is the old rule that merchandiser, purveyor of accommodations or provider of services (above an insignificant size) may do what he likes with his own, may sell or decline to sell, serve or decline to serve, choose between customer and customer at least on the basis of race. State statutes like those prevailing in New York had already set up this rule. Now the federal government enters alongside the state.

Property devoted to other than commercial or productive use is not dealt with in a similar manner. A man may refuse to entertain anyone within his home or admit anyone to ride in his car. Consumption for personal use is an expression of personality, guarded from invasion. Property (in the extruded sense we have been using the term) devoted to production and commerce is not; neither in employment of labor nor in the sale of goods and services can the ancient absolute property right of domination—decision-making in the current phase—be unqualified. What happened is sufficiently clear. The political ideal invested in the Constitution and reflected in the Bill of Rights, and the fourteenth and fifteenth amendments, contemplated individuals whose personality was not to be invaded, save for police purposes designed to protect other personalities from invasion. In the simpler days of the eighteenth century, the state was the principal threat: the Bill of Rights restrained the federal government and by the fourteenth amendment extended the restraints to the state governments. As the twentieth century entered its later half, it was clear that personal freedom could be abridged or invaded by denial of economic facilities offered or provided by privately owned enterprises. Such facilities indeed were chiefly in private hands—overwhelmingly, in fact, offered or conducted by corporations. Yet they were essential to life and personality. The result was gradual, judicial extension of constitutional law, complemented now by such statutes as the Civil Rights Act of 1964, which covers the fields of lodging, restaurant facilities, places of entertainment, establishments serving or offering to serve food, gasoline or other products. The Civil Rights Act does not extend, even remotely, to the whole field of commerce; it does not affect all productive property. Yet the point is clear: such property may by statute, if not by constitutional extension, be made subject to those limitations which inhibit state action to protect individual freedom.

A third state-constraint upon management results from the current interpretation of the antitrust legislation and more specifically the Clayton Act. The Supreme Court has established that any merger which appreciably limits competition is prohibited. The writer considers the policy retrogressive; competition enforced to that extent is more likely to cripple production and distribution than increase it. That, however, is a matter for legislative determination, whether judicial or congressional. The significant fact is that the law endeavors to assure that productive property will not be used to prevent carrying on production along the lines and subject to the conditions of the competitive process as conceived by classical economics. It thus seeks to maintain a picture of civilization to which a powerful current of American thought appears to be committed. Rightly, this is not construed as an invasion of liberty or personal right. It is construed as—and, of course, is—a direct attempt to mold, control or inhibit certain dispositions of productive property, maintaining the historical conception that highly competitive markets are generally beneficial to human liberty. In modern context, the premise may, of course, be disputed.

Yet the enforcement of such a conception unquestionably imposes limitations on the disposition and operation of productive property. Cognate limitations have not yet been applied to property used only for individual consumption. Although the state considers that it can control the framework and bases of production and commerce, it has not attempted (aside from police limitations) to tell a man what or how he should consume; that would constitute an intolerable invasion of his private life.

V. The institution of passive property

Increased size and domination of the American corporation has automatically split the package of rights and privileges comprising the old conception of property. Specifically, it splits the personality of the individual beneficial owner away from the enterprise manager. The "things" themselves—including the intangible elements noted earlier in this essay—"belong" to the corporation which holds legal title to them. The ultimate beneficial interest embodied in a share of stock represents an expectation that a portion of the profits remaining after taxes will be declared as dividends, and that in the relatively unlikely event of liquidation each share will get its allocable part of the assets. The former expectation is vivid; the latter so remote that it plays little part in giving market value to shares. Stockholders do have a right to vote, which is of diminishing importance as the number of shareholders in each corporation increases—diminishing in fact to negligible importance as the corporations become giants. As the number of stockholders increases, the capacity of each to express opinions is extremely limited. No one is bound to take notice of them, though they may have quasi-political importance, similar to that of constituents who write letters to their congressman. Finally, they have a right, difficult to put into operation, to bring a stockholders' action against the corporation and its management, demanding that the corporation be made whole from any damage it may have suffered in case of theft, fraud, or wrongdoing by directors or administrators. Such actions are common, though few stockholders are involved in them. They are a useful deterrent to dishonesty and disloyalty on the part of management.

These shares nevertheless have become so desirable that they are now the dominant form of personal wealth-holding because, through the device of stock exchanges, they have acquired "liquidity"—that is, the capability of being sold for ready cash within days or hours. The stockholder, though no longer the sole residuary legatee of all profits, is the residuary legatee of about half of them, and that is a vast stake.

(Sophisticated estimates indicate that dividends combined with increase in market value of shares have yielded better than 8 per cent per annum during the generation past.) The package of passive property rights and expectations has proved sufficiently satisfactory to have induced an increasing number of Americans to place their savings in this form of property. In 1929 perhaps one million Americans owned common stock. At the close of 1967, a conservative estimate would place that figure at between twenty-two and twenty-three million stockholders. These holdings represent slightly less than one-third of individually owned wealth in the United States. Projecting the trend, one would expect twenty years from now to find between forty and fifty million Americans directly owning shares. The aggregate market value of personally owned shares now approximates 10 to 15 per cent more than the annual personally received income in the United States (the latter will be over 600 billion dollars for the year 1967). We can expect that the total market value of personally owned shares twenty years hence will far surpass the trillion-dollar mark.

Yet this is only the "top level" of passive property-holding. A very large number of shares are not held by individuals, but by intermediate fiduciary institutions which in turn distribute the benefits of shareholding to participating individuals. One of the two largest groups of such intermediary institutions is that of the pension trust funds maintained by corporations or groups of corporations for the benefit of employees; these collect savings in regular installments from employers to be held in trust for their employees and subsequently paid to them as old-age or other similar benefits. The second is the relatively smaller group of institutions known as mutual funds; these buy a portfolio of assorted stocks and sell participations in the portfolio to individuals desiring to hold an interest in diversified groups of stock instead of directly holding shares in one or more companies. Through the pension trust funds not fewer than twenty million (probably a great many more) employees already have an indirect beneficial claim both to the dividends proceeding from shares and to their market value in the pension portfolio—even though their interest is non-liquid, and is received only on retirement, death or (occasionally) other contingency. Perhaps two million holders of shares in mutual funds are likewise indirect beneficiaries, although they receive current return, and can promptly convert their shares into cash.

In addition to these two categories there are other intermediate institutions which are also holders (though less significant) of stocks—namely, life insurance companies which invest about 3 per cent of their assets in stocks, and fire and casualty companies which invest a considerably larger percentage. Comparatively speaking, all these institutions combined probably own a relatively small fraction of all stocks outstanding—perhaps between 5 and 10 per cent. Yet the rapidity of their growth—especially striking in the case of pension trusts—indicates that this form of stockholding is likely to become dominant in future years.

The significance of the intermediate institutions is twofold. First, they vastly increase the number of citizens who, to some degree, rely on the stockholding form of wealth. Second, they remove the individual still further from connection with or impact on the management and administration of the productive corporations themselves.

As might be expected, the law has moved to protect the holders of this form of wealth. It has not unnaturally moved along the lines of the interest that most preoccupies shareholders—that is, "liquidity" (capacity to turn the holding into cash), and market price. Since liquidity turns not on underlying property, but on resale of shares, legal protection is chiefly involved with the processes of the market place. Hence its preoccupation with information enabling buyers and sellers to determine the price at which they are willing to buy or sell. The entire battery of legislation set up by the Securities and Exchange acts has essentially little to do with the conduct of the corporation's affairs beyond requiring regular publication of information considered accurate by accounting standards, and prohibiting speculative activities by corporate administrators. Even more directly, this legislation deals with conduct of the stock exchanges themselves and with practices of their members who buy or sell as brokers for the public.

In both direction and effect, this preoccupation of the Securities and Exchange acts recognizes a new economic fact: that stock markets are no longer places of "investment" as the word was used by classical economists. Save to a marginal degree, they no longer allocate capital. They are mechanisms for liquidity. The purchaser of stock, save in rare instances, does not buy a new issue. The price he pays does not add to capital or assets of the corporation whose shares he buys. Stock markets do not exist for, and in general are not used for (in fact are not allowed to be used for), distribution of newly issued shares. Their rules commonly prevent shares from being listed and traded until *after* they have been sold by some other means. Occasionally, it is true, large new issues are distributed which shortly after make their way into markets (one thinks at once of the American Telephone and Telegraph Company issue of new stock in 1964). But such operations perform an insignificant percentage of the work of stock exchanges. The exchanges are institutions in which shares, arising from investment made long ago, are shifted from sellers who wish cash to buyers who wish stock. Purchases and sales on the New York and other stock exchanges do not seriously affect the business operations of the companies whose shares are the subject of trading.

We have yet to digest the social-economic situation resulting from this fact. Immense dollar values of stocks are bought and sold every day, month and year. These dollars—indeed hundreds of billions of dollars—do not, apparently, enter the stream of direct commercial or productive use. That is, they do not become "capital" devoted to productive use. A seller of stocks more likely desires to buy other stocks than to use the capital for a business he himself owns.

Dr. Paul Harbrecht, at Columbia and now at Detroit University, has been elaborating a theory that we have evolved a new wealth-holding and wealth-circulating system whose liquidity is maintained through the exchanges but is only psychologically connected with the capital gathering and capital application system on which productive industry and enterprise actually depend. If this is the fact, one effect of the corporate system has been to set up a parallel, circulating "property-wealth" system, in which the wealth flows from passive wealth-holder to passive wealth-holder, without significantly furthering the functions of capital formation, capital application, capital use or risk bearing. Yet these functions were the heart of the nineteenth-century "capitalist" system. Both the wealth and the wealth-holders are divorced from the productive—that is, the commercial—process, though, at long last, the estimate of this wealth turns on an estimate of the productiveness, the character and effectiveness of the corporation whose shares are its vehicles.

Now, clearly, this wealth cannot be justified by the old economic maxims, despite passionate and sentimental arguments of neo-classic economists who would have us believe the old system has not changed.* The purchaser of stock does not contribute savings to an

---

* The conclusion and the theory set forth in the first edition of *The Modern Corporation and Private Property* inspired a lively, sometimes passionate, debate among professional economists. *The Quarterly Journal of Economics* published three phases of that debate in Vol. LXXIX, February 1965, pp. 1–51, Professor Shorey Peterson leading the attack, to which I replied, and in which Professor Carl Kaysen took a middle ground. Professor Henry Manne, also a neoclassicist, attacked in an essay, "The Higher Criticism of the Modern Corporation," 62 *Columbia Law Review* 399 (1962). Current volumes adopt the general premises worked out by Dr. Means and myself and carry analysis rather further; for example, *Modern Capitalism: The Changing Balance of Public and Private Power*, Andrew Shonfield (London: Oxford University Press, 1965); *The Economic Theory of Managerial Capitalism*, Robin Marris (New York: Free Press of Glencoe, 1964); *The Industrial State*, J. Kenneth Galbraith (New York: Harper & Row, 1967).

enterprise, thus enabling it to increase its plant or operations. He does not take the "risk" of a new or increased economic operation; he merely estimates the chance of the corporation's shares increasing in value. The contribution his purchase makes to anyone other than himself is the maintenance of liquidity for other shareholders who may wish to convert their holdings into cash. Clearly he cannot and does not intend to contribute managerial or entrepreneurial effort or service.

This raises a problem of social ethics that is bound to push its way into the legal scene in the next generation. Why have stockholders? What contribution do they make, entitling them to heirship of half the profits of the industrial system, receivable partly in the form of dividends, and partly in the form of increased market values resulting from undistributed corporate gains? Stockholders toil not, neither do they spin, to earn that reward. They are beneficiaries by position only. Justification for their inheritance must be sought outside classic economic reasoning.

It can be founded only upon social grounds. There is—and in American social economy, there always has been—a value attached to individual life, individual development, individual solution of personal problems, individual choice of consumption and activity. Wealth unquestionably does add to an individual's capacity and range in pursuit of happiness and self-development. There is certainly advantage to the community when men take care of themselves. But that justification turns on the distribution as well as the existence of wealth. Its force exists only in direct ratio to the number of individuals who hold such wealth. Justification for the stockholder's existence thus depends on increasing distribution within the American population. Ideally, the stockholder's position will be impregnable only when every American family has its fragment of that position and of the wealth by which the opportunity to develop individuality becomes fully actualized.

Privilege to have income and a fragment of wealth without a corresponding duty to work for it cannot be justified except on the ground that the community is better off—and not unless most members of the community share it. A guaranteed annual wage for all, a governmentally assured minimum income, a stockholder's share in the United States distributed to every American family—these are all different ways of giving Americans capacity to settle their own lives rather than having their lives settled for them by blind economic forces, by compulsions of poverty or by regulations of a social-work bureaucracy.

Wide distribution of stockholdings is one way of working toward this.

Such distribution is indeed proceeding—rather dramatically in terms of statistics, all too slowly in terms of social ethics. The generation since 1932 has multiplied the number of direct stockholders tenfold. If indirect stockholdings through intermediate institutions are included, a vast indirect sector has grown up as well. Yet distribution of wealth generally is still in its infancy. One per cent of the American population owns perhaps 25 per cent of all personally owned wealth ° and undoubtedly more than that percentage of common stocks. Plainly we have a long way to go. The intermediate institutions, notably pension trusts, justify themselves not merely because they increase the benefits of the stockholder-position, but because they rationalize it as well. Through direct ownership, Nym who bought railroad stocks twenty years ago lost money, Bardolph who bought A.T.&T. trebled his stake, while Pistol who bought I.B.M. stock has multiplied it fiftyfold. This is an irrational result. The pension trust, possibly holding all of these stocks, distributes the losses and the benefits (the latter being considerably greater) among a broad category of employees.

One would expect therefore that the law would increasingly encourage an ever wider distribution of stocks—whether through tax policy or some other device. It would encourage pension trust or social security trust entry into stockholder position. The time may well come when the government social security funds are invested, not wholly in government bonds as at present, but in a broadening list of American stocks. As social security and pension trusts increasingly cover the entire working population of the United States, the stockholder position, though having lost its ancient justification, could become a vehicle for rationalized wealth distribution corresponding to and serving the American ideal of a just civilization. The institution of passive property has an advantage which, so far as we know, is new to history in that distribution and redistribution of wealth-holding can take place without interruption of the productive process. Ancient Hebrew law required redistribution of land every half-century through the institution of the "Jubilee Year," but ran into operational difficulties, as might have been expected. The great revolutionary movements of 1848 and, in our time, in Russia, China and Cuba involved extreme productive losses, none of which has yet been recouped (though after half a century the Soviet Union may finally be at the point of doing so). The corporate system, accompanied by reasonably enlightened tax policies and aided by continuously growing productivity, can achieve whatever redistribution the American people want.

° *The Share of Top Wealth-holders in National Wealth 1922–56*, Robert J. Lampman (Princeton, N. J.: National Bureau of Economic Research, 1962), p. 208.

Few observers would seriously deny that greater production is inevitable as well as needed. President Lyndon B. Johnson boldly embraced the proposition that "poverty" (referring to families with income of less than $3,000 a year) can and should be abolished, making a first tentative approach toward meeting the problem in 1964. It is scarcely open to question that present and potential productive capacity offers adequate tools to the American economy when and if the American public really desires to "abolish poverty." That is, the tools are at hand insofar as the problems are economic. Actually it is clear that problems deeper than economic—for example, problems of education and automation—will have to be met. What can be said is that the deeper problems cannot readily be met unless productive capacity can be maintained and increased to finance their solution, and unless the present technical organization of wealth can permit the shifting process to go on without interrupting or handicapping production. Both these conditions do exist.

VI. *The institutional economic revolution*

Though its outline is still obscure, the central mass of the twentieth-century American economic revolution has become discernible. Its driving forces are five: (1) immense increase in productivity; (2) massive collectivization of property devoted to production, with accompanying decline of individual decision-making and control; (3) massive dissociation of wealth from active management; (4) growing pressure for greater distribution of such passive wealth; (5) assertion of the individual's right to live and consume as the individual chooses.

Of this revolution, the corporation has proved a vital (albeit neutral) instrument and vehicle. It has become, and now is, the dominant form of organization and production. It has progressively created, and continues to create, a passive form of wealth. It is, in great measure, emancipated from dependence on individual savings and "capital" markets. Nevertheless, like the slave of Aladdin's lamp, it must increasingly follow the mandate of the American state, embodied in social attitudes and in case, statute and constitutional law. This mandate changes and evolves as a consensus is developed on values and their priorities in American life.

This revolution is no longer just a possibility, as was the case when *The Modern Corporation and Private Property* was published in 1932. It is at least halfway along. In historical terms, it is moving rapidly. Some may dread, others may welcome it. But its existence and its advance cannot be seriously denied. The property system has decisively changed and there is no ground for believing the change is reversible. Tentative beginnings are apparent in the companion area of distribution, chiefly through taxation.

A closely related trend (not here discussed) is, of course, emergence of the American state partly as an administrator of wealth distribution, partly as a direct distributor of certain products. In notable areas production for use rather than production for profit is emerging as the norm. Education, scientific research and development, the arts, and a variety of services ranging from roads and low-income housing to nonprofit recreation and television constitute a few illustrative fields. Health will probably be—in part now is—such a field. Increasingly it is clear that these non-commercial functions are, among other things, essential to the continued life, stability and growth of the non-statist corporate enterprise.

In typical American fashion, the revolution has come not through a single ideological or utopian burst, conceived and imposed by a few, but through an evolving consensus that insists equally on enjoying the results of mass production and on the primacy of individual life. It will go forward—as it inevitably must—as fast and as far as that consensus demands.

Conclusion

We are well underway toward recognition that property used in production must conform to conceptions of civilization worked out through democratic processes of American constitutional government. Few American enterprises, and no large corporations, can take the view that their plants, tools and organizations are their own, and that they can do what they please with their own. There is increasing recognition of the fact that collective operations, and those predominantly conducted by large corporations, are like operations carried on by the state itself. Corporations are essentially political constructs. Their perpetual life, their capacity to accumulate tens of billions of assets, and to draw profit from their production and their sales, has made them part of the service of supply of the United States. Informally they are an adjunct of the state itself. The "active"—that is, productive —property of an organization increasingly is prevented from invading personality and freedom, from discriminating in employment and service against categories of men, in recklessly using their market control.

Passive property—notably, stock—increasingly loses its "capital" function. It becomes primarily a method for distributing liquid wealth and a channel for distributing income whose accumulation for capital purposes is not required. The corporation may, and indeed is expected to, retain earnings for the maintenance and enlargement of its capital plant and operations. The stockholder's right to spend the income from or use the liquid value of his shares as he pleases is guarded as a defense of his right to order his own life.

Far beyond this summary, the real revolution of our time is yet faintly perceived. If the current estimate that by 1980 our total productivity will double (approximately 1.2 trillion of 1960 dollars) and personally received income will reach approximately one trillion dollars proves true, the entire emphasis of American civilization will appreciably change. Philosophical preoccupation will become more important than economic. What is this personal life, this individuality, this search for personal development and fulfillment intended to achieve? Mere wallowing in consumption would leave great numbers of people unsatisfied; their demand will be for participation. This means, in substance, a growing demand that significant jobs be available for everyone, at a time when automation may diminish the number of all commercially created jobs as we presently know them. It may well mean that the state would be expected to create jobs wherever a social need is recognized, irrespective of the classic requirement for a commercial base. Is it possible, as Walt Rostow maintains, that the population will merely become bored? Perhaps; but if so, it will be because esthetics, the arts, the endeavor to understand, use and enjoy the thrilling prospects opened by science, and the endless search for meaning, will have tragically lagged far behind economic advance. Not impossibly, the teacher, the artist, the poet and the philosopher will set the pace for the next era.

ADOLF A. BERLE

Columbia University. December, 1967.

IMPLICATIONS OF THE CORPORATE
REVOLUTION IN ECONOMIC THEORY

THE FACT of the corporate revolution is now so widely accepted that statistical evidence is no longer needed to establish its occurrence. But the republication of *The Modern Corporation and Private Property* does raise questions of how reliable its estimates of corporate concentration have proved to be, what has happened in the thirty-five years since the book's publication, and what are the major implications of this revolution as the authors now see them.

The questions of reliability and of subsequent developments are considered in a new statistical appendix. There the various attacks on the statistical findings of the book are examined and the conclusion is reached that the statistics have stood up well. Indeed, on the crucial finding that the 200 largest non-banking corporations controlled somewhere between 45 and 53 per cent of the assets of all non-banking corporations, with 49.2 per cent the actual crude estimate arrived at, a subsequent and much more reliable estimate based on actual examination of the tax returns of the big corporations as filed with the Treasury resulted in a figure of 49.4 per cent for the largest 200. The very close agreement between the crude and the refined figure is, of course, fortuitous. But it is clear that the crude estimate was not misleading.

Developments since *The Modern Corporation* was published have tended to confirm the trends indicated there of increasing concentration, increasing dispersion of stock ownership, and increasing separation of ownership and control.

As the statistical appendix shows, concentration has continued to increase. The 100 largest manufacturing corporations increased their proportion of all manufacturing corporation assets from approximately 40 per cent in 1929 to approximately 49 per cent in 1962, while their proportion of net capital assets increased from 44 per cent in 1929 to 58 per cent in 1962. In the field of public utilities, the Holding Company Act caused a breakup of some of the larger systems and slowed up further concentration, but since 1950 the degree of concentration has been increasing. In the field of transportation, public policy has long stood in the way of railroad mergers. But more recently, approved mergers or acquisition of control has reduced the 42 railroads included in the 1929 list of the largest 200 to 27, and further acquisitions, already approved, when consummated will reduce the list to 18. In the same period air transport has become big business, with 6 airlines which would almost certainly be included in a current list of the largest 200 non-financial corporations.

For non-financial corporations as a whole there has been no recent study to compare with that for 1929. But, as the statistical appendix shows, there can be little question that such a study would show increased concentration, though the rate of increase would be much slower than that of the 1920's.

Subsequent developments have also continued the other two statistical trends indicated in *The Modern Corporation*. As the statistical appendix shows, the ultimate ownership of the big corporations has become ever more widely dispersed, and control has become increasingly separated from ownership. While in 1929 only 88 of the 200 largest corporations were classed as management controlled, by 1963 169, or 84.5 per cent, were so classed. And in 1929, 22 corporations were classed as privately owned or controlled by the owners through majority ownership, while only 5 were so classed in 1963. Thus, the three trends so fundamentally changing the character of the economy— concentration of economic power, dispersion of stock ownership, and separation of ownership and control—have continued over the last thirty-five years. The corporate revolution marches on.

Like the industrial revolution, which established the factory as a predominant form of production and separated the worker from control over the instruments of production, the corporate revolution, separating ownership from control over the instruments of production, has come on us gradually. Its beginnings in this country can be traced back to the early 19th century. Much had been written on the big corporation and its effect on competition in the free market, particularly after the great merger movement at the turn of the century. But neither the magnitude of the institutional revolution nor its profound legal and economic implications had received major attention. In the body of *The Modern Corporation* both the economic and legal characteristics were spelled out and some of the major implications outlined as we saw them at that time.

From the economic point of view, the crucial implication of this corporate revolution was the extent to which it made obsolete the basic concepts underlying the body of traditional economic theory which was then the basis of public policy. Wealth, enterprise, initiative, the profit motive, and competition, each was shown to have become so changed in character with the revolution as to make traditional theory no longer applicable. The conclusion was reached that "New concepts must be forged and a new picture of economic relationships created."

In the thirty-five years since publication, much progress has been made in developing the new concepts and the new picture, but much still remains to be done. The changes in thinking and practice that have been forced by the corporate revolution will be outlined for four major areas of public policy.

First and foremost, both the theory and the policy toward employment have changed. Under traditional theory as it stood at the time *The Modern Corporation* was published, our free enterprise economy was assumed to contain a cybernetic mechanism which would automatically tend to re-establish full employment when any temporary departure occurred. This was the guiding star under which President Hoover went down to defeat in 1932, waiting for recovery, which was "just around the corner."

The New Deal rejected the theory of automatic recovery, at first on pragmatic grounds, and then theory came to back this pragmatism. After World War II the principle of government responsibility prevailed. The Employment Act of 1946 gave the new policy legislative sanction.

Actually, two explanations of persistent unemployment developed and gained wide acceptance. The Keynesian explanation, published in 1936, was concerned with the relation between saving and investment. While it was presented in terms of lending, borrowing, and interest rates, it rested essentially on the fact that under the conditions created by the corporate revolution the bulk of saving and investment was carried on in a dual process conducted by two independent groups of individuals whose actions did not necessarily mesh at full employment. The other explanation was presented by the present writer in 1934 and was concerned with the inflexibility of administered prices. In its essential substance, it rested on the fact that under the conditions created by the corporate revolution most prices were not determined by trading in the market, but by administrative action, and tended to be fixed for considerable periods of time, thus inhibiting any general fall in the price level and converting a general fall in demand into a recession and unemployment.

This is not the place to decide between these theories. What is important is that both had their basis in the changes wrought by the corporate revolution and both supported monetary and fiscal policy as the major instrument for establishing and maintaining the level of aggregate demand necessary for full employment. And both involved a rejection of traditional theory.

In a second area concerned with the economy as a whole, that of inflation, the corporate revolution has brought a wholly new set of problems. These lie entirely outside traditional theory, which provided the conventional wisdom at the time *The Modern Corporation* was published. For an economy of small-scale competitive enterprise and flexible prices, the only form of inflation allowed by theory was one in which a general excess in demand resulted in a general rise in prices and wage rates. In the economy of the modern corporation, a wholly new type of inflation is possible: a rise of administered prices without a general excess of demand. The power to administer prices is also a power within limits to raise prices arbitrarily and in the absence of an increase in demand.

Just such an inflation occurred between 1953 and 1958. In testimony before the Senate Antitrust and Monopoly Subcommittee in 1959, the author pointed out that the 8 per cent rise in the wholesale price index of the preceding five years had occurred in administered prices and that the average of flexible market prices as a group had not risen at all. Yet flexible market prices are by their nature most sensitive to demand, and the industries responsible for the rise were operating far below capacity. This new type of inflation may properly be called "administrative inflation" to distinguish it from demand inflation. That the rise in the wholesale index was not a demand inflation was confirmed by a staff study of the Joint Economic Committee, and it was publicly acknowledged by a leading member of the Federal Reserve Board staff that this was a type of inflation that could not be controlled through monetary policy and the limiting of demand.

This new type of inflation made possible by the corporate revolution presents a major problem of public policy in seeking to achieve full employment. If all prices were determined by supply-and-demand conditions, it would be possible through fiscal and monetary measures to provide that level of demand which would just support full employment without inflation. But well before full employment is reached, administrative inflation is likely to begin. This is a type of creeping inflation which is most unlikely to develop into galloping inflation because it operates to reduce demand. Also, it is a type of inflation that can arise either from the effects of labor's efforts to force wages up faster than productivity, a "cost-push" inflation, or from the effects of management's seeking to widen profit margins, a "profits push" inflation. The 1953–1958 inflation clearly came from management's side, and there is much evidence in the more recent creeping rise in the wholesale index that real wages have, if anything, lagged behind increases in productivity.

But whatever the source of administrative inflation, it poses a major problem of public policy: must a choice be made between price-level stability and less than full employment on the one hand and creeping inflation and a satisfactory level of employment on the other? Or is there some way to prevent administrative inflation and obtain the advantages of price stability and full employment without interfering excessively with the operation of the free-enterprise system?

A third area in which the corporate revolution has forced a change in practice and the need for new theory is that of international trade and the balance of payments. Under traditional theory, stability in exchange rates could be obtained by the use of gold as the basis of each country's money, and any unbalance in payments would automatically be corrected through the flow of gold between countries, accompanied by a rise in the general price level in the gold-receiving country and a fall in the price-wage level in the gold-losing country.

Experience has shown that the measures which, with highly flexible prices and wage rates, would produce a general fall in price level actually produce depression and unemployment. As a result, country after country shifted from the gold standard to the gold-exchange standard, under which gold continued to flow from one country to another to satisfy any minor unbalance in payments. But under the gold-exchange system a country's internal money stock was no longer directly related to its gold holdings, and the price-level effects of gold movement were largely inhibited. This removed the basic mechanism of adjustment which had tended to eliminate any fundamental unbalance in payments in the precorporate economy.

The agonies of England in its recent effort to support the pound and its final devaluation illustrate the problem. When the fundamental unbalance in British payments developed, the government sought to correct it by tightening internal policy at the expense of employment and progress. But even some depression was not enough to match the fundamental unbalance, and the pound had to be devalued.

The international monetary institutions set up after World War II have greatly helped in the handling of short-run unbalances in payments. And the new proposals for international reserves would further lengthen the period during which a country could incur a *temporary* unbalance in payments provided the unbalance was reversed in a later period. But there is nothing automatic in the present system that would tend to correct a fundamental unbalance. Time alone is not enough.

The failure of the automatic price-level adjustment is easily explained by the inflexibility of administered prices. But it presents a problem, brought by the corporate revolution, that is still waiting for a solution. Can a way be worked out to keep the very real advantages of stable exchange rates without the danger of periodic strains and damaging devaluations in one country or another?

The fourth area in which the modern corporation has undermined traditional thinking is in the matter of economic performance. The central body of economic theory taught at the time *The Modern Corporation* was published held that so long as there was competition among producers economic performance would be high. Each producer's selfish interest would be so canalized by market forces that his action would serve the public interest. He would tend to use available resources to produce what the public wanted at the lowest possible cost. There were recognized exceptions as regulation was substituted for competition in the public-utility field and as freedom of enterprise was curbed by such laws as those against theft and the breaching of contracts. But on the whole, theory taught that the actions of Mr. Typical Small Enterprise were so circumscribed by the market that what was good for Mr. Enterprise tended to be good for the public. Within the limits of the competitive market, economic performance could be left to the decision-making of the small enterpriser.

The corporate revolution has changed all that by creating centers of economic power on a scale never previously known. For the most part, competition is no longer among the many. And competition among the few is a radically different thing, as E. H. Chamberlin, in the U.S. and Joan Robinson, in England, pointed out in 1933. The inflexibility of administered prices is itself evidence of market power and presents its problems. But economic power is a much more inclusive concept than is market power alone. It influences the use made of available resources, the safety of the products supplied, the amount of waste products polluting the environment, the conditions of work, as well as the fairness of the wages paid and the prices charged. Competition clearly cannot control the use of this power so that the result is substantially in the public interest. Clearly the public has not received the full benefits of the new drugs which science has developed. And the safety of cars and tires has called for a degree of government control. Society is only just beginning to study the performance of individual industries to see how well they serve the public interest.

At the same time that economic power has built up in the hands of corporate management, the separation of ownership and control has released management from the overriding requirement that it serve stockholders. Profits are an essential part of the corporate system. But the use of corporate power solely to serve the stockholders is no longer likely to serve the public interest. Yet no criteria of good corporate performance have yet been worked out. Should the problems of bad performance be worked on piecemeal, as has been done by the laws concerning theft and breach of contract, drug distribution, and auto safety? Or can criteria for good performance be developed to guide corporate management and inducements be provided to encourage the good? What changes would be needed to make it true that action by corporate management in its own self-interest serves the public interest?

After examining these problems created by the corporate revolution, one can raise the crucial question of whether the system of enterprise which has resulted is worth having. Should the clock be turned back? Or, if it cannot be turned back, is there some alternative system that could better serve the public interest?

The most articulate criticism of the free-corporate-enterprise system *as a system* comes, of course, from the Communists, and the Communist regimes offer the most obvious alternative. Here the major claim is that capitalism exploits the workers. This contention rests on two assertions: first, that capital makes no contribution to the value of production, and second, that capitalists receive a large share of the income generated in production. We need to examine this claim before we can compare the two alternative systems.

Experience in the Communist countries has already undermined the first assertion. Immediately after the Communists came to power in Russia, they acted on the assumption that capital as such made no contribution, and they began to build new plants on a big scale. Then they suddenly awoke to the fact that they had a tremendous number of new plants started but not enough capital to complete them. Labor that could be diverted from producing for current consumption and used to build capital plant and equipment was insufficient. A halt was called on all new construction, and the available labor and materials were thereafter strictly rationed for the completion of those plants that promised the greatest increase in output over input. In capitalist language, they put the available capital into completing those plants that were expected to yield the highest rate of return on the added capital investment. Since that time, capital—the diverting of part of the current productive effort into capital formation—has been carefully rationed into the uses in which the capital would be most productive. This means that, whether they admit it or not, capital is being treated as a resource which has value quite apart from and in addition to the labor it involves.

Some Communist economists are beginning to admit that Marx was wrong on this particular proposition. Thus, when I was in Yugoslavia in 1955, individual economists who were otherwise Marxist agreed that capital had to be treated as a factor that contributed to production and to the value of products. With the increased attention in Russia to the pricing of products in relation to cost, one can expect not only that products requiring more skilled and higher-paid labor will be priced higher than those requiring the same amount of low-paid labor, but also that products requiring the same amount of labor will be priced higher if they require more capital. But whether or not this happens, the rationing of capital is itself an admission that it makes a contribution to value. Of course, who gets this addition to value is quite a different matter, still to be discussed. But it can no longer be said that any payment to capitalists for the use of capital represents exploitation of labor. It would be exploitation only if it was excessive.

The second basis of the exploitation charge is that a large proportion of the income generated in production goes to capital. There is, first, the question of what constitutes a "large" proportion. If one takes wages and salaries paid by all private corporations in 1967 as going to labor and interest, dividends and undistributed profits of the same corporations as going to capital, it will be found that only 12 per cent of the total went to capital. Of course, some of the salary payments went to top management, and in absolute figures these payments are large. But if they were eliminated from the above figures it would still be true that in 1967 capital received little more than 12 per cent of the income from corporate production that was divided between capital and labor, while labor received close to 88 per cent.

Even the 12 per cent looks less exploitive when its disposal is examined. Roughly half the share going to capital stays within the corporation to be reinvested in the business. Of the part distributed as interest and dividends, a larger proportion is paid in personal income taxes than is true for wages and salaries. And some of the remainder is invested in corporate enterprise. If all the 12 per cent had been distributed as wages and salaries and the same amount of capital and tax revenue had been needed, this would have absorbed something like 8 or 9 percentage points of the extra 12 per cent, so that extra worker expenditure on consumption could not be increased by more than 3 or 4 per cent. In the light of an increase in real-wage rates of about 3 per cent a year, it is difficult to find a great deal of general exploitation here.

This does not mean that there are not specific situations in which there is labor exploitation or that there would not be labor exploitation in the absence of labor unions. The public has supported the right of labor to organize in order to provide a countervailing power and has supported collective bargaining even to the point that it has frequently suffered from prolonged lock-outs or strikes. But it would be difficult to make a case that the corporate system as it now operates in the United States is a system which lives or rests on the exploitation of labor.

The real difference between the system operating in Russia today and that in the United States is concerned with power and who makes what decisions.

To get at the essential difference, let us treat the different agencies of production in Russia as if they were separate enterprises similar to U.S. corporations and consider the money flows involving profits. The first thing to notice, then, is that in Russia all the profits of enterprise go to government and in the United States, government, through taxes, takes only approximately half the profits of corporate enterprise. In Russia, government, in effect, returns a part of the income to the enterprises as capital, while in the U.S. roughly half of profits after income taxes are retained by the corporations for investment purposes. Of the quarter of the profits distributed as dividends, a substantial part gets reinvested in enterprise or paid to the government as taxes. Thus the major difference in money flows in the two countries is concerned with that part of profits not reinvested in enterprise or paid to the government—the remaining quarter of profits which gets distributed as dividends in the United States while the corresponding amount goes to government in Russia. This represents only 3 or 4 per cent of the income generated by corporate production in the United States.

The disposal of this 3 or 4 per cent of income makes for a powerful difference in the degree of freedom versus centralized control. In a very real sense the money paid in dividends to stockholders is the price we now pay, not only for supplying part of the capital required by enterprise, but also, and more importantly, for the widespread dispersion of initiative and decision-making. In Russia, the government has to decide who occupies what positions of authority in the industrial hierarchy. In the U.S., boards of directors, mostly self-perpetuating in the largest companies, make such decisions and government does not have to be directly concerned. In Russia, the government, through its agencies, has to decide what to produce and what price to charge. In the U.S., these decisions are decentralized, with both the initiative and the responsibility dispersed. The corporate system in the United States thus gives a freedom and flexibility and room for independent initiative far in excess of that in Russia. It is the great advantage of free enterprise and the traditional basis of our democratic society.

Where the solution to the problems created by the corporate revolution will take the American economy is far from clear. How far is it necessary to go in canalizing the action of big corporate management to bring that action into conformity with the public interest? What role has economic planning to play in a free society? Is the concentration of power in the managements of the large corporations consistent with the maintenance of a democratic society? These are the basic questions which must be faced.

GARDINER C. MEANS

December, 1967.

IT FALLS TO ME to write this preface because I was nominally the Director of a research project financed by the Social Science Research Council of America and carried on under the direction of the Columbia University Council for Research in The Social Sciences. The project called for a study of recent trends in corporate development. A number of lines converged to make such a study appropriate. It was apparent to any thoughtful observer that the American corporation had ceased to be a private business device and had become an institution. In 1928, when the project was launched, the financial machinery was developing so rapidly as to indicate that we were in the throes of a revolution in our institution of private property, at least as applied to industrial economic uses. The writer had ventured a series of technical studies in corporate securities, all of which led to the conclusion that American industrial property, through the corporate device, was being thrown into a collective hopper wherein the individual owner was steadily being lost in the creation of a series of huge industrial oligarchies. Further, this development seemed in many ways a thoroughly logical and intelligent trend; the process could not be reversed. Equally, it seemed fraught with dangers as well as with advantages.

The project called for an associated economist. Mr. Gardiner C. Means undertook a careful statistical and economic analysis of the situation, the theory being that a lawyer and an economist working hand and hand might secure a more fertile result than either working alone. This hypothesis, held by the Social Science Research Council of America and peculiarly by Professor Edwin F. Gay of Harvard, has, I think, been fairly justified, though we may not have succeeded in putting on paper the real benefits of the cooperation. Difficulty in such cooperation is extreme; for technicians in different fields must first agree on a common language; then endeavor to apply their respective methods of approach, keeping in mind the shortcomings and advantages of the different methods; and finally work out conclusions to which both are prepared to subscribe. Since a lawyer is primarily concerned with the justice of the individual case and can never ignore the problem of what ought to be done; and since an economist is primarily descriptive and analytic, the chasm is not easy to bridge. I pay every tribute to Mr. Means' willingness to go more than half way in meeting the language and point of view of a discipline not his own; I have attempted to do likewise.

The Columbia Law School, with that singular freedom which characterizes it, was content to assume the brunt of the Research burden. Through the courtesy of Dean Young B. Smith, we were afforded facilities and opportunities which this book can only meagerly repay.

This book is rather a statement of conclusions than a demonstration of the method by which the conclusions were reached; any other course would make a volume bulky, unreadable, and uninteresting save to the occasional scientist.

The statistical studies in Book I have appeared in fuller form under Mr. Means' name in the *American Economic Review* and in the *Quarterly Journal of Economics.* He has, in addition, a mass of statistical computations which may or may not find print as time goes on. On the legal side I have endeavored to make technical studies of the problems involved, or to have them made by assistants or occasional students for Doctors' degrees at the Columbia Law School. Of these, a good many have already been printed in the various Law Reviews throughout the country; they are referred to in the text, thereby giving the reader access to the technical essays wherein are included careful analyses of substantially all of the cases, statutes and decisions. The principal cases and authorities are separately collected and published under the title of "Cases and Materials in the Law of Corporation Finance" (West Publishing Company, St. Paul, 1930)—a volume of materials gathered as a part of the research project mentioned above, and organized so as roughly to parallel the portions of this book dealing primarily with legal problems. By these methods we have endeavored to avoid overloading this volume unduly with foot-notes which are more likely to suggest the erudition of the author than to enlighten the reader.

In the last four chapters the writers have frankly attempted to speculate on the basis of the recorded data in connection with corporate activities in the field of property interests and finance. These observations must be set aside from the data contained in the foregoing study. From any given body of material, each individual must draw his own conclusions; these are likely to be as diverse as the minds of the men who study them. The writers' own are here set down because it appears to them proper that the deductions and speculations of the students working in the material should be recorded alongside their views as to the underlying facts. In some sense they permit discounting the fact data by exhibiting the bias of the writers, making judgment of their fact-finding truer. In a larger sense, students have no right to refuse a statement or predictions which they draw from their material. The intellectual and scholastic hazards of stating such conclusions are well enough recognized. Feeling as we do that the development here studied is one of the phenomena of the great change in the tide of social organization, and that out of it grows, in large measure, the history of the coming years, it is fair to set forth the direction of the current as we see it.

It is of the essence of revolutions of the more silent sort that they are unrecognized until they are far advanced. This was the case with the so-called "industrial revolution," and is the case with the corporate revolution through which we are at present passing.

The translation of perhaps two-thirds of the industrial wealth of the country from individual ownership to ownership by the large, publicly financed corporations vitally changes the lives of property owners, the lives of workers, and the methods of property tenure. The divorce of ownership from control consequent on that process almost necessarily involves a new form of economic organization of society.

Manifestly the problem calls for a series of appraisals. Is this organization permanent? Will it intensify or will it break up? Mr. Brandeis struggled to turn the clock backward in 1915; Professor Felix Frankfurter is inclined to believe even now that it cannot last. To us there is much to indicate that the process will go a great deal further than it has now gone.

Accepting the institution of the large corporation (as we must), and studying it as a human institution, we have to consider the effect on property, the effect on workers, and the effect upon individuals who consume or use the goods or service which the corporation produces or renders. This is the work of a lifetime; the present volume is intended primarily to break ground on the relation which corporations bear to property.

When these subjects are thought through there will still remain the problem of the relation which the corporation will ultimately bear to the state—whether it will dominate the state or be regulated by the state or whether the two will coexist with relatively little connection. In other words, as between a political organization of society and an economic organization of society which will be the dominant form? This is a question which must remain unanswered for a long time to come.

It is obvious that the corporate system not only tends to be the flower of our industrial organization, but that the public is in a mood to impose on it a steadily growing degree of responsibility for our economic welfare. An endeavor to analyze this institution therefore needs no apology. The authors are merely conscious of the lack of time, ability and strength to do more than make a beginning.

The existence of this study is in large measure due to Professor Edwin F. Gay of Harvard, who molded into concrete form the suggestion that work should be done in this field. In addition, our particular thanks are due to Professor James C. Bonbright of the Columbia University School of Business for much patient revision and constant help; to Mr. George May, head of Price, Waterhouse & Co. and Vice-President of the American Economic Association, whose shrewd comment, wide experience and kindly wit has opened many doors and trains of thought; to Dean Smith of the Columbia Law School for his willingness to embark that institution on an uncharted field of legal-economic work; and to our various assistants, notably Mr. Abram Hewitt and Mr. Blackwell Smith, who did much of the spade work, little of which appears in print but which was essential in permitting us to reach many of our conclusions.

All students of these and allied problems, and we among them, owe a debt to Professor William Z. Ripley of Harvard University, who must be recognized as having pioneered this area.

A. A. BERLE, JR.

New York City, July, 1932.

BOOK ONE

*Property in Flux: Separation of
the attributes of ownership under the
corporate system*

CHAPTER I: PROPERTY

IN TRANSITION

CORPORATIONS HAVE CEASED to be merely legal devices through which the private business transactions of individuals may be carried on. Though still much used for this purpose, the corporate form has acquired a larger significance. The corporation has, in fact, become both a method of property tenure and a means of organizing economic life. Grown to tremendous proportions, there may be said to have evolved a "corporate system"—as there was once a feudal system —which has attracted to itself a combination of attributes and powers, and has attained a degree of prominence entitling it to be dealt with as a major social institution.

We are examining this institution probably before it has attained its zenith. Spectacular as its rise has been, every indication seems to be that the system will move forward to proportions which would stagger imagination today; just as the corporate system of today was beyond the imagination of most statesmen and business men at the opening of the present century. Only by remembering that men still living can recall a time when the present situation was hardly dreamed of, can we enforce the conclusion that the new order may easily become completely dominant during the lifetime of our children. For that reason, if for no other, it is desirable to examine this system, bearing in mind that its impact on the life of the country and of every individual is certain to be great; it may even determine a large part of the behaviour of most men living under it.

Organization of property has played a constant part in the balance of powers which go to make up the life of any era. We need not resolve the controversy as to whether property interests are invariably controlling. The cynical view of many historians insists that property interests have at all times, visible or invisible, been dominant.

Following this grim analysis, one commentator on the rise of corporations observed that they had become the "master instruments of civilization."[1] Another expressed his depression at the fact that the system had at length reached a point definitely committing civilization to the rule of a plutocracy.[2] Still others have seen in the system a transition phase towards ultimate socialism or communism. Acceptance of any of these beliefs may be delayed; but the underlying thought expressed in them all is that the corporate system has become the principal factor in economic organization through its mobilization of property interests.

In its new aspect the corporation is a means whereby the wealth of innumerable individuals has been concentrated into huge aggregates and whereby control over this wealth has been surrendered to a unified direction. The power attendant upon such concentration has brought forth princes of industry, whose position in the community is yet to be defined. The surrender of control over their wealth by investors has effectively broken the old property relationships and has raised the problem of defining these relationships anew. The direction of industry by persons other than those who have ventured their wealth has raised the question of the motive force back of such direction and the effective distribution of the returns from business enterprise.

These corporations have arisen in field after field as the myriad independent and competing units of private business have given way to the few large groupings of the modern quasi-public corporation. The typical business unit of the 19th century was owned by individuals or small groups; was managed by them or their appointees; and was, in the main, limited in size by the personal wealth of the individuals in control. These units have been supplanted in ever greater measure by great aggregations in which tens and even hundreds of thousands of workers and property worth hundreds of millions of dollars, belonging to tens or even hundreds of thousands of individuals, are combined through the corporate mechanism into a single producing organization under unified control and management. Such a unit is the American Telephone and Telegraph Company, perhaps the most advanced development of the corporate system. With assets of almost five billions of dollars, with 454,000[3] employees, and stockholders

[1] Thorstein Veblen, "Absentee Ownership and Business Enterprise," N. Y. 1923.
[2] Walther Rathenau, "Die Neue Wirtschaft," Berlin, 1918.
[3] Annual Report of the American Telephone and Telegraph Company, New York, 1930, pp. 20 and 26, figures as of December 31, 1929. On December 31, 1930 the number of employees had dropped to 394,000 presumably a sub-normal condition.

to the number of 567,694,[4] this company may indeed be called an economic empire—an empire bounded by no geographical limits, but held together by centralized control. One hundred companies of this size would control the whole of American wealth; would employ all of the gainfully employed; and if there were no duplication of stockholders, would be owned by practically every family in the country.

Such an organization of economic activity rests upon two developments, each of which has made possible an extension of the area under unified control. The factory system, the basis of the industrial revolution, brought an increasingly large number of workers directly under a single management. Then, the modern corporation, equally revolutionary in its effect, placed the wealth of innumerable individuals under the same central control. By each of these changes the power of those in control was immensely enlarged and the status of those involved, worker or property owner, was radically changed. The independent worker who entered the factory became a wage laborer surrendering the direction of his labor to his industrial master. The property owner who invests in a modern corporation so far surrenders his wealth to those in control of the corporation that he has exchanged the position of independent owner for one in which he may become merely recipient of the wages of capital.

In and of itself, the corporate device does not necessarily bring about this change. It has long been possible for an individual to incorporate his business even though it still represents his own investment, his own activities, and his own business transactions; he has in fact merely created a legal *alter ego* by setting up a corporation as the nominal vehicle. If the corporate form had done nothing more than this, we should have only an interesting custom according to which business would be carried on by individuals adopting for that purpose certain legal clothing. It would involve no radical shift in property tenure or in the organization of economic activity; it would inaugurate no "system" comparable to the institutions of feudalism.

The corporate system appears only when this type of private or "close" corporation has given way to an essentially different form, the quasi-public corporation: a corporation in which a large measure of separation of ownership and control has taken place through the multiplication of owners.

Such separation may exist in varying degrees. Where the men ultimately responsible for running a corporation own a majority of the voting stock while the remainder is widely diffused, control and

[4] As of December 31, 1930. Standard Corporation Records.

part ownership are in their hands. Only for the remaining owners is there separation from control. Frequently, however, ownership is so widely scattered that working control can be maintained with but a minority interest. The Rockefeller family, for example, is reported to have retained direct or indirect minority interests in many of the Standard Oil Companies; and in the case of the Standard Oil Company of Indiana, this interest, amounting to only 14.5 per cent[5] combined with the strategic position of its holders, has proved sufficient for the control of the corporation. In such a case the greater bulk of ownership is virtually without control. Separation of ownership and control becomes almost complete when not even a substantial minority interest exists, as in the American Telephone and Telegraph Company whose largest holder is reported to own less than one per cent of the company's stock. Under such conditions control may be held by the directors or titular managers who can employ the proxy machinery to become a self-perpetuating body, even though as a group they own but a small fraction of the stock outstanding. In each of these types, majority control, minority control, and management control, the separation of ownership from control has become effective—a large body of security holders has been created who exercise virtually no control over the wealth which they or their predecessors in interest have contributed to the enterprise. In the case of management control, the ownership interest held by the controlling group amounts to but a very small fraction of the total ownership. Corporations where this separation has become an important factor may be classed as quasi-public in character in contradistinction to the private, or closely held corporation in which no important separation of ownership and control has taken place.

Growing out of this separation are two characteristics, almost as typical of the quasi-public corporation as the separation itself—mere size and the public market for its securities. It is precisely this separation of control from ownership which makes possible tremendous aggregations of property. The Fords and the Mellons, whose personal wealth is sufficient to finance great enterprises, are so few, that they only emphasize the dependence of the large enterprise on the wealth of more than the individual or group of individuals who may be in control. The quasi-public corporation commands its supply of capital from a group of investors frequently described as the "investing public." It draws these savings to itself either directly, as individuals purchase stocks or bonds, or indirectly, as insurance companies,

[5] See Table XII, p. 94.

banks, and investment trusts receive these savings and invest them in corporate securities. To secure these funds it must commonly avail itself of an open market in its securities—usually by listing shares on a stock exchange, or, less importantly, by maintaining a private or "unlisted" market. So essential, in fact, is the open market to the quasi-public corporation that it may be considered almost as characteristic of that type of corporation as the separation of ownership from control and the great aggregation of wealth.

These characteristics are not invariable. The private corporation may be, and in a few instances is, exceedingly large; witness the Ford Motor Company, still owned and directed by Mr. Ford and his immediate associates. Private or "close" corporations may and occasionally do avail themselves of a public market for their shares; the Aluminum Company of America, though most of its stock is closely held, has its shares listed on the New York Curb Exchange, and a small fraction of its stock is traded in there. But these instances are so exceptional as to prove the rule. In the overwhelming bulk of cases, corporations fall into the quasi-public class when they represent large aggregations of wealth and their securities are available in the open market; for in such corporations part or most of the owners have almost invariably surrendered control.

Though the American law makes no distinction between the private corporation and the quasi-public, the economics of the two are essentially different. The separation of ownership from control produces a condition where the interests of owner and of ultimate manager may, and often do, diverge, and where many of the checks which formerly operated to limit the use of power disappear. Size alone tends to give these giant corporations a social significance not attached to the smaller units of private enterprise. By the use of the open market for securities, each of these corporations assumes obligations towards the investing public which transform it from a legal method clothing the rule of a few individuals into an institution at least nominally serving investors who have embarked their funds in its enterprise. New responsibilities towards the owners, the workers, the consumers, and the State thus rest upon the shoulders of those in control. In creating these new relationships, the quasi-public corporation may fairly be said to work a revolution. It has destroyed the unity that we commonly call property—has divided ownership into nominal ownership and the power formerly joined to it. Thereby the corporation has changed the nature of profit-seeking enterprise. This revolution forms the subject of the present study.

Examination of the changes produced can properly commence with the new relationships between the owners on the one hand and control on the other, and it is these relationships with which this book will deal. This involves the area roughly termed "corporation finance"—the relations between the corporation as managed by the group in control, and those who hold participations in it—its stockholders, bondholders, and, to some extent, its other creditors. The change in internal organization—the relation of the corporation to its workers, its plant organization and its technical problem of production—we cannot consider at this time. Nor can we here deal with its external relationships, on the one hand with its customers—the terms on which it furnishes to them its products or its services—and on the other hand, with the political state—the government by which it may be in some degree controlled, or over which it may have a measure of dominance. Here we are concerned only with a fundamental change in the form of property, and in the economic relationships which rest upon it.

Outwardly the change is simple enough. Men are less likely to own the physical instruments of production. They are more likely to own pieces of paper, loosely known as stocks, bonds, and other securities, which have become mobile through the machinery of the public markets. Beneath this, however, lies a more fundamental shift. Physical control over the instruments of production has been surrendered in ever growing degree to centralized groups who manage property in bulk, supposedly, but by no means necessarily, for the benefit of the security holders. Power over industrial property has been cut off from the beneficial ownership of this property—or, in less technical language, from the legal right to enjoy its fruits. Control of physical assets has passed from the individual owner to those who direct the quasi-public institutions, while the owner retains an interest in their product and increase. We see, in fact, the surrender and regrouping of the incidence of ownership, which formerly bracketed full power of manual disposition with complete right to enjoy the use, the fruits, and the proceeds of physical assets. There has resulted the dissolution of the old atom of ownership into its component parts, control and beneficial ownership.

This dissolution of the atom of property destroys the very foundation on which the economic order of the past three centuries has rested. Private enterprise, which has molded economic life since the close of the middle ages, has been rooted in the institution of private property. Under the feudal system, its predecessor, economic organization grew out of mutual obligations and privileges derived by various individuals from their relation to property which no one of them owned. Private enterprise, on the other hand, has assumed an owner of the instruments of production with complete property rights over those instruments. Whereas the organization of feudal economic life rested upon an elaborate system of binding customs, the organization under the system of private enterprise has rested upon the self-interest of the property owner—a self-interest held in check only by competition and the conditions of supply and demand. Such self-interest has long been regarded as the best guarantee of economic efficiency. It has been assumed that, if the individual is protected in the right both to use his own property as he sees fit and to receive the full fruits of its use, his desire for personal gain, for profits, can be relied upon as an effective incentive to his efficient use of any industrial property he may possess.

In the quasi-public corporation, such an assumption no longer holds. As we have seen, it is no longer the individual himself who uses his wealth. Those in control of that wealth, and therefore in a position to secure industrial efficiency and produce profits, are no longer, as owners, entitled to the bulk of such profits. Those who control the destinies of the typical modern corporation own so insignificant a fraction of the company's stock that the returns from running the corporation profitably accrue to them in only a very minor degree. The stockholders, on the other hand, to whom the profits of the corporation go, cannot be motivated by those profits to a more efficient use of the property, since they have surrendered all disposition of it to those in control of the enterprise. The explosion of the atom of property destroys the basis of the old assumption that the quest for profits will spur the owner of industrial property to its effective use. It consequently challenges the fundamental economic principle of individual initiative in industrial enterprise. It raises for reexamination the question of the motive force back of industry, and the ends for which the modern corporation can be or will be run.

The corporate system further commands attention because its development is progressive, as its features become more marked and as new areas come one by one under its sway. Economic power, in terms of control over physical assets, is apparently responding to a centripetal force, tending more and more to concentrate in the hands of a few corporate managements. At the same time, beneficial ownership is centrifugal, tending to divide and subdivide, to split into ever smaller units and to pass freely from hand to hand. In other words, ownership continually becomes more dispersed; the power formerly joined to it becomes increasingly concentrated; and the corporate system is thereby more securely established.

This system bids fair to be as all-embracing as was the feudal system in its time. It demands that we examine both its conditions and its trends, for an understanding of the structure upon which will rest the economic order of the future.

CHAPTER II: THE APPEARANCE
OF THE CORPORATE SYSTEM

CORPORATE ENTERPRISE is no new institution. From the days of the joint stock trading companies which built up the merchant empires of England and Holland in the Seventeenth Century, the quasi-public corporation has been well known. Its entrance into the field of industry, however, dates from the early Nineteenth Century. In 1800 the corporate form was used in America mainly for undertakings involving a direct public interest: the construction of turnpikes, bridges and canals, the operation of banks and insurance companies, and the creation of fire brigades. Up to that year only 335 profit-seeking corporations appear to have been formed in the United States, nearly all incorporated in the last decade of the Eighteenth Century. Of these, 219 were turnpike, bridge and canal companies, and another 36 furnished water and fire protection or dock facilities. Banks and insurance companies had just begun to assume corporate form and numbered 67 at the opening of the century. Manufacturing industry lay almost wholly outside the corporate field, being represented by only 6 corporations.[1]

Though some of these early utility corporations were quasi-public in character, their stock being held by what was, for the time, a large number of stockholders, the first important manufacturing enterprise to be so organized dates from 1813. The Boston Manufacturing Company, first of the large New England textile firms, was established at Waltham, Massachusetts, during that year and was in many ways the prototype of the corporations of later date. Though insignificantly small in comparison with the corporate giants of today this company had all their essential characteristics. Within ten years of the date of

[1] Joseph S. Davis, "Essays in the Earlier History of American Corporations," Cambridge, 1917, Vol. II, p. 24.

incorporation, its stock, originally held by eleven stockholders, had become in a sense dispersed. By 1830 the stockholders numbered 76, no individual owned more than 8½ per cent of the stock, it took 12 to establish majority control, and the management lay with a board of directors whose combined holdings amounted to only 22 per cent. Twenty years later there were 123 stockholders, the largest of whom still owned 8½ per cent. Fifty-one per cent of the stock was distributed among 17 individuals while the management held only 11 per cent.[2]

Small though these figures seem in comparison with the hundreds of thousands of stockholders of the American Telephone Company today, they are none the less significant. The number of shareholders represented a very considerable dispersion for the par value of each share was $1,000 and the total number of available shares was small. The paid-in capital of $300,000,—increased in 20 years to $1,000,000,— was a very large sum for industrial enterprise in those days. The size of the industrial plant was correspondingly large in relation to those of competing concerns, and for the first time, all the textile processes, from breaking open the bale of cotton to shipping the finished cloth, were brought under a single direction. Here, too, the "promoter," so important a figure in the corporate system today, clearly appeared. By "selling out to the public," to use the modern phrase, the original organizers freed themselves and a large part of their capital from the fortunes of their first investment and were enabled to go on to organize further similar corporate units. This they did, forming a succession of large textile concerns, all corporate in form, all capitalized at $1,000,000 or more within a few years of organization, all equipped for large scale, mass production including every process, and all publicly held.[8] In every company, ownership rested with the public and direction with a management which owned a relatively small proportion of the stock. In 1842, the stock of one company, the Merrimack, was held by 390 people, including: [4]

> 80 administrators or trustees.
> 68 females.

[2] Derived from the Stock and Dividend Books of the Boston Manufacturing Company, preserved at the Harvard Business School, Cambridge, Massachusetts.
[8] The Merrimack Co. was formed in 1822, the Hamilton in 1825, the Appleton and Lowell Companies in 1828, Middlesex in 1830, Tremont and Suffolk Companies in 1831, the Boott and Massachusetts Companies in 1835 and 1839, all in the single city of Lowell. The same promoters launched similar concerns in other New England towns and founded in 1846 the new textile center of Lawrence. —C. F. Ware, "Early New England Cotton Manufacture," Boston, 1931. Appendix A.
[4] *Ibid,* p. 150.

52 retired business men.
46 merchants.
45 manufacturers and mechanics.
40 clerks, students, and unspecified.
23 lawyers.
18 physicians.
15 farmers.
 3 institutions.

By virtue of their size and widespread ownership, these companies were always distinguished in New England as "The Corporations" in contrast to the small private concerns, though the latter were often incorporated.

The corporate development of this branch of the textile industry stood alone in the industrial field before 1860. Its growth, moreover, was arrested in the years after the Civil War when the corporate system was elsewhere growing apace, so that today, paradoxically, the textile industry is one of the few major industries which is not dominated by great quasi-public corporations.

More general in the ante-bellum period, and more significant for the future development, was the introduction of the corporate system into the railroad field. Railroad construction, involving a heavy initial outlay of capital, almost necessitated recourse to the corporate form. Once the first short lines had been constructed, this form made possible the next step, consolidation into larger systems. The first of the major groupings, the creation of the New York Central Railroad in 1853, was achieved through the devices which the corporation offered. The property of 10 small companies between Albany and Buffalo was transferred to a new corporation by exchange of stock and the 34 million dollars of securities, issued against the combined properties, were dispersed among 2,445 investors in Albany and other cities of New York State. No individual or group held a controlling financial interest in the new corporation.[5] Already the stock of railroad companies was familiar on the public exchanges and by the 'Sixties fights for control of their properties had become either market fights or more sinister legal battles.[6]

Since the Civil War, the quasi-public corporation has come to dominate the railroad field almost completely. Advantages of consolidation and the disastrous effects of competition drove companies into larger and larger units until, in 1930, 14 great systems operated

[5] F. W. Stevens, "The Beginnings of the New York Central Railroad," N. Y., 1926, pp. 352, 382.
[6] C. F. Adams, "Chapters of Erie," Boston, 1871, pp. 11, 13.

86.6 per cent of the first class mileage and 81.7 per cent of all road-road mileage in the country.[7]

Following the lead of the railroads, in the last part of the Nineteenth Century and the early years of the Twentieth, one aspect of economic life after another has come under corporate sway. Banking and insurance companies carried the system over from the earlier years of the century. So also did the public utilities, among which it has become practically universal.[8] Mining and quarrying followed close on the heels of the utilities, being 86.3 per cent corporate in 1902 and 93.6 per cent in 1919.[9] In the latter year, 99 per cent of the wage earners in the copper industry were employed by corporations, 98 per cent in iron ore, 97 per cent in lead and zinc, and 89 per cent in petroleum and natural gas.[10] It should be noted, of course, that the extent to which a field is incorporated is not an exact measure of the presence of the quasi-public corporation and the corporate system, since private corporations are included in the totals. The latter, however, represent in most cases a relatively small proportion of the wealth and activity involved and therefore do not seriously invalidate such figures as an index of the extension of the quasi-public corporation.

Except for the textile corporations mentioned above, the corporate system made slower headway in the manufacturing field. Its growth was stimulated in the period immediately following the Civil War by the enlargement of industrial units and the spread of mass production. In the closing decades of the Nineteenth Century it received a further stimulus from the trust movement of those years. By 1899 the census reported 66.7 per cent of all manufactured products as made by corporations [11] and corporate increase in the Twentieth Century has been most rapid; 87 per cent of goods were so produced by 1919 [12] and it is fair to assume that over 94 per cent of manufacturing is car-

---

[7] Derived from the report of the House Committee on Interstate and Foreign Commerce on the "Regulation of Stock Ownership in the Railroads," 71st Congress, 3rd Session, House Report No. 2789, Feb. 21, 1931, pp. LII, LIV.

[8] In 1922, 28 miles of electric railroads were in the hands of private individuals or partnerships. Census of Elec. Ind., Elec. R. R., 1922, p. 9. All telegraph companies were corporate by 1917. Census of Elec. Ind., Telegraphs, 1917, p. 9. All but $5,000,000 of capital of telephone companies in 1922 was corporate. Census of Telephones, 1922, p. 1. All but $5,200,000 of gross income of all non-municipal electric light and power companies was received by corporations in 1917. (99.0%.) Census of Elec. Ind., Cent. Elec. Lt. & Pr. Sta., 1917, p. 25. In these census figures the Massachusetts Trust is presumably included as a corporation.

[9] Statistical Abstract of the United States, 1925, p. 703.

[10] Abstract of 14th Census of the United States, 1920, p. 1278.

[11] 13th Census of United States, 1910, Vol. VIII, p. 135.

[12] 14th Census of United States, 1920, Vol. VIII, pp. 14, 108.

ried on by corporations at the present time.[13] Wage earners in the employ of manufacturing corporations have increased correspondingly from 65 per cent of those engaged in manufactures in 1899 to 92 per cent (estimated) in 1929.[14] Though in manufacturing, private corporations play a more important role than in the mining and utility fields, the growth in total corporate manufacturing reflects a large measure of growth of quasi-public corporations.

In a few manufacturing industries the transfer to the corporate form has been delayed, but even here the shift is noticeable. In 1920, the men's clothing industry, with a value product of over a billion dollars was only 54.6 per cent corporate, the bread and baking industry only 51.7 per cent, millinery and lace goods 46.9 per cent, automobile repairing 39.1 per cent, women's clothing 32.9 per cent, fur goods 30.1 per cent, cheese-making 20.7 per cent.[15] These are the most important manufacturing industries in which the corporate form has not become overwhelmingly predominant,[16] but in each case the 1920 figure showed a larger proportion of corporate production than the figure of the previous census. There is good reason, moreover, to believe that the recent census will show a very much greater proportion of corporate activity in most of these industries.

In the mercantile field the corporation is only just beginning to come into its own. Exact figures are not here available, but rough estimates place the per cent of wholesale sales made by corporations in 1909 at approximately 30 per cent and at 40 per cent in 1925. In the same sixteen-year period retail sales by corporations grew from 15 to 30 per cent of all retail sales.[17] The latter growth included some additional extension of wholesale corporate trade since in many cases the retail corporation also performed the wholesale function. Though these figures, at best only approximate, may be shown to be in error when the census of 1930 reports a thorough canvass of the mercantile field for the first time, the rapid growth of the corporation in this area cannot be questioned.

This expansion is almost synonymous with the development of the chain store. From 1919 to 1927 sales by chain groceries increased 287

[13] Estimate obtained by projecting trend line based on log of figure for per cent of manufactured products not made by corporations according to the census figures of 1899, 1909, and 1919.

[14] Abstract of 14th Census of the United States, 1920, p. 1021 for 1899 and estimate (see note 13 for method) for 1929.

[15] Abstract of 14th Census of the United States, 1920, pp. 1022–1029.

[16] All industries reported in the Census as having a value product of over $140,-000,000, less than 55 per cent of which was produced by corporations.

[17] Based on figures supplied by the National Bureau of Economic Research.

per cent while sales of 5 and 10 cent store chains grew 160 per cent.[18] The rate of growth of these chain stores is so far in excess of the growth of total retail sales as to represent a noteworthy encroachment of corporate upon private enterprise in distribution.

For the fields of construction and what the census calls "unclassified industries"—*i.e.*, personal services, amusements, rental of business buildings, professional activities of physicians, lawyers, etc.,— accurate figures are not available. Between forty and sixty per cent of all construction appears to be carried on by corporations,[19] and perhaps some 15 to 25 per cent of the unclassified industries.[20] It is impossible to discover the degree of growth in these fields. Certainly there has been a marked increase in the number of moving picture houses owned by corporations, particularly by the big chains, barber and beauty parlors are chained and incorporated to a growing but still small extent, restaurant chains have grown in the last twenty years, and corporations for the owning of business property have extended their operations. It is not possible, however, to measure whether these developments have been more rapid than the total growth of business in these fields.

One of the last areas of non-corporate activity, the field of real estate, shows signs of coming within the corporate sphere. Much real estate is held by private corporations. Real estate corporations such as the Equitable Office Building, Inc., with active securities on the exchanges, have already made their appearance, and a Real Estate Exchange has recently been formed in New York to deal solely in securities of corporations organized to take over real estate.

In agriculture the corporation has made least headway. In 1920, 61.1 per cent of all farms, measured by their value, were operated by the owner, while 34.9 per cent were operated by tenants. Only 4.0 per cent were operated by managers.[21] Presumably corporate farming was entirely restricted to the latter class, though lands held by a corporation and operated not by the corporation but by tenants would be included in the second group.

The operations of the government remain as the only field of economic activity not yet considered. Here, of course, the corporate system with its widely dispersed ownership is not in evidence. It should be noted, however, that even the government is beginning to

[18] National Bureau of Economic Research, "Recent Economic Changes in the United States, N. Y., 1930, p. 362.
[19] Based on figures supplied by the National Bureau of Economic Research.
[20] Rough estimate based on Income Tax data.
[21] 14th Census of United States, 1920, Vol. V, p. 130.

employ the corporate device—witness, for example, the Port of New York Authority. Even here the corporation may become the established form, ultimate ownership and, to the extent that the democratic machinery is effective, ultimate control, vesting with the people.

Thus, in field after field, the corporation has entered, grown, and become wholly or partially dominant. The date of its appearance and the degree of its dominance have in general varied with two factors, the public character of the activity in question and the amount of fixed capital necessary to carry on business. It came first in the fields of public utilities, common carriers, banks and insurance companies (which even in the 1840's were conceded to perform public functions) [22] and last in the areas of personal service and agriculture;—early, with the high fixed capital costs in railways and mines; late, in mercantile pursuits where capital consists to such a large extent of stock on hand. On the basis of its development in the past we may look forward to a time when practically all economic activity will be carried on under the corporate form. And wherever the corporation has become dominant, it has been in its quasi-public, not its private, rôle. It does not simply give a legal clothing to the private enterprise of individuals. It adds a new quality to enterprise—the quality of multiple ownership.

[22] According to Nathan Appleton, leading New England texture manufacturer, Ware, *op. cit.*, p. 290.

CHAPTER III: THE CONCENTRATION

OF ECONOMIC POWER

THE CORPORATE system has done more than evolve a norm by which business is carried on. Within it there exists a centripetal attraction which draws wealth together into aggregations of constantly increasing size, at the same time throwing control into the hands of fewer and fewer men. The trend is apparent; and no limit is as yet in sight. Were it possible to say that circumstances had established the concentration, but that there was no basis to form an opinion as to whether the process would continue, the whole problem might be simplified. But this is not the case. So far as can be seen, every element which favored concentration still exists, and the only apparent factor which may end the tendency is the limit in the ability of a few human beings effectively to handle the aggregates of property brought under their control.

The size of the modern giant corporation is difficult to grasp. Many people would consider large a corporation having assets of a million dollars or an income of $50,000. Measured by the average corporation this idea would be justified. In 1927 two-thirds of all corporations reporting net incomes earned less than $5,000 each.[1] The average non-banking corporation in that year had an income of only $22,000,[2] and gross assets of but $570,000.[3] In comparison with the average corporation the million dollar company would be large. But in comparison to the great modern corporation both are pigmies. On the basis of assets, the American Telephone and Telegraph Company would be equivalent to over 8,000 average sized corporations, and both the United States Steel Corporation and the Pennsylvania Railroad Company to over

[1] Statistics of Income, 1927, p. 19.
[2] *Ibid.* pp. 16 and 17. Non-banking is here used to exclude banks, insurance companies, and investment trusts.
[3] *Ibid.* pp. 371 and 372.

18

4,000. A hundred million dollar company would be equivalent in assets to nearly 200 average corporations. Clearly such great organisms are not to be thought of in the same terms as the average company. Already the Telephone Company controls more wealth than is contained within the borders of twenty-one of the states in the country.

The great extent to which economic activity is today carried on by such large enterprises is clearly indicated by the accompanying list of the two hundred largest [4] non-banking corporations, compiled as of January 1, 1930. Nearly all of these companies had assets of over one hundred million dollars, and fifteen had assets of over a billion dollars. Their combined assets amounted to eighty-one billions of dollars or, as we shall see, nearly half of all corporate wealth in the United States.

These great companies form the very framework of American industry. The individual must come in contact with them almost constantly. He may own an interest in one or more of them, he may be employed by one of them, but above all he is continually accepting their service. If he travels any distance he is almost certain to ride on one of the great railroad systems. The engine which draws him has probably been constructed by the American Locomotive Company or the Baldwin Locomotive Works; the car in which he rides is likely to have been made by the American Car and Foundry Company or one of its subsidiaries, unless he is enjoying the services of the Pullman Company. The rails have almost certainly been supplied by one of the eleven steel companies on the list; and coal may well have come from one of the four coal companies, if not from a mine owned by the railroad itself. Perhaps the individual travels by automobile—in a car manufactured by the Ford, General Motors, Studebaker, or Chrylser Companies, on tires supplied by Firestone, Goodrich, Goodyear or the United States Rubber Company. He may choose among the brands of gas furnished by one of the twenty petroleum companies all actively seeking his trade. Should he pause to send a telegram or to telephone, one of the listed companies would be sure to fill his need.

[4] Largest according to gross assets less depreciation, as reported in Moody's Railroad, Public Utility, and Industrial Manuals. In the cases where a consolidated balance sheet was not given in Moody's, an estimate was made based on the assets of subsidiaries and the assets of the parent corporation minus its investments in affiliated companies. These estimates, while they cannot be perfectly accurate, are sufficiently so for the present purpose. In two cases, no balance sheet of the parent was given but a very rough estimate of the assets controlled was made, based on the bonds and stocks of the parent company and the assets of certain of its subsidiaries. No company is included in the list, a majority of whose voting stock was known to be owned by another corporation.

TABLE I: *The 200 Largest Non-banking Corporations in the United States*

Name	Gross assets on or about Jan. 1, 1930. In millions of dollars
Amusements	
Eastman Kodak Co.	163.4
General Theatre Equipment, Inc. (Fox Theatres)	360.0
Loew's, Inc.	124.2
Paramount Publix Corp.	236.7
Radio Corp. of America	280.0 (est.)
Warner Bros. Pictures, Inc.	167.1
Chemicals	
PETROLEUM	
Atlantic Refining Co.	167.2
Continental Oil Co.	198.0
Gulf Oil Corp.	430.9
Ohio Oil Co.	110.6
Phillips Petroleum Co.	145.3
Prairie Oil & Gas Co.	209.8
Prairie Pipe Line Co.	140.5
Pure Oil Co.	215.4
Richfield Oil Co. of California	131.9
Shell Union Oil Corp.	486.4
Sinclair Consolidated Oil Corp.	400.6
Sinclair Crude Oil Purchasing Co.	111.9
Standard Oil Co. of California	604.7
Standard Oil Co. of Indiana	850.0 (est.)
Standard Oil Co. of New Jersey	1767.3
Standard Oil Co. of New York	708.4
Texas Corp.	609.8
Tide Water Associated Oil Co.	251.4
Union Oil Associates	240.0 (est.)
Vacuum Oil Co.	205.7
OTHER CHEMICALS, SOAP, ETC.	
Allied Chemical & Dye Corp.	277.2
Corn Products Refining Co.	126.7
Du Pont de Nemours & Co.	497.3
International Match Corp.	217.6

Name	Gross assets on or about Jan. 1, 1930. In millions of dollars
OTHER CHEMICALS, SOAP, ETC. (*Continued*)	
Koppers Co.	250.0
Procter & Gamble Co.	109.4
Union Carbide & Carbon Corp.	306.6
Coal	
Consolidation Coal Co.	94.0
Glen Alden Coal Co.	300.0 (est.)
Philadelphia & Reading Coal & Iron Corp.	129.0
Pittsburgh Coal Co.	171.5
Food Products, Drugs, Tobacco, etc.	
DAIRY PRODUCTS	
Borden Co.	174.0
National Dairy Products Co.	224.5
FRUIT	
United Fruit Co.	226.0
MEAT	
Armour & Co.	452.3
Swift & Co.	351.2
Wilson & Co.	98.0
SUGAR	
American Sugar Refining Co.	157.1
Cuban Cane Prod. Co.	101.3
TOBACCO	
American Tobacco Co.	265.4
Liggett & Myers Tobacco Co.	150.3
Lorillard (P.) Co.	110.0
Reynolds Tobacco Co.	163.1
OTHERS	
National Biscuit Co.	133.2
Glass	
Pittsburgh Plate Glass Co.	101.6
Leather	
International Shoe Co.	111.3

TABLE I: *The 200 Largest Non-banking Corporations in the United States (Continued)*

Name	Gross assets on or about Jan. 1, 1930. In millions of dollars
Lumber	
Long-Bell Lumber Corp.	116.1
Mercantile	
Drug, Inc. (United Drug Co.)	158.0
Great Atlantic & Pacific Tea Co.	147.3
Kresge Co.	109.5
Macy (R. H.) & Co.	97.0 (est.)
Marshall Field & Co.	137.2
Montgomery Ward & Co.	187.5
Sears, Roebuck & Co.	251.8
United Stores Corp. (United Cigar Stores)	161.5
Woolworth & Co.	165.4
Metal Products	
AUTOMOBILES	
Chrysler Corp.	209.7
Ford Motor Co.	761.0
General Motors Corp.	1400.0 (est.)
Studebaker Corp.	134.2
ELECTRICAL EQUIPMENT	
General Electric Co.	515.7
Westinghouse Electric & Manufacturing Co.	253.9
MACHINERY	
Deere & Co.	94.6
International Harvester Co.	384.0
Singer Manufacturing Co.	210.0 (est.)
United Shoe Machinery Corp.	94.1
OTHERS	
American Can Co.	191.3
American Car & Foundry Co.	119.5
American Locomotive Co.	106.2
American Radiator & Standard Sanitary Corp.	199.4
Baldwin Locomotive Works	98.8
Crane Co.	115.9

Name	Gross assets on or about Jan. 1, 1930. In millions of dollars
Metals	
ALUMINUM	
Aluminum Co. of America	300.0
COPPER & LEAD	
American Smelting & Refining Co.	241.0
Anaconda Copper Mining Co.	680.6
Kennecott Copper Corp.	337.8
National Lead Co.	108.4
Phelps Dodge Corp.	124.7
IRON & STEEL	
American Rolling Mill Co.	104.3
Bethlehem Steel Corp.	801.6
Cliffs Corp.	98.0
Crucible Steel Co. of America	124.3
Inland Steel Co.	103.2
Jones & Laughlin Steel Corp.	222.0
National Steel Corp.	120.8
Republic Iron & Steel Co.	331.7
United States Steel Corp.	2286.1
Wheeling Steel Corp.	128.3
Youngstown Sheet & Tube Co.	235.7
Paper	
Crown Zellerbach Corp.	117.7
International Paper & Power Co.	686.5
Minnesota & Ontario Paper Co.	90.3
Public Utilities (Grouped according to associated companies)	
COMMUNICATIONS	
American Telephone & Telegraph Co.	4228.4
Associated Telephone Utilities Co.	95.9
International Telephone & Telegraph Corp.	521.2
Western Union Telegraph Co.	332.2
ELECTRICITY AND GAS	
American Commonwealths Power Corp.	184.4
American Water Works & Elec. Co.	378.5

TABLE I: *The 200 Largest Non-banking Corporations in the United States (Continued)*

Name	Gross assets on or about Jan. 1, 1930. In millions of dollars
ELECTRICITY AND GAS (*Continued*)	
Associated Gas & Electric Co.	900.4
New England Gas and Electric Association	108.7
Railway and Bus Associates	112.2
Central Public Service Co.	199.5
Cities Service Co.	989.6
Consolidated Gas Co. of New York	1171.5
Consolidated Gas, Elec. Lt. & Power Co. of Baltimore	135.9
Detroit Edison Co.	296.1
Duke Power Co.	212.1
Edison Electric Ill. Co. of Boston	156.3
Electric Bond & Share Co.	756.0
American Gas & Electric Co.	431.0
American Power & Light Co.	754.1
Electric Power & Light Corp.	560.0 (est.)
National Power & Light Co.	500.0 (est.)
INSULL GROUP	
Commonwealth Edison Co.	440.0 (est.)
Middle West Utilities Co.	1120.0 (est.)
Midland United Co.	298.1
North Amer. Light & Power Co.	308.4
Peoples Gas, Light & Coke Co.	192.1
Public Service Co. of Northern Illinois	190.0
KOPPERS CO. GROUP	
Brooklyn Union Gas Co.	123.7
Eastern Gas & Fuel Associates	158.7
Lone Star Gas Corp.	109.0
North American Co.	810.3
Pacific Gas & Elec. Co.	428.2
Pacific Lighting Corp.	203.4
So. California Edison Co., Ltd.	340.6
Stone & Webster, Inc.	400.0 (est.)
Tri-Utilities Corp.	346.0
UNITED CORPORATION GROUP	
Columbia Gas & Electric Corp.	529.2

Name	Gross assets on or about Jan. 1, 1930. In millions of dollars
ELECTRICITY AND GAS (*Continued*)	
UNITED CORPORATION GROUP (*Continued*)	
Commonwealth and Southern Corp.	1133.7
Niagara Hudson Power Corp.	756.9
Public Service Corp. of New Jersey	634.6
United Gas Improvement Co.	802.0
United Light & Power Co.	520.1
United States Electric Power Corp.	1125.8
Utilities Power & Light Corp.	373.1
Railroads (*Grouped according to associated companies*)	
Alleghany Corp.	1600.0 (est.)
Erie Rd. Co.	560.9
Kansas City Southern Ry. Co.	146.1
New York, Chicago & St. Louis R. Co.	350.0 (est.)
Wheeling & Lake Erie Ry. Co.	104.1
Atchison, Topeka & Santa Fe Ry. Co.	1135.4
Atlantic Coast Line R. Co.	840.0 (est.)
Baltimore & Ohio Rd. Co.	1040.8
Chicago & Alton Rd. Co.	161.8
Reading Co.	565.0 (est.)
Western Maryland Ry. Co.	168.2
Chicago & Eastern Illinois Ry. Co.	97.4
Chicago Great Western Rd. Co.	149.2
Chicago, Milwaukee, St. Paul & Pacific Rd. Co.	776.1
Chicago & North Western Ry. Co.	641.0
Chicago, Rock Island & Pacific Ry. Co.	477.4
Chicago Union Station Co.	96.8
Delaware & Hudson Co.	269.4
Delaware, Lackawanna & Western R. Co.	189.3
Denver & Rio Grande Western Rd. Co.	223.4
Florida East Coast Ry. Co.	123.6
{ Great Northern Ry. Co.	812.4
{ Northern Pacific Ry. Co.	813.9
Chicago, Burlington & Quincy Rd. Co.	645.4
Spokane, Portland & Seattle Ry. Co.	140.2

TABLE I: *The 200 Largest Non-banking Corporations in the United States (Continued)*

Name	Gross assets on or about Jan. 1, 1930. In millions of dollars
Railroads (Continued)	
Missouri-Kansas-Texas Rd. Co.	314.0
New York Central Rd. Co.	2250.0
New York, New Haven & Hartford R. Co.	560.8
Boston & Maine Rd. Co.	256.4
Pennsylvania R. Co.	2600.0 (est.)
Lehigh Valley Rd. Co.	226.0
Norfolk & Western Ry. Co.	497.0
Wabash Ry. Co.	334.6
St. Louis-San Francisco Ry. Co.	439.9
St. Louis Southwestern Ry. Co.	139.4
Seaboard Air Line Ry. Co.	283.1
Southern Pacific Co.	2156.7
Southern Ry. Co.	655.5
Union Pacific Rd. Co.	1121.1
Illinois Central Rd. Co.	680.9
Virginian Ry. Co.	152.7
Western Pacific Rd. Corp.	156.0 (est.)
Real Estate	
U. S. Realty & Improvement Co.	124.6
Rubber	
B. F. Goodrich Co.	163.6
Firestone Tire & Rubber Co.	161.6
Goodyear Tire & Rubber Co.	243.2
United States Rubber Co.	307.8
Textiles	
American Woolen Co.	113.9
Traction	
Boston Elevated Ry. Co.	109.7
Brooklyn & Manhattan Transit Co.	288.5
Chicago Rys. Co.	108.2
Hudson Manhattan R. Co.	131.7
Interborough Rapid Transit Co.	458.6
Philadelphia Rapid Transit Co.	95.6

Name	Gross assets on or about Jan. 1, 1930. In millions of dollars
Traction (*Continued*)	
Third Avenue Ry. Co.	110.0 (est.)
United Rys. & Elec. Co. of Baltimore	96.7
Transportation	
International Mercantile Marine Co.	100.0 (est.)
Pullman, Inc.	315.5

Perhaps, on the other hand, the individual stays in his own home in comparative isolation and privacy. What do the two hundred largest companies mean to him there? His electricity and gas are almost sure to be furnished by one of these public utility companies: the aluminum of his kitchen utensils by the Aluminum Co. of America. His electric refrigerator may be the product of General Motors Co., or of one of the two great electric equipment companies, General Electric and Westinghouse Electric. The chances are that the Crane Company has supplied his plumbing fixtures, the American Radiator and Standard Sanitary Corp. his heating equipment. He probably buys at least some of his groceries from the Great Atlantic and Pacific Tea Co.—a company that expected to sell one-eighth of all the groceries in the country in 1930 [4a]—and he secures some of his drugs, directly or indirectly, from the United Drug Company. The cans which contain his groceries may well have been made by the American Can Company; his sugar has been refined by one of the major companies, his meat has probably been prepared by Swift, Armour, or Wilson, his crackers put up by the National Biscuit Company. The newspaper which comes to his door may be printed on International Paper Company paper or on that of the Crown Zellerbach Corporation; his shoes may be one of the International Shoe Company's makes; and although his suit may not be made of American Woolen Company cloth, it has doubtless been stitched on a Singer sewing machine.

If he seeks amusement through a radio he will almost of necessity use a set made under a license of the Radio Corporation of America. When he steps out to the movies he will probably see a Paramount,

[4a] Wall Street Journal, Nov. 25, 1929.

Fox, or Warner Brothers' picture (taken on Eastman Kodak film) at a theatre controlled by one of these producing groups. No matter which of the alluring cigarette advertisements he succumbs to he is almost sure to find himself smoking one of the many brands put out by the "big four" tobacco companies, and he probably stops to buy them at the United Cigar store on the corner.

Even where the individual does not come in direct contact, he cannot escape indirect contact with these companies, so ubiquitous have they become. There are few articles of consumption to whose production one of the big companies has not to some extent contributed. The International Harvester Company and the Deere Company, plowmakers, have aided in the production of most of the bread that the American eats, to much of the cotton he wears and to many of the other agricultural products he consumes. It is almost impossible to obtain electric power from a local utility without receiving service from generating equipment supplied by one of the two big electric equipment companies. Few industrial products are made without the aid at some point in the process of steel derived from one of the big companies. And nearly every article involves transportation by one of the big railroads, either in the state of a raw material or that of a finished product.

While these companies play an integral part in the business of the country, their dominant position becomes apparent only when we seek to examine their importance in relation to the whole of the American economy. Here we must turn to the tool of statistics for only thus can we grasp the picture of our economic life as a whole. To make a statistical comparison of the relative importance of the large corporations, it is first necessary to decide upon a measure of importance. Since this study is primarily concerned with property, we have taken wealth, the economic equivalent of property, as the criterion of "importance" and have further assumed that the gross assets [5] controlled by a corporation are roughly proportional to its wealth. Wherever possible, however, the results obtained have been checked by the use of a second measure of importance—net earnings.[6]

In seeking to present a picture of the relative positions of these

[5] Gross assets less depreciation. In some balance sheets depreciation is subtracted from assets and in others it is included as a liability. Both practices are legitimate, but the latter results in a larger figure for gross assets. An adjustment has, therefore, been made where necessary to obtain gross assets exclusive of depreciation.

[6] Statutory net income as compiled by the Treasury Department. This consists of the untaxed net income derived by a corporation directly from its business operations.

large corporations, four economic areas will be examined: (1) the New York stock market; (2) all corporate wealth; (3) all business wealth; and (4) the national wealth.

In the New York stock market there can be no question of the dominant position of the large corporation. Taking the list of stocks published weekly by the "Commercial and Financial Chronicle" and covering all but the most inactive stocks traded on the New York Stock Exchange in a normal week, 130 out of the 573 independent American corporations represented can be classed as huge companies, each reporting assets of over one hundred million dollars.[7] These 130 companies controlled more than 80 per cent of the assets of all the companies represented. In the following table, these corporations are grouped by size showing the total assets held by each group and the per cent which this represents of the assets of all the corporations covered.[8]

Size measured by gross assets	Number of companies	Gross assets held by group	Per cent of total assets represented
Under $50,000,000	372	$ 7,325,000,000	10.9
$50–$100,000,000	71	4,950,000,000	7.4
Over $100,000,000	130	54,714,000,000	81.7
Total	573	$66,989,000,000	100.0

[7] The stocks of 678 corporations were included in the list published by the "Commercial and Financial Chronicle" in the issue selected, that of the typical week of March 9, 1929. Of these, 76 were subsidiaries of other corporations on the list, 21 were foreign corporations and 8 were financial corporations. When a corporation listed on the exchange was a subsidiary of a corporation not listed, the parent was regarded as represented on the exchange. The assets of the listed corporations were obtained in Moody's Manuals for 1928 and 1929.

[8] A similar study was made for the independent companies listed on the New York Curb Exchange, using the curb transaction list from the same issue of the "Commercial and Financial Chronicle." Unfortunately, the study was first made for a different purpose which involved only the companies in existence in 1927 and a compilation of asests as of that date. For this reason it does not include many companies which should be added. As the correction would probably not make a radical difference in the set of percentages, the uncorrected results are given below:

Size measured by gross assets	Number of companies	Gross assets held by group	Per cent of total assets represented
Under $50,000,000	371	$3,731,000,000	24.3
$50–$100,000,000	31	2,308,000,000	15.0
Over $100,000,000	37	9,338,000,000	60.7
Total	439	$15,377,000,000	100.0

Besides showing the overwhelming importance of the huge corporation, this table shows what is perhaps of even greater significance, the relative unimportance of the medium-sized corporation having assets between $50,000,000 and $100,000,000 and as a group controlling less than 8 per cent of the total assets represented. The small corporations—and in this day of industrial giants the reader must not be shocked by the reference to all corporations with assets less than $50,000,000 as small—though numerous, do not hold an important position. It is noteworthy, however, that practically half the corporations included had less than $30,000,000 assets and as a group controlled less than 6 per cent of the total.[9]

When we compare the combined assets of the two hundred largest non-banking corporations with the assets of all non-banking corporations, their dominant role is further emphasized. These companies, 42 railroads, 52 public utilities, and 106 industrials, each with assets over ninety million dollars, had combined assets at the beginning of 1930 of $81,074,000,000.[10] According to an estimate based on Income Tax figures, the total assets of all non-banking corporations at the beginning of 1930 amounted to $165,000,000,000.[11] Thus the two hundred big companies controlled 49.2 per cent or nearly half of all non-banking corporate wealth, while the remaining half was owned by the more than 300,000 smaller companies.

The same dominant position of the large companies is shown when we compare the net income of the largest companies with the net income of all corporations. In 1929, the most recent year for which Income Tax statistics have been published, the largest two hundred non-banking corporations, each with an income of over $5,000,000, received 43.2 per cent of the income of all non-banking corporations.[12]

Even this figure, however, tends to minimize the importance of the big companies. To a very considerable extent the Income Tax statistics, on which it is based, fail to include as part of the income of

[9] See Appendix A for a more detailed table of companies according to size.

[10] In the 26 cases where a consolidated balance sheet was not given in Moody's an estimate was made based on the assets of subsidiaries and the assets of the parent corporation minus its investments in affiliated companies. These estimates, while they cannot be perfectly accurate, are sufficiently so for the present purpose. In two cases, no balance sheet of the parent was given but a very rough estimate of the assets controlled was made, based on the bonds and stocks of the parent company and the assets of certain of its subsidiaries.

[11] This estimate was arrived at by making an estimate of the gross assets of all non-banking corporations on Dec. 31, 1929, according to the method described in "The Large Corporation in American Economic Life," American Economic Review, Vol. XXI, March, 1931, pp. 15 and 16.

[12] See Table IV.

wealth at the end of 1928 amounted to $360,062,000,000.[16] If we assume an increase equal to the average of the previous six years we should have $367,000,000,000 as the national wealth in 1929. Since the total assets of the two hundred big companies in that year amounted to $81,077,000,000,[17] they controlled roughly 22 per cent of the total wealth of the country. The lower relative importance of the large corporation in comparison to the national wealth is in large measure due to the importance of agricultural land and improvements, residential real estate, personal property including automobiles, and large volume of government property.

To recapitulate, the following table gives the results of the foregoing analysis:

Relative Importance of Large Corporations

(*On or about January 1, 1930*)

	Results obtained by actual computation	Probable limits
Proportion of corporate wealth (*other than banking*) controlled by the 200 largest corporations	49.2%	45–53%
Proportion of business wealth (*other than banking*) controlled by the 200 largest corporations	38.0%[1]	35–45%
Proportion of national wealth controlled by the 200 largest corporations	22.0%	15–25%

[1] Unadjusted for unconsolidated income tax returns.

It is apparent from these figures that a very considerable portion of the industrial wealth of the country has been concentrated under the control of a relatively few huge units. There were over 300,000 non-financial corporations in the country in 1929. Yet 200 of these, or less than seven-hundredths of one per cent, control nearly half the corporate wealth.

It must further be remembered that the influence of one of these huge companies extends far beyond the assets under its direct control.

[16] The Conference Board Bulletin, No. 38, (February 25, 1930), p. 303, National Industrial Conference Board, New York.

[17] The error due to including bills receivable in gross assets is not sufficiently large in comparison to the probable error in the estimate of national wealth to warrant making an adjustment.

Smaller companies which sell to or buy from the larger companies are likely to be influenced by them to a vastly greater extent than by other smaller companies with which they might deal. In many cases the continued prosperity of the smaller company depends on the favor of the larger and almost inevitably the interests of the latter become the interests of the former. The influence of the larger company on prices is often greatly increased by its mere size, even though it does not begin to approach a monopoly. Its political influence may be tremendous. Therefore, if roughly half of corporate wealth is controlled by two hundred large corporations and half by smaller companies it is fair to assume that very much more than half of industry is dominated by these great units. This concentration is made even more significant when it is recalled that as a result of it, approximately 2,000 individuals out of a population of one hundred and twenty-five million are in a position to control and direct half of industry.

The actual extent to which the concentration of power has progressed is striking enough. More striking still, however, is the pace at which it is proceeding. In 1909, the assets of the 200 then largest non-banking corporations amounted to only $26.0 billion.[18] By 1919 they had reached $43.7 billion, an increase of 68 per cent in ten years. In the next ten years from 1919 to 1929 they increased to $81.1 billion, an increase of 85 per cent.

The growth of 150 identical corporations included in the largest 200 companies in both 1919 and 1928 is given in Table II.

The assets of 44 identical railroads increased from $18 billion in 1919 to $23 billion in 1928 or 24 per cent; 71 identical industrial corporations increased from $14 billion to $23 billion in the same period, a growth of approximately 58 per cent in nine years. In the public utility field, as is well known, the rate has been vastly more rapid. In the same nine years the assets of 35 identical utilities grew from $6 billion to $18 billion, or nearly three times. The more rapid growth of the utilities approximately compensates for the slow growth of the railroads, and the total for the 150 corporations shows a growth from $39 billion to $63 billion, or an increase of practically 63 per cent.

Though the growth of the large corporations shown in these tables is rapid, it is truly significant only if it has been more rapid than the growth of all industrial wealth. We have already discussed the difficulty in estimating the total industrial wealth for each year; but, as we have seen, more accurate material is available with reference to the wealth of corporations. Here again the distinction between banking and non-

[18] See Table III.

TABLE II: *Gross Assets of 150 Identical Corporations Common to Both 1919 and 1928 List of 200 Largest American Corporations*

Year	Gross assets as of Dec. 31 in million dollars [1]			
	44 Rail-roads	71 Indus-trials	35 Public utilities	150 Corpo-rations
1919	18,480	14,288	6,017	38,785
1920	20,535	16,186	6,393	43,114
1921	20,186	15,590	6,745	42,521
1922	20,643	15,962	7,757	44,362
1923	20,409	17,174	8,749	46,332
1924	20,839	17,703	9,814	48,356
1925	21,272	19,111	11,508	51,891
1926	21,881	20,569	13,562	56,012
1927	22,462	21,154	15,580	59,192
1928	23,026	22,675	17,703	63,404
Increase 1919–1928	24%	58%	194%	63%
Annual Rate of Growth 1919–1928 [2]	2.4%	5.2%	12.3%	5.6%
Increase 1924–1928	9%	28%	80%	31%
Annual Rate of Growth 1924–1928 [2]	2.3%	6.0%	15.9%	7.0%

[1] Derived from Moody's Railroad, Public Utility and Industrial Manuals.

[2] Compounded annually.

banking corporations is necessary, especially in view of the rapid growth of investment trusts which have been included, for the present purpose, with banks. Where industrial activity is concerned, there is reason to exclude such companies from consideration. In examining the growth of the 200 largest corporations, the increase in their gross assets has been accepted as a reasonable measure of growth. In measuring the growth of all non-financial corporations, no accurate

TABLE III: *Comparison of Growth of Large Corporations with Growth of All Corporations*

	200 largest non-financial corporations		All non-financial corporations	
Year	Gross assets as of December 31 [1] (million dollars) (a)	Annual rate of growth [2] (per cent) (b)	Estimated wealth as of December 31 (million dollars) (c)	Annual rate of growth [2] (per cent) (d)
1909	$26,063 ⎫		$ 63,303 [3] ⎫	
1919	43,718 ⎪	5.1		3.0
1920	48,436 ⎪		90,507 [4] ⎬	
1921	47,762 ⎭			
1922	49,729	4.1	⎫	
1923	51,886	4.2	⎬	4.3
1924	54,337	4.7	102,658 [5] ⎭	
1925	58,317	7.2	⎫	4.8
1926	63,404	8.7	112,435 [6] ⎭	
1927	67,165	5.9	117,693 [7]	4.5
1928	73,139	8.6	124,334 [8]	5.7
1929	81,074	10.6	131,500 [8]	5.8
1909–1928		5.4		3.6
1921–1928		6.1		4.4
1924–1928		7.7		4.9

[1] For method of obtaining figures see text.

[2] Where an interval of more than a year intervenes between successive figures, the annual rate of growth is figured on a basis which gives a rate compounded annually.

[3] Estimate obtained by determining the per cent growth in the capital stocks and indebtedness of all non-financial corporations between December 31, 1909 (Annual Report of Commissioner of Internal Revenue, 1910, pp. 69 and 74) and December 31, 1924 (Statistics of Income, 1925, pp. 31, 43 and 46). In the latter year the fair value of all capital stocks was used, as it was somewhat larger than total par value even for those corporations reporting par value. This percentage was then applied to the estimated wealth of non-financial corporations on December 31, 1924.

[4] Estimate of non-financial corporate wealth made by the Federal Trade Commission and based upon the capital stock tax returns for approximately December 31, 1921, as compiled by the Treasury Department. (National Wealth and Income, Federal Trade Commission, p. 134.) This figure includes real estate, buildings, and equipment as reported and estimates for cash and inventory. Figures cover all corporations.

[5] Figures for real estate, building, equipment, cash and inventory of all non-financial corporations as tabulated by the Treasury Department (Statistics of Income, 1925,

p. 40) plus an adjustment for wealth of corporations whose balance sheets were not tabulated. Adjustment was made by assuming the wealth of corporations whose assets were not tabulated was in the same proportion to the fair value of their stock as the wealth of corporations tabulated to the fair value of their stock (*ibid.*, p. 31).

[6] Real estate, buildings, etc., of non-financial corporations (Statistics of Income, 1926, pp. 360 and 390) adjusted for corporations whose balance sheets were not tabulated. This adjustment was made on the basis of the proportion of balance sheets tabulated in each income class. As over 99 per cent of all but the very smallest corporations appear to have been tabulated, the error in estimation cannot be large (*ibid.*, pp. 356, 358, 360, and 398).

[7] Same basis as ([6]) (Statistics of Income, 1927, pp. 371, 372, 380 and 382).

[8] Same basis as ([6]), except that 97 per cent of balance sheets were assumed to be tabulated. (Statistics of Income, 1928, pp. 32, 380, and 386 and Statistics of Income, 1929, pp. 25 and 332.)

---

figures for gross assets are available. For certain years, notably 1921, 1924, and 1926 to 1929, a figure which the Federal Trade Commission has designated as "wealth used in corporate business" can, however, be employed as a satisfactory measure of growth. This item includes only cash, inventory, land, buildings and equipment. In each of these years the figure is based upon the data supplied from tax returns, and, to make the data for the different years comparable, certain adjustments have been necessary as explained in the footnotes of Table III. With these adjustments, the figures for different years become reasonably comparable and should indicate with a fair degree of accuracy the rate of increase of all corporate wealth exclusive of that of banking corporations. For the year 1909 less satisfactory material is available; but an estimate, involving a very much larger margin of error, has been made for that year.

When the rates of growth of the wealth of all non-financial corporations and of the assets of the 200 largest corporations are thus compared, they show the large corporations as a group to be growing very much more rapidly than all corporations. For the period from 1909 to 1928 their annual rate of growth has been 5.4 per cent, while that of all corporations (assuming the estimates are reliable) has amounted to only 3.6 per cent, and for corporations other than the largest 200 only 2.0 per cent. The large corporations would thus appear to be increasing in wealth over 50 per cent faster than all corporations or over two and one-half times as fast as smaller corporations. From 1921 to 1928 the annual rate of growth of the large corporations has been 6.1 per cent compared with 4.4 per cent for all corporations or 3.1 per cent for the smaller companies. From 1924 to 1928, a period of most rapid growth, the annual rates were respectively 7.7 per cent for the large, 4.9 per cent for all, and only 2.6 per cent for corporations other than the largest 200, indicating that the large corporations were growing more than half again as fast as all corporations and three times as fast as smaller corporations.

This very much more rapid rate of growth of the big companies in comparison to other companies is equally evident when we examine the proportion of the income of all non-banking corporations which has been reported each year by the 200 companies reporting the largest incomes.[19]

For 1921 the results are misleading as in that year, the year of depression, the net income of all corporations was extremely low, and on purely statistical grounds, one would expect the proportion received by the corporations reporting the largest income to be very much greater than normal. In the remaining years, however, there is no reason to think that the figures are not reasonably comparable for different years. The results run roughly parallel to those obtained when the growth in assets was examined. Thus, while the years from 1920 to 1923 show no noticeable growth in the proportion of net income received by the 200 largest, from 1924 to 1929 there is a very marked increase in the proportion of all corporate income going to the 200 largest, increasing from 33.4 per cent in 1920 to 43.2 per cent in 1929 or from an average of 33.5 in the years 1920–1923 to an average of 40.4 in the years 1926–1929.

This increase in the proportion received by the large companies could theoretically be explained on two grounds other than the actual growth of the large corporations. If they had obtained an increasing rate of return on their capital in comparison with the smaller companies, the increase in the proportion of income could be explained. It could likewise be explained on the ground that for a large number of subsidiary corporations the net income was not consolidated with the parent in the earlier years and was so consolidated in the later years. This latter explanation, however, could at most account for only a very small part of the increase, since approximately the same proportion of all non-financial corporate dividends were reported as received by non-financial corporations in 1927 as in 1922,[20] indicating that subsidiaries were reported as separate corporations to approximately the same extent throughout the period.

It is quite conceivable that an important part of the increase is explained by the greater profitableness of large corporations; but the fact that the change coincides roughly with the change shown for

[19] See Table IV.
[20] 20.3 per cent in 1922 and 20.5 per cent in 1927. Derived from Statistics of Income, 1922, pp. 18, 19 and 22, and *ibid.*, 1927, pp. 312 and 315.

TABLE IV: *Growth of Large Corporations as Indicated by Relation of Their Statutory Net Income to That of All Corporations* [1]

	Net income of all non-financial corporations (million dollars)	Estimated net income of 200 largest non-financial corporations (million dollars)	Per cent by largest 200 corporations	Estimated net income of 800 next largest non-financial corporations (million dollars)	Per cent by next largest 800 corporations
1920	$6,899	$2,307	33.4	$1,305	19.0
1921	3,597	1,354	37.6	708	19.6
1922	6,076	1,958	32.2	1,151	19.0
1923	7,453	2,445	32.8	1,386	18.6
1924	6,591	2,378	36.0	1,247	19.0
1925	8,060	2,993	37.1	1,522	18.9
1926	8,337	3,335	40.0	1,564	18.7
1927	7,459	2,865	38.4	1,360	18.2
1928	8,646	3,493	40.4	1,618	18.7
1929	9,456	4,081	43.2	1,808	19.1
Average 1920–1923	$6,006	$2,015	33.5	$1,137	18.9
Average 1926–1929	$8,474	$3,444	40.7	$1,587	18.7

[1] Derived from Statistics of Income for the respective years. Net income of all non-financial corporations equals statutory net income of all corporations reporting net income less that of financial corporations reporting net income. Income for the largest 200 was estimated by taking the net income of all non-financial corporations reporting income over $5,000,000 including nearly 200 companies and adding to this an estimate of the income of additional companies to make the total of 200. In each case the few additional companies were assumed to have a net income of $5,000,000. (If the average income of the added companies had been $4,500,000 it would have lowered the estimate in 1927 only from 38.4 to 38.2 per cent. In other years the change would have been very much less. As in each year there were approximately 800 companies having incomes between $1,000,000 and $5,000,000, it is unlikely that the average income of the few companies necessary to make up the 200 largest would have been below $4,500,000 and was probably closer to $5,000,000. The assumption of the latter figures would not, therefore, lead to appreciable error.

Income for the next largest 800 was estimated by taking the income of all non-financial corporations reporting statutory net income of over $1,000,000 (approximately 900 corporations each year) and adding an estimate of the income of addi-

tional companies to make a total of 1,000, the extra companies being assumed to
have an income of $1,000,000. From the resulting figure the estimated income of
the largest 200 was subtracted. (Error due to the probability that the additional
companies had an average income of somewhat less than $1,000,000 would be
negligible. If the average in 1927 had been $900,000 it would have reduced the
percentage only from 18.2 to 18.1. As there were nearly 1,000 corporations having
incomes between $500,000 and $1,000,000, the average income of the added companies must have been more nearly $1,000,000 than $900,000. In other years the
error would have been even less.)

corporate wealth tends to strengthen the conclusion that the large
corporations have increased greatly both their proportion of the wealth
and their proportion of the income of all corporations.

Though it is not possible to obtain figures for the growth of
industrial wealth, we have already seen that the corporation has become increasingly important in industry after industry. Presumably a
constantly increasing proportion of all industrial wealth has come
under corporate sway.[21] If that be the fact, the proportion of industrial
wealth controlled by the 200 corporations has been increasing at a
rate even more rapid than their proportion of all corporate wealth.

The relative growth of the wealth of the large corporations and
the national wealth can only be very roughly calculated. As we have
indicated, national wealth is a difficult concept to define, and all
estimates of national wealth must be, at best, approximate; so that too
much reliance should not be placed on any comparison of the growth
of corporate wealth with that of national wealth. Between 1922 and
1928 the estimates by the National Industrial Conference Board [22]
indicate a growth in national wealth of 12.5 per cent compared with the
growth in assets [23] of the 200 largest corporations of 45.6 per cent, or
annual rates of growth of 2.0 per cent and 6.3 per cent respectively.[24]
While the estimates based on the 1930 census figures may be considerably higher than those of the Conference Board, the estimates of the
latter for 1928 would have to be increased by over 30 per cent to make
the rate of increase in the national wealth equal to that of the 200

[21] The 1899 census reported 66.7 per cent of all manufactured products are made
by corporations, as against 87.0 per cent in 1919. An extension of trend based
on the log of the figure for the per cent of manufactured products not made
by corporations according to the census figures of 1899, 1909, and 1919 indicates that in 1929 approximately 94 per cent of all manufactured products were
made by corporations. Basis figures obtained from 14th Census of the U. S., vol.
viii, pp. 14 and 108.
[22] National Industrial Conference Board, Conference Board Bulletin No. 38
(February 25, 1930), p. 303.
[23] The use of the gross assets of corporations rather than their tangible wealth is
reasonable, since the comparison is primarily for noting changes in relationship
rather than an absolute relationship.
[24] Compounded annually.

corporations. There can, therefore, be little doubt that the wealth of the large corporations has been increasing at a very much more rapid rate than the total national wealth.

To summarize the conclusions with relation to growth:

(1) On the basis of gross assets, the large corporations appear to have been growing between two and three times as fast as all other non-financial corporations.
(2) This conclusion is supported by the figures of corporate income.
(3) Since an increased proportion of industrial wealth presumably continues to come under corporate sway, the proportion of industrial wealth controlled by the large corporations has been increasing at a rate even faster than the proportion of corporate wealth controlled by them.
(4) Since estimates of national wealth are extremely approximate it is not possible to determine the growth in the proportion of national wealth controlled by the large corporations, but there can be little question that the proportion has been increasing at a rapid rate.

Just what does this rapid growth of the big companies promise for the future? Let us project the trend of the growth of recent years. If the wealth of the large corporations and that of all corporations should each continue to increase for the next twenty years at its average annual rate for the twenty years from 1909 to 1929, 70 per cent of all corporate activity would be carried on by two hundred corporations by 1950.[25] If the more rapid rates of growth from 1924 to 1929 were maintained for the next twenty years 85 per cent of corporate wealth would be held by two hundred huge units. It would take only forty years at the 1909–1929 rates or only thirty years at the 1924–1929 rates for all corporate activity and practically all industrial activity to be absorbed by two hundred giant companies. If the indicated growth of the large corporations and of the national wealth were to be effective from now until 1950, half of the national wealth would be under the control of big companies at the end of that period.

Whether the future will see any such complete absorption of economic activity into a few great enterprises it is not possible to predict. A glance at Table III will show that the rate of growth has not been uniform. The years from 1921 through 1923 showed little more growth by the large corporations than by all, though this slackening may reflect only a breathing spell after the excessive growth of the war years. One would expect, moreover, that the rate of concentration

[25] Assuming 49.2 per cent of non-banking corporate wealth was held by the largest 200 in 1929 and applying the rates of growth indicated in Table III.

would slacken as a larger and larger proportion of industry became absorbed and less remained to be added. The trend of the recent past
indicates, however, that the great corporation, already of tremendous
importance today, will become increasingly important in the future.

This conclusion is still further confirmed when we examine the
ways in which the growth of the large companies takes place and
compare their growth by each method with that of other companies.
A given corporation can increase the wealth under its control in three
major ways: by reinvesting its earnings, by raising new capital through
the sale of securities in the public markets, and by acquiring control of
other corporations by either purchase or exchange of securities. While
there are numerous other ways by which an increase could take place,
such as private sale of securities to individuals, these three so far outweigh other methods that they alone need to be considered.

A comparison of the savings of large corporations with those of
all corporations indicates that the big companies as a group save a
larger proportion of their net income. In the six-year period from 1922
to 1927 inclusive, 108 corporations (all of the 200 largest for which
consolidated statements could be obtained for each year) saved 38.5
per cent of their net income available for dividends.[26] In the same
period, all corporations combined saved only 29.4 per cent of their
net income.[27] Since the earnings of the large corporations are included
as an important proportion in the earnings of all corporations and since
these large companies saved a larger than average percentage of earnings, the remaining corporations, mainly smaller companies, must have
saved a proportion very much smaller than average, probably less than
25 per cent of their earnings. The importance of this method of growth
is indicated by the fact that roughly a quarter of the growth of the
large corporations was derived from earnings between 1922 and 1927.

Of much greater importance as a source of relative expansion has
been the second method—the raising of new capital in the public
markets. Over 55 per cent of the growth of the large companies has
been made possible by the public offering of additional securities,[28] a
fact which particularly concerns us here since these offerings are all
made to the public investor, and since the dependence of these corporations on new capital is undoubtedly one of the strongest factors
determining the relation between those who control the corporations

[26] See Appendix B.

[27] This difference in rate of saving is probably not an indication of greater liberality
in paying dividends on the part of the small corporations but an indication of
their greater liability to loss. For both groups, the net income for the group included the net income of those making a profit minus the losses suffered by the
remainder.

[28] See Appendix C.

and their investing stockholders. Here again the large corporation increases the wealth under its control by this means of expansion to a much greater extent than the smaller companies. From 1922 to 1927 inclusive, a sample study indicates that two-thirds of all public offerings of new securities (as reported by the "Commercial and Financial Chronicle"—excluding banking companies) were made by the two hundred largest companies or their subsidiaries.

The third and more spectacular method of growth of the large corporations is by consolidation or merger. Within the eleven years, 1919 through 1929, no less than 49 corporations recorded among the largest two hundred at one time or another during the period have disappeared by merging with other large companies on the list.[29] It would be an extensive task to chronicle all the smaller companies which the companies on our list have absorbed. A list of a few of the more important industrial mergers in 1928 and 1929 involving only one big company will be found in Appendix E. Roughly twenty per cent of the growth of the largest companies which we have been observing can be attributed to additions through merger, a growth which effects a reduction in the corporate wealth lying outside the control of the largest group.

The growth in the assets of the two hundred largest corporations in the six-year period from 1922 to 1927 inclusive is given below, as well as estimates of the manner of growth.

Estimated savings out of earnings	$ 5,748,000,000	26.5%
Estimated new capital from sale of securities	11,813,000,000	55.0%
Estimated growth as a result of mergers	4,000,000,000	18.5%
	$21,561,000,000	100.0%
Estimated reduction from reappraisals, etc., *and error in estimates*	$ 2,000,000,000	
Net growth in assets, 1922–1927, inclusive	19,561,000,000	

One question yet remains—are these companies likely to survive? It is sometimes said that consolidations of great magnitude sooner or later, more often sooner, go into a period of decline,—that beyond a certain point the organization breaks down, and the whole falls of its own weight. There appears, however, to be little foundation for such a suggestion. Examination of the condition in 1928 of the two hundred companies which were largest in 1919 shows the following: [30]

[29] For list of these, see Appendix D.

[30] A study of the present status of the two hundred companies included as the largest in the list for 1910 yield percentage results per unit of time almost identical with those for the 1919 list.

Of the 200 largest corporations in 1919:—

  23 merged with larger companies.[31]
154 were included in list of largest 200 corporations in 1928.
  21 remained large and active concerns though 7 of them went through reorganization.
  2 liquidated or the equivalent.
  ___
200

This table shows 25 companies actually disappearing in nine years, or a rate of disappearance of 1.4 per cent a year. If this were the normal rate of disappearance it would indicate an average expectancy of over 70 years of further life. At the same time the disappearance of a corporation through merger does not indicate that its organization has broken down and that it is about to fall into dissolution; it passes, but does not die. If we regard the two liquidated companies as the only ones which actually disappeared, we would have a dissolution rate of 1 per cent in nine years or an average expectancy of 900 years of life, either as an independent concern or as an integral part of a larger enterprise. On the other hand if we apply the rates of merger and of dissolution simultaneously they indicate that at the end of 360 years sixteen of the two hundred companies would have disappeared through dissolution and all the remaining companies would have merged into a single corporation having a life expectancy of over 1000 years. Furthermore, if the changes in the nine years are a promise of the future, half of the companies included in the 1919 list of 200 companies will also be represented in a list of the largest two hundred compiled a century hence, ten directly and ninety as absorbed units in these ten.

These figures are, of course, an unwarranted extension into the future of the trend of nine years from 1919 to 1928. They serve, however, to indicate that there is little in the history of the 200 companies in the nine-year period considered to suggest that the large corporation has a short life cycle ending in dissolution.

In conclusion, then, the huge corporation, the corporation with $90,000,000 of assets or more, has come to dominate most major industries if not all industry in the United States. A rapidly increasing proportion of industry is carried on under this form of organization. There is apparently no immediate limit to its increase. It is coming more and more to be the industrial unit with which American economic, social, and political life must deal. The implications of this fact challenge many of the basic assumptions of current thought.

[31] See Appendix F.

(1) Most fundamental of all, it is now necessary to think, to a very important extent, in terms of these huge units rather than in terms of the multitude of small competing elements of private enterprise. The emphasis must be shifted to that very great proportion of industry in the hands of a relatively few units, units which can be studied individually and concretely. Such studies will reveal the operation of half of industry and what is more important, that half which is likely to be more typical of the industry of the future.[32]

(2) Competition has changed in character and the principles applicable to present conditions are radically different from those which apply when the dominant competing units are smaller and more numerous. The principles of duopoly have become more important than those of free competition.

(3) An increasing proportion of production is carried on for use and not for sale. With the increase in the large companies, a larger proportion of goods are consumed by the producing organization in the process of making further goods. To this extent the calculus of cost versus quality would presumably be solved in the interest of producing a product which would yield the maximum use per unit of cost rather than the maximum profit per unit of investment. Under the latter incentive the consumer is only incidentally offered the product which will give him the most use per unit of cost unless he himself is easily able to measure usefulness. Adulteration, shoddy goods, and goods of lower quality than would be economically desirable are frequent under the incentive for profit. To the extent that production is for use by the producing organization there is no such incentive.[33]

(4) The nature of capital has changed. To an increasing extent it is composed not of tangible goods, but of organizations built in the past and available to function in the future. Even the value of tangible goods tends to become increasingly dependent upon their

[32] For instance, it seems likely that a study of the directors and senior officers of the 200 largest companies, their training, social background, and other characteristics, would reveal more of vital importance to the community than a study of those at the head of thousands of smaller companies. The same would be true of the ownership of the large companies, their labor policies, their price policies, their promotion practices, etc. This is not to suggest that the practices of the large companies would be typical of the smaller companies, but rather that they would be factually more important.

[33] For instance, it is to the advantage of the American Telephone and Telegraph Company to have its subsidiary, the Western Electric Company, make the best possible vacuum tubes for the innumerable repeater sets in use on its long distance lines. On the other hand, it might be to the advantage of a corporation making tubes for sale to the public to make second-grade tubes which would wear out quickly and allow a second sale at a second profit to be made.

organized relationship to other tangible goods composing the property of one of these great units.

(5) Finally, a society in which production is governed by blind economic forces is being replaced by one in which production is carried on under the ultimate control of a handful of individuals.[34] The economic power in the hands of the few persons who control a giant corporation is a tremendous force which can harm or benefit a multitude of individuals, affect whole districts, shift the currents of trade, bring ruin to one community and prosperity to another. The organizations which they control have passed far beyond the realm of private enterprise—they have become more nearly social institutions.

Such is the character of the corporate system—dynamic, constantly building itself into greater aggregates, and thereby changing the basic conditions which the thinking of the past has assumed.

---

[34] Approximately 2,000 men were directors of the 200 largest corporations in 1930. Since an important number of these are inactive, the ultimate control of nearly half of industry was actually in the hands of a few hundred men.

CHAPTER IV: THE DISPERSION

OF STOCK OWNERSHIP

ACCOMPANYING THE CONCENTRATION of economic power, growing out
of it, and making it possible, has come an ever wider dispersion of
stock ownership. This in turn has brought about a fundamental change
in the character of wealth,—in the relation between the individual
and his wealth, the value of that wealth and the nature of property
itself. Dispersion in the ownership of separate enterprises appears to
be inherent in the corporate system. It has already proceeded far, it
is rapidly increasing, and appears to be an inevitable development.

As is to be expected, the process of stock dispersion has proceeded furthest in the very large companies. The stockholder lists of
the largest railroad, the Pennsylvania Railroad, the largest public
utility, the American Telephone and Telegraph Company, and the
largest industrial, the United States Steel Corporation, show in each
case that the principal holder in 1929 owned less than one per cent of
the outstanding stock. The most important holdings reported were,
respectively, .34 of one per cent, .70 of one per cent, and .90 of one
per cent.[1] In these companies no single individual holds an important
proportion of the total ownership. Even the aggregate holdings of the
twenty largest stockholders of the Pennsylvania Railroad amounted in
1929 to only 2.7 per cent, of the Telephone Company to 4.0 per cent,
and of the Steel Company to 5.1 per cent. Below the first twenty, the
amount held by each stockholder dropped off rapidly to insignificant
proportions. The twentieth holder of Railroad stock owned but .07 of
one per cent, of Telephone stock .09 of one per cent, and of Steel stock
but .09 of one per cent.[1] The remainder of the half million Telephone

[1] See Table XII, pp. 99 and 100.

stockholders, the 196,119 stockholders of the Railroad and the 182,585 holders of Steel stock were negligible as individual holders.

In the dispersion of stock these companies are in the lead but are not alone. In many large companies the largest stockholding represents a small proportion of the total ownership while the number of stockholders is legion. According to information covering 1929, the following companies are comparable to the three described above:

Company	Size of largest holding	Number of stockholders
Atchison, Topeka & Santa Fe Ry. Co.	.76%	59,042
Chicago, Milwaukee, St. Paul & Pacific Rd. Co.	1.36	12,045
General Electric Co.	1.50	60,374
Delaware & Hudson Co.	1.51	9,003
Southern Pacific Co.	1.65	55,788
Boston Elevated Ry. Co.	1.66	16,419
Southern Ry. Co.	1.92	20,262
Consolidated Gas Co., of N. Y.	2.11	93,515
Great Northern Ry. Co.	2.12	42,085
Northern Pacific Ry. Co.	2.13	38,339
Missouri-Kansas-Texas Rd. Co.	2.23	12,693
Union Pacific Rd. Co.	2.27	49,387
Baltimore & Ohio Rd. Co.	2.56	39,627
Western Union Tel. Co.	2.74	23,738

The fact that these companies are for the most part railroads and utilities does not indicate that this condition is absent in the industrial field. Only the greater difficulty of obtaining information on industrial companies prevents the demonstration of the same situation in that area. Various companies for which information was secured from private sources showed similar small single holdings and very large numbers of stockholders, but the confidential nature of this information prevents its being here set forth in detail.

In the large companies in which the dispersion of ownership has not proceeded to the point of eliminating all strong stock interests, the most common condition is that of wide ownership of the bulk of the stock with a substantial minority held by a single interest. In many cases the largest stockholder is a second corporation which is itself widely owned. Thus, in 1930, the Pennsylvania Railroad was itself, or through subsidiaries, the largest single stockholder, though not a

TABLE v: *144 Out of 200 Largest Companies Distributed According to Number of Stockholders* [1]

	Railroads	Public utilities	Industrials	Total
Under 5,000	10	5	5	20
5,000–19,999	16	11	26	53
20,000–49,999	8	5	26	39
50,000–99,999	3	10	9	22
100,000–199,999	1	3	3	7
200,000–500,000		3		3
Total	38	37	69	144

[1] Derived from Table XII.

majority holder, in the Norfolk & Western Railway, the Wabash, the Western Maryland and the New York, New Haven & Hartford Railroad, while the second largest holding was insignificant. Similarly, the Electric Bond & Share Company was the largest single holder in at least three large public utility companies.

Where it is not possible to discover the size of the largest holdings, some measure of the degree to which a corporation has become publicly owned may be obtained by examining the size of its stockholder list. Though a large list is not necessarily an indication of the extent to which large holdings have disappeared, it is a measure of the degree to which public participation has progressed. The stockholder lists of 144 companies for which information could be obtained [2] out of the 200 largest companies described above revealed the fact that only 20, representing less than 5 per cent of the assets of the 144 companies, each had less than 5000 stockholders, while as many as 71 companies had over 20,000.[3] More than half the assets represented belonged to companies with 50,000 stockholders or more. In the aggregate these companies reported 5,839,116 stockholders of record. Among the remainder of the 200 largest companies, for which exact information could not be secured, very many are known to be widely owned and only six are believed to be so closely held that there are less than 1000 stockholders. Furthermore it is likely that even these companies will at some date in the future be sold out in part or in whole to public investors. Only 4 of the 200 companies (exclusive of 4 jointly controlled by listed com-

[2] Excluding companies jointly owned by two or more other big companies.
[3] See Table V.

TABLE VI: *Stockholdings by Management*

Officers' and Directors' proportionate holdings of common and preferred stock in 1922 by industries arranged in order of holdings for comparison with size of corporations involved.[1]

Approximate number of companies [2]		Total par value of stock held by management		Average par value of total outstanding stock per corporation	
		Com-mon	Pre-ferred	Common	Preferred
44	Steam railroads	1.2	.1	$ 52,402,000	$11,799,000
22	Gas	1.4	.4	8,063,000	4,079,000
36	Other mining and quarrying	1.8	8.2	7,777,000	17,000
378	Trans. & other public utilities	2.1	.7	7,839,000	1,858,000
46	Electric light & power	4.2	1.8	4,457,000	1,675,000
132	Mining and quarrying	4.5	6.2	4,479,000	681,000
102	Telegraph and telephone †	5.3	13.4	1,441,000	46,000
53	Petroleum mining	5.3	2.7	3,686,000	775,000
24	Electric railroads	5.4	8.4	3,390,000	399,000
6	Chemical and allied substances *	6.3	.3	138,546,000	2,889,000
43	Coal mining	8.4	9.4	2,989,000	1,064,000
4367	All industries	10.7	5.8	1,715,000	361,000
16	Metal and metal products	11.4	12.0	35,729,000	15,084,000
1363	Manufacturing	15.0	9.6	2,367,000	547,000
275	Food products	17.5	5.3	1,392,000	443,000
1203	Finance	22.0	23.1	433,000	18,000
698	Other manufacturing	22.7	10.6	1,408,000	506,000
140	Other public utilities	23.4	24.7	354,000	23,000
13	Rubber, rubber goods, etc.	39.0	2.1	794,000	1,705,000
192	Textile products	42.9	17.2	363,000	89,000
41	Leather products	44.7	6.1	645,000	387,000
950	Trade	48.4	19.7	224,000	25,000
172	Service	49.7	21.6	106,000	14,000
70	Agriculture and related industries	55.9	61.2	146,000	3,000
122	Lumber and wood products	56.9	37.3	250,000	18,000
99	Construction	67.6	46.3	107,000	14,000

† Does not include the largest telephone or the largest telegraph company.

° Mostly petroleum mining. The figure is presumably dominated by one of the Standard Oil units.

[1] Derived from Federal Trade Commission, National Wealth and Income, p. 159, Table 90. The table is based on data furnished to the commission from 4367 representative corporations.

[2] Approximated by applying percentage of corporations reported by Federal Trade Commission, *ibid.* p. 145, to number of corporations reported by Treasury Department, Statistics of Income, 1922, p. 16.

---

panies) did not have their stocks listed on an organized stock exchange.[4]

Among companies smaller than the largest two hundred, the dispersion of stock ownership has often progressed to a considerable degree though as is to be expected it has nowhere reached the extent evident among the biggest companies. In a small group of forty-two companies with assets ranging from $6,000,000 to $80,000,000 for which information could be obtained, six reported over ten thousand and the remaining twenty-seven had from five hundred to five thousand.[5] An added indication of extensive public investment in securities of smaller companies is to be found in the large number of such companies whose stocks are actively traded on the New York Stock Exchange. As we have seen, half of the stocks whose prices were regularly reported by the Commercial and Financial Chronicle in 1929 were those of companies with assets under $30,000,000 while one hundred of these had less than $10,000,000 assets.

Still further light is throw on the ownership of smaller companies in a study made by The Federal Trade Commission in 1925.[6] Their report covered the stockholdings of the directors and officers of 4,367 corporations selected in a manner to give a cross section of all industry and representing approximately one-eighth of the capital stock of all corporations. The capital stock of these companies amounted on the average to less than $2,000,000, indicating that the bulk of the companies included were extremely small in comparison to the truly big companies. Yet the directors and officers of these companies owned on the average only 10.7 per cent of their common and 5.8 per cent of their preferred stocks. This suggests a very considerable ownership of these smaller companies by those not directly connected with their man-

[4] Stocks having trading privileges on the New York Curb Market were treated for the present purpose as listed. The four companies not listed were:—

Virginian Railway Company   Ford Motor Company
Florida East Coast Railway Company   Koppers Company.

[5] See Appendix F.

[6] Federal Trade Commission, National Wealth and Income, p. 159, Table 90.

TABLE VII: *Stockholders of the Three Largest American Corporations*

Dec. 31	American Telephone and Telegraph Co.	Pennsylvania Railroad	United States Steel Corp.[7] (common only)
1931	642,180 [10]	241,391 [5e]	174,507 [10]
1930	567,694 [10]	207,188 [5d]	145,566 [10]
1929	469,801 [8]	196,119 [5]	120,918 [10]
1928	454,596 [6]	157,650 [5a]	100,784
1927	423,580	143,249 [5b]	96,297
1926	399,121	142,257 [5c]	86,034
1925	362,179	140,578 [4]	90,576
1924	345,466	145,174	96,317
1923	281,149	144,228	99,779
1922	248,925	137,429	93,789
1921	186,342	141,699	107,439
1920	139,448	133,068	95,776
1919	120,460	117,725	74,318
1918	112,420	106,911	72,779
1917	87,000	100,038	51,689
1916	71,000	90,388	37,720
1915	66,000	93,768	45,767
1914	60,000	91,571	52,785
1913	57,000	88,586	46,460
1912	50,000	75,155 [3]	34,213
1911	48,000	73,165	35,011
1910	41,000	65,283	28,850
1909	37,000	56,809	18,615
1908	26,000	58,273	21,093
1907	23,000	57,226	28,435
1906	19,000	40,153 [2]	14,723
1905	18,000	40,385	20,075
1904	17,000	42,230	33,395
1903	16,000	42,437	37,237
1902	12,000	28,408	24,636
1901	10,000		15,887
1880		13,000 [1]	

[1] "The Growth and Development of the Pennsylvania Railroad Co.," H. W. Schotter (Philadelphia, 1927), p. 11.

[2] *Ibid.*, p. 186.
[3] *Ibid.*, p. 303.
[4] *Ibid.*, p. 415.
[5] Standard Corporation Records, (a) as of May 1, 1929; (b) as of May 1, 1928; (c) as of Feb. 1, 1927; (d) as of April 1, 1930; (e) as of Oct. 1, 1931.
[6] Standard Corporation Records.
[7] Wall Street Journal, October 26, 1929. (Common stock only.)
[8] Annual Report, 1929, p. 19.
[9] Bell Telephone Securities, 1929, issued by Bell Telephone Securities Co., New York, p. 10. (Derived from chart.)
[10] Standard Corporation Records. (Common stock only.)

agement. More important is the indication contained in the figures, that as the size of the company increases the tendency to dispersion increases. It is not possible to group the companies directly according to size, since the results of the Commission study were reported in the form of averages for each industry, thus grouping small and large companies. When the industries are arranged in order of the average size of the management's holdings of stock, however, the proportion held by the officers and directors is seen to vary in almost exactly inverse ratio to the average size of the companies under consideration. With only two major exceptions, the larger the size of the company, the smaller was the proportion of stock held by the management.[7] In the railroads, with common stock averaging $52,000,000 per company, the holdings of the management amounted to 1.4 per cent, and in the third industry, miscellaneous mining and quarrying, it amounted to 1.8 per cent. Only where the companies are small did the managements appear to hold important stock interests. The holdings of the latter amounted to less than 20 per cent except in industries with companies having an average capital under a million dollars while but three industrial groups, each composed of companies averaging less than $200,000, showed directors and officers owning more than half the stock.

It is clear, then, that the dispersion of ownership has gone to tremendous lengths among the largest companies and has progressed to a considerable extent among the medium sized. Further, it may be said that in general the larger the company, the more likely is its ownership to be diffused among a multitude of individuals.

It is also clear that the dispersion is a continuing process. Here again the evidence of the largest companies is striking. Table VII shows the growth during the last thirty years in the number of stockholders of the three largest companies.

[7] See Table VI.

The Telephone Company's shareholders have increased by leaps and bounds until in three short decades the 10,000 owners of 1901 have become the 642,180 owners of 1931.[8] The Pennsylvania Railroad had eight times the number of stockholders in 1931 that it had in 1902. The United States Steel Company, though its stockholder list has fluctuated more than that of the other two, has shown a similar proportionate increase. Once the process of distribution is well under way, the evidence of these companies indicates that it tends to proceed swiftly and far.

A similar tendency for stockholders to increase markedly is revealed among the thirty-one representative large companies for which information since 1900 was available. (Appendix G.) As line 5 in the accompanying chart graphically shows, the increase here has been most rapid. Likewise the estimated total of all stockholders of all corporations, has grown almost as rapidly, from 4 millions in 1900 to some 18 millions in 1928. (Table VIII.)

An approximate idea of the number of book stockholders in different industries in 1922 can be obtained from estimates based on the average par value of stock per holder for a sample group of companies representing in the aggregate nearly one-eighth of corporate capital.[9] Since 1922 the number of railroad book stockholders has declined slightly to approximately 884,000 in 1930.[10] The number of book stockholders of other public utilities have increased at a most rapid rate while the number of stockholders in other industrial groups has increased to a considerable extent.

In dealing with these figures of book stockholders it should be noted that they represent estimates of the combined stockholder lists of all corporations in the country or in an industry, not the number of individuals in the country or in the industry who own stock since one person often owns the stock of several companies. It is with the stockholder lists that we are concerned here, for they indicate the tendency for individual corporations to be owned by an ever-increasing number of investors.

In recent years, two comparatively new developments have contributed in very large measure to the increase in the number of stock-

[8] See Chart I.
[9] See Table IX.
[10] The number of book stockholders of Class I railroads at the beginning of 1930 was 840,000. ("Regulation of Stock Ownership in Railroads," p. XLIX.) Since 5 per cent of the railroad mileage in the country is controlled by other than Class I roads, a proportionate addition to the stockholders of Class I roads has been made to obtain an estimate of the total number of railroad book stockholders.

1. *Pennsylvania Railroad Co.*
2. *United States Steel Corp.*
3. *American Telephone & Telegraph Co.*
4. *Index of Total Book Stockholders.*[1]
5. *Book stockholders of thirty-one representative companies.*
6. *Book stockholders of thirty-one representative companies excluding American Telephone & Telegraph Co.*

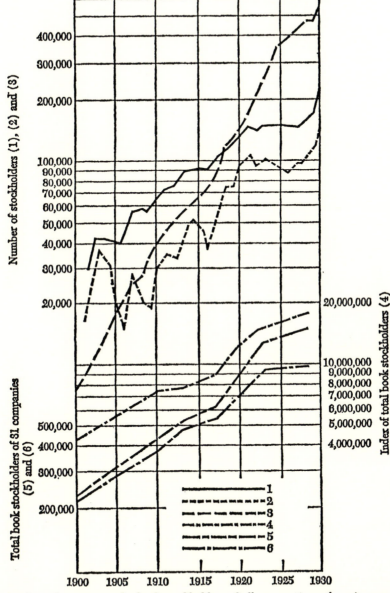

[1] For the index covering the book stockholders of all corporations, there is reason to question the rapidity of the growth shown between 1900 and 1910. The index is based on data for a very small number of companies in 1900, and is dominated by the American Telephone and Telegraph Company which increased very rapidly in number of stockholders.

TABLE VIII: *Estimated Number of Book Stockholders of American Corporations*[1] *(1900–1928)*

Year	Total capital stock of all corporations in the United States	Average no. of $100 par value shares per stockholder	Estimated no. of stockholders in the United States	Annual rate of increase (compounded annually)
1900	$61,831,955,370	140.1	4,400,000	
1910	64,053,763,141	86.3	7,400,000	5.2%
1913	65,038,309,611	87.0	7,500,000	.5%
1917	66,584,420,424	77.3	8,600,000	3.5%
1920	69,205,967,666	57.3	12,000,000	12.0%
1923	71,479,464,925	49.7	14,400,000	6.2%
1928	91,881,243,985 [2]	51.0 [3]	18,000,000	4.5%

[1] As compiled and computed by H. T. Warshow (*op. cit.*, p. 28) for 1900–1923 and compiled by the present writer for 1928 on a comparable basis. The relative accuracy of Mr. Warshow's estimate is suggested by the estimate of the number of book stockholders in 1922 made by the present writer on the basis of quite different basic figures compiled by the Federal Trade Commission (see Table IX). By interpolation, Mr. Warshow's figures indicate 13,600,000 book stockholders in 1922. The Federal Trade Commission figures covering approximately one eighth of corporate capital indicate 13,564,000. While the almost identical results must be looked upon as fortuitous, the figure arrived at is not likely to be wide of the mark.

[2] Statistics of Income, 1927, p. 373.

[3] The wide use of no-par stock makes both the figure for total stock of all corporations and the estimate of the average shares per stockholder less reliable than in earlier years.

holders—ownership by customers and ownership by employees. Neither of these developments, however, appears likely to affect an appreciable proportion of all stock ownership.[11] Customer ownership campaigns which have found their greatest popularity in the public utility field, have only been of an appreciable importance since 1919. According to figures published by the National Electric Light Association, less than 45,000 individual sales were made to utility customers between 1914 and 1919. Thereafter customer ownership campaigns became increasingly popular until a maximum was reached with a total of 294,000 separate sales in 1924.[12] Since that year sales have declined somewhat

[11] For a more extensive discussion of this point, see G. C. Means, "The Diffusion of Stock Ownership in the United States," Quarterly Journal of Economics, Vol. XVIV (August, 1930) pp. 567–570.

[12] See Appendix I.

NOTE: *The estimates for particular industries are subject to greater possible error than that for industry as a whole.*

Industry	Par value of outstanding stock [2]	Average par value per stockholder in sample	Estimated number of book stockholders	Per cent of capital of industry included in sample
Agriculture and related industries	$ 1,126,682,000	$ 8,764	128,000	.9
Mining and quarrying	8,775,456,000		2,043,000	
Coal mining	1,330,822,000	11,991	111,000	12.5
Petroleum mining	3,126,591,000	3,428	912,000	7.4
Other mining and quarrying	4,318,043,000	4,229	1,020,000	5.6
Manufacturing	23,411,383,000		3,074,000	
Food products	3,876,290,000	4,576	846,000	12.5
Textile products	2,510,313,000	11,300	222,000	3.4
Leather products	695,597,000	4,448	157,000	6.1
Rubber, rubber goods, etc.	623,981,000	3,092	202,000	5.1
Lumber and wood products	1,161,528,000	14,888	78,000	2.8
Chemical and allied substances [3]	2,937,217,000	11,333	258,000	13.3
Metal and metal products	6,839,215,000	9,213	741,000	8.9
Other manufacturing	4,767,242,000	8,358	570,000	27.1
Construction	727,316,000	9,307	78,000	1.7
Transportation and other public utilities	17,532,293,000		3,293,000	
Steam railroads	8,369,924,000	8,687	965,000	34.5
Electric railroads	1,500,308,000	3,831	392,000	6.1
Electric light and power	1,493,406,000	2,925	511,000	19.3
Gas	909,826,000	3,854	242,000	29.4
Telegraph and telephone	1,787,935,000	3,774	473,000	8.6
Other public utilities	3,470,894,000	4,896	710,000	1.6
Trade	7,659,325,000	8,032	954,000	3.2
Service	1,549,218,000	4,138	374,000	1.4
Finance	12,922,003,000	3,579	3,620,000	4.2
All Industries	$73,703,676,000	$ 5,435	13,564,000	11.9

[1] Derived from National Wealth and Income, pp. 145, 146, and 213, and Statistics of Income, 1922, pp. 40 and 41.

[2] No par stock taken at fair value.

[3] Mostly petroleum refining.

in importance, being approximately 217,000 in 1930, while the value of annual sales has declined from a maximum of $297,000,000 in 1925 to approximately $135,000,000 in 1930. Total sales to utility customers from 1914 to the end of 1929 numbered 2,000,000, but so many of these were additional sales to the same people and so many purchasers have undoubtedly sold their stock, that the number of persons added to the stockholder lists has probably been nearer one million than two, while their total holdings of stock obtained by direct purchase amount to less than 1½ per cent of all corporate stocks. Furthermore the annual sales to customers have dropped to such a point that this proportion is only just being maintained. The force of the movement seems already to have been spent. While the number of customer owners will undoubtedly continue to increase, there is little to indicate that their holdings will represent an important proportion of corporate wealth.

The movement toward employee ownership appears to have followed a similar course. According to a comprehensive study made by The National Industrial Conference Board, only 89 companies had adopted employee stock purchase plans prior to 1919, and new companies were adopting such plans at the rate of approximately nine per year.[13] After 1919, they became much more popular and were introduced into 24 additional companies in 1919, 46 in 1920 and 51 in 1923, their peak year. Since that time the number of new companies adopting such plans each year has fallen off until in 1926, the last full year covered by the Conference Board study, only 13 companies were added to the list of those undertaking sales to employees. By the middle of 1927, approximately 800,000 employees had become stockholders and owned stock having a market value of $1,000,000,000, or approximately one per cent of all corporate stocks then outstanding. As is the case of customer ownership, it is quite possible, not to say probable, that the number of employee stockholders will increase, yet there is nothing to suggest that their ownership will involve an increasing proportion of industry.

The rise in popularity of these two movements was undoubtedly due in a considerable measure to the influence of Federal taxation. Both developed most vigorously during a period in which the weight of the Federal surtaxes was such as to make the individual with a large income an extremely poor market for corporate securities.[14] The difficulty of obtaining new capital from the usual sources was thus

[13] See Appendix J.
[14] For an extensive discussion of this point see "The Diffusion of Stock Ownership in the United States," *loc. cit.*, pp. 574–590.

increased and a new market for corporate securities was sought in the man of smaller income, the employee and the local customer. With the subsequent reduction in surtaxes the large owner has again taken his place in the market as a source for new capital,[15] a fact which may explain the lessening volume of sales to customers and employees. Factors other than taxation must have played a part in the rise and partial decline of these two movements. What is most significant here, however, is that these two developments have been somewhat episodic in character, a fact which suggests that the tendency of stock to become dispersed throughout the community is more fundamental than any particular form which the dispersion may take.

The passing of ownership from the hands of the managing few to the hands of the investing many raises the question of who these multitudinous investors may be, from what income classes they are drawn—in other words, who the owners of the nation's industries now are. An answer to this question may be found in the Statistics of Income, compiled from Federal income tax returns. This record shows that in 1929, 73.7 per cent of corporate dividends were received by six hundred thousand persons (597,003) reporting taxable income of $5,000 or more. Of the remainder, approximately 10 per cent was reported by individuals with an income below $5,000 but filing an income tax return, including for the most part individuals with an income above the taxable minimum of $3,500 for married and $1,500 for single persons. The remaining 16 per cent was presumably received by those not required to file income tax returns. The total number of stockholders in the country in that year probably lay between 4 and 7,000,000 persons.[16] The distribution of this ownership (as indicated by dividends received) among different income groups was as shown in table on the next page. This shows the great extent to which persons of small or moderate means must be stockholders of corporations.

The income tax returns show not only the present distribution of ownership among economic groups but the changes which have occurred in the last decade. Since the start of the record in 1916, it appears that there has been a major shift in the ownership of industry from people of large incomes to those of moderate means. This change is clearly shown in Chart II. In 1916, over 57 per cent of all corporate dividends (excluding those received by other corporations) were received by individuals reporting the 25,000 largest incomes. In 1921, this group reported only 35 per cent of all dividends. At the same time, individuals reporting other than the 100,000 largest incomes, those

[15] See pp. 61–62.
[16] See Appendix K.

Distribution of Dividends Among Various Income Groups in 1929

Size of taxable income	No. of individual stockholders included in income group [1]	Per cent of all dividends received by group	Per cent cumulated from above
Over $1,000,000	513	5.74%	5.74%
$100,000 to $1,000,000	14,303	19.02%	24.76%
$25,000 to $100,000	87,762	23.97%	48.73%
$5,000 to $25,000	494,425	24.88%	73.61%
Under $5,000	3,5–6,500,000 [2]	26.28%	100.00%

[1] It is not possible to determine accurately the number of individuals in each income group who actually received dividends. The Treasury Department reports that only 516,029 individuals out of 913,597 with incomes over $5,000 actually received dividends. For simplicity, it has been assumed here that the 397,568 individuals not receiving dividends are included in the group reporting taxable income under $25,000. It is probable that no serious error results from this assumption.

[2] Estimated—See Appendix K.

with an income of less than $13,000 in 1916 and less than $20,000 in 1921, increased their proportion of all dividends from 22 per cent in 1916 to 44 per cent in 1921. In the former year, half of all dividends were reported by 15,000 individuals, while in the latter year it required the combined dividends of 75,000 individuals to cover half of all dividends received. So large a shift in corporate ownership in the brief period of five years is a change of almost revolutionary proportions. In small part, it can be explained by the efforts of the rich owner of stocks to avoid income taxes without disposing of his securities, but for the most part, it must represent a true shift in corporate ownership. It appears to have been due, in a large measure, to the heavy surtaxes on large incomes during the war and post-war period, which as already suggested made the large income receiver a poor market for risk bearing securities, and to some extent, induced him to shift into tax-exempt issues. The general significance of this shift from the rich to the less well to do cannot at this time be confidently determined. Does it represent a permanent change in the ownership of industrial wealth comparable to the shift in land ownership which was an outgrowth of the French Revolution? Does it indicate a trend toward still greater participation in ownership by the less well to do? Or is it a temporary condition which will reverse itself in the near future?

CHART II: *Distribution in Ownership of Corporate Stocks as Reflected in Dividends Received by Different Income Groups*

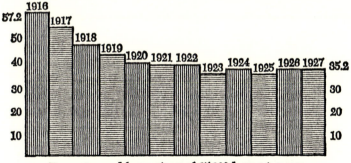

Per cent owned by receivers of 25,000 largest incomes

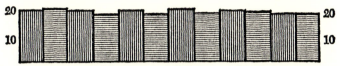

Per cent owned by receivers of 75,000 next largest incomes

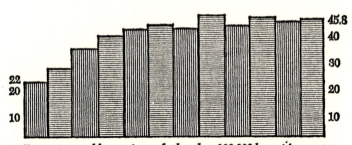

Per cent owned by receivers of other than 100,000 largest incomes

Since 1921, the income tax returns show no further shift in the direction of the smaller owner. Rather, the distribution of stock ownership among income groups appears to have remained fairly constant. Whether this indicates a change in trend, and we are about to see ownership pass again to the higher income class, or whether it is merely a pause in a constant trend which was disproportionately accelerated by the heavy income taxes, it is too early to say. The answer, however, may depend upon two conditions which immediately concern us here —the treatment of the small investor by those in control of corporate affairs, and the existence of other fields for the investment of his savings. Is the man of moderate means to remain a corporate investor voluntarily or involuntarily? Is he to receive such treatment that his confidence will be retained and he will remain a market for corporate securities? Or, on the other hand, is he going to be forced to continue in the corporate field by the closing of all other avenues to the investment of his savings?

The answer depends on a balance of two factors, the need of the corporation on the one hand and the desires and opportunities of the investor on the other. The corporation from time to time is almost sure to be faced with the necessity of raising new capital. If it is a growing concern, it will have to call upon the public frequently and for considerable amounts. We have already seen that over half of the recent phenomenal growth of the great corporations was achieved through the raising of new capital in the public markets. The investor may look forward to the likelihood that the corporate system will in the future continue to call for his savings; he will, in fact, probably find his place in the system determined more by that fact than by any other single feature for if he is to continue to be a supplier of capital for the extension of corporate enterprise, his confidence must be maintained. Just how good his treatment must be in order to ensure his investment will presumably depend upon his general willingness or reluctance to save, and on the other opportunities for investment which present themselves to him. It is thus worth our while to consider just what opportunities there may be at the present time and what they are likely to be in the future.

Within recent years approximately half of all the savings of the community have gone into corporate securities—almost entirely the securities of quasi-public corporations. Of the investments reported in all of the probated estates subject to inheritance tax in 1928, 58.5 per cent consisted of corporate securities. Of the remainder, 33.2 per cent was real estate and 8.3 per cent government bonds.[17] These are the three principal fields for investment which do not involve adding the labor of the investor to the use of his savings in order to produce a return. Corporate investment is here seen to lead by a wide margin with real estate holding an important second place.

The estates here listed fall predominantly in the higher income brackets and show, as one would expect, a somewhat larger proportion of investment in corporate securities than would appear were smaller estates more extensively included. Of that part of the national wealth in 1922 which could represent investment, only 43 per cent appears

[17] See Appendix L.

to have been represented by corporate securities, while 46 per cent was in real estate and 11 per cent in government issues.[18] The former set of figures, however, probably give a truer picture of the savings which are invested apart from the individual's labor, for an important proportion of the national wealth consists of investments in land which the owner farms. The income tax returns bear out this conclusion, though here again the lowest income groups are excluded and the highest groups show the largest corporate investments. These returns for 1922 show 54.2 per cent of the income from property to have been derived from corporate securities, as against 34.8 per cent from real estate and 11 per cent from government obligations.[19] Approximate though these figures are, since income is not exactly proportionate to investment and other variations arising from the income tax technique enter in, the conclusion seems certainly warranted that corporations represented very much more than half of the national savings apart from those directly employed by the owner. Some of these corporate investments are in private companies but unquestionably the bulk are in quasi-public corporations.

As in every other aspect of the corporate system which we have discussed, the trend here again appears to be toward the expansion and intrenchment of the system—in this case by drawing to itself not only a large but an increasing proportion of the national savings. Here again the figures are only approximate, but the trend appears sufficiently distinct to be accorded a measure of consideration. Whereas in 1922, 54.2 per cent of reported income from investment appears to have been received from corporate securities, the corresponding figure for 1927 stood at 62.8 per cent.[20]

We cannot project into the future the trend here indicated because the figures are not a sufficiently accurate measure to record any more than a direction. They do not establish a rate of growth. The likelihood of a reversal of trend, however, seems so slight as not to require our serious attention. There is nothing in the future of real estate as we can see it today to promise added attractions to the investor, though an important share of savings can go into this field each year at much the same rate as in the past. The field of government securities is distinctly limited unless the government should itself enter business. To think that the individual will place his savings in private business on a large scale in defiance of the ever-spreading corporate system is again to expect the most improbable. Two serious alterna-

[18] See Appendix M.
[19] See Appendix N.
[20] See Appendix N.

tives only remain, the export of capital through loans to foreign governments, foreign industry, etc., and the failure of the community to save at all. With the international extension of the corporate system, however, investment in foreign industry tends to be still within the system, and the field of foreign government securities is limited. If the community is to save, it thus appears that it will, in large measure, be obliged to invest in corporate securities. It matters little whether that investment be direct or through the medium of insurance companies, banks, and investment trusts, which in turn place these savings at the disposal of corporate managements. The destination of the savings remains the same. It is evident, therefore, that so long as the present trend continues, and there is no apparent reason why it should not, the corporate system will be in a position, if not actually to conscript savings, at least to absorb a very considerable part of them, leaving the investor little choice but to entrust his accumulation to it.

We must conclude, then, that parallel with the growth in the size of the industrial unit has come a dispersion in its ownership such that an important part of the wealth of individuals consists of interests in great enterprises of which no one individual owns a major part. A rapidly increasing proportion of wealth appears to be taking this form and there is much to indicate that the increase will continue. More and more, our thinking must be in terms of this type of wealth. Here again the change is such as to require a reexamination of basic concepts.

(1) Most fundamental of all, the position of ownership has changed from that of an active to that of a passive agent. In place of actual physical properties over which the owner could exercise direction and for which he was responsible, the owner now holds a piece of paper representing a set of rights and expectations with respect to an enterprise. But over the enterprise and over the physical property —the instruments of production—in which he has an interest, the owner has little control. At the same time he bears no responsibility with respect to the enterprise or its physical property. It has often been said that the owner of a horse is responsible. If the horse lives he must feed it. If the horse dies he must bury it. No such responsibility attaches to a share of stock. The owner is practically powerless through his own efforts to affect the underlying property.

(2) The spiritual values that formerly went with ownership have been separated from it. Physical property capable of being shaped by its owner could bring to him direct satisfaction apart from the income it yielded in more concrete form. It represented an extension of his own personality. With the corporate revolution, this quality has been

lost to the property owner much as it has been lost to the worker through the industrial revolution.

(3) The value of an individual's wealth is coming to depend on forces entirely outside himself and his own efforts. Instead, its value is determined on the one hand by the actions of the individuals in command of the enterprise—individuals over whom the typical owner has no control, and on the other hand, by the actions of others in a sensitive and often capricious market. The value is thus subject to the vagaries and manipulations characteristic of the market place. It is further subject to the great swings in society's appraisal of its own immediate future as reflected in the general level of values in the organized markets.

(4) The value of the individual's wealth not only fluctuates constantly—the same may be said of most wealth—but it is subject to a constant appraisal. The individual can see the change in the appraised value of his estate from moment to moment, a fact which may markedly affect both the expenditure of his income and his enjoyment of that income.

(5) Individual wealth has become extremely liquid through the organized markets. The individual owner can convert it into other forms of wealth at a moment's notice and, provided the market machinery is in working order, he may do so without serious loss due to forced sale.

(6) Wealth is less and less in a form which can be employed directly by its owner. When wealth is in the form of land, for instance, it is capable of being used by the owner even though the value of land in the market is negligible. The physical quality of such wealth makes possible a subjective value to the owner quite apart from any market value it may have. The newer form of wealth is quite incapable of this direct use. Only through sale in the market can the owner obtain its direct use. He is thus tied to the market as never before.

(7) Finally, in the corporate system, the "owner" of industrial wealth is left with a mere symbol of ownership while the power, the responsibility and the substance which have been an integral part of ownership in the past are being transferred to a separate group in whose hands lies control.

CHAPTER V: THE EVOLUTION OF CONTROL

AS THE OWNERSHIP of corporate wealth has become more widely dispersed, ownership of that wealth and control over it have come to lie less and less in the same hands. Under the corporate system, control over industrial wealth can be and is being exercised with a minimum of ownership interest. Conceivably it can be exercised without any such interest. Ownership of wealth without appreciable control and control of wealth without appreciable ownership appear to be the logical outcome of corporate development.

This separation of function forces us to recognize "control" as something apart from ownership on the one hand and from management on the other. Hitherto we have talked in familiar terms about the corporation, about its size, about the ownership of its stock. Though we have described a new form of economic organization, our description has been made up of familiar parts. Control divorced from ownership is not, however, a familiar concept. It is a characteristic product of the corporate system. Like sovereignty, its counterpart in the political field, it is an elusive concept, for power can rarely be sharply segregated or clearly defined. Since direction over the activities of a corporation is exercised through the board of directors, we may say for practical purposes that control lies in the hands of the individual or group who have the actual power to select the board of directors, (or its majority), either by mobilizing the legal right to choose them— "controlling" a majority of the votes directly or through some legal device—or by exerting pressure which influences their choice. Occasionally a measure of control is exercised not through the selection of directors, but through dictation to the management, as where a bank determines the policy of a corporation seriously indebted to it. In most cases, however, if one can determine who does actually have the power to select the directors, one has located the group of individuals who for practical purposes may be regarded as "the control."

When control is thus defined a wide variety of kinds and conditions of control situations can be found—forms derived wholly or in part from ownership, forms which depend on legal devices, and forms which are extra-legal in character.

Five major types can be distinguished, though no sharp dividing line separates type from type. These include (1) control through almost complete ownership, (2) majority control, (3) control through a legal device without majority ownership, (4) minority control, and (5) management control. Of these, the first three are forms of control resting on a legal base and revolve about the right to vote a majority of the voting stock. The last two, minority and management control are extra legal, resting on a factual rather than a legal base.

Control through almost complete ownership

The first of these is found in what may be properly called the private corporation, in which a single individual or small group of associates own all or practically all the outstanding stock. They are presumably in a position of control not only having the legal powers of ownership, but also being in a position to make use of them and, in particular being in a position to elect and dominate the management. In such an enterprise, ownership and control are combined in the same hands.

Majority control

Majority control, the first step in the separation of ownership and control, involves ownership of a majority of the outstanding stock.[1] In the case of a simple corporate structure, the ownership of a majority of the stock by a single individual or small group gives to this group virtually all the legal powers of control which would be held by a sole owner of the enterprise and in particular the power to select the board of directors.[2] Certain powers of control, such as the power to amend the charter or to discontinue the enterprise, may require more than a simple majority vote and to that extent the majority exercises less control than a sole owner. Further, the powers of control may be

[1] Where a corporation has subsidiaries, majority control as here used would involve the ownership of stocks representing more than half of the equity interest in the consolidated enterprise.

[2] Where a minority of the stockholders have the power to select a minority of the board, their loss of control over the enterprise may be less, though it must in any case be very considerable.

to a slight extent curbed by the existence of a compact minority which is ready to question the policy or acts of the majority both directly, at stockholders' meetings and in the courts. Where all stock except that held by the majority interest is widely scattered, on the other hand, majority ownership (in the absence of a "legal device") means undiminished actual control. At the same time, the concentrating of control in the hands of a majority means that the minority have lost most of the powers of control over the enterprise of which they are part owners. For them, at least, the separation of ownership and control is well nigh complete, though for the majority the two functions are combined.

If the separation of ownership and control had progressed no further than this, the problems resulting from it would not have assumed major proportions. A large group of individuals cannot combine their capital effectively in a single enterprise without a loss of control by some members of the group. Clearly it would not be possible for each member to exercise the major elements of control over the enterprise. The disadvantages of the "liberum veto" are too great to make unanimous action practicable. The granting of control to a majority of stockholders has therefore been a natural and generally acceptable step. Presumably many if not most of the interests of a minority owner run parallel to those of the controlling majority and are in the main protected by the self-interest of the latter. So far as such interests of the minority are concerned, this loss of control is not serious.[3] Only when the interests of majority and minority are in a measure opposed and the interests of the latter are not protected by enforceable law are the minority holders likely to suffer. This, however, is a risk which the minority must run; and since it is an inevitable counterpart of group enterprise, the problems growing out of it, though they may be most acute in isolated cases, have not taken on major social significance.

Among the largest corporations, however, the separation of ownership and control has passed far beyond the separation represented in majority control. In a truly large corporation, the investment necessary for majority ownership is so considerable as to make such control extremely expensive. Among such corporations, majority control is conspicuous more by its absence than by its presence. More often control is maintained with a relatively small proportion of ownership.

[3] This assumes that the individuals in control are reasonably competent. If the control were incompetent the fact that the interests of majority and minority were parallel would be of little protection to the latter.

Control through a legal device

In the effort to maintain control of a corporation without ownership of a majority of its stock, various legal devices have been developed. Of these, the most important among the very large companies is the device of "pyramiding." This involves the owning of a majority of the stock of one corporation which in turn holds a majority of the stock of another—a process which can be repeated a number of times. An interest equal to slightly more than a quarter or an eighth or a sixteenth or an even smaller proportion of the ultimate property to be controlled is by this method legally entrenched. By issuing bonds and non-voting preferred stock of the intermediate companies the process can be accelerated. By the introduction of two or three intermediate companies each of which is legally controlled through ownership of a majority of its stock by the company higher in the series, complete legal control of a large operating company can be maintained by an ownership interest equal to a fraction of one per cent of the property controlled. The owner of a majority of the stock of the company at the apex of a pyramid can have almost as complete control of the entire property as a sole owner even though his ownership interest is less than one per cent of the whole.

In recent years the Van Sweringen brothers have been notably successful in using this device to create and retain control of a great railroad system. Through an intricate series of pyramided holding companies they gathered together vast railroad properties extending nearly from coast to coast. As the system was built up the structure of holding companies was simplified until at the beginning of 1930 it was not unduly complex. The major ramifications are shown in Chart III. By this pyramid an investment of less than twenty million dollars has been able to control eight Class I railroads having combined assets of over two billion dollars. Less than one per cent of the total investment or hardly more than two per cent of the investment represented by stock has been sufficient to control this great system.[4]

The rapidity with which the pyramided structure allows the investment to be reduced while control is maintained is shown by the figures on the chart. The Van Sweringen investment represented 51 per cent of the capital in the General Securities Corporation, eight per cent of the capital of the Alleghany Corporation, four per cent of the

---

[4] At certain points in the pyramid, notably in the case of the Alleghany Corporation, control is maintained by ownership of a large minority interest rather than by means of majority control. This is a form of control which will be discussed later.

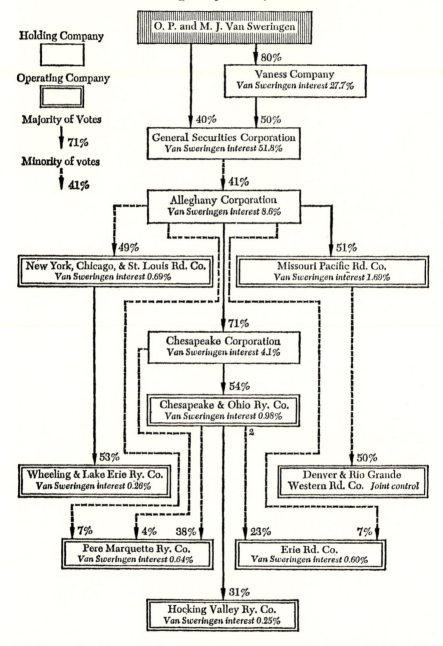

Holding Company

Operating Company

Majority of Votes

↓ 71%

Minority of votes

↓ 41%

O. P. and M. J. Van Sweringen

↓ 80%

Vaness Company
Van Sweringen interest 27.7%

↓ 40% ↓ 50%

General Securities Corporation
Van Sweringen interest 51.8%

↓ 41%

Alleghany Corporation
Van Sweringen interest 8.6%

↓ 49% ↓ 51%

New York, Chicago, & St. Louis Rd. Co.
Van Sweringen interest 0.69%

Missouri Pacific Rd. Co.
Van Sweringen interest 1.69%

↓ 71%

Chesapeake Corporation
Van Sweringen interest 4.1%

↓ 54%

Chesapeake & Ohio Ry. Co.
Van Sweringen interest 0.98%
[2]

↓ 53% ↓ 50%

Wheeling & Lake Erie Ry. Co.
Van Sweringen interest 0.26%

Denver & Rio Grande
Western Rd. Co. *Joint control*

↓ 7% ↓ 4% 38% ↓ ↓ 23% ↓ 7%

Pere Marquette Ry. Co.
Van Sweringen interest 0.64%

Erie Rd. Co.
Van Sweringen interest 0.60%

↓ 31%

Hocking Valley Ry. Co.
Van Sweringen interest 0.25%

1 As of April 30, 1930. Based on RSOR chart opposite p. 878
2 Held via Virginia Transportation Co., which was 100% owned by Chesapeake & Ohio Ry. Co.

Chesapeake Corporation, less than one per cent of the great operating company, the Chesapeake and Ohio Railway, and but a quarter of one per cent of the latter's operating subsidiary, the Hocking Valley Railway. In the last named company over 99¾ per cent of the investment represented ownership without control. For the system as a whole, less than one per cent of the ownership represented combined ownership and control. For the most part the two functions were exercised by separate groups.

This same pyramiding has been extensively employed in building up most of the great public utility systems. By its use legal control can be maintained with an extremely small investment. Through it, legal control can be effectively divorced from legal ownership and factual power can be exercised over great aggregates of wealth with almost no ownership interest therein.

A second legal device for retaining control with a small investment is the use of non-voting stock. This is a comparatively new device, but one which has received so much comment as to be thoroughly familiar. It consists in so arranging the rights attached to different classes of stock that most of the stock is disfranchised, (at least so far as the voting for directors is concerned) and only a very small class, or a class representing a very small investment is permitted to vote. Ownership of just over half of this privileged class is sufficient to give legal control and virtually all the powers of majority ownership. For many years it has been possible in certain states to issue non-voting preferred stock. This has frequently been done without causing serious objection, presumably in part because the issue of common stock is as a rule very much larger than the corresponding issue of preferred stock and in part because the self-interest of the common stockholders has been regarded as ample protection for the interests of the preferred holders.

Only recently have statutory changes made it possible to issue common stock which has no voting rights. Perhaps the most notable example is the non-voting common stock of the Dodge Brothers, Inc., issued in 1925. In this case neither the preferred nor four-fifths of the common stock was entitled to vote in the election of directors. By owning 250,001 shares of voting common representing an investment of less than two and one-quarter million dollars, Dillion Read and Company was able to exercise legal control over this hundred and thirty million dollar concern.[5]

---

[5] Moody's Industrials, 1928, p. 49. The common stock was carried on the books of the company at less than $9 per share including capital surplus. Dodge Brothers stock has since been acquired by Chrysler Corp.

In contrast to non-voting preferred, the use of non-voting common stock has met with considerable disfavor.[6] Both the New York Stock Exchange and the New York Curb have refused to list new issues of non-voting common stock; for practical purposes, this would seem to have eliminated the use of this device on any large scale in the immediate future.

A similar device is, however, being employed which may perhaps be considered a variant of the non-voting stock. This consists of issuing to the controlling group a very large number of shares of a class of stock having excessive voting power, *i.e.*, voting power out of proportion to the capital invested. A striking use has been made of this device in the case of the Cities Service Company. In 1929 this corporation sold to H. L. Doherty and Company one million shares of a $1 par preferred stock. Each share of this stock was entitled to one vote in the election of directors. Yet each share of common stock outstanding was entitled to only $\frac{1}{20}$ vote per share. Twenty-seven per cent of the votes could be cast by the million shares of preferred. Since the other classes of stock were widely distributed (81,470 holders of preferred and 377,988 holders of common stock on June 15, 1930) the excessive voting power given to this cheap stock practically nullified the voting privilege of the regular stockholders. By the use of this device a million dollar par value of stock held virtual control over assets of approximately a billion dollars.[7]

The same device was formerly employed by the group in control of the Standard Gas and Electric Company. Each share of $1 par preferred stock of that company had as much voting power as a $50 par common share. In 1929, the million shares of the cheap stock were able to cast 41 per cent of the votes outstanding. Here again a million dollar par value of stock presumably representing a million dollars of investment was able to exercise practical control over one billion dollars of assets.[8]

In addition to these ways of securing legal control through direct or indirect ownership of the voting majority, a further device must be considered which does not involve even ownership of a voting majority. This is the familiar practice of organizing a voting trust. It involves the creation of a group of trustees, often a part of the man-

[6] See, for instance, W. Z. Ripley, "Main Street and Wall Street," Boston, 1927.

[7] Moody's Public Utilities, 1930, p. 1998.

[8] Standard Corporation Records, April 29, 1929. In the latter part of 1929 this method of control was replaced by one depending on an extremely complex holding company set up. New York Times, March 24, 1930, and Moody's Public Utilities, 1930.

agement, with the complete power to vote all stock placed in trust with it. When a majority of the stock is held in trust, as is usually the case, the trustees have almost complete control over the affairs of the corporation yet without any necessary ownership on their part. The stockholders, meantime, receive, in place of their stock, trust certificates entitling them to share in such disbursements as the directors may choose to distribute. In the recent organization of the (then) ninety million dollar Pennroad Corporation, the organizing group—the Pennsylvania Railroad management, used this device to guarantee complete control. The stock of the newly formed corporation was placed in a voting trust and the stockholders of the railroad were offered the privilege of furnishing capital by purchase of voting trust certificates.[9] The purchasers of these certificates acquired the position of owners without the power even as a group to control their own enterprise.

The voting trust, more completely than any device we have hitherto considered, separates control from all ownership interest. Originally bitterly opposed by the law and held illegal by the courts on the ground that the vote could not be separated from the stock, it came to be permitted by statutory provision in most states. Such statutes, however, commonly limited the period during which the trust agreement could run to some term of years, in New York State to a maximum of ten years. But even where the duration has been limited, the voting trustees might entrench themselves beyond the reach of the stockholders for a longer period by arranging for renewal of the trust for additional terms at their own discretion. The Interborough Rapid Transit Company is perhaps the most striking case. The voting trust agreement provided for a duration of five years, but was renewable for five successive periods of five years each without any further action on the part of the holders of voting trust certificates.[10] Legal control could thus be prolonged for a period of thirty years.

Control through a voting trust differs from the other forms of legal control, and from the forms of factual control which we shall examine, in that it is fixed, defined, and inalienable, with certain definite and well recognized responsibilities attached. Under the other arrangements so far discussed, control may be bought or sold; may pass by inheritance in case of death; its location may not be generally known (in fact, frequently it is not) and its holder has never stood up in public and assumed the definite obligations of its possession. Control through a voting trust is open, not easily transferred, and therefore

[9] Standard Corporation Records, July 22, 1929, p. 6730.
[10] Standard Corporation Records, Special Reports Section, May 9, 1929.

responsible. Presumably, it is this open acceptance of responsibility which has reduced the criticism of the voting trust, making it an effective device for maintaining control without ownership. Perhaps for the same reason it has not been extensively employed in the larger corporations, since those individuals desiring to control a company may not wish to assume the responsibilities and liabilities which a trust would impose upon them.

Control based on a legal device, whether by pyramiding, by a special class of voting stock or by a voting trust is almost as secure as control through sole or majority ownership even though it involves little ownership interest. In case of failure, legal control may be lost. Only under the most unusual conditions can an individual or group in legal control of a prosperous business become so entangled in a situation that they can extricate themselves only by surrendering this control. In 1930, Mr. Fox was apparently forced to surrender his majority holding of the special classes of voting stock in Fox Films and in Fox Theatre Corporations as a result of the short term debts which had been incurred in expanding these enterprises and the pressure of creditors after the stock market crash. In spite of the fact that the companies were reputed to be highly profitable, the capital necessary to fund the debts of the corporation and prevent foreclosure was forthcoming only when Mr. Fox disposed of his legal control.[11] Such a combination of circumstances is rare; we can reasonably say that so long as a corporation is not actually bankrupt, legal control stands every chance of being maintained, whether it rests on sole ownership, majority ownership or legal device.

The methods of control so far discussed have all involved a legal status. In each case factual control has rested primarily upon the more or less permanent possession of the legal power to vote a majority of the voting stock. Yet such control has been held in connection with different proportions of ownership. At one end of the scale ownership and control have been wholly combined. At the other end of the scale ownership and control have been wholly separated. Any degree of combination or separation might be arranged with control based on a legal status.

In the typical large corporation, however, control does not rest upon legal status. In these companies control is more often factual, depending upon strategic position secured through a measure of ownership, a share in management or an external circumstance important to the conduct of the enterprise. Such control is less clearly

11 New York Times, April 8, 1930. Also New York Times and Wall Street Journal from December 7, 1929 to April 8, 1930.

defined than the legal forms, is more precarious, and more subject to accident and change. It is, however, none the less actual. It may be maintained over a long period of years, and as a corporation becomes larger and its ownership more widespread, it tends towards a position of impregnability comparable to that of legal control, a position from which it can be dislodged only by a virtual revolution.

As in the case of legal control, factual control apart from legal control may involve varying degrees of ownership, though never more than 50 per cent of the voting stock.[12] It may rest to a very considerable extent on the ownership of a large minority stock interest, or, when stock ownership is widely distributed, it may lie in the hands of the management. No sharp dividing line exists between these two situations, but so far as they can be distinguished, they may properly be referred to as minority control and management control.

Minority control

The first of these, minority control, may be said to exist when an individual or small group hold a sufficient stock interest to be in a position to dominate a corporation *through their stock interest*. Such a group is often said to have "working control" of the company. In general, their control rests upon their ability to attract from scattered owners proxies sufficient when combined with their substantial minority interest to control a majority of the votes at the annual elections. Conversely, this means that no other stockholding is sufficiently large to act as a nucleus around which to gather a majority of the votes. Where a corporation is comparatively small and the number of stockholders is not great, minority control appears to be comparatively difficult to maintain. A rival group may be able to purchase a majority of the stock or perhaps only a minority large enough to attract the additional votes necessary to obtain control in a proxy fight. The larger the company and the wider the distribution of its stock, the more difficult it appears to be to dislodge a controlling minority. As a financial operation it would be practically impossible for an outside interest to purchase a majority of the stock of the General Motors Corporation; even a Rockefeller would think twice before endeavoring to purchase a majority ownership of the Standard Oil Company of Indiana. Likewise the cost of mobilizing the votes of tens or hundreds of thousands of stockholders by circularizing them and perhaps conducting a publicity campaign, must be such as to prevent any but the most wealthy from seeking this method of seizing control from an

[12] Over 50% of the voting stock would presumably involve legal control.

existing minority. This is especially the case where the existing control can charge to the corporation the costs of its fight to maintain its position, while the outsider must conduct a fight at his own private expense.

There is, however, a serious limitation on minority control. This is the possibility that the management may be antagonistic. So long as the affairs of the corporation run smoothly, minority control may be quietly maintained over a period of years. But in time of crisis, or where a conflict of interest between the control and the management arises, the issue may be drawn and a proxy fight to determine control may demonstrate how far dependent upon its appointed management the controlling group has become. The management is, in most cases, elected annually at a stockholders' meeting, notice of which must be sent to every stockholder entitled to vote. With this notice is usually sent a proxy slip which the stockholder is requested to sign and return. By doing so he creates the two or three people named in the proxy his agents, and empowers them to vote his shares at the annual meeting. In selecting the proxy committee the corporate management is in a position to name men who will be subservient to it; and where the management has been selected by the controlling minority, it will, as a matter of course, select a proxy committee which will serve the interests of this minority. The normal apathy of the small stockholder is such that he will either fail to return his proxy, or will sign on the dotted line, returning his proxy to the office of the corporation. In the ordinary course of events, only one such request is received by the stockholders at the time of each election. The proxy votes are then used to rubber stamp the selections already made by those in control. But if the management should resist and refuse the proxy machinery to the minority group in control, such a group has only the expensive recourse of sending out a duplicate set of proxies and bidding for the stockholder's support in opposition to the management. When such a fight for control is joined, factual power is once more dependent on legal power and the stockholders by their votes or by their choice of proxy committees decide the issue.

In recent years the most striking illustration of this fight for control was presented by the open warfare between Mr. John D. Rockefeller, Jr., and the management of the Standard Oil Company of Indiana. Mr. Rockefeller actually held 14.9 per cent of the voting stock.[18] He had been in substantial control of the company for years. Colonel Stewart, the chairman of the board of directors and undeniably the

---

[18] Either directly, through members of his family or through charitable institutions. See Table XII.

driving force behind much of that company's activity, displeased Mr. Rockefeller in connection with certain transactions which were the subject of discussion during the administration of President Harding. He asked Colonel Stewart to resign; Stewart refused and did not grant to Mr. Rockefeller the use of the proxy machinery at the following annual election of directors. Thereupon Mr. Rockefeller waged a most dramatic proxy battle against him. He circularized the stockholders at considerable expense, asking for proxies. He engaged the most eminent legal talent to guard against any "technical mistakes." He brought to bear the tremendous influence of his standing in the community. The Wall Street Journal pointed out at the time that the fight marked the first time the Rockefeller domination in a large Standard Oil unit "had been really in question." [14] In opposition, Colonel Stewart obtained the full support of the existing board of directors and sought the support of the 16,000 employees who were stockholders. At this most opportune moment the company declared a 50 per cent stock dividend.[15] The issue was for long in grave doubt. Four days previous to the election both sides are reported to have claimed the support of a majority, the one of votes and the other of stockholders. In the final election of directors, Mr. Rockefeller won, 59 per cent of the votes outstanding or 65 per cent of the votes cast being in favor of his candidates. Control may be said to have remained in his hands.[16] Colonel Stewart's connection with the company was brought to a close.[17]

The basis for Mr. Rockefeller's success in this fight must be a matter of conjecture, but, though his ownership of stock formed the nucleus about which he attracted support, the outcome did not rest on ownership alone. He appears to have won partly because the public in general sided with him in his view of the transaction to which Stewart had been a party, and still more, perhaps, because Mr. Rockefeller's own standing in the community commanded the confidence of a large body of stockholders. The difficulty and cost of dislodging the management, however, emphasizes the precarious nature of control resting on the ownership of a minority of the voting stock,—a control

[14] Wall Street Journal, January 11, 1929.

[15] Even though a stock dividend may have little effect on the value of the stockholdings of the individual, the psychological effect may be great.

[16] 5,519,210 shares voted against Colonel Stewart and 2,954,986 shares in favor. 9,284,688 shares were outstanding. New York Times, March 8, 1929. The figures reported by other papers were substantially the same.

[17] This dramatic fight was fully reported by the daily press between January 10 and March 8, 1929. See particularly:—the Wall Street Journal, January 10, January 11 and March 8; the New York Times, January 12, January 30, March 3 and March 8.

which would appear in ordinary times to be adequately safeguarded,—and further emphasizes the importance of the management to any effective minority control.

This case has been described in detail because it probably marks the dividing line between minority control and management control. If Mr. Stewart had won the fight we could say that management without appreciable ownership was in the saddle. As it is, we may say that Mr. Rockefeller is in control, to a considerable degree through his ownership of a minority interest of 14.9 per cent and in part through less tangible factors. Could other men with less prestige and financial power have retained control with but a 15 per cent ownership? Could Mr. Rockefeller have retained control if his ownership had been appreciably less? Here would seem to be control based on the minimum of ownership which would allow it to be held separate from the titular management.

Management control

The fifth type of control is that in which ownership is so widely distributed that no individual or small group has even a minority interest large enough to dominate the affairs of the company. When the largest single interest amounts to but a fraction of one per cent—the case in several of the largest American corporations—no stockholder is in the position through his holdings alone to place important pressure upon the management or to use his holdings as a considerable nucleus for the accumulation of the majority of votes necessary to control.

We have already seen that the largest stockholder of the Pennsylvania Railroad held but 34 hundredths of one per cent of the total stock outstanding.[18] The next largest holder owned but 2 tenths of one per cent while the combined holdings of the twenty largest owners amounted to only 2.7 per cent of the total stock. There were only 236 stockholders holding over 500 shares each (.004 per cent) and their combined holdings amounted to less than five per cent of the total. Clearly no individual or small group was in a position to dominate the company *through stock ownership,* a fact still further emphasized by the heterogeneous character of the list of largest holders.

It is further striking that no directors or officers were included among the largest twenty holders. Not a single director or officer held as much as one-tenth of one per cent of the total stock. The combined

[18] See Table X.

TABLE X: *20 Largest Stockholders of the Pennsylvania Railroad Co.*
(as of Dec. 31, 1929) [1]

	No. of shares held	Proportion of total shares
Penn. Rd. Employees Provident & Loan Association	39,350	.34%
William M. Potts	23,738	.20%
J. Marshall Lockhart	22,500	.19%
Fahnestock & Co.—held for Fahnestock family	16,848	.15%
Estate of Henry H. Houston	16,000	.14%
The Home Insurance Co.	16,000	.14%
General Education Board	15,882	.14%
Haygart Corp. (Adams Express), Investment trust	15,400	.13%
English Assoc. of American Bond & Share Holders	15,264	.13%
Celia Sibley Wilson	15,000	.13%
Estate and family of Marcus Loew	13,600	.12%
Travelers Insurance Co.	13,500	.12%
Estate of John J. Emery	13,000	.12%
Jas. Capel & Co., Brokers	12,686	.11%
Sterling Securities Corp.	12,000	.11%
Harris, Upham & Co. (partners acct.)	11,250	.10%
Kuhn, Loeb & Co. (for own acct.)	10,000	.09%
Girard Trust Co. (for own acct.)	10,000	.09%
1 unidentified individual	10,000	.09%
Mrs. E. S. Woodward	8,500	.07%
	310,518	2.70%

[1] "Regulation of Stock Ownership in Railroads," pp. 142, 143. Total shares outstanding December 31, 1929—11,495,128.

holdings of all the directors could not have amounted to more than 7 tenths of one per cent and were presumably very much less.[19] Certainly in terms of relative interest the holdings by the directors were negligible.

[19] Not a single director is included among the individuals whose holdings are given in the Congressional Reports but the 19 largest unnamed holders combined (there were 19 directors) had but .7 of one per cent. Presumably most of the directors held amounts of stock too small) to be included in this group. See "Regulation of Stock Ownership in Railroads," pp. 142 and 143.

The same lack of any concentrated holdings or large holdings on the part of the directors appears to exist in the case of the Telephone and the Steel corporations.[20] In neither of these companies does the largest stockholder own as much as one per cent of the outstanding stock while the twenty largest Telephone holders owned 4.6 per cent and the twenty largest Steel, 6.4 per cent. These lists differ from the list of the Pennsylvania stockholders in that in the latter adjustment has been made for stock held by brokers and by nominees, while in these lists no such adjustment has been possible. The brokerage accounts represent the holdings of a multitude of individuals. At the same time, the largest individual holders may have stock in brokerage accounts or in the name of nominees. If adjustment for these items were made, it might increase the proportions held by the few very largest holders but would probably reduce considerably the holdings of the largest 20.[21] It is clear, therefore, that in these companies, also, no small group of individuals have sufficient stockholdings to dominate *through stock ownership.*

In these companies the directors appear to have a somewhat larger proportionate interest. The reported holdings of the directors of the Steel Corporation in 1928 are given in Table XI. Two directors were included in the largest 20 holders and the combined holdings of directors amounted to 1.4 per cent of the outstanding stock. In the Telephone Company, one director with .48 of one per cent of the stock was among the largest 20 holders. Furthermore, it is possible that the directors owned stock which was actually held in the name of brokers or nominees, though the amount thus owned does not appear likely to have been great in these particular companies.

In such companies where does control lie? To answer this question, it is necessary to examine in greater detail the conditions surrounding the electing of the board of directors. In the election of the board the stockholder ordinarily has three alternatives. He can refrain from voting, he can attend the annual meeting and personally vote his stock,[22] or he can sign a proxy transferring his voting power to certain individuals selected by the management of the corporation, the proxy committee. As his personal vote will count for little or nothing at the meeting unless he has a very large block of stock, the stockholder is practically reduced to the alternative of not voting at

[20] For the 20 largest stockholders of these companies, see Appendices.
[21] The 20 largest holders of the Pennsylvania Railroad held 3.5 per cent before adjustment and only 2.7 per cent after adjustment.
[22] The use of a personal proxy to represent only the particular stockholder is for this purpose equivalent to his personal attendance at the stockholders' meeting.

TABLE XI: *United States Steel Corporation*

Stockholdings of Board of Directors [1]

Director	1928			1927		
	Pfd. shares	Com. shares	Total shares	Pfd. shares	Com. shares	Total shares
G. F. Baker	500	77,000	77,500	500	49,950	50,450
G. F. Baker, Jr.		10,001	10,001		1,001	1,001
W. J. Filbert	1,904	1,688	3,592	1,904	1,134	3,038
Samuel Mather		1,121	1,121		801	801
T. Morrison	4,000	1,401	5,401	4,000	1,001	5,001
J. S. Phipps		1	1		1	1
N. L. Miller		1,001	1,001		3,450	3,450
P. Roberts, Jr.	110	1	111	110	1	111
M. C. Taylor		40,100	40,100		40,001	40,001
Robert Winsor	1	700	701	1	500	501
E. J. Buffington	693	753	1,446	693	1,133	1,826
J. A. Farrel	4,850	603	5,453	4,950	315	5,265
J. P. Morgan	105	1,261	1,366		901	901
Total Stock held by Directors	12,163	135,631	147,794	12,158	100,189	112,347
Stock Outstanding [2]	3,102,811	7,116,235	10,719,046			
Per cent of Outstanding held by Directors	.4%	1.9%	1.4%			

[1] New York Times, April 17, 1928.
[2] Standard Corporation Records, 1929.

81

all or else of *handing over his vote to individuals over whom he has no control and in whose selection he did not participate.* In neither case will he be able to exercise any measure of control. Rather, control will tend to be in the hands of those who select the proxy committee by whom, in turn, the election of directors for the ensuing period may be made. Since the proxy committee is appointed by the existing management, the latter can virtually dictate their own successors. Where ownership is sufficiently sub-divided, the management can thus become a self-perpetuating body even though its share in the ownership is negligible.[23] This form of control can properly be called "management control."

Such management control, though resting on no legal foundation, appears to be comparatively secure where the stock is widely distributed. Even here, however, there is always the possibility of revolt. A group outside the management may seek control. If the company has been seriously mismanaged, a protective committee of stockholders may combine a number of individual owners into a group which can successfully contend with the existing management and replace it by another which in turn can be ousted only by revolutionary action. Thus, the unsuccessful management of the Childs' restaurant chain was expelled by the action of a minority group after the former had made itself thoroughly unpopular, so it was charged, by trying to turn its patrons into vegetarians.[24] Likewise, the management of the Youngstown Sheet and Tube Company appears to have found itself confronted with the alternative of giving way to the newly created minority interest of a group of individuals headed by Cyrus S. Eaton or of seeking support from some other source. In this case, the price of escaping the impending minority control was apparently thought to be the complete sacrifice of independence through merger with the Bethlehem Steel Corporation.[25]

[23] The nearest approach to this condition which the present writer has been able to discover elsewhere is the organization which dominates the Catholic Church. The Pope selects the Cardinals and the College of Cardinals in turn select the succeeding Pope.

[24] See New York Times and Wall Street Journal, February 1 to March 8, 1929, particularly advertisements appearing in the former on February 16, 18 and 20, 1929 and the newspaper reports of the proceedings at the annual stockholders' meeting published in both periodicals on March 8, 1929.

[25] See New York Times and Wall Street Journal, March 10, to April 12, 1930 and reports of subsequent litigations as given in the same periodicals between April and December, 1930. If the merger with Bethlehem had been successful, most of the existing management of the Youngstown company would presumably have retained their position of management, if not of control. Such is not likely to have been the case under Eaton control. This was clearly brought out by the testimony

Both the cases cited involve an active battle in which the stockholders were called in to cast the deciding vote. More often control is quietly exercised over a period of years without any active contest such as would give the stockholders an opportunity to choose between two contesting groups. For the most part the stockholder is able to play only the part of the rubber stamp. Occasionally he may have the opportunity to support an effort to seize control, a position not unlike that of a populace supporting a revolution. In either case, the usual stockholder has little power over the affairs of the enterprise and his vote, if he has one, is rarely capable of being used as an instrument of democratic control. The separation of ownership and control has become virtually complete. The bulk of the owners have in fact almost no control over the enterprise, while those in control hold only a negligible proportion of the total ownership.

Sometimes factual control is not found in the hands of any single group. We have seen how dependent a controlling minority may be upon the cooperation of the management and how a controlling management may have to accede in a measure to the demands of a strong minority in order to maintain its measure of control. It is not unusual for two or more strong minority interests to enter into a working arrangement by which they jointly maintain control; or a minority and a management may combine as "the" control. In such cases we may say that control is divided and can refer to the situation as "joint control." [26]

Corporate control thus appears in many forms—relatively defined and relatively stable legal positions, loosely defined and somewhat more precarious factual situations. Each form is not complete in itself and exclusive of others. Several bases may reinforce each other. Thus the controlling management of the Consolidated Gas, Electric Light & Power Company of Baltimore, feeling its control endangered by a growing minority interest, organized a voting trust, broke up the threatening minority, and then terminated the trust at the end of a year when it appeared to be no longer necessary, returning to their old basis of management control. [27] In this case, a group with factual

---

of Mr. Campbell, Pres. of the Youngstown Sheet and Tube Co., at the Youngstown Trial.

[26] It must of course be apparent that whenever two or more individuals exercise power (or important powers) over an enterprise such that each must adjust his action with regard for the position of the other, we have a case of "joint control." For the present purpose, "joint control" is used to apply only where groups with radically different interests share "control."

[27] New York Times, June 26, 1929 and M. P. U. 1930.

control reinforced its position by the temporary use of a legal device. On the other hand factual control may be limited to the point where it can scarcely be exercised. The pressure from creditors when a firm is financially insecure may go to the point where a bondholders' committee itself may be considered to have control.

The separation of ownership and control among the 200 "largest" American corporations

With these various types of legal and factual control in mind, an effort has been made to discover how far each type exists among the largest American corporations. For this purpose the list of the two hundred largest companies was classified according to type of control and the degree of separation of ownership and control.[28] Necessarily such a classification is attended by a large measure of error. In many cases no accurate information is available, the result being at best an inference drawn from fragmentary evidence. In many other cases the management of the corporation itself would be puzzled to answer the question "Who is in control?" This is particularly true of corporations subject to "joint control." In these cases not infrequently several men or groups of men maintain positions partly by reason of their ownership of a portion of the corporation's stock; partly by reason of their personal influence; partly because they are connected with institutions or interests whose antagonism might be dangerous to the corporate welfare or whose favor might be to its advantage. Out of this mass of imponderables their position is secure for the time being. But an outsider cannot estimate, and the insider frequently does not know, which of the various elements, if any, is dominant.

In seeking to classify according to the type of control, reasonably definite and reliable information was obtained for nearly two-thirds of the companies. Legal devices such as holding companies, voting trusts and non-voting common stock are accurately reported in the manuals. Where a stock is not listed or traded on any public exchange, that fact may be taken to indicate the lack of an important public interest in the stock of the company. In many cases, the exact holdings of the principal interests have been reported—particularly in the railroad field.

Where reliable information has not been directly available it has been necessary to depend upon newspaper reports—not necessarily accurate in themselves—but valid when supported by evidence from

[28] Table XII.

other sources.[29] It was reported in the New York Times,[30] for example, that an important interest in the United States Rubber Company had been acquired by the du Pont interests in 1928. This evidence, unsatisfactory in itself, was supported by later reports that du Pont interests had formed the Rubber Securities Corporation and placed in it their holdings of United States Rubber stock,[31] and by the replacing of the former president of the company by Mr. F. B. Davis, Jr., a director of E. I. du Pont de Nemours Company and formerly president and general manager of one of its subsidiaries.[32] Further, the Wall Street News reported that the du Pont family held 14 per cent of the voting stock early in 1928.[33] The number of stockholders in January, 1929 was reported as 26,057.[34] Since the Rubber Securities Corporation had a total capital stock amounting to less than the value of the stocks of the United States Rubber Company necessary to give majority control, and since the list of stockholders was so large, it was assumed that the du Pont interests did not hold a majority of the outstanding stock. This was supported by other evidence of a less precise nature. On this basis, the United States Rubber Company was classed as controlled by a minority interest.

Many of the corporations could not be so accurately classified. The dividing line between control by a minority interest and control by the management is not clear, and many companies had to be classed as doubtful. Thus, with regard to the Allied Chemical and Dye Corporation, Standard Corporation Records reports that in 1927 the Solvay American Investment Corporation was formed under the control of Solvay and Company of Belgium to hold 18.1 per cent of its outstanding stock,[35] and there is no report of a change in its holdings

[29] The use of newspapers as a source of information deserves a word of comment. The ordinary news sections of a paper are usually read as a matter of interest while the financial sections are very much more likely to be read as, in part, a basis for action on the part of the reader. Accuracy therefore becomes important to the reader. A financial page which was continuously inaccurate should soon come to be known as such, and be avoided. The two papers here particularly employed, the New York Times and the Wall Street Journal, have excellent reputations for accuracy and in general can be relied upon even though particular statements may be inaccurate because of typographical or other error. Information based on a series of statements by these papers in regard to financial matters should within reason be accepted as reliable.

[30] New York Times, April 16, 1928.

[31] Wall Street Journal, Dec. 7, 1929.

[32] Standard Corporation Records, April 24, 1920.

[33] Wall Street News, April 19, 1928.

[34] Standard Corporation Records, April 24, 1929.

[35] Ibid., Sept. 18, 1929.

TABLE XII: Control of the 200 Largest Corporations

A. PRIVATE OWNERSHIP AND CONTROL—NO IMPORTANT STOCKHOLDINGS BY PUBLIC

Size in millions of dollars of assets	Corporation	Ownership	Source of information	No. of stockholders Dec. 1929
	Railroads			
$ 123.6	Florida East Coast Ry. Co.	Estate of Mary L. (Flagler) Bingham	RSOR 344	8
152.7	Virginian Ry. Co.	Estate of H. H. Rogers	RSOR 317	343
276.3				
	Public Utilities			
108.7	New England Gas & Elec. Association[1]	Assoc. Gas & Elec. officials	SCR 1930	
112.2	Railway & Bus Assoc.[1]	Assoc. Gas & Elec. interests	MPU 1930	
220.9				
	Industrials			
300.0 Est.	Aluminum Co. of America	Mellon Interests hold over 80% of stock	SCR 1929	
761.0	Ford Motor Co.	Ford family own all stock	NYT 4/11/29	
430.9	Gulf Oil Corp. of Pa.	Mellon Interests hold over 90% of stock	WSJ 7/8/29	12,368 [2]
147.3	Great Atlantic & Pac. Tea Co. of America	Closely held	M. Ind. 1930	
222.0	Jones & Laughlin Steel Corp.	Jones & Laughlin families & associates	M. Ind. 1930	
250.0 Est.	Koppers Co. of Del.	Mellon interests	NYT 9/17/29	
90.3	Minnesota & Ontario Paper Co.	Mr. Backus & associates	WSJ 3/20/30	
120.8	Nat'l Steel Corp.	Appears to be closely held	M. Ind. 1930	
2,322.3				
2,819.5				

[1] These two companies are part of the Assoc. Gas & Electric System and it is possible that they should be regarded as subsidiaries of the latter.

[2] As of Dec. 1928.

Size in millions of dollars of assets	Corporation	Owner of Majority	Source of information	No. of stockholders Dec. 1929
	Railroads			
283.1	*Seaboard Air Line Ry. Co.*[1]	Underwriting Syndicate headed by Dillon, Read & Co.	RSOR 313	4,870 [2]
283.1				
	Public Utilities			
212.1	*Duke Power Co.*	Duke trusts & associates (Trusts hold 43.7%)	MPU 1930	
158.7	*Eastern Gas & Fuel Associates*	Koppers interests	WSJ 10/2/29	
109.0	*Lone Star Gas Corp.*	Crawford interests	SCR 1930	7,000
479.8				
	Industrials			
97.0 Est.	*R. H. Macy & Co.*	Bulk believed to be closely held	Private	
137.2	*Marshall Field & Co.*	Bulk believed to be closely held	M. Ind. 1930	
124.7	*Phelps Dodge Corp.*	Bulk held by Dodge family & associates		
210.0 Est.	*Singer Mfg. Co.*	Bulk believed to be closely held	NYT 3/14/29	3,359
115.9	*Crane Co.*	Bulk believed to be closely held		
94.6	*Deere & Co.*	Bulk believed to be closely held		4,451 [3]
779.4				
1,542.3				

[1] Large holdings in the hands of an underwriting syndicate are, as a rule, temporary prior to sale of securities to the investing public.
[2] As of April 1930.
[3] As of October 1929.

TABLE XII: Control of the 200 Largest Corporations (Continued)

C. CONTROL BY A LEGAL DEVICE—BULK OF STOCK BELIEVED TO BE OWNED BY PUBLIC

Size in millions of dollars of assets	Corporation	Legal device	Source of information	No. of stockholders Dec. 1929
	Railroads			
1,600.0 Est.	Alleghany Corp.[1]	Pyramiding	RSOR 882	24,511
	Public Utilities			
184.4	*Amer. Commonwealths Power Corp.*[1]	Non-voting Common stock	MPU 1930	3,000 [2]
378.5	Amer. Water Works & Elec. Co.	Voting Trust	SCR 1931	
900.4	Assoc. Gas & Elec. Co.	Non-voting Common stock	MPU 1930	190,139 [3]
989.6	Cities Service Co.	Special Vote-Weighted Pref.	MPU 1930	459,458
458.6	Interborough Rapid Transit Co.	Voting Trust	MPU 1930	
95.6	Phila. Rapid Transit Co.	Pyramiding	MPU 1930	50,000
346.0	Tri-Utilities Corp.	Pyramiding	MPU 1930	
520.1	United Light & Power Co.[1]	Non-voting Common stock	MPU 1930	
1,125.8	U. S. Elec. Power Corp.[1]	Pyramiding & Special stock	MPU 1930	51,322
373.1	Utilities Power & Lt. Corp.	Non-voting Common & Voting Trust	MPU 1930	36,236
5,372.1				

[1] Control maintained by a large minority holding of voting stock.
[2] As of June 1930.
[3] Whole system as of June 1930.
[4] As of February 1930.

C. CONTROL BY A LEGAL DEVICE—BULK OF STOCK BELIEVED TO BE OWNED BY PUBLIC (*Continued*)

Size in millions of dollars of assets	Corporation	Legal device	Source of information	No. of stockholders Dec. 1929
	Industrials			
265.4	Amer. Tobacco Co.	Non-voting Common stock	M. Ind. 1930	30,459
98.0	Cliffs Corp.	Voting Trust & Pyramiding	M. Ind. 1930	
117.7	Crown Zellerbach Corp.	Voting Trust	WSJ 10/19/29	
360.0	Gen'l Theatre Equipment, Inc.	Pyramiding, non-voting Common, & Voting Trust	M. Ind. 1930	
217.6	Int'l Match Corp.	Pyramiding	M. Ind. 1930	
150.3	Liggett & Myers Tobacco Co.	Non-voting Common stock	M. Ind. 1930	12,219
163.1	R. J. Reynolds Tobacco Co.	Non-voting Common stock	M. Ind. 1930	
486.4	Shell Union Oil Corp.	Pyramiding	M. Ind. 1930	
240.0 Est.	Union Oil Associates	Pyramiding	M. Ind. 1930	
161.5	United Stores Corp.	Pyramiding, Special stock & Voting Trust	M. Ind. 1930	13,712 [5]
2,260.0				
9,232.1				

[5] Parent and Subsidiaries.

TABLE XII: *Control of the 200 Largest Corporations* (*Continued*)

D. MINORITY CONTROL THROUGH OWNERSHIP OF AN IMPORTANT MINORITY BLOCK OF STOCK—REMAINING STOCK BELIEVED TO BE WIDELY DISTRIBUTED

Size in millions of dollars of assets	Corporation	Minority interest	Size of holding	Source of information	Character of ultimate control	No. of stock- holders Dec. 1929
	Railroads					
840.0 Est.	Atlantic Coast Line Rd. Co.	Atlantic Coast Line Co. Associated interests	27.10% 11.79%	RSOR 283	Pyramiding	12,850 [1]
97.4	Chicago & Eastern Illinois Ry. Co.	Estate of Thomas F. Ryan	38.13%	RSOR 255	Minority	2,071
149.2	Chicago Great Western Rd. Co.	Patrick H. Joyce	23.4%	RSOR 452	Minority	6,409 [2]
189.3	Dela. Lackawanna & Western Rd. Co.	Baker & Vanderbilt families	17.85%	RSOR 134	Minority	6,943
560.9	Erie Railroad Co.	Alleghany Corp. (and sub.)	30.41%	RSOR 878	Pyramiding	6,538
680.9	Illinois Central Rd. Co.	Union Pacific Rd. Co. (and sub.)	28.97%	RSOR 353	Management	20,152
146.1	Kansas City Southern Ry. Co.	Alleghany Corp.	20.8%	RSOR 878	Pyramiding	3,746
350.0 Est.	N.Y., Chicago & St. Louis Rd. Co.	Alleghany Corp.	49.5%	MRR 1930	Pyramiding	7,787
497.0	Norfolk & Western Ry. Co.	Penn. Rd. Co. (and sub.)	43.30%	RSOR 170	Management	12,068
139.4	St. Louis Southwestern Ry. Co.	N.Y. Investors, Inc. & associates	36.03%	RSOR 364	Pyramiding	1,265

[1] Whole system.
[2] As of February 1930.

D. MINORITY CONTROL THROUGH OWNERSHIP OF AN IMPORTANT MINORITY BLOCK OF STOCK—REMAINING STOCK BELIEVED TO BE WIDELY DISTRIBUTED (Continued)

Size in millions of dollars of assets	Corporation	Minority interest	Size of holding	Source of information	Character of ultimate control	No. of stock-holders Dec. 1929
334.6	Wabash Ry. Co.	Penn. Rd. Co. (and sub.)	48.93%	RSOR 164	Management	4,719
168.2	Western Maryland Ry. Co.	B & O. Rd. Co.	43.10%	RSOR 211	Management	2,653 [2]
156.0 Est.	Western Pacific Rd. Corp.	Arthur Curtis James (through holding Co.)	38.61%	RSOR 482	Minority	5,500 [3]
4,565.4	**Public Utilities**					
431.0	Amer. Gas & Electric Co.	Elec. Bond & Share Co.	16.2%	SCR 1931	Management	13,064
754.1	Amer. Power & Light Co.	Elec. Bond & Share Co.	20.2%	SCR 1931	Management	
123.7	Bklyn. Union Gas Co.	Koppers-Mellon Interests	26.3%	NYT 3/16/30	Minority	4,859
529.2	Columbia Gas & Elec. Corp.	United Corp.	20.8%	MPU 1930	Management	46,100
1,138.7	Commonwealth & Southern Corp.	Am. Super-power Corp.	12.7%	SCR 1931	Management	107,000 [4]
		United Corp.	5.1%	MPU 1930		
440.0 Est.	Commonwealth Edison Co.	United Gas Improvement Co.	2.7%	MPU 1930		
		In Treasury of Subsid.	5.8%	SCR 1930		
		Insull Utility Invest. Inc.	12.6%	SCR 1931	Pyramiding	
		Corporation Securities of Chi.	4.3%	SCR 1931		

[2] As of February 1930.

[3] As of December 1928.

[4] Approximate figure as of May 1930.

TABLE XII: Control of the 200 Largest Corporations (Continued)

D. MINORITY CONTROL THROUGH OWNERSHIP OF AN IMPORTANT MINORITY BLOCK OF STOCK—REMAINING STOCK BELIEVED TO BE WIDELY DISTRIBUTED (Continued)

Size in millions of dollars of assets	Corporation	Minority interest	Size of holding	Source of information	Character of ultimate control	No. of stockholders Dec. 1929
296.1	Detroit Edison Co.	No. American Co.	20.6%	SCR 1931	Pyramiding	13,726
560.0 Est.	Elec. Power & Light Corp.	Elec. Bond & Share Co.	23.4%	SCR 1931	Management	
1,120.0 Est.	Middle West Utilities Co.	Insull Utility Investments, Inc.	28.4%	SCR 1931	Pyramiding	296,389 [1]
500.0 Est.	Nat'l Power & Light Co.	Electric Bond & Share Co.	45.7%	SCR 1931	Management	
756.9	Niagara Hudson Power Corp.	United Corp.	22.1%	NYJ 3/3/31	Management	73,702 [5]
810.3	North American Co.	Central States Elec. Corp. & subs. or affil.	24.4%	MPU 1930	Pyramiding	
428.2	Pacific Gas & Elec. Co.	No. American Co.	20.0%	SCR 1931	Pyramiding	47,528 [6]
203.4	Pacific Lighting Corp.			Private	Minority	61,131
						7,765
192.1	Peoples Gas Light & Coke Co.	[Insull Utility Investments, Inc. / Corporation Securities Co. of Chicago]	23.0% / 5.2%	SCR 1931	Pyramiding	7,298

[1] Whole system.
[5] As of March 1930.
[6] As of April 1930.

D. MINORITY CONTROL THROUGH OWNERSHIP OF AN IMPORTANT MINORITY BLOCK OF STOCK—REMAINING STOCK BELIEVED TO BE WIDELY DISTRIBUTED (Continued)

Size in millions of dollars of assets	Corporation	Minority interest	Size of holding	Source of information	Character of ultimate control	No. of stockholders Dec. 1929
190.0	Public Service Co. of Northern Illinois	Middle West Utilities Co. (through sub.) Insull Utility Investments, Inc.	over 31.4%	SCR 1931	Pyramiding	4,821 [7]
			8.1%	SCR 1931		
		Corporation Securities Co. of Chicago	1.7%	SCR 1931		
802.0	United Gas Improvement Co.	United Corp.	27.0%	MPU 1930	Management	90,054 [2]
Industrials						
167.2	Atlantic Refining Co.	Blair & Co. and associates	about 20%	NYT 8/4/28	Minority	
94.0	Consolidation Coal Co.	John D. Rockefeller, Jr.	35.8%	NYT 5/25/28	Minority	19,000
497.3	E. I. duPont de Nemours & Co.	du Pont family	30.0%	M. Ind. '28	Minority	36,238
1,400.0 Est.	General Motors Corp.	E. I. duPont de Nemours & Co. (& sub.)	32.6%	M. Ind. '30	Pyramiding	189,600
243.2	Goodyear Tire & Rubber Co.	Cyrus S. Eaton & Assoc.	27.5%	Keane's 1930 SCR 1931	Pyramiding	46,025

2 As of February 1930.

7 Preferred stocks only as of November 1930.

94

TABLE XII: *Control of the 200 Largest Corporations* (*Continued*)

D. MINORITY CONTROL THROUGH OWNERSHIP OF AN IMPORTANT MINORITY BLOCK OF STOCK—REMAINING STOCK BELIEVED TO BE WIDELY DISTRIBUTED (*Continued*)

Size in millions of dollars of assets	Corporation	Minority interest	Size of holding	Source of information	Character of ultimate control	No. of stockholders Dec. 1929
103.2	Inland Steel Co.	Cyrus S. Eaton & Assoc.	26.1%	SCR 1931	Minority	
124.2	Loew's Inc.	Gen'l Theatre (thru affl.)	48.5%	WSJ 2/21/30	Pyramiding	
209.8	Prairie Oil & Gas Co.	Petroleum Corp. of Amer.	23.8%	SCR 1931	Pyramiding	
850.0 Est.	Standard Oil Co. of Indiana	Rockefeller interests	14.5%	WSJ 1/15/29	Minority	81,022
1,767.3	Standard Oil Co. of N. J.	Rockefeller interests	about 20%	NYT 4/26/29	Minority	104,000 [3]
708.4	Standard Oil Co. of N. Y.	Rockefeller interests	about 20%		Minority	55,804
251.4	Tide Water Associated Oil	Executives of company thru Holding Co.	about 20%	NYT 6/3/30	Minority	32,286
307.8	U. S. Rubber Co.	du Pont family			Minority	25,486
205.7	Vacuum Oil Co.	Rockefeller interests	about 20%	NYT 4/26/29	Minority	

[3] As of May 1930.

E. JOINT CONTROL BY TWO OR MORE MINORITY INTERESTS—LARGE PUBLIC INTERESTS

Size	Corporation	Minority interest	Size of holding	Source of information	Character of ultimate control	No. of stockholders Dec. 1929
	Railroads					
256.4	Boston & Maine Rd. Co.	N.Y., N.H. & H. R. R. Co., through Holding Co.				
226.0	Lehigh Valley Rd. Co.	Pennroad Corp.	29.20%	RSOR 90	Management	14,349
		Pennsylvania Rd. Co. (through sub.)	16.00%		Management	
565.0 Est.	Reading Co.	Wabash Ry. Co.	30.19%	RSOR 268	Management	6,338
			19.10%		Management	
791.0		Baltimore & Ohio Rd. Co.	34.26%	RSOR 194	Management	8,576
		N.Y. Central Rd. Co. (and Sub.)	25.01%		Management	
	Utilities					
199.5	Cen. Pub. Ser. Co.	Public Utility Holding Co.	over 25%	MPU 1930	Pyramiding	36,865 [1]
		A. E. Pierce & Co.	large int.		Minority	

[1] Subsidiaries only.

TABLE XII: Control of the 200 Largest Corporations (Continued)

E. JOINT CONTROL BY TWO OR MORE MINORITY INTERESTS (Continued)

Size	Corporation	Minority interest	Size of holding	Source of information	Character of ultimate control	No. of stockholders Dec. 1929
298.1	Midland United Co.	Commonwealth Edison Co. / Peoples Gas Light & Coke Co. / Public Service Co. of Nor. Ill. / Middle West Utilities Co.	over 40%	MPU 1930	Pyramiding	84,835 [2]
		United Gas Improvement Co.	16.7%	MPU 1930	Management	
308.4	N. Amer. Light & Power Co.	N. American Co. (in voting trust) / Middle West Utilities Co. (in voting trust)	over 50%	SCR 1931	Pyramiding / Pyramiding	19,770
634.6	Pub. Serv. Corp. of N. Jersey	United Gas Improvement Co. / United Corp.	27.1% / 14.3%	MPU 1930	Management / Management	83,720
	Industrials					
280.0 Est.	Radio Corp. of America	Gen. Electric Co. / Westinghouse Elec.	32.1% / 19.2%	M. Ind. 1930	Management / Management	60,000 [3]

[2] Including subsidiaries.

[3] Approximate only.

F. JOINT CONTROL BY A MINORITY AND THE MANAGEMENT—LARGE PUBLIC INTEREST

Size	Corporation	Minority interest	Size of holding	Source of information	Character of ultimate control	No. of stock-holders Dec. 1929
	Railroads					
477.4	Chic., Rock Island & Pac. Ry. Co.	St. Louis-San Francisco Ry. Co.				
560.8	N. Y., N. H. & H. Rd. Co.	Penn. Rd. Co. & Penn-road Corp.	14.22%	RSOR 495	Management	15,865
1,038.2			13.24%	RSOR 110	Management	29,965
	Industrials					
140.5	Prairie Pipe Line Co.	Petroleum Corp. of America	13.7%	SCR 1931	Management Pyramiding	9,179

97

TABLE XII: *Control of the 200 Largest Corporations* (*Continued*)

G. MANAGEMENT CONTROL—NO SINGLE IMPORTANT STOCK INTEREST

Size	Corporation	Largest stockholders or stockholding family and 2nd largest stockholder	Size of largest holding	Size of 2d largest holding	Size of 20th largest holding	Holdings by 20 largest holders	Source of information	No. of stockholders Dec. 1929
1,135.4	Atchison, Topeka & Santa Fe Ry. Co.	Mills Family Rockefeller foundation	.76%	.74%	.18%	6.1%	RSOR 443	59,042
1,040.8	Baltimore & Ohio Rd. Co.	Union Pac. Rd. Co. Alien Property Custodian	2.56%	1.02%	.12%	8.7%	RSOR 183	39,627
776.1	Chicago, Milwaukee, St. Paul & Pac. Rd. Co.	Director General of Rds.[1]	1.36%	1.29%	.16%	11.9%	RSOR 399	12,045 [2]
641.0	Chicago & North Western Ry. Co.	Edw. S. Harkness Vanderbilt Family Union Pac. Co. (thru sub.)	3.45%	2.45%	.17%	14.7%	RSOR 375	15,706
269.4	Delaware & Hudson Co.	B. P. Trenkman Home Insurance Co.	1.51%	.97%	.38%	12.4%	RSOR 95	9,003
812.4	Great Northern Ry. Co.	Arthur Curtis James Geo. F. Baker, Jr.	2.12%	.94%	.20%	9.5%	RSOR 384	42,085
314.0	Missouri-Kansas-Texas Rd. Co.	Partner, Lodenberg, Thalman & Co. Reorganization Managers	2.23%	1.40%	.23%	11.2%	RSOR 419	12,693
2,250.0	New York Central Rd. Co.	Union Pac. Rd. Co. (thru sub.) Vanderbilt Family	5.35%	4.78%	.13%	19.3%	RSOR 123	54,122 [3]

[1] On the assumption that the largest stockholders had converted their expired voting trust certificates.
[2] As of April 1930.
[3] As of February 1930.

G. MANAGEMENT CONTROL—NO SINGLE IMPORTANT STOCK INTEREST (Continued)

Size	Corporation	Largest stockholders or stockholding family and 2nd largest stockholder	Size of largest holding	Size of 2d largest holding	Size of 20th largest holding	Holdings by 20 largest holders	Source of information	No. of stockholders Dec. 1929
813.9	Northern Pacific Ry. Co.	Arthur Curtis James / Emma B. Kennedy	2.13%	1.20%	.20%	10.8%	RSOR 391	38,339
2,600.0 Est.	Pennsylvania Rd. Co.	Penn. Rd. Employees' Provident & Loan Assn. / William M. Potts	.34%	.20%	.07%	2.7%	RSOR 143	196,119
439.9	St. Louis–San Francisco Ry. Co.	Speyer & Co. account / J. W. Davis & Co. account	4.01%	3.98%	.21%	20.0%	RSOR 487	15,865
2,156.7	Southern Pacific Co.	Dodge Family thru holding company / Arthur Curtis James	1.65%	1.37%	.13%	12.1%	RSOR 501	55,788
655.5	Southern Ry. Co.	Milbank Interests / Eli B. Springs	1.92%	1.83%	.40%	10.0%	RSOR 321	20,262
1,121.1	Union Pacific Rd. Co.	N. V. M. tot B. van het A. F.[4] / Harriman Family	2.27%	1.85%	.24%	10.4%	RSOR 425	49,387
15,026.2								
Public Utilities								
4,228.4	Amer. Tel. & Tel. Co.	Sun Life Assurance Co. / Geo. F. Baker	.60%	.47%	.09%	4.0%	WSJ 4/11/30	469,801
109.7	Boston Elevated Ry. Co.	Curtis & Sanger (broker) / R. L. Day & Co.	1.66%	1.55%	less than .30%		WSJ 4/5/30	16,419

[4] N. V. Maatschappij tot Beheer van het Administratiekantoor Fondsen, Amsterdam, Holland.

TABLE XII: *Control of the 200 Largest Corporations (Continued)*

G. MANAGEMENT CONTROL—NO SINGLE IMPORTANT STOCK INTEREST (*Continued*)

Size	Corporation	Largest stockholders or stockholding family and 2nd largest stockholder	Size of largest holding	Size of 2d largest holding	Size of 20th largest holding	Holdings by 20 largest holders	Source of information	No. of stockholders Dec. 1929
1,171.5	Consol. Gas Co. of N. Y.	Sun Life Assurance Co. United Corp.	2.11%	1.50%	less than 40%		NYT 3/16/30 MPU 1930	93,515
756.0 [5]	Electric Bond & Share Co.	Elec. Bond & Share Sec., Inc. Part of Employee Stock Purchase Plan	4%	less than 2%			SCR 1931	95,000
332.2 / 6,597.8	Western Union Tel. Co.	Morgan, Turner & Co. Johnson & Co.	2.74%	1.9%			NYT 4/11/31	23,738
Industrials 515.7	General Electric Co.	Elec. Securities Corp. (An Employees' Investment Co. and subsidiary to Gen. Elec. Co.)	about 1.5%				WSJ 3/19/28	60,374
2,286.1 / 2,801.8	United States Steel Corp.	George F. Baker	.74%		.09%	5.1%	NYT 4/22/30	182,585

[5] Assets of American and Foreign Power Co. only.

Size	Corporation	Situation	Character of ultimate control	Source of information	No. of stockholders Dec. 1929
	Railroads				
161.8	Chicago & Alton Rd. Co.	On Dec. 31, 1929 in hands of receiver. Subsequently the B. & O. R. Co. acquired property at foreclosure sale.		RSOR 215	2,265
104.1 265.9	Wheeling & Lake Erie Ry. Co.	Stock having 53.34% of voting power was held by a trustee with limited powers for the joint benefit of the New York, Chicago & St. Louis Rd. Co. and the Alleghany Corp.		RSOR 259	
	Public Utilities		Pyramiding		
108.2	Chicago Rys. Co.	In hands of receivers.		MPU 1930	389

TABLE XII: *Control of the 200 Largest Corporations* (*Continued*)

I. JOINTLY CONTROLLED BY OTHER COMPANIES—VIRTUALLY NO PUBLIC INTEREST

Size	Corporation	Controlling companies	Size of holding	Character of ultimate control	Source of information	No. of stock-holders Dec. 1929
	Railroads					
645.4	Chicago, Burlington & Quincy Rd. Co.	Great Northern Ry. Co.	48.5%	Management	RSOR 406	425
		Northern Pacific Ry. Co.	48.5%			
		Stock for both in hands of a trustee				
96.8	Chicago Union Station Co.	Chicago, Burlington & Quincy Rd. Co.	25%	Management	MRR 1930	4
		Chicago, Milwaukee, St. Paul & Pacific Rd. Co.	25%	Management		
		Pennsylvania Rd. Co. & sub.	50%	Management		
223.4	Denver & Rio Grande Western Rd. Co.	Alleghany Corp. (through sub.)	50%	Pyramiding	RSOR 476	1,556[1]
		Western Pacific Rd. Co.	50%	Minority		
140.2	Spokane, Portland & Seattle Ry. Co.	Great Northern Ry. Co.	50%	Management	RSOR 394	12
		Northern Pacific Ry. Co.	50%	Management		
1,105.8						
	Industrials					
111.9	Sinclair Crude Oil Purchasing Co.	Sinclair Consolidated Oil Corp.	50%	Management	M. Ind. 1930	
		Standard Oil Co. of Indiana	50%	Minority		

[1] All but two of stockholders are owners of the preferred which is virtually non-voting.

TABLE XII: *Control of the 200 Largest Corporations (Continued)*

J. MAJORITY OF STOCK BELIEVED TO BE WIDELY DISTRIBUTED AND WORK-
ING CONTROL HELD EITHER BY A LARGE MINORITY INTEREST OR BY THE
MANAGEMENT, PRESUMABLY THE FORMER

Size	Corporation	Number of stockholders December 1929
	Railroads	
	None	
	Public Utilities	
95.9	Associated Telephone Util. Co.	8,278
131.7	Hudson Manhattan Rd. Co.	3,522 [1]
400.0 Est.	Stone & Webster, Inc.	15,000 [2]
110.0 Est.	Third Ave. Ry. Co.	1,170 [3]
96.7	United Rys. & Elec. Co. of Balt.	1,955
834.3		
	Industrials	
277.2	Allied Chemical & Dye Corp.	
104.3	American Rolling Mill Co.	10,113
241.0	Amer. Smelting & Ref. Co.	20,110
198.0	Continental Oil Co.	
126.7	Corn Products Refining Co.	10,000 [4]
124.3	Crucible Steel Co. of America	7,657
101.3	Cuban Cane Products Co.	
300.0 Est.	Glen Alden Coal Co.	
100.0 Est.	International Mercantile Mar. Co.	
111.3	International Shoe Co.	6,426
109.5	S. S. Kresge Co.	12,050
116.1	Long-Bell Lumber Corp.	3,500 [4]
108.4	National Lead Co.	9,786
110.6	Ohio Oil Co.	7,796 [5]
236.7	Paramount Publix Corp.	13,589
145.3	Phillips Petroleum Co.	12,025
171.5	Pittsburgh Coal Co.	3,872
101.6	Pittsburgh Plate Glass Co.	4,000 [4]
109.4	Procter & Gamble Co.	14,581
331.7	Republic Iron & Steel Corp.	
604.7	Standard Oil Co. of Calif.	55,077 [6]
124.6	U. S. Realty & Improvement Co.	
167.1	Warner Bros. Pictures, Inc.	11,157
128.3	Wheeling Steel Corp.	3,630
4,249.6		

[1] As of March 1930.
[2] Over this amount.
[3] As of October 1929.
[4] Approximately.
[5] As of February 1930.
[6] As of December 1928.

TABLE XII: *Control of the 200 Largest Corporations (Continued)*

K. MAJORITY OF STOCK BELIEVED TO BE WIDELY DISTRIBUTED AND WORK-ING CONTROL HELD EITHER BY A LARGE MINORITY INTEREST OR BY THE MANAGEMENT, PRESUMABLY THE LATTER

Size	Corporation	Number of stockholders December 1929
	Railroads	
	None	
	Public Utilities	
288.5	Bklyn. Man. Transit Co.	10,700 [1]
135.9	Consol. Gas, Elec. Lt., & Pr. Co. of Baltimore	
156.3	Edison Elec. Ill. Co. of Boston	14,878
521.2	Inter. Tel. & Tel. Corp.	53,594
340.6	So. Calif. Edison Co., Ltd.	119,418
1,442.5		
	Industrials	
191.3	American Can Co.	
119.5	American Car & Foundry Co.	17,152 [2]
106.2	American Locomotive Co.	21,564
199.4	American Radiator & St. San. Corp.	20,404
157.1	American Sugar Refining Co.	20,690
113.9	American Woolen Co.	
680.6	Anaconda Copper Mining Co.	95,050
452.3	Armour & Co. (Ill.)	80,000 [3]
98.8	Baldwin Locomotive Works	8,100 [4]
801.6	Bethlehem Steel Corp.	75,876
174.0	Borden Co.	17,167
209.7	Chrysler Corp.	36,000 [5]
158.0	Drug, Inc.	29,124 [6]
163.4	Eastman Kodak Co.	32,807
161.6	Firestone Tire & Rubber Co.	
163.6	B. F. Goodrich Co.	15,000 [5]
384.0	International Harvester Co.	40,200 [5]
686.5	International Paper & Pr. Co.	37,849
337.8	Kennecott Copper Corp.	31,009 [7]
110.0	P. Lorillard Co.	10,000 [5]
187.5	Montgomery Ward & Co.	45,852
133.2	National Biscuit Co.	19,881

[1] As of December 1928.

[2] As of July 1929.

[3] As of October 1930.

[4] As of May 1930.

[5] Approximately.

[6] As of January 1927.

[7] As of December 1927.

TABLE XII: *Control of the 200 Largest Corporations* (*Continued*)

**K. MAJORITY OF STOCK BELIEVED TO BE WIDELY DISTRIBUTED AND WORK-
ING CONTROL HELD EITHER BY A LARGE MINORITY INTEREST OR BY THE
MANAGEMENT, PRESUMABLY THE LATTER** (*Continued*)

Size	Corporation	Number of stockholders December 1929
224.5	National Dairy Products Corp.	31,074
129.0	Phila. & Reading Coal & Iron Corp.	
315.5	Pullman, Inc.	30,162 [8]
215.4	Pure Oil Co.	37,000 [9]
131.9	Richfield Oil Co. of Calif.	17,256 [10]
251.8	Sears, Roebuck & Co.	27,700 [11]
400.6	Sinclair Consolidated Oil Corp.	27,601 [11]
134.2	Studebaker Corp.	26,451
351.2	Swift & Co.	47,000
609.8	Texas Corp.	65,898
306.6	Union Carbide & Carbon Corp.	28,780
226.0	United Fruit Co.	27,960
94.1	United Shoe Machinery Corp.	18,051 [12]
253.9	Westinghouse Elec. & Mfg. Co.	44,004
98.0	Wilson & Co.	9,800 [14]
165.4	F. W. Woolworth Co.	19,416 [13]
235.7	Youngstown Sheet & Tube Co.	
9,133.6		

[8] As of April 1930.
[9] As of March 1929.
[10] As of January 1930.
[11] As of December 1928.
[12] As of March 1926.
[13] As of October 1929.
[14] Approximately.

TABLE XIII: *Summary According to Type of Ultimate Control of 200 Largest Corporations*

Type of Control	Number of corporations				Proportion of companies by industrial groups			
	Rail-roads	Public utilities	Indus-trials	Total	R.R.	P.U.	Ind.	Total
I Private Ownership	2	2	8	12	5%	4%	8%	6%
II Majority Ownership	1	3	6	10	2%	6%	6%	5%
III Minority Control	4½	7½	34½	46½	11%	14%	32%	23%
IV Legal Device	7½	19	14½	41	18%	36%	14%	21%
V Management Control	26	19½	43	88½	62%	38%	40%	44%
In Receivership	1	1		2	2%	2%		1%
Total	42	52	106	200	100%	100%	100%	100%
IV & V Management Control or Legal Device involving a small proportion of total ownership	33½	38½	57½	129½	80%	74%	54%	65%

Type of Control	Wealth of corporations (in million dollars)				Proportion of wealth by industrial groups			
	Rail-roads	Public utilities	Indus-trials	Total	R.R.	P.U.	Ind.	Total
I Private Ownership	276	221	2,869	3,366	1%	1%	9%	4%
II Majority Ownership	283	480	779	1,542	1%	2%	3%	2%
III Minority Control	704	1,261	9,258	11,223	3%	5%	31%	14%
IV Legal Device	3,852	9,406	4,307	17,565	15%	37%	14%	22%
V Management Control	19,675	14,291	13,142	47,108	79%	55%	43%	58%
In Receivership	161	108		269	1%			1%
Total	24,951	25,767	30,355	81,073	100%	100%	100%	100%
IV & V Management Control or Legal Device involving a small proportion of total ownership	23,527	23,697	17,449	64,673	94%	92%	57%	80%

TABLE XIV: *Summary According to Type of Immediate Control of 200 Largest Corporations*

Type of control	Railroads		Public utilities		Industrials		Total		Distribution	
	No. companies	Assets in million dollars	No. companies	Assets in million dollars	No. companies	Assets in million dollars	No. companies	Assets in million dollars	According to companies	According to assets
I Private Ownership	2	276	2	221	8	2,870	12	3,367	6%	4%
II Majority Ownership	1	283	3	480	6	779	10	1,542	5%	2%
III Minority Control										
(a) Known to be controlled	13	4,309	17	9,271	14	6,929	44	20,509	22%	26%
(b) Thought to be so controlled			5	834	24	4,250	29	5,084	14½%	6%
IV Legal Device	1	1,600	10	5,372	10	2,260	21	9,232	10½%	12%
V Management Control										
(a) Known to be controlled	14	15,026	5	6,598	2	2,802	21	24,426	10½%	30%
(b) Thought to be so controlled	9	3,191	5	1,442	39	9,934	44	11,376	22%	14%
Joint Control	2	266	4	1,441	3	532	16	5,164	8%	6%
Special Situations			1	108			3	374	1½%	6%
Total	42	24,951	52	25,767	106	30,356	200	81,074	100%	100%

107

since that time. In 1929 three of the ten directors of the Allied Chemical and Dye Corporation were also directors of the Solvay American Investment Corporation. The stock of the former is known to be widely held. Recently the New York Times reported that the above investment company was its largest stockholder.[36] On the basis of this information the company was classed as doubtful but presumably minority controlled.

For some other cases in the doubtful group, little information was obtained and the companies were classified on a basis of general "street knowledge." The possible error in this group is therefore considerable. On the whole, information could be most readily obtained for the railroads and public utilities since regulation of these fields has required a greater publicity of accounts and has yielded important government reports. Explicit information on the railroads was available from the very competent study of the ownership of railroads already referred to and made under the direction of Dr. Walter M. W. Splawn, Special Counsel to the House Committee on Interstate and Foreign Commerce.[37] Less information was available with respect to the utilities, except where one company owned stock of another. The industrials are undoubtedly the least accurately classified.[38]

In the process of classification, certain arbitrary judgments had to be made. Corporations which appeared to be owned to the extent of 80 per cent or more by a compact group of individuals were classed as private and those in which the public interest appeared to be larger than 20 per cent but less than 50 per cent were classed as majority owned. Companies were regarded as controlled by a legal device only where there appeared to be a very considerable separation of ownership and control. A mild degree of pyramiding or the issuance of non-voting preferred stock was disregarded. The dividing line between minority and management control was drawn roughly at 20 per cent, though in a few special instances a smaller holding was credited with the power of control. It is notable that in none of the companies classed under management control was the dominant stock

[36] New York Times, April 24, 1931.

[37] "Regulation of Stock Ownership in Railroads," *loc. cit.*

[38] Dr. Splawn's report not only gave accurate data with respect to the railroads but served indirectly to support the data obtained in the other two fields. Before his report was published, the present writer had gathered information on the largest 200 companies in 1927 and classified them according to type of control. Comparison of the results insofar as railroads were concerned with the data supplied by Dr. Splawn showed almost no cases of inaccurate classification. While this applies only to the railroads, it suggests that the data relied upon for classification is essentially satisfactory.

interest known to be greater than 5 per cent of the voting stock. Cases falling between 20 and 5 per cent were usually classed as joint minority-management control. Perhaps others should be classed in this category.

Many cases were found in which the immediate control of a corporation was exercised by a second corporation through a dominant minority stock interest.[39] When the controlling corporation was itself management controlled, the first company was classed as minority in its immediate, but management in its ultimate control. If the controlling company was controlled otherwise than by the management, the first company was classed as minority in its immediate control, but pyramided in its ultimate control. Likewise in the case of joint control, insofar as ultimate control was concerned, each such company was treated as if it were two companies of half the size, one controlled by each group sharing the control. Thus a company that was jointly controlled by a minority and the management would be classed in ultimate control as one-half company minority controlled and one-half company management controlled. Only five companies had to be subdivided in this manner.

With these reservations as to the source of the material, and the method of handling it, let us examine the type of control exercised over the 42 railroads, the 52 public utilities, and the 106 industrials which compose the list of 200 largest companies at the beginning of 1930,[40] remembering that their combined wealth amounted to nearly half of that of non-banking corporate wealth. Of these companies ultimate control appeared to be:

	By number	By wealth
Management control	44%	58%
Legal device	21%	22%
Minority control	23%	14%
Majority ownership	5%	2%
Private ownership	6%	4%
In hands of receiver	1%	negligible
	100%	100%

While these percentages do not reflect a static condition and while in many cases they are based only on careful guesses, their cumulative

[39] A corporation controlled by another corporation through majority ownership or a legal device was classed as a subsidiary of the latter and disregarded except where an important element of pyramiding entered in.

[40] Given in detail in Table XII.

effect is such as to indicate the great extent to which control of these companies rests on some factor other than ownership alone, and more striking still, the extent to which the management has itself become the control. That 65 per cent of the companies and 80 per cent of their combined wealth should be controlled either by the management or by a legal device involving a small proportion of ownership indicates the important extent to which ownership and control have become separated. Only 11 per cent of the companies and 6 per cent of their wealth involved control by a group of individuals owning half or more of the stock interest outstanding.

Of the three groups concerned, the separation of ownership and control has become most nearly complete in the railroads and utilities. Out of 42 railroads, 26 were management controlled or controlled through minority interests by other roads which were in turn management controlled. Thus 62 per cent of the railroads and 79 per cent of their assets involved this high degree of separation of ownership and control. In addition $7\frac{1}{2}$ roads were ultimately controlled by pyramiding ($5\frac{1}{2}$ being in the Van Sweringen System) indicating a total of 80 per cent of the railroads and 94 per cent of their wealth controlled by individuals lacking an important proportion of the total ownership.

The public utilities show a greater use of legal devices. Three were controlled by voting trusts, in one case combined with non-voting common stock. Three others were controlled by non-voting stock and two by the issue of special vote-weighted stock. Two were controlled by pyramided structures, while in most of the utilities a greater or less degree of pyramiding was found. In all 19 of the 52 utilities were classed as ultimately controlled by a legal device, while $19\frac{1}{2}$ were classed as ultimate management control. Thus 74 per cent of the companies and 92 per cent of their wealth involved control without important ownership.

The separation appears to have progressed least far in the case of the industrials. Even in this field, however, the separation has assumed considerable importance. According to the classification of industrials, which it must be remembered is more subject to error than either of the foregoing groups, 54 per cent of the companies and 57 per cent of their wealth were controlled either by a legal device or by the management.

It is apparent that, with the increasing dispersion of stock ownership in the largest American corporations, a new condition has developed with regard to their control. No longer are the individuals in control of most of these companies, the dominant owners. Rather, there are no dominant owners, and control is maintained in large measure apart from ownership. As has been indicated, control as something apart from ownership on one hand and from management on the other is a new concept ill-defined in practice. It deals with a condition which exists only relatively and one on which information is of the most approximate character. Probably the condition of "joint control" which appears only rarely on the above list is more characteristic of the big corporation than is indicated, control in fact being not a single clearly defined phenomenon local to an individual or small group, but an element in the organization of industry which is broken up and appears in various forms. It may be held to a greater or less extent by a wide variety of individuals. We are justified, however, in treating it here as a single factor; because, whether whole or divided, whether dependent upon proxy machinery, legal device, a measure of ownership, or a strategic position astride the management, it has in very considerable extent become separate from ownership. Formerly assumed to be merely a function of ownership, control now appears as a separate, separable factor.

CHAPTER VI: THE DIVERGENCE OF INTEREST BETWEEN OWNERSHIP AND CONTROL

THE FOREGOING chapters have indicated that the corporate system tends to develop a division of the functions formerly accorded to ownership. This calls for an examination of the exact nature of these functions; the inter-relation of the groups performing them; and the new position which these groups hold in the community at large.

In discussing problems of enterprise it is possible to distinguish between three functions: that of having interests in an enterprise, that of having power over it, and that of acting with respect to it. A single individual may fulfill, in varying degrees, any one or more of these functions.

Before the industrial revolution the owner-worker performed all three, as do most farmers today. But during the nineteenth century the bulk of industrial production came to be carried on by enterprises in which a division had occurred, the owner fulfilling the first two functions while the latter was in large measure performed by a separate group, the hired managers. Under such a system of production, the owners were distinguished primarily by the fact that they were *in a position* both to manage an enterprise or delegate its management and to receive any profits or benefits which might accrue. The managers on the other hand were distinguished primarily by the fact that they operated an enterprise, presumably in the interests of the owners. The difference between ownership and management was thus in part one between position and action. An owner who remained completely quiescent towards his enterprise would nevertheless remain an owner. His title was not applied because he acted or was expected to act. Indeed, when the owner acted, as for instance in hiring a manager or giving him directions, to that extent the owner managed his own enterprise. On the other hand, it is difficult to think of applying the title "manager" to an individual who had been entirely quiescent.

112

Under the corporate system, the second function, that of having power over an enterprise, has become separated from the first. The position of the owner has been reduced to that of having a set of legal and factual interests in the enterprise while the group which we have called control, are in the position of having legal and factual powers over it.

In distinguishing between the interests of ownership and the powers of control, it is necessary to keep in mind the fact that, as there are many individuals having interests in an enterprise who are not customarily thought of as owners, so there may be many individuals having a measure of power over it who should not be thought of as in control. In the present study we have treated the stockholders of a corporation as its owners. When speaking of the ownership of all corporations, the bondholders are often included with the stockholders as part owners. The economist does not hesitate for certain purposes to class an employee with wages due him as temporarily a part owner. All of these groups have interests in the enterprise. Yet a laborer who has a very real interest in a business in so far as it can continue to give him employment is not regarded as part owner. Nor is a customer so included though he has a very real interest in a store to the extent that it can continue to give him good services. Of the whole complex of individuals having interests in an enterprise, only those are called owners who have major interests and, before the law, only those who hold legal title. Similarly, the term control must be limited for practical purposes to those who hold the major elements of power over an enterprise, keeping in mind, however, that a multitude of individuals may exercise a degree of power over the activities of an enterprise without holding sufficient power to warrant their inclusion in "control."

Turning then to the two new groups created out of a former single group,—the owners without appreciable control and the control without appreciable ownership, we must ask what are the relations between them and how may these be expected to affect the conduct of enterprise. When the owner was also in control of his enterprise he could operate it in his own interest and the philosophy surrounding the institution of private property has assumed that he would do so. This assumption has been carried over to present conditions and it is still expected that enterprise will be operated in the interests of the owners. But have we any justification for assuming that those in control of a modern corporation will also choose to operate it in the interests of the owners? The answer to this question will depend on the degree to which the self-interest of those in control may run parallel to the interests of ownership and, insofar as they differ, on the checks on the use of power which may be established by political, economic, or social conditions.

The corporate stockholder has certain well-defined interests in the operation of the company, in the distribution of income, and in the public security markets. In general, it is to his interest, first that the company should be made to earn the maximum profit compatible with a reasonable degree of risk; second, that as large a proportion of these profits should be distributed as the best interests of the business permit, and that nothing should happen to impair his right to receive his equitable share of those profits which are distributed; and finally, that his stock should remain freely marketable at a fair price. In addition to these the stockholder has other but less important interests such as redemption rights, conversion privileges, corporate publicity, etc. However, the three mentioned above usually so far overshadow his other interests as alone to require consideration here.

The interests of control are not so easily discovered. Is control likely to want to run the corporation to produce the maximum profit at the minimum risk; is it likely to want to distribute those profits generously and equitably among the owners; and is it likely to want to maintain market conditions favorable to the investor? An attempt to answer these questions would raise the whole question of the nature of the phenomenon of "control." We must know the controlling individual's aims before we can analyze his desires. Are we to assume for him what has been assumed in the past with regard to the owner of enterprise, that his major aim is *personal profits?* Or must we expect him to seek some other end—prestige, power, or the gratification of professional zeal?

If we are to assume that the desire for *personal profit* is the prime force motivating control, we must conclude that the interests of control are different from and often radically opposed to those of ownership; that the owners most emphatically will not be served by a profit-seeking controlling group. In the operation of the corporation, the controlling group even if they own a large block of stock, can serve their own pockets better by profiting at the expense of the company than by making profits for it. If such persons can make a profit of a million dollars from a sale of property to the corporation, they can afford to suffer a loss of $600,000 through the ownership of 60 per cent of the stock, since the transaction will still net them $400,000 and the remaining stockholders will shoulder the corresponding loss. As their proportion of the holdings decrease, and both profits and losses of the company accrue less and less to them, the opportunities of profiting at the expense of the corporation appear more directly to their benefit. When their holdings amount to only such fractional per cents as the holdings of the management in management-controlled corporations, profits at the expense of the corporation become practically clear gain to the persons in control and the interests of a profit-seeking control run directly counter to the interests of the owners.

In the past, this adverse interest appears sometimes to have taken the extreme form of wrecking a corporation for the profit of those in control. Between 1900 and 1915 various railroads were brought into the hands of receivers as a result of financial mismanagement, apparently designed largely for the benefit of the controlling group, while heavy losses were sustained by the security holders.[1]

Such direct profits at the expense of a corporation are made difficult under present laws and judicial interpretations, but there are numerous less direct ways in which at least part of the profits of a corporation can be diverted for the benefit of those in control. Profits may be shifted from a parent corporation to a subsidiary in which the controlling group have a large interest. Particularly profitable business may be diverted to a second corporation largely owned by the controlling group. In many other ways it is possible to divert profits which would otherwise be made by the corporation into the hands of a group in control. When it comes to the questions of distributing such profits as are made, self-seeking control may strive to divert profits from one class of stock to another, if, as frequently occurs, it holds interests in the latter issue. In market operations, such control may use "inside information" to buy low from present stockholders and sell high to future stockholders. It may have slight interest in maintaining conditions in which a reasonable market price is established. On the contrary it may issue financial statements of a misleading character or distribute informal news items which further its own market manipulations. We must conclude, therefore, that the interests of ownership and control are in large measure opposed *if* the interests of the latter grow primarily out of the desire for personal monetary gain.

Into the other motives which might inspire action on the part of control it will not profit us to go, though speculation in that sphere is tempting. If those in control of a corporation reinvested its profits

[1] See Chicago & Alton Railway Co.   12 I. C. C.   295–1907
          Pere Marquette Railway Co.   44 I. C. C.   1–1914
          Chicago, Rock Island & Pacific   36 I. C. C.   43–1915
          New York, New Haven & Hartford   31 I. C. C.   32–1914
          St. Louis & San Francisco Ry. Co. 29 I. C. C.   139–1914

All of these roads went into receivership or were in financial difficulties as a direct or indirect result of financial management of highly questionable sort.

in an effort to enlarge their own power, their interests might run directly counter to those of the "owners." Such an opposition of interest would also arise if, out of professional pride, the control should maintain labor standards above those required by competitive conditions and business foresight or should improve quality above the point which, over a period, is likely to yield optimum returns to the stockholders. The fact that both of these actions would benefit other groups which are essential to the existence of corporate enterprise and which for some purposes should be regarded as part of the enterprise, does not change their character of opposition to the interests of ownership. Under other motives the interests of owner and control may run parallel, as when control seeks the prestige of "success" and profits for the controlled enterprise is the current measure of success. Suffice it here to realize that where the bulk of the profits of enterprise are scheduled to go to owners who are individuals other than those in control, the interests of the latter are as likely as not to be at variance with those of ownership and that the controlling group is in a position to serve its own interests.

In examining the break up of the old concept that was property and the old unity that was private enterprise, it is therefore evident that we are dealing not only with distinct but often with opposing groups, ownership on the one side, control on the other—a control which tends to move further and further away from ownership and ultimately to lie in the hands of the management itself, a management capable of perpetuating its own position. The concentration of economic power separate from ownership has, in fact, created economic empires, and has delivered these empires into the hands of a new form of absolutism, relegating "owners" to the position of those who supply the means whereby the new princes may exercies their power.

The recognition that industry has come to be dominated by these economic autocrats must bring with it a realization of the hollowness of the familiar statement that economic enterprise in America is a matter of individual initiative. To the dozen or so men in control, there is room for such initiative. For the tens and even hundreds of thousands of workers and of owners in a single enterprise, individual initiative no longer exists. Their activity is group activity on a scale so large that the individual, except he be in a position of control, has dropped into relative insignificance. At the same time the problems of control have become problems in economic government.

BOOK TWO

Regrouping of Rights: Relative legal position of ownership and "control"

CHAPTER I: EVOLUTION OF THE

MODERN CORPORATE STRUCTURE

AS PROPERTY has been gathered under the corporate system, and as control has been increasingly concentrated, the power of this control has steadily widened. Briefly, the past century has seen the corporate mechanism evolve from an arrangement under which an association of owners controlled their property on terms closely supervised by the state to an arrangement by which many men have delivered contributions of capital into the hands of a centralized control. This has been accompanied by grants of power permitting such control almost unexplored permission to deprive the grantors at will of the beneficial interest in the capital thus contributed. It is necessary to glance at this phase of legal history, since without it no fair comprehension of the present system can be attained. At the same time certain checks and balances, partly legal and partly economic, have come into existence. They also, and their effectiveness, must be examined in due course.

The evolutionary phase of the modern corporation in recent legal history has been both protracted and confused. Protracted, because it has been accomplished not by any great change either in concept or in statutory enactment, but rather by a long process of grant of management powers piecemeal. The aggregate of these various grants makes up the charter of almost absolute power which the control, commonly through the management, asserts today. Confused, because the various accretions of power appear partly in statutory amendments over more than a century, partly in decisions purporting to declare the common law; partly in statutory enactments which purport to recognize or declare the common law; partly in clauses inserted in the charters; partly in powers merely assumed by lawyers and managements which, becoming traditional, work their way into the system.

It would be both impracticable and unnecessary to review the entire process.[1] The major lines of the development must, however, be indicated.

American law inherited the corporation from English jurisprudence in the form in which it stood at the close of the Eighteenth Century. At that time a corporation was considered as a "franchise" (Norman-French "privilege"): i.e., the very existence of the corporation was conditioned upon a grant from the state. This grant created the corporation and set it up as a legal person independent of any of the associates. Not infrequently the same grant gave to the corporation other privileges such as a monopoly to run a ferry; a franchise to maintain a railway line in a particular place; a sole right to trade in the Hudson Bay area. Such privileges, except in the case of railways, public utilities and banks, have largely passed out of the picture today. The real privilege [2] which the state grants is that of corporate entity—the right to maintain business in its own name, to sue and be sued on its own behalf irrespective of the individuals; to have perpetual succession—i.e., to continue this entity although the individuals in it changed. From all this necessarily flowed a limited liability of the associates. Since only the entity was liable for debts, which did not attach to the various individuals, it followed that a stockholder

---

[1] The writers compared studies of the legal development of corporations in the states of Alabama, Arizona, California, Connecticut, Delaware, Illinois, Indiana, Maine, Maryland, Massachusetts, New Jersey, New York, Pennsylvania, Rhode Island and Virginia. This material, of interest primarily only to students of legal history, would occupy approximately 600 printed pages. Only a skeleton is given in the present chapter. The material is on file at the Columbia Law School. Prior to 1820 the history of corporate development is substantially covered in J. S. Davis, "Essays in the Early History of American Corporations," (2 vols.) Cambridge, 1917.

[2] The quality of "privilege" at this point becomes elusive, to say the least. More accurately, the associates are granted a legal convenience, in that they may use the courts without writing the name of every shareholder into their papers. The reverse process—that of liability to be sued under a single name, is manifestly not advantageous to them, but is rather a measure of fairness to their opponents.

"Limited liability" again need not be assumed as a state-granted privilege. A clause could be put in every contract by which the apposite party limited his right of recovery to the common fund: the incorporation act may fairly be construed as legislating into all corporate contracts an implied clause to that effect. The only real question turns on non-consensual liabilities—such as liability for negligent injury by a corporate agent—a liability which, however, is in large measure within the control of the state anyhow. It would be quite as fair to assume that a corporation act operated as a limitation of the plaintiff's right to recover as to claim the limitation as a "privilege" for the defendant. Admiralty, bankruptcy and other divisions of law furnish illustrations of limitations on the right of recovery which legal scholars have never felt it necessary to justify by theories of grants of "privilege" to the ship or the bankrupt.

was not normally liable for any of the debts of the enterprise; and he could thus embark a particular amount of capital in the corporate affairs without becoming responsible beyond this amount, for the corporate debts.

At the same time, the document of grant (commonly called the "charter," or today the "certificate of incorporation") embodied the outlines of the arrangement among the associates. It set up the number of shares of stock, and the officials to whom the immediate management of the corporate enterprise was to be delegated; indicated by whom these officials were to be selected and under what conditions; and included provisions establishing both how the business was to be conducted and how the profits were to be distributed, and how the assets were to be disposed of on ultimate dissolution. As a result, each corporate "charter" was the product of a threefold negotiation involving the state and the combined associates, and between the groups of associates acting for themselves. It was recognized as a "contract" and has been consistently so dealt with in American law. The classic statement, (which does not bear analysis), envisaged the result as a contract between the corporation and the state, the stockholders and the corporation, and the stockholders *inter sese*.[8] Of course, the state as a sovereign, does not usually enter into contracts in the ordinary commercial sense. It is impossible to have a contract which at once creates the corporation and embodies a bargain between the corporation and the state, since a contract presupposes two parties capable of contracting before the negotiations begin. There may have been and probably was something resembling a real contract between the associates in early days, since they must have agreed among themselves as to the management of the enterprise and the distribution of the proceeds in a manner justifying the use of the word "contract" in its ordinary sense.

As in the Eighteenth Century negotiations for these contracts were carried on with the crown, so in America they were carried on with the sovereign power of the various states as successors to the crown. In practice this meant the state legislature. Prior to 1811, substantially every contract was separately legislated into the law of the state by a

[8] "The charter of a corporation having a capital stock is a contract between three parties and forms the basis of three distinct contracts. The charter is a contract between the state and the corporation; second, it is a contract between the corporation and the stockholders; third, it is a contract between the stockholders and the state." (2 Cook on Corporations, 5th Ed., section 492; 1 Clark & Marshall, "Private Corporations," section 271f).

Quoted with approval in *Garey et al. v. St. Joe Mining Company*, 32 Utah 497, 91 P. 369 (1907), and often referred to thereafter.

separate act; most charters continued to be specially legislated until well into the Nineteenth Century. To be valid, therefore, the arrangements between the associates themselves, and the powers granted to the corporate management had to be thoroughly thrashed over with the state authorities. During this period, the arrangement may be described as a "State controlled" agreement; since the various legislatures were required to approve every item in the transaction, and in fact they used their power to regulate severely the arrangements entered into.[4]

With a lively appreciation of the possibilities of the corporate mechanism, during the first half of the Nineteenth Century, the various states erected a series of protections. They were thinking primarily of three groups: the general public, the corporate creditors, and (to a less extent), the corporate shareholders. At this time there seems to have been no thought that shareholding might become so common as to make shareholders' interests a consideration in protection of the public at large though the English experience with the South Sea Bubble a century before might have suggested caution. Shareholders were supposed to be capitalists reasonably able to protect themselves. Nevertheless the protections erected served to assist shareholders almost as much as any other group.

The typical protections were three:

(1) The enterprise was required to be defined and was carefully limited in scope. This acted as a check on the management of the corporation. In theory this was probably designed to prevent corporations from dominating the business life of the time; to the shareholder, however, it meant that he knew the particular enterprise, or at the widest, the type of business in which his capital was to be embarked.[5]

[4] For a fair example of this see as an illustration the charter of the Submarine Armour Company, N. Y. Laws of 1838, ch. 153, p. 108.

This charter provided with extreme care the exact property which the corporation could own and the maximum amount thereof; the exact capital which it could have, the minimum which it must have in cash before it could commence business; the precise methods by which its business transactions could be carried on; and a very careful (if somewhat loosely drawn) indication of the line of its future development.

[5] Certain states (notably Ohio) up to relatively recently maintained the "single purpose rule," i.e., that a corporation could be lawfully organized under the General Act only for one stated purpose. This, however, was not general; and in fact was legislated out of existence even in Ohio in 1927. The more important states, notably New Jersey, permitted the corporation to name in its charter more than one purpose and to use all of them; see for example, *Orpheum Theatre & Realty Company v. Brokerage Company,* 197 Missouri Appeals 661; 1 Illinois Law Bulletin, p. 42; Palmer, "Company Law," 11th edition, p. 64–66; *Zabriskie v. Hackensack Railroad,* 18 N. J. Eq. 178: (this last case held that the charter might

(2) The contributions of capital were rigidly supervised. The corporation was not allowed to commence business until a certain amount of its shares had been "paid-up." It is probably at this period that such legislators expected such payment to be in cash. At the same time it was contemplated that all additional shares issued should be paid for at a fixed minimum rate—viz., the "par value" of these shares. The penalty for failure to do so was, among other things, that any shareholder who acquired shares without paying in the fixed minimum, presumably in cash, was liable to creditors to pay the balance in the event that the corporation became insolvent; but the Attorney General of the state could also enforce this requirement if he felt it necessary, which he frequently did not.[6] This was designed frankly to protect creditors—the fear being that a corporation would run up bills and having no contributed capital would be unable to pay them. To the shareholder, however, it meant a certain protection against dilution of his interest. Every shareholder was required to contribute not less than a stated amount for his share; and the result was that "free" stock or stock which did not represent the minimum contribution could not legally be issued. This served as a powerful safeguard for his *pro rata* interest in the corporate assets.

(3) A rigid capital structure was set up. Shares even in those early days could be classified to some extent into preferred and common stock; but the entire system had to be carefully laid out, embodied in the charter, and passed upon by the legislature; so that the participations were thoroughly scrutinized by the state authorities; and their number and incidence were at all times subject to careful control.

On the top of these the common law added a few safeguards on its own behalf.[7]

(4) Under the jurisprudence of the time, residual control—i.e., decisions affecting the general interest of the group, lay in the shareholders or in a specified proportion. The management of the enterprise was by contract commonly delegated to the board of directors; but any change in the capital structure or in the nature of the enterprise, or any amendment of the arrangement had to be passed upon by the

---

set out the purpose; and that this, once incorporated in the charter, could not be changed except in detail).

See also [H. W.] Ballantine on Corporations: Chicago, 1927, p. 683; *Sherman v. S. K. D. Oil Company*, 185 California 534.

[6] See for example *Floyd v. State*, 177 Alabama 109—(Proceeding by *quo warranto* to annul a charter where insufficient payment for stock had been accepted by the officers).

[7] These were rules worked out by American judges on analogies, real or supposed, served from English cases.

shareholders. In the event of any fundamental change the vote had to be unanimous, thus giving every shareholder a considerable degree of control over the policies of the corporation.[8]

(5) Likewise, the common law asserted that the shareholders had the sole right to invest new monies in the enterprise; and they worked this out by granting to each shareholder a pre-emptive right to subscribe to any additionally issued stock of the corporation. This rule, evolved by the Massachusetts courts in *Gray v. Portland Bank* (3 Massachusetts, 363 (1807))—the foundation of the present "law of pre-emptive rights," was assumed to be sweeping and absolute.

(6) In general dividends were permitted to be paid only out of surplus profits arising from the operations of the business.[9] This may have been an American invention, the English law not having laid down any clear principle until the latter half of the Nineteenth Century;[10] but the result was that whenever a distribution of profits did take place, it represented in theory a real profit; the capital could not be frittered away in small payments to the contributors.[11] The rule was designed to protect creditors—i.e., to maintain the integrity of the capital subscribed for the purpose of paying corporate debts,[11a]— or rather to prevent its impairment through payments to shareholders; but it also operated to maintain a sound financial position for the shareholders.

Even at this period it was possible to qualify a good many of these protections by contract; but as the state insisted on supervising the contract, and was not favorably impressed by innovations, the

[8] See Angell & Ames, "Corporations" (1832).

[9] Irrespective of charter or statutory provisions, some American courts so held: *Davenport v. Lines*, 72 Conn. 118, 128 (1899) citing Morawetz on Private Corporations (1st ed.) Sec. 344; Thompson on Corporations, vol. 2, Sec. 2152. To the same effect, see Machen: "Corporations" (1st ed.) vol. II, Sec. 1313. But some charters, and most early incorporation laws covered the point, either in terms or by imposing an individual liability to creditors on directors who paid such dividends.

[10] A summary of the English rule is given in Palmer's Company Law (13th Ed. 1929, by A. F. Topham, K. C., pp. 224–229). The English courts undertook to make a distinction between "fixed capital" and "circulating capital" along the lines once laid down by Adam Smith; and, of course, encountered the difficulties necessarily involved in the fact that "capital" was being used in a sense quite different from that contemplated by the corporation lawyers.

[11] The wasting-asset corporation is, of course, an exception.

[11a] See Sir W. S. Gilbert's comment on the first British Companies Act in the Bab Ballads (6th Ed., Macmillan, London, 1914) p. 490

"They start off with a public declaration
To what extent they mean to pay their debts;
That's called their Capital; if they are wary
They will not quote it at a sum immense."

corporate mechanism was rigid and carefully protected. The effect was to set up a business organism conducting a limited enterprise, with participations settled in advance, and safeguarded either by the statutory contract or by the common law in various ways. Investors could and did place their reliance at least partly on the state, since in theory the state would sanction no contract which was not approximately fair to all concerned including the shareholders.

The arrangement had one effect which would not be important today save that it still colors legal thinking.

Where an entity is created by the state and the state carefully and explicitly lays down rules of conduct for it, the assumption is naturally made that anything permitted to the organism has been expressly sanctioned by the sovereign power. As a result, much of the jurisprudence of the time turned purely on the question of power, and very little else was considered important. If, under the contract, a thing could be done, there was definite state authorization for the action taken, irrespective of its merits; if it was designed to prohibit the doing of a thing, presumably this prohibition would appear expressly or impliedly in the charter.[12] It was accordingly fashionable to believe that anything which a corporation had express power to do, it could rightfully do, the state having sanctioned the existence of such power and thus having declared a policy that anything done under it was rightfully done. Today, of course, this principle has, in large measure, disappeared, though it is not infrequent even at present to find the old doctrine argued as justification when the granted power is being unconscionably exercised.[13]

We have the picture of a group of owners, necessarily delegating certain powers of management, protected in their property rights by a series of fixed rules under which the management had a relatively limited play.[14] The management of the corporation indeed was thought of as a set of agents running a business for a set of owners; and while

[12] See, for instance, the charter granted by the New York legislature in 1833 to the Sagg-Harbor Wharf Company (Laws of New York, 1833, chap. 169), laying down, not merely the lines of incorporation, but also rules for the general conduct of the wharf business. For a still more striking illustration, see the Act of April 24, 1832 (New York Laws of 1832) incorporating the New York and Erie Railroad Company; amended by Chap. 182, New York Laws of 1833. Among other restrictions, business could not be commenced until $1,000,000 had been paid in on the road's stock; the whole route of the road had to be surveyed before "the construction of any section thereof shall be undertaken," and so forth.

[13] See, for example, *Davis V. Louisville Gas & Electric Co.* (Delaware) 142 Atlantic, Rep. 654, 1929. (Permission to change rights of preferred stock contained in the general law, *held* indicative of a state policy in favor of such changes.)

[14] The picture probably was not unfair up to, say, 1835. The number of shareholders was few; they could and did attend meetings; they were business-men; their vote meant something.

they could and did have wider powers than most agents, they were strictly accountable and were in a position to be governed in all matters of general policy by their owners. They occupied, in fact, a position analogous to that of the captain and officers of a ship at sea; in navigation their authority might be supreme; but the direction of the voyage, the alteration of the vessel, the character of the cargo, and the distribution of the profits and losses were settled ahead of time and altered only by the persons having the underlying property interest.

The gradual breaking up of this rigid situation, always in the direction of granting to the management or to a small proportion of the owners a wider latitude of power, roughly accompanies the appearance of large scale production and the growth in number of shareholders. Yet the parallel is so distant that it could not be safely followed. Devices, adopted one after the other, which have resulted in centralized power are in many cases quite consistent with the interests of the owners, merely granting them additional conveniences. The right to a defined enterprise begins to recede with the adoption by states of general incorporation laws. These resulted in the elimination of the legislature from negotiations attending the formation of the corporate contract. In place of a body which scrutinized, controlled and might prescribe arrangements, there was substituted a state official, usually the secretary of state, who was obliged to file a document, or charter, which complied with the state laws. The "contract" was thus drafted by the incorporators; and as will appear these individuals presently assumed a position in which they did not even remotely purport to represent the ultimate suppliers of capital. New York passed such a law in respect to the manufacturing enterprises in 1811 (Laws of 1811, chapter 67) though the *purposes* were more or less limited and the capital was to be not greater than $100,000. In 1837 the first really modern type of statute made its appearance in Connecticut (1837) permitting incorporation "for any lawful business," Maryland following closely thereafter (Laws of 1838, chapter 267) permitting general incorporation for manufacturing and mining; after which the general incorporation principle was successively taken up by New Jersey (revised statutes of New Jersey 1846, 142); Pennsylvania (Public Laws, 1849, p. 563); Indiana and Massachusetts (1851);

Carried over into the quasi-public corporation of to-day, the old theory becomes illusory in the extreme. A management is hardly checked by "majority votes" under the present system of "control" (*supra*, pp. 86–7); the shareholders' vote being given by proxy, the proxy being, in substance, little more than a functionary of the management save in the rare case of a fight for control.

Virginia (1852); Maine (1862); Arizona (1866); New York (see Revised Statutes of 1836, 2nd Ed. 220–224).

A good many of these laws were of a limited type. The prototypes of the more modern general corporation acts may be listed as follows: Connecticut 1837, Virginia 1860, California 1863, Arizona 1866, Maryland 1868, Illinois 1872, Pennsylvania 1874, New York and New Jersey 1875, Maine 1876, Rhode Island 1893, Delaware 1899, Massachusetts 1902, Alabama 1903. The effect of these statutes is substantially to permit the incorporation of any lawful business with certain excepted classes. And as in most states "any lawful business" was not limited to any one business but to as many businesses as the incorporators might name, the rule of a single defined enterprise may be said to disappear, though the effect was neither immediately realized nor immediately permitted by the courts in all cases.

Thus, through a long process of legal change beginning in 1837 and becoming approximately complete by the end of the Nineteenth Century, the general incorporation law had become the instrument under which corporate charters were created. These led to changes in the entire system, neither suspected nor designed at the time, which have been revolutionary in corporation law.

When it was necessary to negotiate with the state legislature for a charter, inevitably that charter was a matter of very general discussion. The proponents of the charter—a promoting group or the like— were required to justify every clause of it to outsiders; they were thus checked at every point and the resulting document had some semblance of having been examined with a view to protecting all of the interests involved.[15] This automatic check vanished with the general corporation act. Today, a promotion group goes to its attorneys; requests a charter which will give the widest possible latitude of power both in the enterprises which the corporation may carry on, and in the apportionment of interests through stock holdings and the like; in the privacy of their attorneys' offices, the document is made up, revised and ultimately approved by its proponents; it is then filed in the office of a secretary of state and remains buried there for practical purposes from then on. Actually, no one knows its contents save the

[15] It can hardly be said that the protection proved effective in many cases. Too often special charters were the result of clever politics or private influence; and, in many cases, of sheer corruption. The various battles over the New York Central and the Erie Railroad (see F. C. Hicks, "High Finance in the Sixties," New Haven, 1929) and, indeed, over many of the special railway charters, indicated that the state could become an accomplice in fraud as well as a bulwark of protection. But it should be observed that the process was at least open and notorious; something could be done about it.

incorporators themselves, their attorneys and the appropriate clerks in the office of the Secretary of State. Were general incorporation laws rigid in their requirements as to defining the nature of the enterprise, or the capital structure and the rights of the participants, this might be of little significance. In fact, as we shall see, practically every rigid requirement has been broken down, until in substance the general incorporation law today permits the originating group to write their own contract on the very broadest of terms.

This would be fair enough if no one was involved outside of the incorporating group. But the charter actually contemplates that every stockholder will be bound by it and by any modification of it and by the general incorporation act, and by every modification of that. Such stockholders are, in large measure, about to be drawn from the general investiing public, who are not represented when the charter is drawn; while the incorporating group is likely to represent the interests of those who intend to maintain control of the corporation when formed. The respective rights and powers of each will, in large measure, be defined by this charter; the result being that a so-called "contract" intended to govern the rights of two sets of parties is drawn exclusively by one party who naturally considers his own interest. The other party not only does not participate in the negotiations but in practice never even sees the document. This naturally leads to the result that the management will have as complete latitude and as little liability as possible; as large a power to arrange and rearrange participations in its own interests as can be secured; and that the prospective shareholder will have as little power and as few enforceable rights as can conveniently be arranged.[16]

The weakening of control by stockholders over the direction of the enterprise

It has been observed that under the original corporate situation there was a large amount of residual control in the shareholding group. A weakening of this control is a study by itself; only the major steps can be noted here. We are here concerned with that branch of the corporate power which had primarily to do with carrying on the

[16] A fair example is the charter drafted by Messrs. Sullivan & Cromwell, attorneys, New York City, for the Shenandoah Corporation (1929), one of the larger investment trusts; or, somewhat earlier, by Root, Clark, Howland & Buckner, for the Dodge Brothers, Inc. (1926); but these are merely illustrations, the practice of these offices in New York being substantially the same as that employed by most specialists in corporation papers.

business for which the concern was organized. The direct manifestation of the shareholders' power in this regard was and is his right to vote.

This begins to weaken with the right to vote by proxy. Designed probably as a convenience to the absent shareholder, it was a century ago denied to the shareholder save where by special provision it was inserted,[17] but its apparent convenience speedily led to the inclusion of this right in every charter or in the appropriate section of the incorporation act. The growth of corporations, the dispersion of shareholders, the manifest impossibility for the vast majority of shareholders to attend meetings, have made the right to vote, in reality, a right to delegate the voting power to someone else—and the proxy is almost invariably a dummy chosen either by the management, by the "control," or by a committee seeking to assume control. The proxy machinery has thus become one of the principal instruments not by which a stockholder exercises power over the management of the enterprise, but by which his power is separated from him.

The second major change was the disappearance of the principle that shareholders had the right to remove directors at will. This power, included in some early statutes [18] was also apparently permitted at common law and so noted by Chancellor Kent.[19] The statutory provisions have disappeared; the common law principle today is otherwise.[20] Once in office directors can serve out their term without any effective interference by the shareholders until the next election save where the charter includes a specific power of removal—a rare circumstance in the case of all but subsidiary corporations. Directors are thus supreme during their time. Directly with this goes the principle always recognized and now considered controlling, that directors, while in office, have almost complete discretion in management; and most of the general corporation acts in terms so provide. Further, the unanimous consent of shareholders was required to permit the management to put into effect certain policies. While such unanimous vote normally was not necessary for the ordinary running of the concern, nevertheless, it was held that no stockholder could be bound by the result of any vote which was "inconsistent" with the object

[17] *Philips v. Wickham*, 1 Paige 590 New York (1829).
[18] New York, Laws of 1828, see 2 R. S. 462, chapter VIII, Section 33.
[19] II Kent Commentatories 298, (13th ed.); Angell & Ames: "Corporations," 1832, 248. The power was called amotion.
[20] Cook, "Corporations," 8th ed., 1923, vol. III, Section 624; *Taylor v. Hutton*, 43 Barbour 195 (New York) 1864.

and purpose for which the body corporate was organized.[21] As a result any striking change in the kind of business for which the corporation was organized became impossible without unanimous consent. Otherwise it was thought that an investment in a corporation would be a wild speculation exposing the owners of the stock to all sorts of risks in all sorts of projects not set forth or appearing in the act of incorporation.

General corporation acts today allow amendment in practically every case in this regard by a majority, commonly two-thirds, frequently less.[22] But even the necessity of such an amendment is commonly avoided, since the draftsman of the corporate charter will usually put in several pages of statement of businesses into which the corporation may go with the intent to permit them to do substantially anything and everything. The present corporation's objects and the nature of the business in which (so far as the charter goes) it can engage are commonly limited only by the imagination of its organizing attorneys and their ability to embrace the world within the limits of the English language.

In the later Nineteenth Century appeared the principle that *all* controlling powers of shareholders might be more or less permanently delegated. The issue was fought out on the question of voting trusts, which involved complete delegation of the voting power for a period of years. Of doubtful legality on their first appearance they presently were definitely authorized by statute.[23]

Concomitantly with this appears the privilege granted to corporations to create certain classes of stock altogether without the right to vote; [24] and the most drastic step, (though it does not so appear

[21] Angell & Ames, "Corporations" (1855) p. 581; *Abbott v. American Hard Rubber Co.*, 33 Barbour 578, 592 (New York, 1861).

[22] See for example: Alabama: Laws of 1888, p. 20 (amendment allowed by two-thirds majority); Maine: Laws of 1902, chapter 229 (amendment allowed by majority); Massachusetts: Laws of 1903, p. 437 (amendment by two-thirds majority); New York: Stock Corporation Law, 1923, Sec. 36, 37 (amendment allowed by varying votes, not, however, less than the majority); and so forth. A similar provision appears in practically every general incorporation law in the country.

[23] Indiana: Laws of 1889, p. 91; New York: Laws of 1901, ch. 355 (five year voting trust permitted); New York Stock Corporation Law, Sec. 50, 1923; term set at ten years (N. Y. Laws 1925, ch. 120); Maryland (voting trust for five years permitted), Laws of 1908, Ch. 240, §77, term raised to ten years, Laws of 1927, Ch. 581; Delaware, (voting trusts permitted not exceeding ten years), Laws of 1931, Ch. 129, Sec. 6, p. 467.

[24] Indiana: see Burns: Ann. Indiana Sts., II, 4832, 4836 (preferred stock only). Pennsylvania: Laws of 1921, May 25, P. L. 1159, §1, §4. See Purdon's Pa. Sts. Am. Title 15, §§161, 164; New York: Laws of 1923, Ch. 787, §5; Delaware: Laws of 1929, Ch. 135, Sec. 5.

at first sight), is the grant of power to a majority to authorize the sale or lease of the entire property of the corporation without unanimous vote, thereby handing over the enterprise to a different management altogether beyond the control of the former participants in it. At common law any dissenter could prevent this.[25]

So through various statutory changes, general permission to incorporate and inclusion in charters of increasing grants of power to the management, the stockholders' position, once a controlling factor in the running of the enterprise, has declined from extreme strength to practical impotence. The legal changes probably have merely recognized the underlying economic fact. It is fairly probable that the reason for the weakening of the shareholder's position lay as much in his inability to manage as in the obvious willingness of the "control" to take over the task.

The elimination of the state supervision over contributions of capital

The special charter commonly required that the corporation could not in any case commence business unless a certain amount of capital had been paid in; and, further, that every share issued must represent a contribution of a stated minimum—viz., its par value. It is probable though not certain that the original statutes contemplated this payment in cash. The principle was the sporting one that no person should be allowed to share in the profits who had not contributed to the original fund. This, the most persistent rule in American corporation law, continued well through the Nineteenth century; the principle was laid down by the standard commentator in 1886 that "every stockholder in a corporation is entitled to insist that every other stockholder shall contribute his ratable part of the company's capital for the common benefit; . . . It would be a plain violation of the equitable rights of those stockholders who have contributed or who have incurred a liability to contribute the amount of their shares in full, to allow any person to have the benefits of membership without adding the amount of their shares to the company's capital." [26]

The rule was given teeth by providing that in the event that the corporation was unable to pay its debts, every stockholder receiv-

---

[25] *Abbott v. Hard Rubber Co.,* 33 Barbour, 578 (New York, 1861); *People v. Ballard,* 141, (New York, 269, 1892). A situation presently rectified by many statutory provisions.

[26] Morawetz: "Corporations," (1886), Sec. 286; *Macon etc. R. R. Co. v. Nason,* 57 Georgia 314 (1876).

ing shares without paying par value should be personally liable up to the amount of the par value of the stock received by them.[27] And in respect to par value shares, this situation in general still survives though, as will appear, it has been notably weakened. The legalistic theories supporting the rule primarily revolve around the protection of creditors; but the principal effect was to enforce an equitable contribution from each shareholder; the result being powerfully to protect each contributor of capital from a dilution of his participation through the issue of participations to non-contributors.

The rule was weakened almost at once by determination in the courts that stock could be issued for property as well as cash.[28] In any event, statutes presently incorporated this principle, no doubt on the theory that if a corporation could issue stock for cash and promptly use the cash to buy property, it might as well be given power to issue the stock directly for the property. On its face this would not seem to weaken the rule. Examination will disclose, however, that it left a latitude open to the management, since the management could fix the valuation of the property.

Valuation of anything other than cash always raises some questions; valuation of intangible assets is largely a matter of opinion; over-valuation is extremely difficult to prove. The judicial and statutory history of the power sufficiently indicates where it led. One group of courts held, and holds today, that "board of directors are required to value the property as its true value," [29] which meant that the court would itself appraise the property paid in for the stock and settle accounts on the basis of its own appraisal. By various gradations which flow one into another, and assisted by repeated statutory amendments the majority of courts came to the conclusion that the job of valuation was too difficult for them, and instead of looking at the actual value, they would look at the state of mind of the directors. If the directors "acted in good faith" or did not "consciously over value" or "were not fraudulent," the stock was validly issued and the mere fact that the property turned out not to be worth (as of the time of the transaction) the par value of the stock issued for it would not upset the transaction or impose a liability on the recipients of the stock. At its extreme this rule would mean that the more in-

[27] See H. W. Ballantine: "Corporations," Sec. 210 (Chicago, 1927).

[28] Though not generally determined this seems to have been recognized by the cases as early as 1856 in the United States. Cook, writing in 1898 indicates this as the common law rule (Cook on Corporations, Sec. 18, edition of 1898).

[29] *Farwell v. Great Western Telegraph Co.*, 161 Illinois, 522; *Trust Co. v. Turner*, 111 Iowa 664.

Dodd, D. L.: "Stock Watering," (N. Y. 1930) Chap. III.

competent the board of directors, the greater their power to dilute stock; since their over-valuation, however foolish or inequitable, would nevertheless be innocent.[80] The rule finally broke down completely with the advent of non-par stock, first adopted in 1912 in New York, and subsequently becoming general. As to this there is no rule either at statute or common law requiring any fixed minimum contribution. On its face non-par stock may be issued to one group for $100 per share; to another group for $1 per share; the common statutory provision being that non-par stock may be issued for such consideration as the directors in their discretion may determine; [81] and there is no liability to creditors which will enforce any different rule. In practice, as we shall see, both law and usage are once more imposing certain checks on this power to dilute.

But we have seen the rule of a fixed minimum contribution run the gamut from an insistence that each shareholder contribute the par value of his shares in cash, down to a situation in which the law *prima facie* requires no minimum contribution, and *prima facie* at least not even an equal contribution from each shareholder.

Diminution of the right to invest additional monies in the enterprise

In 1807, by a sweeping decision, the Massachusetts Court evolved the doctrine that every shareholder had a "pre-emptive right" to subscribe to additional issues of stock in the proportion which his shareholdings bore to the total number of shares outstanding.[82] The economics of this decision were simple enough. If two or more men enter into an enterprise and it is successful, and they desire to make an additional investment in it, reaping the additional profits therefrom, the right to do so is theirs alone. No one of them can insist that the fruits of this demonstrated success be shared with a new partner. The future as well as the present belongs to this particular group.

Seeking to translate this into terms of corporation law, the Massachusetts Court observed that every shareholder was entitled to his *pro rata* share of control or voting power; and also to his *pro rata* share in the assets of the corporation (which might include a surplus); and consequently they created the pre-emptive right.

This had a double effect. When new shares were issued, if the price for them were fixed so as to dilute the book values of the

---

[80] The cases on these rules are collected in Ballantine, "Corporations," Chicago, 1927, Sec. 207.

[81] See for example, New York Stock Corporation Law, Sec. 10.

[82] *Gray v. Portland Bank,* 3 Massachusetts, 363 (1807).

existing shares, each shareholder could retain his position by subscribing to his proportion of the forthcoming issue. The result would leave his book value and his proportion of the earning power and voting power undisturbed. If unable to take up his shares he could at least approximately assure himself against loss by selling or assigning his right to subscribe to the new shares. This principle at once embedded itself in all corporation law and survives down to the present time. It is recognized as one of the shareholders' most valuable rights; in certain corporations, as, for instance, the American Telephone and Telegraph Company, its existence enhances the value of the outstanding stock. It is in fact an automatic device preventing dilution of assets.

Once created, the rule was assaulted from three sides. In the first place, an exception to it was created by certain courts, notably New York,[33] which limited the pre-emptive right to a case where shareholders had authorized an amendment increasing the number of share *authorized in the original charter.* This left it open to avoid the pre-emptive right by merely authorizing in the charter many more shares than were to be issued at the commencement of business.

Stock issued for property is likewise not subject to the pre-emptive right. No logical reason can be assigned for this exception, which came into the law through the hasty decision of a New Jersey Vice Chancellor, who was obliged to rule upon the point, having no more time for consideration than the lunch hour between sessions of court;[34] but it was promptly availed of by the Bar, and is recognized today despite its lack of logic.[35] There is thus a power of dilution unchecked by pre-emptive right in some states where the stock issued is already authorized, and where the stock is issued for property.

The final attack on this right consists in the insertion in many charters of a clause under which a shareholder limits or waives his pre-emptive right in advance—a provision specifically permitted by the general corporation laws of certain states, notably Delaware.[36]

The pre-emptive right, however, is not dead since there are many

---

[33] See *Archer v. Hesse,* 164, New York Appellate Division, 493, (1914); a rule finally limited severely by the New Court of Appeals in *Dunlay v. Garage Co.,* 253 N. Y. 274 (1930).

[34] *Meredith v. New Jersey Zinc Co.,* 55 New Jersey Equity 211, see *Wall v. Utah Copper Co.,* 79 N. J. Eq., 17 (1905), where the same Vice Chancellor recognized his mistake; see also A. H. Frey: "Stockholders' Pre-emptive Rights" (1929) 38 Yale L. J. 563.

[35] *Thom v. Baltimore Trust Co.,* 148 Atlantic 234 (Maryland (1930)).

[36] Delaware General Corporation Law, Section 5, par. 10 (Amendment enacted 1927, and subsequently carried forward.)

old line corporations who need cash, whose charters do not include waivers of pre-emptive rights, and whose original authorized stock has long since been issued. Modern corporations, however, avail themselves of the several devices to avoid the pre-emptive right, viz., the authorization of more stock than they presently need to issue; the issuing of stock for property and the waiver of the right.

Indeed, as the classification of stock becomes increasingly complex, it becomes more and more difficult to mould the pre-emptive right so that it will accomplish its original function of maintaining the stockholders' respective ratable shares in book value and voting power strength. The vote has become increasingly unimportant. Complex corporate structures have made ratable values increasingly difficult to ascertain and maintain, as has been pointed out by Professor A. H. Frey.[37] The trend appears to be to eliminate the right altogether. Older companies are still bound to grant it by old charters; other companies (notably public utilities) though not so bound, find it useful to float stock pursuant to an issue of "rights," the granting of which is optional by the corporation itself.

Modification of restrictions on dividends

The old corporation law in America clung to the principle that dividends should not be paid out of capital; nor when capital was impaired. New York, for instance, provided that Directors should be guilty of a misdemeanor unless the dividends were declared out of surplus net profits "arising from the operation of the business." [38] Definitions of "capital" vary widely. Their result, however, was in each case to establish a fixed minimum which had to be paid in; and the fund from which dividends might be paid had usually to be an amount over that. Most states did not require that the surplus should "arise out of the operation of the business"; but they did require unimpaired capital (however defined) as a prerequisite of dividend payment.

This was the situation up to the close of the Nineteenth Century. Then a number of attacks were made on it from various angles. One of these was the evolution of "paid-in-surplus" which in substance means that when shares are issued, only a portion of the contribution of the shareholder is set up as capital, and the balance is set up as

[37] "Shareholders' Pre-emptive Rights" (1929) 38 Yale L. J. 563.
[38] New York Penal Law, Sec. 64. It was amended, however, by the New York Laws of 1924, chapter 221, so as to provide that directors should not make a dividend "except from surplus."

paid-in-surplus. Where the shares have par value, this is accomplished by inducing the shareholder to pay more than par, the surplus over par being set up as paid-in-surplus. Where non-par shares are dealt with, the Directors have discretion (save perhaps in New York) to set up such portion of the issue price of the shares as they choose as capital, the balance being surplus. Paid-in-surplus today is in general available for the payment of dividends; and a shareholder may thus receive what he believes is a dividend but what is in effect a repayment of the issue price of shares contributed either by him or by someone else, not representing any real profits from the enterprise.

Statutory provisions in some instances, especially Delaware, permit the payment of dividends despite the fact that the capital has been cut into by losses.[39] The management can thus so arrange the capital structure that payments for shares may be distributed as dividends even though the enterprise has in the aggregate earned no profits and although its operations at the date of making the dividend show a deficit.

The elimination of the right to a fixed capital structure and a fixed place therein

The early corporation laws authorized a specific capital structure, and the place of each shareholder in this capital structure was carefully defined. It could not, under the then existing law, be changed without that shareholder's consent, save in a very limited degree. Since the subject must be gone into elsewhere, the history of the decline and fall of the fixed right need only be touched on here.

Prior to the advent of the general corporation acts, a charter was supposed to be a contract brought into existence by the legislative act of the state. In order to change it a legislative act amending the charter had to be passed. The place of any individual shareholder in that contract was peculiar to him, and the legislation changing it was a law impairing the obligation of a contract and so unconstitutional under the rule of the famous Dartmouth College case.[40]

States promptly took care of their rights in the premises by inserting in every charter that they reserved the right "to alter, amend, or repeal," such charter or any provisions thereof at will.

[39] See Delaware: revised code, chapter 65, Sec. 31, as amended by law of March 22, 1929. This, in substance, permits payment of dividends where there is no surplus and where capital has been impaired, provided the corporation has made current profits within the previous two years.

[40] 4 Wheaton (U. S.) 518, (1819) which held that a charter once granted by a state could not subsequently be altered, amended or repealed.

But a charter was also a contract between the associates as against each other and it did not follow that because the state could not change the contract it could not change the contract between the associates themselves. On this subject jurisprudence is still divided, a few courts insisting that the state's right is paramount (though manifestly the state has little, if any, interest in this phase of the corporate contract); the majority maintaining that this is an affair for the shareholders to settle between themselves.[41]

Corporate managements, foreseeing that it might become desirable to change the particular position of any class of shareholders, inserted in their charters a power to amend the corporate contract in respect to the contract-rights, preferences, participations, voting power, and so on, of any class of shares. In theory this permitted the actions of the majority to change the position of any shareholder. Even this did not settle the issue; and clauses were accordingly in-

[41] Ballantine, "Corporations," p. 818, observes that this has been "the subject of much diversity of opinion," which is mild to say the least.

The Supreme Court (*Tomlinson v. Jessup*, 15 Wallace 454, 1872) upheld an amendment by a state eliminating exemption from taxation formerly contained in the charter. This, of course, was the state acting in respect of an agreement affecting itself. *Greenwood v. Union Freight Company*, 105 W. S. 13, 1881, affirmed a decree upholding a Massachusetts statute repealing a franchise consisting of an exclusive right to run tracks through the streets of Boston and granting this right to the defendant. The effect was to wipe out the value of the stockholders' investment. *Zabriskie v. Hackensack Railroad*, 18 N. J. Eq. 178, denied the right of the state to amend a charter extending the line of the defendant's railway beyond the limits set forth in the original charter. *Garey v. St. Joe Mining Company*, 32 Utah 497, upheld a statute passed after the organization of the corporation in question permitting a majority of the shareholders to convert non-assessable stock into assessable stock and to levy assessments thereon. Here the state was changing the arrangement between the private shareholders. A contrary result, denying the right of the state in a similar situation was ruled in *Somerville v. St. Louis Mining & Milling Company*, 46 Montana 268 (1912). *Davis v. Louisville Gas & Electric Company*, 142 Atlantic 654 (Delaware, 1928) upheld a statute passed after the corporation was organized, permitting amendment by the stockholders cutting down rights of certain classes of stock, and based its reasoning (unnecessarily) on the paramount right of the state because "the problem of financing corporate needs is so vital to the continuance in existence of corporations created under the Act, the matter of stock, its kinds, classifications, and relative rights is so intimately associated with that problem, that it is difficult to escape the conclusion that the charter and the statutory regulations defined by the legislature for the meeting of that problem might very well be regarded as affected with a public interest and concern." These cases and others like them (collected by Ballantine, "Corporations," Sec. 279, p. 818ff) almost run the entire gamut. Generally speaking, the state's right is paramount so far as it has to do with privileges granted by the state, and the state may always change or repeal these. In other matters, the state's right is likely to be limited to incidental amendments, except under the Delaware doctrine quoted above, which is, of course, susceptible of indefinite expansion.

serted in substantially all of the incorporation acts, providing for such amendment or for the "reclassification" of any class of outstanding shares; and in modern corporate charters there is not infrequently included a provision that each shareholder accepts in advance any future changes or additions to the incorporation acts. The stockholder is thus in the position of having assented (on the record at least) to future changes in his contract made by appropriate amendment pursuant to the charter, and existing corporation law, and also modifications made by any subsequent amendment pursuant to any *future* incorporation act.

This, of course, leaves the shareholder virtually at the mercy of an adverse majority, and in some instances even of a minority which has control. If his contract be to receive an 8 per cent cumulative preferred dividend, and to have a preference on distribution of the corporate assets equal to $100 per share, his contract may be amended reducing his 8 per cent dividend to 3 per cent and his preference from $100 to $50.

The common law has wrestled with this situation without conspicuous success. Some states, notably New Jersey, striving valiantly to maintain the rule of fixed participation, have evolved a doctrine of "vested rights," which means merely that the courts will not permit certain kinds of changes to be made.[42] Others take the extreme view that the stockholder has surrendered his right to a fixed participation, has bought into a situation in which his right today may be taken away tomorrow, and that he is obliged to swallow his loss.[43] Most courts really deal with each situation on its facts, conceding that the change can be made, but insisting on a showing that the change really works out to the benefit of the complaining stockholder, or that compensating participations are to be given him in exchange for any loss imposed through the change in his contractual rights.

But the result is that no shareholder can be certain that his position will remain the same. If he be a preferred stockholder he may find his preference cut down; if he be a common stockholder he may find his participation cut in two; in each case the modification being made pursuant to the vote of a majority of shareholders mobilized by the control.

---

[42] *Lonsdale v. International Mercantile Marine Company*, 139 Atlantic 50 (N. J. 1927).

[43] *Davis v. Louisville Gas & Electric Company*, 142 Atlantic 654 (Delaware 1928); *Morris v. Public Utilities Company*, 14 Del. Ch. 136 (1923); *Yoakum v. Providence Biltmore Hotel Company, et al.*, 34 F. (2d) 533, 1929.

Limitation of rights in the future of the enterprise

A late phase of the dilution of the stockholder's position appears in the creation of securities known as "stock purchase warrants." These are options to subscribe to stock in the enterprise at a fixed price; the options running for long terms and frequently *in perpetuum.* Permission to create such securities in their final form appear in the Delaware Corporation Law (amendments of 1929).[44] These instruments have not been the subject of legal scrutiny. Under the Delaware law they need not be made matters of public record; their terms are at the discretion of the Directors; their number is unlimited; and they may be issued at any time. The result of the options is to give the holders a "call" on unissued stock of the corporation at a fixed price. Manifestly, if the corporation has grown and its equities have increased, the warrant holder may claim a portion of these increased values by demanding a share of stock at a price far below such values. For instance, if 100,000 shares of stock are issued today at $100 and at the same time warrants to subscribe to an additional 100,000 shares also at $100 are put out, the warrant holders virtually have acquired a "call" on any increase in the equity of the corporation over and above $100 per share. Put differently, the stockholders of the corporation instead of being entitled to all of the increase, may have half of that increase taken from them by the warrant holders. For, should the equities of the corporation increase in value from $10,000,000 to $20,000,000 *prima facie* the shares would be worth $200. Warrant holders, however, could insist on the issue to them of an additional 100,000 shares at a price of $100. The equities of the corporation would then be $30,000,000, and each shareholder would find his share worth $150.

The ultimate fate of these instruments remains in doubt both legally and financially; but there can be no doubt that freedom to issue them weakens the position of the stockholder still further.

The foregoing is not by any means a complete analysis of the legal history of a share of stock. Only a few main currents have been indicated. The trend, however, is sufficiently plain. A share of stock was once a fixed participation in property accompanied by a considerable degree of control over that property. Today it is a participation stripped of many of its original protections, and subject to indefinite variation. With this introduction we may consider the more

[44] Laws of 1929, Chap. 135, §6.

important attributes of shares of stock in a modern corporation and the powers which the control has over them. We must also consider the various checks and balances which appear to be emerging in the common law, restoring in some slight degree some measure of protection. What we have here been observing is the corporation in transition. From a tight organization analogous to an overgrown partnership it has emerged into a tremendous unit whose major preoccupation is distinctly not with the interests of its shareholders.

The trend has plainly been from accentuation of the interests of contributors of capital towards the accentuation of the powers of control. How these are secured, and how they work, and the legal limits, if any, on them, must form the balance of our study of the law of the subject.

CHAPTER II: POWER OVER

PARTICIPATIONS ACCRUING TO

SHARES OF STOCK

IT IS HERE designed to examine the position of a share of stock under the modern corporate structure as modified by common law doctrines, with primary reference to its participation rights in the assets.[1] This

[1] Insofar as rights of participation in the corporate earnings coincide with the rights of participation in the corporate assets, they are included here. Problems of participation in the corporate income as such, however, must be reserved for comment in a following chapter.

It should be noted that the term "assets" as used by lawyers and others appears to have a multiple personality. At times it refers to the particular objects (and rights) which in their organized relationship make up an enterprise. A pro-rata share in such assets (for instance, one millionth of a factory building plus one millionth of a series of machines plus one millionth of a fleet of delivery trucks, etc.) would have almost no meaning to a shareholder. It would be practically impossible to have new capital added through sale of securities to outsiders and yet have each former stockholder maintain his asset portion. Only when the term assets is used to refer to a fund of value,—perhaps a sum of values, measured in a chosen unit (money), does pro-rata share come to have meaning. The introduction of value, however, brings with it a multitude of meanings which attach to that concept and the fund of value referred to as "assets" may, therefore, refer to quite different things. Most commonly, the value fund referred to is "book value," i.e., the assets as arrived at by the accountant through the application of his statistical technique and frequently "book value," or something closely analogous, is the concept back of assets in much of legal thinking. When the question is pushed, however, it usually appears that the value fund may bear little relation to book value, being rather the value fund which the whole enterprise represents—still involving a vague concept, but one which frequently leads to results different from "book value."

Since an effort suitably to define assets would itself involve a comprehensive study and since the actual definition adopted would only occasionally affect the present study, the term assets will here be used in the somewhat ambiguous sense of a fund of value without further definition. Wherever a concrete definition of "assets" might be adopted which would invalidate the discussion in these pages a footnote will be appended giving notice to that effect.

involves consideration of those powers which have become vested in a board of directors or, in some instances, in a portion of the stockholders, whereby this participation can be shifted or reduced without the security holder's acquiescence.

The corporate contract was originally regarded as establishing a set of more or less rigid participations. Of these, the most important were a fixed share in the assets of the corporation and a share in its earnings. In the simplest corporate structure, where only one class of stock was outstanding, the participation accruing to each share was on a *pro rata* basis; it could be easily calculated by dividing the amount of the assets and the amount of the earnings per year by the number of shares outstanding, the quotient being respectively the assets back of each share of stock and the earnings per share. By the specific clauses in the corporate contract, other classes of stock could be created having a greater or less participation, either in assets or in earnings; and perhaps combining with these participations a preference insuring such shares a prior claim on the assets, or a prior claim on the earnings, or a prior claim on dividends declared out of the earnings, or, in fact, almost any arrangement in this regard which the draftsman of the corporate contract might think fit. Whatever the participations might be in a particular case, they were originally established and sanctioned by the state through the medium of a special legislative charter. It followed that such participations could not easily be changed.

Evolution toward complete freedom of contract in corporate charters and the disappearance of the state as a regulating factor in their drafting, has caused a disappearance of the apparent rigidity. This was not caused by any single change in the nature of shares of stock. It has arisen through the adoption, one by one, of a series of mechanisms which, when combined, have thrown into the hands of the board of directors (acting in some instances under appropriate authority from a majority of the shares exercised by the "control"), extremely wide powers in varying the original rigid *pro rata* participation in assets and in earnings.

The mechanisms referred to fall into two broad classes.

i. Mechanisms have been made available permitting the "dilution" of participations—i.e., the reduction of the *pro rata* part of assets and earnings accruing to each share through the issue of additional shares not representing a corresponding contribution to the corporate capital. Here devices deleting the old common law "pre-emptive right," serve to remove from the shareholder his guarantee of an opportunity either to preserve his ratable position, or else, to the extent that he has lost that position, to secure compensation through the sale of his pre-emptive right.

II. Mechanisms likewise have been made available permitting directors to issue securities having a variable or unascertained claim on the corporate assets and earnings; notably: (a) Statutory authorization of the virtually unlimited issue of options to purchase stock running over very long periods of time and even perpetually; (b) statutory authorization of "blank" stock whose preferences and participation may subsequently be declared by the board of directors; and (c) issuance of securities convertible at the option of the corporation.

Subsidiary mechanisms appear from time to time, to be discussed in their place. In this field no one device is controlling. Rather, the board of directors can use a combination of several of them, manipulating their moves as chess men are moved on a board, the result appearing as the combination works itself out in play.

I. DILUTED PARTICIPATIONS

Par value shares

The law originally required a fixed minimum contribution to the assets of the corporation from every purchaser of stock of the original issue. This minimum was the par value of the shares issued.[2] The active sanction was an imposition by law of a supposed liability in favor of creditors [3] where the par value of the shares had not in fact been paid in some form which the law would recognize.[4] Frequently, the

[2] N. Y. Laws, 1892, c. 688, §42; N. J. Laws, 1906, p. 732. The present New York Statute is Stock Corporation Law (1923) c. 787, §69. See *Gamble v. Queens County Water Co.*, 123 N. Y. 91, 106, 25 N. E. 201, 205 (1890); *Stone v. Young*, 210 App. Div. 303, 306, 206 N. Y. Supp. 95, 97 (1924).

[3] *Cf. Welton v. Saffery*, [1897] A. C. 299, where the sanction was in favor of stockholders settling rights *inter se*.

[4] See, *e.g.*, 21 Del. Laws, 1898–9, c. 273, §14, repealed 22 Del. Laws, 1901, c. 166. §1, reenacted and amended as 22 Del. Laws, 1901, c. 166, §20; 22 Del. Laws, 1903, c. 394, §20; N. J. Laws, 1896, p. 284; N. J. Comp. Stat. (1911), Corporations, §21; N. Y. Stock Corporation Law (1923) c. 787, §70.

Cases applying such statutes include: *Kelley v. Killian*, 133 Ill. App. 102 (1907); *Herbert v. Duryea*, 34 App. Div. 478, 54 N. Y. Supp. 311 (1898), aff'd, 164 N. Y. 596, 58 N. E. 1088 (1900); *Stevens v. The Episcopal Church History Co.*, 140 App. Div. 570, 125 N. Y. Supp. 573 (1910); *Stone v. Young, supra*, note 2; see *Scoville v. Thayer*, 105 U. S. 143, 154 (1881); *Camden v. Stewart*, 144 U. S. 104, 113, 12 Sup. Ct. 585, 590 (1892).

liability could not be collected on technical grounds,[5] but the danger was always present. The requirement of payment was doubly specified. In the first place, the quality of consideration turned in for the shares was regulated.[6] Thus, payment was first required in cash; later, in property, contracts, services, and intangible items. The first effective power legally to dilute shares of stock came when the directors were empowered to "value" or appraise property or items other than cash, with a view to determining whether they constituted adequate payment of the par value of the shares issued for them.[7] The second requirement was temporal. "Services rendered," when used to pay for stock, were required to have been rendered *after* the formation of the corporation—*i.e.*, work done prior to the date of the incorporation, or services rendered in forming it, were not recognized. This rule, in substance, still holds.[8]

The rule that "par" value must be paid is of course arbitrary. Where the asset value of each share of stock in the corporation is

[5] *Handley v. Stutz*, 139 U. S. 417; 11 Sup. Ct. 530 (1891) (market conditions made issue below par only way corporation could raise money); *Bent v. Underdown*, 156 Ind. 516, 60 N. E. 307 (1901) (articles of incorporation recorded with Secretary of State having given notice to creditors, stockholders not liable for unpaid balance of subscription stock partially paid for); *Deadwood First Nat. Bank v. Gustin Minerva Cons. Min. Co.*, 42 Minn. 327, 44 N. W. 198 (1901) (subsequent issue below par creates no right in favor of creditors whose debt arose prior to the issue); *Tracy v. Yates*, 18 Barb. 152 (N. Y. 1854) (stockholder not liable for debts contracted before his purchase of stock); cf. *Scoville v. Thayer*, 105 U. S. 143 (1881); *Utica Fire Alarm Telegraph Co. v. Waggoner Watchman Co.*, 166 Mich. 618, 132 N. W. 502 (1911); *Hollander v. Heaslip*, 222 Fed. 808 (C. C. A. 5th, 1915); *Johnson v. Tenn. Oil Co.*, 74 N. J. Eq. 32, 69 Atl. 788 (1908).

[6] N. Y. Laws, 1838, p. 108. On the meaning of "cash" under such a statute, see *People v. Railway Comm.*, 81 App. Div. 242, 81 N. Y. Supp. 20 (1903), aff'g, without opinion, 175 N. Y. 496, 67 N. E. 1088 (1903); *Coddington v. Conaday*, 157 Ind. 243, 61 N. E. 567 (1901); *Hopgoods v. Lusch*, 123 App. Div. 23, 107 N. Y. Supp. 331 (1907); cf. *Furlong v. Johnson*, 239 N. Y. 141, 145 N. E. 910 (1924); 2 Cook on Corporations (1923) c. II, §17.

[7] For an excellent treatise on this whole area in corporation law see Dodd, "Stock Watering; The Judicial Valuation of Property for Stock Issue Purposes" (1930); see also 2 Cook on Corporations (1923) c. II, §18; 5 Thompson on Corporations (3d ed. 1927) §3956 (payment in services), §3967 (payment in transfer of inventions, patents and plays), §§3975–4009 (payment in property).

[8] *Herbert v. Duryea, supra*, note 4; *American Macaroni Corp. v. Saumer*, 174 N. Y. Supp. 183 (Sup. Ct. 1919); cf. *Freeman v. Hatfield*, 172 App. Div. 164, 158 N. Y. Supp. 350 (1st Dept. 1916); *B & C Electrical Const. Co. v. Oeven*, 176 App. Div. 399, 163 N. Y. Supp. 31 (4th Dept. 1917), aff'd, 227 N. Y. 569, 126 N. E. 927 (1919); *Lothrop v. Goudeau*, 142 La. 342, 76 So. 794 (1917); *Stevens v. The Episcopal Church History Co., supra*, note 4. But cf. *Morgan v. Bon Bon*, 222 N. Y. 22, 118 N. E. 205 (1917). As to the power to issue stock in payment for promotion services where consent thereto is given by stockholders, see 5 Thompson on Corporations (3d ed. 1927) §3966 (implying that if the amount is reasonable, there is the power—*quaere* whether this accurately states the rule).

$1,000 and its par value is $100, it is an obvious dilution of the outstanding shares to issue new shares at 100. The effect of such dilution manifestly is to decrease the asset value of each share of stock previously outstanding below 1,000 and to set at far beyond 100 the asset value of each new share of stock issued. Equally, the earning power of each share suffers. As it has become customary to reduce par values, so that the situation in which asset value exceeds par value has become increasingly familiar, this power of dilution at times appears to be really drastic.[9] In some situations the par value is fixed so low that the possibility of dilution is emphasized: an instance is the Union and United Tobacco Corporation, incorporated in Maryland in 1926, having 255,000 shares of stock outstanding, each share having a par value of one cent! The book value, and probably the asset value, of each share of stock in 1928 was more than $12 per share. This case is extreme, but many corporations, especially older ones, have achieved a position in which the asset value of their shares so far transcends the par value as to make the requirement that at least par be paid in, useless so far as protection of the *pro rata* share of assets and earnings of the existing shareholders is concerned.

The remaining step is to permit the directors to issue at will shares authorized in the charter. This can be accomplished either by charter or statute, and is commonly permitted by both. Normally, shares authorized but unissued may be validly sold by the officers of the corporation upon resolution of the board of directors.[10]

Non-par value shares

Requirement of a fixed minimum contribution was eliminated with the general adoption of the non-par value laws after 1912.[11] These

[9] And so recognized by the Special Committee of the New York Stock Exchange, though in a different connection. "Coincident with the development of the stock dividend, there has taken place the development of the less than $100 par and of the no par value stock, together with the practice of having a large capital or paid-in surpluses; and these relatively new conceptions have led with increasing frequency to the corporate practice of partial or complete recapitalization through the form of so-called 'split-ups.'" Report of the Special Committee on Dividends of the New York Stock Exchange (1929) pt. 4, par. 4.

[10] E.g., "Shares of capital stock of this corporation without nominal or par value of any class or classes, hereto or hereafter authorized, may be issued by this corporation from time to time for such consideration as may be fixed from time to time by the board of directors." Certificate of Incorporation of the United Corporation (incorporated January 7, 1929, under the laws of Delaware).

[11] E.g., Cal. Civ. Code (1923) §290(b), as amended by Laws, 1927, p. 1307, §3; Del. General Corporation Law (1915) §§5, 14, 20, as amended by Laws, 1929, c. 135, §§6, 11; Ill. General Corporation Act (1919) §§31, 32, as amended

laws did not at once reach the result, requiring in their early versions that a fixed minimum be paid in behind each share. The typical requirement of today is that of New York [12] which permits non-par stock to be sold for such consideration as may be fixed in the charter or as may be determined by vote of the shareholders; or, if the charter shall so provide, as may be fixed by the board of directors from time to time by appropriate resolution. Naturally, save in exceptional cases, charters adopt the latter alternative and permit directors to fix the price. It is, in fact, a very rare case when such power is withheld from directors.

Thus, by the terms of the statute and the charter-contract, authority is commonly handed over to the board of directors to dilute at will. If there are any limitations on this (and there are [13]), they come only from some common law check or balance on an apparently absolute power of dilution granted to the directors, involving both asset value and shares in earnings. Only one further move is necessary to insure the apparent completeness of the power. This is the inclusion of a clause in the charter that any subscriber to shares of stock in the corporation "waives" in advance any right he may have to require the directors so to exercise their discretion in fixing the price of new issues as to safeguard the asset value and earning participations of the outstanding shares. The writers have discovered no charter which has gone this far. But the entire history of corporation law shows that as soon as the common law develops a check on absolute management power granted by statute or contract, a clause has made its appearance in the charter attempting to negate such right.[14] Accordingly, the suggested development seems likely.

---

by Laws, 1921, p. 365; Ohio Gen. Code (1926) §8623-17, as amended by Laws, 1929, p. 13; Md. Code Pub. Gen. Laws (1924) Art. 23, §§39, 40, 45, as amended by Laws, 1927, c. 581; Mass. Gen. Laws (1921) c. 156, §§6(e), 14; N. J. Comp. Stat. (1910) pp. 1667, 1668, §§120–123, as amended by Laws, 1926, pp. 542, 543; N. Y. Stock Corporation Law (1923) §12. See generally, Parker, "Corporation Manual" (1930) §8.

The effect of these laws in deleting the requirement of a minimum contribution was discussed in *Johnson v. Louisville Trust Co.*, 293 Fed. 857 (C. C. A. 6th, 1923); *Atlantic Refining Co. v. Hodgman*, 13 F. (2d) 781 (C. C. A. 3d, 1926). For a general discussion of non-par stock, see *Bodell v. General Gas & Electric Corp.*, 15 Del. Ch. 119, 132 Atl. 442 (1926); Berle, "Studies in the Law of Corporation Finance" (1928) c. iv.

[12] *Supra* note 11.

[13] See *infra*, Book II, Chapter 7.

[14] See, *e.g.*, *Davis v. Louisville Gas & Electric Co.*, 142 Atl. 654 (Del. 1928) (waiver by shareholders of any right to object to changes in the corporate charter pursuant to subsequent acts of the legislature). Charters commonly include waiver of the directors' disability to deal with their own corporation, grant of sole dis-

"Parasitic" shares

Corporation laws permit the evolution of a capital structure under which the issue of additional shares of stock automatically dilutes certain participations, and adds to the value of others. This is accomplished by creating a capital structure under which one class of stock, say class *A*, is entitled as a class to receive two-thirds of the net earnings, and another class, say class *B*, is entitled to receive the remaining one-third. In such case, the issue of each additional share of class *A* stock means of course that the earnings on additional capital received by the corporation automatically accrues two-thirds to that share of stock and one-third to the class *B* stock. Or, to put it differently, class *B* takes up one-third of the earning power of all new capital invested. By appropriate issue of class *A* stock, without concurrent increase of class *B*, the class *B* shares, acting as parasites, automatically absorb to themselves a portion of the earning power of the capital received for the shares of class *A* as they go out. This kind of structure is found with sufficient frequency to make its incidents a real problem.

On this simple base, any number of variations may be worked out. For instance, class *A* stock may be entitled, upon liquidation of the assets, to receive $100 before the class *B* shares receive anything, and thereafter class *B* and class *A* may share equally by classes, or perhaps the remaining balance is divided among the class *A* and the class *B*, share for share. Here the class *A* stock is protected up to the $100 liquidating value; but any accretions of value in the assets of the corporation over that amount pass in part to the class *B* shares. Such a structure is not unfamiliar in corporations such as investment trusts and in many utility holding companies, whose principal object is to acquire securities or equities which may increase in value. The idea, of course, is to permit a class *B* stock, representing relatively little contribution, to share in increases of assets or earning power derived from contributions paid in by the class *A* shareholders—i.e., to obtain a part of the profits made by speculation with money supplied by others. It is unnecessary unduly to detail the various devices which may be worked out along these lines; the device is simple, and its application obvious.

Oddly enough, the first appearance of this in the law was probably inadvertent. When preferred stock first became popular it was cus-

---

cretion to the directors to determine consideration for stock purchase warrants, waiver of pre-emptive rights, *etc. ad infinitum.* For an instructive example, see Certificate of Incorporation of the United Corporation, *supra* note 10.

tomary to grant to each a preference equal to $100 per share on liquidation. The incorporators doubtless intended that this was all such stock should receive. But the law proceeded on the logical principle that every share of stock was entitled to equal participation for all purposes, except as specifically limited; the court accordingly construed this contract in some instances as meaning that the preferred stock should receive $100 on liquidation and thereafter should share ratably with the common.[15] In result, as every share of common stock increased the assets of the corporation, the sale of each such share correspondingly increased the ultimate liquidation value of the preferred—a result probably not intended.[16] This situation was, of course, speedily met by the inclusion of wording in charters indicating plainly that such preferred stock was to receive on liquidation $100 and no more.[17] Modern participating shares are not drawn with any such

[15] *In re Bridgewater Navigation Co.*, L. R. [1888] 39 Ch. Div. 15, order modified [1889] 14 App. Cas. 525 (the articles contained no provisions as to the distribution of assets on the winding-up of the company). Priority in the distribution of assets is not incidental to the ownership of preferred stock, not even with respect to the relation of the stockholders *inter se*. In the absence of statutory or contractual provisions giving a preference to such stock over common stock in the distribution of the assets, preferred stockholders are on an equal footing with the common stockholders. *Lloyd v. Pennsylvania Electric Vehicle Co.*, 75 N. J. Eq. 263, 72 Atl. 16 (1909); *People v. New York Building-Loan Banking Co.*, 56 Misc. 23, 100 N. Y. Supp. 459 (Sup. Ct. 1906). Preferred stockholders may, however, by agreement be given a preference over common stockholders in the capital of a corporation, and such preference will be given effect upon dissolution of the corporation. *Hamlin v. Continental Trust Co.*, 78 Fed. 664 (C. C. A. 6th, 1897); *People ex rel. Recess Exporting & Importing Corp. v. Hugo*, 191 App. Div. 628, 182 N. Y. Supp. 9 (1920); *Drewry-Hughes Co. v. Throckmorton*, 120 Va. 859, 92 S. E. 818 (1917); *Re Espuela Land & Cattle Co.* [1909] 2 Ch. Div. 187; *cf. Re National Telegraph Co.* [1914] 1 Ch. Div. 755, not followed in *Re Fraser & Chalmers* [1919] 2 Ch. Div. 114 (following the *Espuela Land & Cattle Co.* case).

[16] Which led several courts to hold that the fair construction of the preferred stock provision meant that their $100 preference expressed all they were to get. *Williams v. Renshaw*, 220 App. Div. 39, 220 N. Y. Supp. 532 (3d Dept. 1927); *Marrow v. Peterborough Water Co.*, 4 Ont. L. Rep. 324 (1920). These holdings are *contra* to the rule of the *Bridgewater Navigation Co.* case, *supra* note 15.

[17] "Upon any dissolution, liquidation or winding up of the corporation, whether voluntary or involuntary, or upon any reduction of that portion of the capital of the Corporation that has been set up out of the consideration received for any of the shares of the Common Stock of the Corporation, followed presently by the distribution to stockholders of assets of the Corporation which have been constituted surplus by such reduction, the holders of the First Preferred Stock of every series shall be entitled to receive out of the assets of the Corporation One Hundred Dollars ($100) per share, plus an amount equal to accrued dividends, before any distribution of the assets to be distributed shall be made to the holders of Preference and/or common stock of the Corporation; but they shall be entitled to no further participation in such distribution. After payment to the holders of the First Preferred Stock of the full preferential amounts hereinbefore provided

inadvertence; and the parasitic quality which appears in many classes of shares, operating, of course, as an automatic dilution of the asset value behind each contributing share, is usually the result of a very definite plan on the part of the organizing group.

Shifting of assets from group to group within the corporation—paid-in surplus

Paid-in surplus as a mechanism for granting control to the directors over asset values of shares of stock is a late invention. Legal analysis of this device has not proceeded far enough to permit any dogmatic statements, no modern case of importance having reached a court of last resort, and no legal essay having yet been written.[18]

Technically, paid-in surplus is a contribution made by the purchaser of a share of stock over and above that part of the purchase price which the law requires the corporation to set up on its books as "capital." Capital is here used in the legalistic sense only; it is that amount of the purchase price which the law requires the corporation to segregate on its books, and over which the law throws certain restrictions: viz., that it cannot be used for the purchase of the corporation's own stock [19] and that it cannot be paid out as dividends.[20] The

---

for, the holders of the First Preferred Stock as such shall have no right or claim to any of the remaining assets of the Corporation, either upon any distribution of surplus assets or upon dissolution, liquidation or winding up. The remaining assets to be distributed, if any, upon a distribution of surplus assets, or upon dissolution, liquidation or winding up, shall be distributed among the holders of the Preference Stock and/or the common stock of the Corporation." Certificate of Incorporation of the United Corporation, *supra* note 10.

[18] "Corporate surplus, paid in or what not, and particularly the right to declare dividends therefrom, is also in process. This question has mainly arisen since 1925. A somewhat sketchy treatment in this volume reflects the laziness of the judicial mind about it. To an economist, paid-in surplus certainly can be made to cover a multitude of situations, not to say sins. It may vary from license to commit larceny, to the situation where purchasers of shares pay in a premium to equalize surplus already earned and accumulated on existing shares. William Z. Ripley, Book Review (1931) 31 Columbia Law Rev. 1220, 1222.

[19] *Crandall v. Lincoln*, 52 Conn. 73 (1884); Levy, "Power of a Corporation to Purchase Its Own Stock" (1930) 15 Minn. L. Rev. 1; Ballantine on Corporations (1927) §66.

[20] *Merchants Insurance Co. v. Schroeder*, 39 Cal. App. 226, 178 Pac. 540 (1918), with which *cf. Dominguez Land Corporation v. Dougherty*, 196 Cal. 453, 238 Pac. 697 (1925); *Whittenberg v. Federal Mining and Smelting Co.*, 15 Del. Ch. 147, 133 Atl. 48 (1926); *Coleman v. Booth*, 268 Mo. 64, 186 S. W. 1021 (1916); see N. Y. Penal Law (1909) §664, as amended by Laws, 1924, c. 221; Del. General Corporation Law (1929) §34; Weiner, Amount Available for Dividends (1929) 29 Columbia Law Rev. 906, 912; Berle, "Studies in the Law of Corporation Finance" (1928) pp. 70–71. *Cf.* note 25, *infra*.

economist and the accountant quarrel violently and with reason over this legalistic interpretation, some holding that the restrictions which the law applies to "capital" as so interpreted, should be applied equally either to the assets which the corporation intends to devote permanently to the conduct of its business (as distinguished from those which it expects to distribute from time to time) or else to the entire amount of contributions made by individual shareholders for their participations. Accountants lean peculiarly to the latter view. To the lawyer, however, "capital" means that amount which by reason of some statute [21] or rule of common law, the corporation was obliged to segregate, and maintain intact, save for possible impairment through business operations. Anything over this sum contributed on original issue of shares is "paid-in surplus."

When thoroughly analyzed, paid-in surplus develops into a more complex item. It may partake of any one of four characteristics.

(a) It may be a contribution over and above the "capital" item, made by an incoming shareholder to equalize a surplus fund already accumulated in the operation of the business, thus putting him on a par with older shareholders. For instance, if a corporation started life having shares with $100 par value fully paid and then, through successful operations, accumulated a surplus fund of $50 per share, the sale of additional shares at 100 to outsiders would represent a

[21] See, e.g., "Any corporation may by resolution of its board of directors determine that only a part of the consideration which shall be received by the corporation for any of the shares of its capital stock which it shall issue from time to time shall be capital; provided, however, that, in case any of the shares issued shall be shares having a par value, the amount of the part of such consideration so determined to be capital shall be in excess of the aggregate par value of the shares issued for such consideration having a par value, unless all the shares issued shall be shares having a par value, in which case the amount of the part of such consideration so determined to be capital need be only equal to the aggregate par value of such shares. In each such case the board of directors shall specify in dollars the part of such consideration which shall be capital. If the board of directors shall not have determined (a) at the time of issue of any shares of the capital stock of the corporation issued for cash, or (b) within sixty days after the issue of any shares of the capital stock of the corporation issued for property other than cash what part of the consideration for such shares shall be capital, the capital of the corporation in respect of such shares shall be an amount equal to the aggregate par value of such shares having a par value, plus the amount of consideration for such shares without par value. The capital of the corporation may be increased from time to time by resolution of the board of directors, directing that a portion of the net assets of the corporation in excess of the amount so determined to be capital be transferred to capital account. The board of directors may direct that the portion of the excess net assets so transferred shall be treated as capital in respect of any shares of the corporation of any designed class or classes. The excess, if any, at any given time, of the total net assets of the corporation over the amount so determined to be capital shall be surplus." Del. General Corporation Law (1929) §14 as amended by Laws, 1929, c. 135, §6.

mere dilution of this surplus fund. If the outsider is required to pay an additional $50 per share the law calls this "paid-in surplus." In a business sense, however, it is merely his contribution to equalize the surplus fund accumulated for the benefit of others; a business man would regard it as only sensible that this item should be thrown into the earned surplus hotchpot, to be treated exactly as earned surplus. The only case on the subject so holds.[22]

(b) A paid-in surplus item will also arise where the corporation, through statutory proceedings, has reduced its capital stock—i.e., gone through the necessary steps to obtain permission from the state to reduce that amount of assets restricted by the legal inhibitions on capital referred to above. Thus, if a share of stock having $100 par value is reduced to $50 par and actually prior to this operation the assets amounted to $100 per share, an item of surplus equal to $50 per share arises. Though not paid in at inception as surplus it is now classed as "paid-in surplus." [23] This is obviously an operation looking towards liquidation of a part of the contributions originally made by the shareholders; and the business sense of the transaction would seem to indicate that it could be distributed only to the shares whose capital had thus been reduced and perhaps not at all, if thereby the security behind senior issues would be lessened. The law is yet unsettled on the point.

(c) Where one corporation sells all of its assets to another corporation, organized perhaps for that purpose, the second corporation may and frequently does desire to perpetuate the situation existing before the sale. Thus, where a corporation has, let us say, $1,000,000 par value stock outstanding and a surplus of $500,000, and it sells these assets to a second corporation which likewise wishes to issue shares having a par value of $1,000,000, the second corporation will emerge with a capital liability of $1,000,000, a surplus item of $500,000, and assets of $1,500,000. The surplus item is "paid-in"—i.e., it was not earned from the operations of the business of the new corporation. Yet it was originally earned; and the whole intent of the transaction is to place the new corporation in the same situation with respect to both capital and surplus as was the old. The enterprise has, in a word, merely changed its legal clothes. The business sense of this transaction

[22] *Equitable Life Assurance Society v. Union Pacific R. R. Co.* (1914) 212 N. Y. 360, 106 N. E. 92.
[23] See Ohio General Corporation Act (1929) §§8623–8639 (reduction of stated capital), §8640 (distribution of excess assets); *Small v. Sullivan*, 245 N. Y. 343, 157 N. E. 261 (1927) (reduction by consolidation); *Hoyt v. E. I. Du Pont de Nemours Powder Co.*, 88 N. J. Eq. 196, 102 Atl. 666 (1917).

would be to carry the surplus item as earned surplus in the new corporation just as it was carried before the sale of the assets. The law remains unsettled.[24]

(d) The real problem arises where surplus is paid in by persons buying stock on original issue, without relation to any existing paid-in surplus, and without any actual intent as to its use. Evolved from the three previous situations, the new device has attained a vogue which indicates a serious change in technique. Where the corporation has only one class of shares outstanding the consequences are, perhaps, not grave. In case such surplus is distributed, the recipients will be precisely the holders of the stock (or their transferees) who contributed it. There is, of course, the danger that through declaration of such surplus, piecemeal, as dividends, a fictitious market value may be given to the stock to which it is not economically entitled; the use

[24] In *Hood Rubber Co. v. Commonwealth*, 238 Mass. 369, 131 N. E. 201 (1921), a corporation by amendment changed 50,000 shares of common stock of $100 par value each, to 100,000 shares of non-par common stock, and provided for an exchange on the basis of two new shares for one old one. A tax was collected, over the corporation's protest, on an alleged increase of capital stock. The corporation sued for the rebate of this tax, and the court held that recovery should be granted, saying at page 372, "The treasury of the corporation is not thereby to be enriched by cash, property, services, or the remission of its obligation for expenses. . . . It is a simple exchange of one token for another token or several other tokens representing the same thing. The capital stock remains the same. The number of fractions into which it is divided alone is increased." It did not appear in that case whether there was a surplus; and the stockholders had taken pains to state in the authorizing resolution that the conversion of par shares into non-par shares should be "without any capitalization or impairment of any existing surplus accumulated and undistributed profits." In view of this definite statement of intent, the case seems plainly right. On the same day the same court decided *Olympia Theatres v. Commonwealth*, 238 Mass. 374, 131 N. E. 204 (1921) in which a capital of 80,000 shares with a par value of $50 per share was changed to 80,000 shares with no nominal or par value. Thereafter, the 80,000 non-par shares were increased to 250,000 non-par shares, leaving 170,000 shares of unissued stock, and the old stockholders received a share of non-par stock for a share of par stock. The court characterizing the *Hood Rubber* case said, at pages 376–377, "Any theory by which an excise was exacted for the change of the eighty thousand shares of common stock, each with a par value of $50, into an equal number of shares without par value, was unsupported by the statutes then in existence. That is settled by *Hood Rubber Co. v. Commonwealth, ante*, 369, just decided." This statement seems unduly broad. If in the *Hood Rubber* case there had been no declaration of intent to preserve the existing capital account as it then stood, and the non-par shares had been permitted to capitalize the existing surplus, there might very well be a basis for imposing such excise. The court, of course, in its *dictum* had not in its mind the problem here considered. It does not follow that the conversion of a par share results in fixing the same amount of capital behind each share.

Pennsylvania appears to provide by statute that on reorganization, or conversion of par stock into non-par stock, the absorptive power of the non-par

of some such arrangement has in fact characterised many dubious schemes.[25] Again, combined with the device of non-par stock, stock dividends may be regularly declared; and (since the directors have full power to determine how much surplus shall be transferred to capital account upon issue of non-par shares as dividends) it may and frequently does occur, that corporations issue dividends payable in stock of their own company,[26] possibly represented in fact by transfer of only a trifling amount of paid-in surplus capital—the result being that the stockholder's *pro rata* share of assets does not really change, though he has a constantly multiplying number of shares of stock. The securities market does not, as yet, appear sufficiently sophisticated to discount this situation, with the result that serious danger may be involved in purchasing shares of stock in corporations having a paid-in surplus and a policy of regular stock dividends. Such "stock dividends" apparently constitute a return on the shares; equally they may be thought of as involving no return at all or as representing a return only to the extent that actual profits have been earned and added to capital account. The New York Stock Exchange has been led recently to regulate this practice by insisting that "regular" stock dividends shall be declared only when they represent actual and adequate

---

shares shall not "freeze" any accumulated surplus. Pa. Laws, 1919, p. 914 *et seq.,* §3; "For the purposes of this act the 'stated capital' of a corporation issuing shares without nominal or par value, shall be the capital with which the corporation will begin business, as stated in the certificate of incorporation or reorganization or the joint agreement of merger or consolidation, plus any net additions thereto or minus any net deductions therefrom; provided that 'stated capital' shall not include any net profits or surplus earnings, so long and during such period as the same may be paid out in dividends under the provisions of Section 8 of this act . . ." §8 provides that dividends shall not be paid out of anything except net profits or surplus earnings. It thus appears that in Pennsylvania the capital with which the corporation begins business is the capital fund, until added to by some formal act. Even so, dividends cannot be paid out of paid-in surplus, this not being net profits or surplus earnings.

[25] It is interesting to note that various states in the early stages contemplated payment of dividends only out of "surplus net earnings arising from the operation of the business"—that is, only from actual earnings. This was the rule in New York (New York Penal Law, (1909) §664) until an amendment (Laws of 1924, Chapter 221). The amendment struck out the requirement that earnings should be paid only from surplus net earnings arising from the operation of the business, and permitted making of payments out of "surplus." The apparent object of the change was specifically to permit payment from paid-in surplus.

[26] Examples of companies following this policy—North American Company, Auburn Automobile Company, Shenandoah Corporation. The exact amount transferred from surplus to capital in respect of each share distributed as dividends usually does not appear until long after the dividend has been paid. Central States Electric Corporation worked out a bond, the interest on which could be paid at the option of the bondholder in stock of the debtor company.

transfer of earnings from surplus to capital account.[27] The law seems to impose no check for limitation.

The real danger inherent in "paid-in surplus" appears where the corporation has more than one class of stock outstanding. Under the law, so far as at present developed, paid-in surplus is, *prima facie,* available for all the purposes for which other surplus can be used. It can apparently be paid out as dividends at the will of the directors, despite the fact that it is really a contribution of assets and not an accumulation of earnings. If, therefore, a corporation has both class A and class B stock outstanding—the class A stock has been issued for $100 per share of which $50 is set up as "capital" and $50 as paid-in surplus, and the class B stock has been issued for ten cents a share,— there is nothing to prevent the directors from commencing to pay dividends at once to both class A and class B out of the earned surplus item contributed by purchasers of class A. In substance, this means that a portion of the contribution made by the class A shareholders is at once diverted and distributed to the class B shareholders. In a word, a part of the asset value behind the class A shares is at once distributed to the class B as "dividends."

The practice is too recent, and the analysis too incomplete, to permit generalizations. The most important justification for paid-in surplus of the fourth type appears to be where a corporation elects instead of borrowing money, to finance part of its needs by preferred stock.[28] In such case, the limited preference dividends on preferred stock are really a substitute for interest payments. Preferred stockholders usually insist on having dividends paid regularly. Without some reasonable assurance of this, preferred stock cannot be sold. If the senior financing were handled through a bond or note issue, the corresponding interest would have to be paid, irrespective of whether the corporation was earning money or not; and the capital contributions of the junior stockholders could and would be used for this

[27] See, *e.g.,* the restrictions on the use of paid-in surplus funds required by a ruling of the Governing Committee of the New York Stock Exchange, April 30, 1930: "Accounting should be adapted to the end that this account should show at any given time the exact amount of realized undistributed earnings, either from date of organization, or, in the event of recapitalization, from some fixed stated date. The fact that state laws may permit stock dividends to be paid without any charge against earnings or earned surplus or with only a nominal charge has no bearing upon the correct accounting procedure to be followed." See further, Report of Special Committee on Dividends of the New York Stock Exchange, *supra* note 9.

[28] A good many real estate companies endeavor to do precisely this. Certain of the Fred F. French Company units, for example, use preferred stock in lieu of second mortgage money.

purpose. Preferred stockholders, in the case supposed, are really replacing bondholders; and a provision, at least for a limited time, for payment of their dividends out of capital contributions of junior shares seems neither unnatural or necessarily undesirable. The junior shares are in reality merely paying rent for the capital they hire; the rent (as usual) commences before the profits begin to come in.

Beyond this, it would seem that there is little justification for the use of paid-in surplus at the outset. The only other result is to grant to the directors almost unlimited power to transfer contributions of assets from one group to another group; perhaps, to a group which has little or no right to receive them under standards either of business or ethics. It is considered probable that the law will ultimately regulate the use of paid-in surplus; upon a case properly presented, the courts might enjoin unreasonable use today. Pending the necessary decision on the subject, the question will remain a moot point among lawyers.

Paid-in surplus is dangerous because in large measure the public investor neither knows of its existence nor understands what it means. He may be contributing surplus without knowing it. In New York, unless the charter explicitly requires a stated sum to be set up in respect of each non-par share as "capital," all of the payment for non-par shares is deemed to be "capital"; [29] and probably in a New York corporation, under the usual clauses, payment for non-par shares on original issue must be credited to the capital fund. Outside of New York, however, this is not the general rule. In Delaware, for example, the directors may fix the consideration for which non-par shares are to be issued, specifying how much is to be set up as capital and how much as paid-in surplus. The buyer of stock will not normally know what these figures are. In Delaware, also, where stock is issued for property the directors do not even have to specify in advance what shall be done with the capital account. They are allowed sixty days

[29] New York Stock Corporation law (1923) §12, requires that the charter shall contain *verbatim* one of the two following statements, where non-par stock is authorized:

A. "The capital of the corporation shall be at least equal to the sum of the aggregate par value of all issued shares having par value, plus $ (the blank space being filled in with some number representing one dollar or more), in respect to every issued share without par value, plus such amounts as, from time to time, by resolution of the Board of Directors, may be transferred thereto";

B. "The capital of the corporation shall be at least equal to the sum of the aggregate par value of all issued shares having par value, plus the aggregate amount of consideration received by the corporation for the issuance of shares without par value, plus such amounts as, from time to time, by resolution of the Board of Directors, may be transferred thereto."

after the transaction, to settle how much shall be capital and how much paid-in surplus.[30] Here the recipient of the stock has not even the possibility of knowing in advance whether he is contributing to a paid-in surplus fund or not.

When this device is united to that of classified shares, of which some classes may be parasitic, it is plain that the power to settle how much of the issue price of shares shall be paid-in surplus, coupled with the power to distribute such surplus as dividends, forms an important accretion in management power to apportion assets as between shareholder and shareholder. Capable of legitimate use, it is also fraught with the possibility of tremendous abuse; whether the benefits outweigh the dangers will not be known for some time to come. Justifications may appear for uses which seem indefensible now; apparently legitimate uses may prove unsound.

It would appear that the principal uses of paid-in surplus of this fourth type are two. First, it is used to pay dividends on preferred stock during the formative period—in other words, to pay rent for capital before profits come in. Secondly, it is used to protect the earned surplus when the time comes to pay back the capital represented by preferred shares.

This latter use is worth a word. Preferred shares under the modern capital structure are frequently redeemable—i.e., they can be bought in for cash at the option of the corporation. Many corporation statutes permit payments made for preferred shares to be deducted, at least in part, from capital account, thereby preserving unimpaired the surplus account, leaving it available for dividends.[31] But there is a limitation. In the states referred to, when preferred shares are redeemed or retired, the *par* value of each share so redeemed may commonly be charged against capital account. Where *non-par* shares are redeemed, the amount of the "capital represented by" such shares may be similarly charged. The latter phrase has never been judicially construed; it has been assumed, without justification, to mean (in respect of each share) the total amount received for that class of preferred stock, divided by the number of shares outstanding. But preferred stock is commonly redeemable only at a premium—say at 110 for a share of stock having a par value of 100. When, therefore, the corporation pays $110 to redeem a share of preferred stock representing $100 of contribution to capital, the extra $10 has to come from something. It cannot come out of the capital account. If it can be paid only out of earned surplus, the operation might reduce the earned surplus so far

[30] Delaware General Corporation Law, §14, *supra* note 21.
[31] See, for example, Delaware General Corporation Law (1929) §27.

that payment of dividends upon the junior shares might be prevented. Accordingly, corporations set up paid-in surplus, thereby protecting their earned surplus account from drains occasioned by retirement.[82] In this aspect, the paid-in surplus fund permits the transfer of part of the contribution of junior shareholders to the preferred shareholders, in order to help pay them out of the picture. Though capable of abuse, this is commonly a legitimate process. Directors do not ordinarily issue preferred stock save as a means of hiring capital; they do not ordinarily redeem preferred stock save when opportunity allows them either to hire capital elsewhere at a lower rate, or to free the corporation of a burdensome prior charge on income. The use of the junior stockholders' contributions for this purpose is probably to their advantage.

Shifting of participations—mergers

A final method of dilution is that of merging the corporation with another corporation, and issuing shares in a new corporation or in the merging corporation in lieu of the shares of the corporation merged. This amounts to a forcible exchange of participations in one concern for participations in a larger concern. It may be assumed that the bulk of such mergers are on a fair basis. This, however, is not invariably true. In a relatively recent instance the Public Service Corporation of New Jersey purchased large stock holdings in a number of smaller utility concerns. It then caused these concerns to lease their facilities to the Public Service Corporation of New Jersey at a rental carrying a fixed dividend on their shares of stock. Such a lease represented the definite obligation of the parent corporation, thus furnishing a security roughly equivalent in safety of income to a junior mortgage bond. Still later it undertook to merge these companies into itself, offering its preferred stock in exchange for stock of the companies thus absorbed. A preferred stock dividend is not an obligation analogous to a rental, and is far less safe. Under the sponsorship of a New York banking house (Roosevelt & Son), a series of stockholders' committees were formed; they forced a ruling on the point in the New Jersey courts.[83] The court held that such a merger constituted too great a change in the preferential position of the asset value underlying each share of stock of the small corporations and forbade the transaction. Here the dilution was less in quantity of assets than in quality; the asset value

[82] See Berle, "Cases and Materials in the Law of Corporation Finance" (1930) p. 394 et seq.
[83] Outwater v. Public Service Corporation of New Jersey, 103 N. J. Eq. 461, 143 Atl. 729 (1928).

behind each share of stock would, at least at the time, have remained substantially the same, but the risk would have been materially increased—as was proved in 1930–31 by the market fate of Public Service Co. of New Jersey, preferred.

The simplest form of dilution exists where one of the two corporations sells all its assets to the other in return for shares of stock of the buyer representing a far greater proportion of the outstanding stock than the assets sold bear to the assets of the merged enterprise. The selling corporation then dissolves, and distributes the shares of stock received in payment ratably among its shareholders. Here the shareholders of the buying concern suffer, as their asset value is diluted through the distribution of an undue number of shares of stock to the shareholders of the selling concern. The effect is precisely the same as where shares of stock are sold below asset value to outsiders. Where a sufficient demonstration can be made of the inequity of the exchange, courts will prohibit the transaction.[34] But since the judgment of the directors as to the fairness of the exchange is given a great deal of weight,[35] they have in this device a very real power of dilution.

Dilution through merger, however, commonly involves something more than action of the directors. A favorable vote of at least a majority and sometimes two-thirds of the voting shareholders is usually required by statute.[36] Consequently, this type of dilution can be carried through only with the active assistance of the "control."

Variation of participations [37]*—purchase by the corporation of its own stock*

Corporations are generally able to purchase shares of their own stock [38] though the power is uniformly limited to the amount of surplus funds.

[34] *Jones v. Missouri Edison Electric Co.*, 144 Fed. 765 (C. C. A. 8th, 1906).

[35] *Cf. Donald v. American Smelting & Refining Co.*, 61 N. J. Eq. 50, 48 Atl. 786 (1901) (involving purchase of property for stock).

[36] For a collection of these statutes, see Parker, "Corporation Manual" (1931) §46.

[37] We have already noted one of the mechanisms for the increase of asset value and earning power behind certain shares of stock in the discussion of "parasitic" shares, *supra* p. 159.

[38] This is true both at common law and under most statutes. For a discussion of the common law rule, see (1926) 10 Corn. L. Q. 371; Ballantine on Corporations (1927) §66. Substantially all of the cases have been collected by Mr. Irving J. Levy of the New York Bar, in a study made at the Columbia Law School under the direction of the writer, and reprinted in (1930) 15 Minn. L. Rev. 1. Mr. Levy comes to the conclusion that there should be legislative prohibition against the use of this power. For a technical examination of the subject, the reading of this essay is suggested. Writers on corporation law divide on the practice. *Cf.* Mora-

So long as surplus funds only can be used for this purpose,[39] the scope of the power is limited. United, however, to the paid-in surplus device—and remembering that the paid-in surplus may be made as large as the organizing group at the outset or the directors thereafter choose to make it—it becomes obvious that the power is far reaching.

The effect of the power on asset value either for increase or reduction lies in the fact that the surplus fund may be used to buy stock in the open market at the discretion of the board of directors and at a time when they deem the price favorable. If purchased above its asset value, the effect is to decrease the asset value behind every remaining share; if purchased below asset value, the effect is to increase this value. The former use is infrequent, though the famous endeavor of the National City Bank to "support" its stock at 400 or thereabouts through purchases by its affiliate, the National City Company, of shares of the Bank's own stock in the open market far above book value, comes at once to mind. Purchase at prices below book value in order to increase asset value per share is, however, by no means unusual; many "investment trusts" have resorted to the practice in order to strengthen the asset value behind their shares.

Carried to an extreme, the practice would permit a board of directors in a depressed market to use all of the surplus funds of the corporation (including paid-in surplus), to retire shares which are temporarily depressed. This carries with it the danger that a management seeking to strengthen its own share holdings, or to make an asset showing per share more favorable than operations would permit, might deliberately depress the stock, or at least sanction an erroneous open market appraisal, for the sole purpose of gathering in as much cheap stock as its surplus fund would stand, thereby increasing the relative participations of all remaining holders. In other words, they might strengthen the corporation through a process of veiled manipulation of shares of their own stock. This involves placing the board of directors, marketwise, in a position so directly adverse to the share-

wetz, "Private Corporations" (2d ed. 1886) §§112–113; Machen, "Corporations" (1908) §§514 *et seq.* 626; Wormser, "Power of a Corporation to Buy Its Own Stock" (1917) 24 Yale L. J. 177. It is unnecessary here to go into the history of the doctrine; from the time when the power came into existence, courts recognized that it was subject to limitations by reason of the fact that the corporation directors might misuse their fiduciary powers. See *Luther v. Luther Co.,* 118 Wis. 112, 94 N. W. 69 (1903); *Borg v. International Silver Co.,* 11 F. (2d) 143 (S. D. N. Y. 1926). The power is usually exercised by the officers of the company under authority conferred by resolution of the board of directors

[39] Some statutes so restrict the power. N. D. Comp. Laws Ann. (1925) §4531; Okla. Rev. Laws (1921) §5320; see Levy, *op. cit. supra* note 38, at 16.

holders whom they nominally represent, as to create a situation which seems, on its face, unsound.[40] On the other hand, there is something to be said for permitting a corporation to buy shares of its own stock, especially where the market machinery has temporarily broken down. During the panic of November, 1929, many corporations were urgently asked to use their surplus funds for such purchase. The incidental effect was to shift the asset values of the remaining outstanding shares. But the motive was to provide market purchases for shares of stock, and to keep running the mechanism of the public market. It is difficult to regard this process as anything other than a legitimate use; it was, in fact, the only available means of safeguarding a decent market appraisal for the bulk of the stockholders.

Removal of stockholders' safeguards—deletion of the pre-emptive right

The pre-emptive right was originally conceived as a necessary outgrowth of a property interest in a participation in the corporate assets. The owner was not bound to permit any part of these to be transferred to an outsider; and he was entitled to the benefits of the whole enterprise. If the enterprise had demonstrated that it could earn more than the normal return on capital, he was entitled to the opportunity to invest his capital in this demonstrably profitable way. Accordingly, the pre-emptive right was considered as safeguarding his (a) voting right and (b) his relative participation. In this last aspect it was a shorthand automatic device to protect him from dilution. If the book value of his shares of stock amounted to $150, and a new share was about to be sold at $100, if an outsider bought it, the $50 surplus was split between the old stockholder and the newcomer. If the shareholder bought the new share, his participation remained the same. In any true analysis, the pre-emptive right is analogous to a dividend. It represents the right to secure an additional portion either of the present surplus or of the future earning power of the corporation, or both; if sold, it represents a means of converting into present cash the value of a part of such earning power or surplus.

This was well enough so long as all shares represented participations in surplus. The emergence of preferred stock which had only a

---

[40] Apparently the New York Stock Exchange has taken this view, at least in connection with investment trusts. On May 26, 1930, a ruling was announced by the Listing Committee forbidding the purchase by so-called "investment trusts" of their own shares of stock save in exceptional circumstances. New York Times, May 27, 1930. These circumstances were not defined by the Exchange. A report of any purchases actually taking place was required to be made at once. See Berle, "Liability for Stock Market Manipulation" (1931) 31 Columbia Law Rev. 264.

limited dividend right, and only a limited participation in the capital assets, however, gave rise to a tremendous confusion. In one case on the subject which suggests a real understanding of the problem [41] the holder of a preferred stock limited both in dividends and in participation in the capital assets sued to demand a pre-emptive right in a new issue of convertible preferred stock. The new issue had no voting power. Vice-Chancellor Lane, in a concise opinion, pointed out that since the only object of the pre-emptive right was to protect either an interest in accumulated surplus or a ratable voting power, and since the complaining shareholder had no interest in the surplus and would obtain no voting power, the reason for the rule fell. He accordingly denied a pre-emptive right. Other jurisdictions struggling with this question, have not fared so happily.[42] The fact today is, of course, that the voting right is apt to be negligible; and the real argument for the pre-emptive right turns on the participation which the shareholder has in assets and in earning power. If both are limited, as is frequently the case with preferred stock, the thrust of the pre-emptive-right rule would seem to have failed.

The common stockholder or participating shareholder, on the other hand, is vitally interested. The pre-emptive right is, for him, the great safeguard against dilution. It is true that the courts would probably safeguard him even where such right does not exist, if he brought the proper law suit. But a law suit is of little use to a small shareholder; the expense is too great. To him one automatic right is worth a thousand law suits. Corporations organized in a time when pre-emptive rights were carefully protected, and which have scrupulously maintained them, have found their stock appreciating for that very reason—American Telephone & Telegraph Company stock is a notable example.

But where the classification of stock is carried to the extreme lengths now prevalent it becomes almost, if not wholly, impossible to work out a rule which will do justice to the situation. The case of participating preferred stocks—stocks which, let us say, have a cumulative preferred dividend of $4 per share, and after the common stock has received $4 then receive another $3 per share, and thereafter divide equally with the common stock, or any one of the thousand

[41] *General Investment Co. v. Bethlehem Steel Corporation*, 88 N. J. Eq., 237, 102 Atl. 252 (1917).
[42] *Jones v. Concord & Montreal R. Co.*, 67 N. H. 119, 30 Atl. 120 (1891); *Jones v. Concord & Montreal R. Co.*, 67 N. H. 234, 30 Atl. 614 (1892); *Thomas Branch & Co. v. Riverside & Dan River Cotton Mills*, 139 Va. 291, 123 S. E. 542 (1924) (in which the pre-emptive right was recognized in the holders of participating, preferred as to dividend, stock).

similar arrangements which have been worked out,—may need something analogous to a pre-emptive right; but no simple mathematical formula can be devised. A pre-emptive right here is as likely to be unjust as just, and it may fail of its purpose completely. This has led a recent writer on the subject to consider pre-emptive rights in cases of complex classification as merely anomalous.[43]

The modern trend in corporate financing has been to cut the Gordian knot altogether. The pre-emptive right introduced too many problems. Everything in the nature of stock is, under the law, *prima facie* entitled to such right; and the right applies to every security which the corporation can issue which either is stock or is convertible or reducible into stock. Accordingly, stockholders are entitled to a pre-emptive right in convertible bonds, and probably in connection with stock purchase warrants; they have similar rights in respect of any combination of stock and warrants, bonds and warrants, or bonds or stock convertible into other stock. The machinery of getting out pre-emptive rights is arduous, sometimes expensive, and likely to create market difficulties. Accordingly, clauses began to appear in statutes as noted above,[44] permitting corporations to cut off the pre-emptive right by inclusion of a proper statement in their charter. One such law (Delaware) provides that no shareholder shall have any pre-emptive right unless it is specifically granted him in the certificate of incorporation. A typical certificate drawn under this law provides that,

"No stockholder shall be entitled as a matter of right to subscribe for, purchase or receive any shares of the stock or option warrants of the corporation which it may issue or sell, whether out of the number of shares authorized by this Certificate of Incorporation or by amendment thereof or out of the shares of the stock of the Corporation acquired by it after the issuance thereof, nor shall any stockholder be entitled as a matter of right to purchase or subscribe for or receive any bonds, debentures or other obligations which the corporation may issue or sell that shall be convertible into or exchangeable for stock or to which shall be attached or appertain any warrant or warrants or other instrument or instruments that shall confer upon the holder or owner of such obligation the right to subscribe for or purchase from the corporation any shares of its Capital Stock. But all such additional issues of stock option warrants or of bonds, debentures or

---

[43] H. S. Drinker, "Preëmptive Right of Shareholders" (1930), 43 Harvard Law Review, 586; see also Morawetz, "Preëmptive Right of Shareholders" (1928), 42 Harvard Law Review, 186; A. H. Frey, "Shareholders' Pre-emptive Rights" (1929) 38 Yale Law Journal 563. The principal cases are collected in Berle: "Cases and Materials in the Law of Corporation Finance," pages 309–354.

[44] *Supra* note 14.

other obligations convertible into or exchangeable for stock or to which warrants shall be attached or appertain or which shall confer upon the holder the right to subscribe for or purchase any shares of stock may be issued and disposed of by the Board of Directors to such persons and upon such terms as in their absolute discretion they may deem advisable."

The deletion of this pre-emptive right leaves the field clear for the directors to exercise all of the powers of dilution which turn on the issue of additional stock. Whatever legal limitations on their power may remain, the automatic check has been removed.

Even where the pre-emptive right exists, it is subject to the exception (noted in Chapter I of this Book) that it does not apply to the issue of stock for property; [45] and in a minority of jurisdictions, notably New York, it does not necessarily apply to the issue of shares already authorized but unissued.[46]

With these exceptions, and with the direct elimination of the pre-emptive right through the statutes and charter provisions, the corporation utilizing all of the modern devices will grant to its directors a substantially untrammelled power through the issue of stock and the determination of its price to regulate the asset value behind each share.

II. UNASCERTAINED PARTICIPATIONS

An extreme grant of power has been taken and secured by directors where statutes have permitted corporate charters to authorize the issue of securities whose precise claim on the corporate earnings and

[45] See Note, Berle, "Cases and Materials in the Law of Corporation Finance" (1930) p. 344.

[46] *Dunlay v. Avenue M. Garage & Repair Co., Inc.*, 253 N. Y. 274, 170 N. E. 917 (1930); *Archer v. Hesse*, 164 App. Div. 493, 150 N. Y. Supp. 296 (1st Dept. 1914). Manifestly the subscriber to the first share of stock can not impress his claim as to a pre-emptive right on every other share thereafter. The corporation has to start somehow. On the other hand there is the possibility of fostering a practice of building up tremendous reservoirs of authorized but unissued stock free of the pre-emptive right. The rule arrived at in the *Dunlay* case was that the pre-emptive right does not attach to shares of stock issued "to be used in the business of the corporation rather than the expansion of such business beyond the original limits"; the inference being that where such stock is issued for "expansion beyond original limits" a pre-emptive right applies. This distinction is not of great practical use since there is no clear line between the use of capital "in the business" and in the "expansion of the business." Probably one vigorous significance of this case is that where on original issue the sellers of the stock of the corporation state in the prospectus, "authorized capital stock 1,000,000 shares; amount to be presently issued 100,000 shares," or the like (which is common practice in prospectuses today), they have themselves indicated the line between shares issued for the contemplated business of the corporation and shares reserved for "expansion." At least, this is a possible result.

assets is not to be ascertained until later. Three classes of such securities have already made their appearance, viz., stock purchase warrants, "blank" stock, and securities convertible at the option of the corporation.

Stock purchase warrants [47]

Stock purchase warrants are perhaps the most widely distributed of this class of security. Very little is known about them, either as a matter of finance or as a matter of law. They have not been in existence long enough to permit the formation of any intelligent judgment as to their value; their legal position differs widely from their present economic use. Nominally, a stock purchase warrant is an option, permitting the holder to subscribe to one or more shares of the capital stock of the issuing corporation at a price stated in the warrant (which may vary during the period of the option); the term of the option being either limited or perpetual. Of recent years, the trend has been toward the perpetual option warrant, first legalized by an amendment to the Delaware Corporation law in 1929.[48]

By hypothesis, a stock purchase warrant constitutes a privilege to the holder to become a stockholder upon payment of the purchase price. If this price is less than the asset value per share of the class of stock in respect of which the warrant was issued, a dilution necessarily occurs when the warrant is exercised.[49] But unless the

[47] A study was made under the direction of one of the writers by Messrs. Russell G. Garner and Alfred R. Forsythe: "Stock Purchase Warrants and 'Rights,'" Southern California Law Review, April and June, 1931, Volume IV, No. 5, pages 269–292; Volume IV, No. 5, pages 375–392. This study, which traces the presently ascertainable status of these rights, likewise includes a reprint of all of the principal forms in current use. In view of the extremely arbitrary quality inherent in a stock purchase warrant, the authors in their conclusion considered it "a fair question, whether, in view of the directors' duty to protect the stockholders, the directors ever can issue warrants naming the present set price over the objection of a stockholder"; and an option to purchase shares of the corporation at, say, $100 per share, though fair today, may be grossly inequitable to the shareholders ten years from now.

[48] Delaware General Corporation Law (1929) §14, last paragraph. Prior to 1929, Delaware law did not expressly permit the creation of rights or bonds; the legality of perpetual warrants was therefore doubtful, to say the least. In 1929, the law was amended to permit the issuance of options "unlimited in duration." This was shocking to most students at the time, but the Delaware Act in this respect merely legalized what had already been done by certain daring New York offices, and within a few months perpetual warrants became so common as to excite little comment.

[49] Professor Berle and I disagree on the question of when the dilution of assets takes place. I believe that a clearer understanding of a warrant transaction in

market value of the stock is higher than the option price, the warrant will not be exercised, since it would be cheaper to purchase the stock in the open market. Where the warrant is exercised long after its issue date (assuming the corporation to have been prosperous), a dilution is almost certain to take place. This has led some students to describe stock purchase warrants as the potential right to a continuous dilution of the stock until all existing warrants are exhausted. Obviously, if a corporation has 100,000 shares of stock issued and outstanding, and has warrants representing options on another 100,000 shares, and prior to the exercise of any options the book value of each share of stock is 150, while the option price is 100, the effect of exercising the options will be to take half of the excess over the option price from the old shareholders, and to present it to the new shareholders. For this reason, potentially, the power to issue warrants and the power to exercise them when issued, represents a drastic power over the asset values underlying the existing shares of stock.

Under the typical prevailing statute, the power to issue such warrants is vested solely in the board of directors; [50] and, unless the corporation charter otherwise provides, the directors are subject to no control. A stockholder buying shares in a Delaware corporation is

---

reached by regarding the *issue* of a warrant as producing a dilution of assets unless the warrant brings to the corporation sufficient additional funds). The difference turns largely on the meaning of a pro-rata share in assets. If "assets" are to be defined as book value, and if a pro-rata share amounts to the book value divided by the number of shares outstanding, Professor Berle's position is unassailable. On the other hand, if "pro-rata share in assets" means the stockholder's share in a property which is valuable primarily because it is expected to earn an income in the future then the free gift to any other person of a right to share in any part of these prospective earnings lessens the original stockholder's share in the property and thus dilutes the assets represented by his share of stock. Such a definition would indicate that a stock purchase warrant—an option to share in the future earnings of a company—tended to dilute the assets represented by a share of stock at the time of issue unless an appreciable sum were paid into the corporation treasury as a result of its issue.

When a purchase warrant is exercised the pro-rata share in assets (as above defined) represented by an existing share of stock is simultaneously increased through the cancellation of the warrant and decreased by the issue of stock at less than its asset value.

When such a warrant is exercised, however, the market value of the stock must tend to exceed the market price of the warrant by approximately the amount to be paid into the corporation by its exercise unless the warrant holder is willing to accept a financial loss.

If the market values fairly represent the share in assets represented respectively by the stock and warrants before the latter were exercised, there would be no change in the amount of assets represented by each share before and after the transaction.—G. C. M.

[50] Del. General Corporation Law (1929) §14.

thus subject to this variation in his rights whenever the directors, by simple resolution, choose to exercise it.[51] A charter can, of course, be drawn preventing the exercise of such power; but the writers have come across no case in which this has been done. Substantially similar provisions exist in Maryland [52] and in New Jersey; [53] New York has not yet sanctioned the practice. In an extreme form it appears in the corporate structure of the American & Foreign Power Company, which has an authorized capital of several classes of preferred stock and 10,000,000 shares of common stock. Of the common stock, 1,413,000 shares were outstanding as of April 30, 1929; option warrants calling for 3,619,000 shares were outstanding at the same time. In other words, warrants were outstanding calling for more than twice the total amount of existing issued common stock.

In practice, stock purchase warrants and particularly perpetual warrants have run a curious and almost incomprehensible course. Though their interest in any distributions by a corporation can be realized only by exercising the warrants, thereby securing the underlying shares at the option price, in practice they are rarely exercised. Despite this fact, they maintain market values, which to the uninitiated seem inexplicable. The market theory appears to be that to hold an option warrant is equivalent to holding a long position in the stock; but that, as it costs less to buy an option than to buy the stock itself, the option is entitled to sell at a premium. Consequently, if the option is to purchase stock at 10, and the stock itself is selling at 20, the option warrant will not sell at 10 (the market price minus the option price), but at 10 plus a premium representing the chance of further appreciation of the underlying stock. So long as this situation exists, it is never profitable to buy the option and convert it into the stock. The option warrant will always be a little ahead. In practice, the option warrant prices have often run so consistently ahead that relatively few shares of stock seem to have been issued against such warrants other than at or near their expiration; perpetual warrants have rarely been exercised. This had led certain observers in the New York market to suggest that the real result of an option warrant is to create a pure gambling counter, since it will never be exercised, and will consequently never have any impact on the corporation's assets. In view of the extremely short experience with perpetual warrants, generalization is impossible. While they may persist as perpetual

[51] See Berle, "Investors and the Revised Delaware Corporation Act" (1929) 29 Columbia Law Rev. 563, 565.

[52] Md. Code (Bagby, Supp. 1929) §§41, 44, 45, as amended by Laws 1929, c. 565.

[53] N. J. Comp. Stat. (Supp. 1931) §47-18, as amended by Laws 1930, c. 123.

gambling counters, there is no guarantee that a changing security or business cycle may not tell a different story.[54] For the purpose accordingly of long term holdings, there is an unexplained element of danger in those corporations whose structure is heavily loaded with stock purchase warrants. If prosperous, dilution may take place at any time.[55]

Legally, option warrants are subject to a number of serious objections which have not been worked out. The first is the chance that they may be held to be pure gambling contracts, not designed to represent any actual delivery of the stock. The second is that at the time when the stock purchase warrants are issued, particularly if they are perpetual, it is almost beyond human wisdom to set any fair price on such options. A board of directors issuing them (or bankers buying them) must necessarily fix a price determined solely by what the traffic will bear; and a stockholder who chooses to step in and enjoin the transaction on the ground that the price bore no relation to the ultimate participation, may very easily succeed in so doing. In the third place, they share the weakness of convertible bonds. If, when the time comes, the corporation either has not the stock to deliver or does not wish to deliver it, the remedies of the shareholder are nothing if not obscure. Courts will probably not decree the issue of the stock. The amount of damages they would grant to the disappointed holder is as yet unascertained.

"Blank" stock

This device, even newer than stock purchase warrants, has created a potentiality almost wholly unrecognized by directors; and the ultimate use to which the device will be put remains problematic.[56]

[54] The proper open market appraisal of an option warrant is an exceedingly complex problem in mathematics. A few of the simpler calculations which must be made are these: the warrant is worth the market price of the stock, less the option price, plus a premium for the fact that less funds are required to "carry" the warrants; minus a discount for the fact that the warrants do not share in dividends; plus or minus a factor for the chance of appreciation of the underlying stock (limited, however, by the fact that arbitrage operations will always prevent the warrant from sinking below the market price, minus the option price); minus the potential depreciation in the value of the share of stock occasioned by the option owing to dilution through the operation of the warrant itself; this last factor being varied by the probability of the number of warrants exercised at any given time; and so forth.

[55] Again the reader must be reminded that this is a legal view. From the economic viewpoint, loss in value occurs when warrants are issued and not at the time of exercise. The existence of a heavy load of warrants reduces the present value of the stock. Their exercise seems unlikely to lessen the value of the existing stock.—G. C. M.

[56] See Berle, op. cit. supra note 50, at 565.

"Blank" stock was evolved out of the desire to create authorized but unissued preferred stock under an arrangement giving the directors the power to vary the dividend rate set out in the charter prior to the issue of such stock. This, of course, was perfectly legitimate. Preferred stock is frequently used for senior financing, much as are bonds or debentures. From time immemorial, it was required to be described in the certificate of incorporation. If, therefore, a preferred stock was authorized but unissued, carrying an 8 per cent cumulative dividend rate, at a time when the money market permitted the issuance of such stock on a 6 per cent basis, either the stock had to be sold at a premium (a difficult thing to do) or the charter had to be amended, entailing all of the formalities of a stockholders' meeting and a proper stockholders' vote. If the authorized preferred stock carried a 5 per cent dividend rate at a time when the market required not less than 6 or 7 per cent to promote the sale, the stock could only be sold at a heavy discount. Consequently, it was desired to permit the directors, without going through the formality of amending the charter, to vary the dividend rate. Presently, it seemed desirable to permit directors to vary other qualities of the stock itself, permitting them to mould such stock into the form most adapted to the company's financing at the time. This culminated in the Delaware device of 1929 (Section 5, sub-section 4; Section 13), which amounts to a statutory permission to corporations to set up in their charters classes of stock whose designations, preferences, and relative participating rights and any limitations on them, may be determined by the board of directors of the corporation, if the certificate of incorporation so states. In result, the corporation emerges with "blank" stock, which constitutes, in fact, a blank check on the corporate assets and the corporate earnings, to be filled in by the directors at will.

This, of course, is far broader than the power merely to adjust a dividend rate to the prevailing rates for capital hire in the market. The power is complete; the directors are granted at least apparent authority to issue stock in such a way as to vary the *pro rata* asset share of all outstanding stock; to vary their dividend participations; to vary their relative voting strength; in short, to do pretty much as they will with the existing shareholders. The writers have come across no certificate which has not, to some extent, limited the power of directors in that regard; either because the power was not realized, or, because its existence seemed too drastic even for the corporate organizers of today. The typical certificate grants specific power to the directors to determine the dividend rate, an optional redemption price, sinking fund, conversion provisions, and the like,—leaving directors with a sufficiently wide latitude, but still less sweeping than that made possible under the statute.

The legality of this class of security remains undetermined. Undeniably, such securities are valid as far as they go. It does not seem probable, however, that the grant of power as appearing in the Delaware statute can be used safely by directors. It may well be that the common law will so strictly circumscribe the power as to make it less dangerous than it at present appears.[57] Unless some such circumscription is evolved, the directors in any such corporation have one of the most absolute grants of power over property beneficially owned by others that is known to the common law.

Securities convertible at the option of the corporation

A new form of security is beginning to make its appearance, though so little is known about it that at present it can hardly be discussed. These are securities convertible at the option not of the holder, but of the corporation, into other securities. The Associated Gas & Electric Company has supplied the outstanding example of such securities.

The power to convert a security, of course, connotes the probability that the power will be exercised when such conversion is most favorable to the "control." The evolution of this type of security accordingly opens new fields in the practice of control of underlying asset values; and the significance of such devices is likely to increase.

The mechanisms reviewed above do not by any means exhaust all the powers of control which exist over the asset value of shares of stock. They are merely the principal ones. In combination they are sufficiently far-reaching to demonstrate the point that the participation which any share of stock has in the corporate earnings and assets may, under appropriate corporate structure, be dependent largely on the will of the directors or the "control." And it is noticeable that the bulk of these powers can be exercised by the directors without the shareholders' vote—that is, without invoking the machinery of "control."

The basic theory underlying all of these mechanisms is that of a free contract. The purchaser of stock in the corporation is considered to have agreed to and accepted all of the provisions of the underlying corporation act and of the corporate charter; and probably to have accepted also all future amendments of the corporation law and of the charter.[58] He is thus deemed to have agreed to the existence and use of all of the mechanisms mentioned in this chapter, and several

[57] See Berle, *op. cit. supra* note 13, *passim*.
[58] *Davis v. Louisville Gas & Electric Co.* (1928) 142 Atl. 654 (Delaware).

more besides. Accordingly, when the directors vary his participation in assets, and he objects, he is faced with a doctrine which accuses him of having directly agreed to the situation in which he finds himself. Of course, the "contract" is a fiction of law; shareholders do not bargain with their corporation and strike an agreement on the terms of the corporation law and the charter before the stock is sold. They almost certainly did not read the corporate charter, and probably would not have understood it if they had; and would be entirely helpless in the face of the provisions of a complicated corporation act.[59]

The only conclusion that can be drawn is that the share of stock as at present known, while it represents in a sense a participation in corporate assets, does so subject to so many qualifications that the distinctness of the property right has been blurred to the point of invisibility. For protection the stockholder has only a set of expectations that the men who compose the management and control will deal fairly with his interest. He must rely for the most part, not on legal rights, but on economic significances,—on an accumulation of conditions which will make it desirable or advantageous, for the purposes of the administration of the corporation, to recognize a participation more or less meeting his expectations.

[59] In the course of his practice of the law, one of the writers has never come across a shareholder who had read the corporation charter, let alone the underlying corporation act. In practice, only counsel for the organizing group have thoroughly digested either the one or the other, until a controversy arises.

CHAPTER III: POWERS OVER

THE ROUTING OF EARNINGS AS

BETWEEN SHARES OF STOCK

OF COGNATE IMPORTANCE is a series of powers acquired by directors and, to a less extent, by the "control," to apportion earnings more or less at will among shares of stock. The devices for apportioning assets as between shares of stock, reviewed in the previous chapter, of course affect earnings also. Asset value is of direct interest to a shareholder only when the corporation liquidates—a rare occurrence, save in bankruptcy—or when the corporation is sold entire to another corporation—a situation which occurs sufficiently often to make it a real factor in the situation—or in the case of a true merger. But earnings often follow the asset values; and accordingly, while a shift in such values may not immediately affect the return on any given share, over a period of years, it almost inevitably shifts the *pro rata* claims on earnings, and changes *pro rata* distributions by way of dividends. Hence, in considering powers over the distribution of corporate earnings, all of the powers over asset participations must be considered as included, though their effect may be indirect.

Direct powers of apportioning earnings are less well developed than powers over asset participation. This is perhaps, because the practice is more modern; or possibly, because such powers are more readily discernible by the public investor and consequently are more jealously watched. But they are rapidly evolving.

Control through determination of the time of
distribution of earnings

The primary device permitting the directors to control participations in earnings arises out of an ancient and fundamental common law right. This was the right of directors to determine the *time* when dividends should be paid; and refrain from declaring dividends when, in their judgment, the corporate purposes could be subserved by retaining earnings in the business.[1] Only one limitation has been imposed by the law on this process. Earnings must not be withheld to an unreasonable degree. But "unreasonable" is a word admitting of very wide latitude; in practice, save under exceptional circumstances, no lawyer advises a shareholder to sue to compel declaration of dividends on the ground that they had been unreasonably withheld. Almost any sensible showing by the board of directors that they intended to expand, or foresaw difficulties, or envisaged opportunities, would defeat the action. The time rarely comes when it can be made to appear that a corporation does not need additional working capital.

If, therefore, the *right* of a stockholder to receive a participation in income could be made to depend on the time when it was payable, the management could acquire a very real power to steer earnings. Such a tie-up has at length emerged.

Non-cumulative preferred dividends [2]

The best known direct power to route earnings arises where the corporate capital structure includes a class of non-cumulative preferred stock. Such stock commonly has a limited dividend—say 7 per cent—payable in preference and priority to any dividends payable upon junior stock. There is, commonly, a provision that no dividends may be declared upon the junior stock in any year in which the preferred stock has not received its full dividend. Latent in this situation, however, is the possibility that in any year the directors may decline to declare dividends on both classes of stock. If, in fact, there are earnings in any year which can be applied to payment of the dividends on the non-cumulative preferred, the directors by simply withholding such dividends, can set up an earned surplus fund.

Here a dispute entered the law.[3] One group of cases held that

[1] Morawetz, Corporations, 2nd Ed., Section 447; *Dodge v. Ford Motor Co.*, 204 Mich. 459 (1919); *Hunter v. Roberts, Thorp & Co.*, 83 Mich. 63; *N. Y. L. E. & W. R. R. Co. v. Nickals*, 119 U. S. 296 (1886).

[2] For a statement of the problem, see Berle: "Studies in the Law of Corporation Finance," Chapter V, republished from 23 Columbia Law Review, 360.

[3] Perhaps partly as a result of the article cited in the preceding note, though more likely as a result of *Bassett v. U. S. Cast Iron Pipe Co.*, 74 N. J. Eq., 668 and *Moran v. U. S. Cast Iron Pipe Co.*, 95 N. J. Eq. 389. The two views are well contrasted in *Barclay v. Wabash Ry.*, 30 Fed. (2nd) 260, Judge Manton taking the view that the stockholder had not lost his right to a dividend merely because of the delay; Learned Hand taking the view that if the dividend were not declared, it was forever lost.

such earnings, even though withheld, must ultimately be applied to the holders of the preferred stock—that is, a mere failure of the directors in any year to declare and pay earned dividends does not mean that the holder of such stock has forfeited all right to dividends for that year. A contrary view insisted that the right of the preferred shareholders to dividends for any year simply ceased to exist if the directors elected not to declare dividends—thus leaving the share in earnings granted to such stock at the mercy of a whim of the board of directors. This controversy continues, though the latter view apparently prevails; the last word on the subject (*Wabash Railroad v. Barclay*, 280 U. S. 197 (1930)), was said by Mr. Justice Holmes, who, writing for the United States Supreme Court, held that, although the preferred stock had not received dividends for previous years in which they were earned, common dividends could be paid in any year in which the preferred had been paid one year's stipulated dividend.[4] In other words, back dividends, though earned, did not have to be made up. The Supreme Court did not, however, determine whether the surplus accumulated by withholding dividends from the non-cumulative preferred did or did not belong to the preferred stock, thus leaving one of the fundamental questions still open.

The dispute in the law turns on a simple issue. A contract by which preferred stockholders receive dividends or not, depending on the whim of the directors, sounds hardly reasonable. Intelligent construction of the non-cumulative arrangement would seem to be that if there have been earnings, available for payment of non-cumulative dividends, these must be either paid out to the non-cumulative preferred stockholders, or, if withheld, must be piled up in a dividend credit from which dividends can ultimately be paid to such stock. Lawyers are divided on the point. Business arrangements out of court have been made on both theories—some corporations declining to recognize any right of the non-cumulative preferred stock in earnings accumulated by withholding their dividends;[5] others, recognizing the right of such stock to so much of the surplus as had been accumulated by withholding earned dividends which could have been, but were

---

[4] A decision vigorously criticized by Prof. Clifford M. Hicks "The Rights of Non-Cumulative Preferred Stock—a Doubtful Decision by the United States Supreme Court," 5 Temple Law Quarterly 538 (1931). This article reviews substantially all the cases on both sides of the controversy. Practically speaking, the Supreme Court settled the law on the point; its decision in the *Wabash* case has already been followed in Massachusetts, *Joslin v. Boston & Maine R. R.*, (Mass.) 175 N. E. 156 (1931).

[5] For instance, the arrangement made with holders of non-cumulative preferred stock of American Linseed Co. when it was finally merged with a larger corporation.

not, declared to them. A fair proportion of the business community in recent years (though this was not always the case) has assumed that distribution of earnings to non-cumulative preferred stock rests in the direct control of the directors; and that the directors, by declining to declare dividends, in any year, can thereby cut off the right of non-cumulative preferred to share at all in earnings of that year. Junior shares in that case are necessarily deprived of receiving any dividend for the year, but it is a temporary privation they can well afford to suffer, since in the following year, (under this theory) earnings withheld from the preferred stock may be declared and paid out to the common or junior shares.[6]

Participating preferred stocks

This non-cumulative preferred stock dispute would be of relatively little importance, if it did not bear on another group of securities, steadily growing in scope. Non-cumulative preferred stock is not popular; it commonly is born out of reorganizations in which disappointed creditors or former stockholders more or less unwillingly take such stock, *faute de mieux,* in a bad situation.

And yet, the far more popular "participating preferred stock" of today, (often disguised under the designation "class A stock") is little more than a non-cumulative preferred stock in fact.[7] Thus the class A stock of the Continental Baking Corporation is entitled to $8 per share before the class B receives anything; and thereafter the class A and class B stock share equally. This amounts to a non-cumulative preferred stock with an additional participation attached. Variations on this theme are many, but the principle is always the same. A dividend

---

[6] In its simplest form, the situation works out thus: Assume a corporation with $1,000,000 par value of 7% non-cumulative preferred, and 10,000 shares of non-par common. In 1925 it earns $100,000; in 1926 it earns $100,000; in 1927 it earns $100,000; in 1928 it earns $100,000; in 1929 it earns $100,000; in 1930 it earns $100,000. During these years, it declares no dividends.

In 1931, it declares $70,000 (one year's dividend on the preferred) and declares $530,000 dividends on the common.

If the preferred dividend had been declared annually, the preferred stockholders during the period would have received $420,000; leaving only $180,000 available for the common.

Most non-cumulative preferred and participating preferred stock structures permit this type of manipulation.

[7] For instance:

Continental Baking Corp.	Class A stock
Armour Co. (of Illinois)	Class A stock
General Baking Co.	Class A stock
Ward Baking Corp.	Class A stock

which may be declared or withheld at the will of the board of directors, when earned but withheld, if lost forever, results in sluicing earnings into a general fund. From this the accumulated earnings can be declared out in part to other classes of stock. The result is a situation in which the power of the directors to withhold earnings, consitutes power to deprive one group of shareholders of their share in the earnings, and to hand over this share to another class, if the directors so choose.

The legal rules relating to non-cumulative preferred stock and the dispute noted above, obviously apply by analogy in the participating preferred field also. How far directors have direct power to apportion earnings where the capital structure includes a participating preferred stock, necessarily abides the ultimate determination of the non-cumulative controversy. Many charters, (especially recent ones) in specific terms grant to the directors complete and absolute power in withholding dividends.[8] They directly authorize the management to deprive certain classes of stock of all or part of earnings.

The same mechanism has been extended to other classes of securities. Income bonds, the interest upon which is dependent upon its declaration by the directors, are one example. Such interest is frequently non-cumulative, payable only to the extent that it is earned and actually declared by directors. Participating bonds, in which bondholders are entitled to receive additional distributions out of the earnings of the corporation when the directors so declare, are of like quality.

Parasitic stock [9]

The lines of control here follow closely those set forth in the previous chapter, except that an added factor is needed. The directors must be able to control the surplus account to a greater or less degree.

The simplest type-situation here is a class of stock—say class A—entitled *as a class* to two-thirds of the earnings, accompanied by another—say class B—entitled *as a class* to one-third of the earnings.[10]

[8] For instance, the charter of the Southern Railway (see *Norwich v. Southern Ry. Co.*, 11 Va. L. Reg. (U. S.) 203); and probably, that of the Erie Railway; also Associated Gas & Electric Co.

[9] This field is not covered by decided case law. Only occasionally, legal discussions of the problems involved are available in the courts. The financial use of the device is so wide, however, that until something appears to the contrary, the financial practice must be taken as the state of affairs.

[10] Stock of this character may legally be issued: see *Grausman v. Porto Rican American Tobacco Co.*, 95 N. J. Eq. 154 (1923); affirmed on other grounds, 95 N. J. Eq. 223.

In the supposed case it would appear at first blush that the earnings are automatically routed as soon as earned; for each dollar earned is necessarily split, two-thirds to class A and one-third to class B. But the directors may increase the number of shares of class A stock outstanding. The capital gathered by selling the additional shares will, presumably, be put to work by the corporation, and should result in increased earnings. One-third of these earnings at once is available for apportionment to the class B stock. The directors, through their discretion to issue additional shares of one or the other class of stock, may thus vary the income of each class as they choose. And if they declare dividends payable in stock, by determining which class of stock they will issue as stock dividends, they may still further effect the ultimate destination of income. The arithmetic computations indicating the breadth of this power may be left to a footnote; the result is obvious.[11]

Still further, by controlling the surplus account, the directors may not inconsiderably effect the routing of earnings. They may, for example, use the surplus account to buy in and retire shares of stock

[11] To take a slightly different type of structure, let us assume a corporation with 10,000 shares of class A stock entitled to $7 a year cumulative preferred dividends and thereafter entitled to a dividend share for share, equal to one-third of the dividends declared on class B. The junior stock consists of 10,000 shares of class B.

In case the corporation earns $110,000 per year, and it is all declared out, the class A will receive $70,000 (its preference); a dividend can then be declared out of the remaining $40,000 equal to $3 per share (30,000) on the class B and an additional dividend of $1 per share may be declared on the class A (one-third of the dividend declared to each class B share).

Assume that the directors during the following year doubled the number of class B shares; and the earnings remain approximately the same. $70,000 goes to the class A; of the remaining $40,000 earnings, the directors may declare a dividend of slightly over $1.70 on each share of class B and a dividend of approximately $.57 on each share of class A. As between the classes, the share of class B has been increased from 30,000 to slightly over 34,000—a shift of about 11%; while the share of class A (over and above its preferred claim) has been dropped from $1 to less than $.60.

Conversely, let us suppose the same case but the directors elect to double the class A shares. Let us assume that on the additional capital they earn at the same rate as previously—that is, that the earnings of the corporation are doubled. We now have a capital structure of 20,000 shares of class A; 10,000 shares of class B; and earnings of $220,000 per year. Of this, $140,000 goes to class A to satisfy its preference. Of the remaining $80,000, the directors may declare somewhat over $3.60 per share on the class B—a total of $36,000 to the class, as against $30,000 before; while the class A shares will receive slightly over $1.20 per share in addition—that is, rather more than $24,000. But class A has contributed twice the capital. The class B has increased in proportion. This computation could be carried on indefinitely. It is possible to work out a share of stock which increases its advantage (relative to the capital contribution which it has made) on almost any given change in capital structure.

either of class A or of class B, depending on the class of stock they intend to strengthen or weaken at the time.[12] Since the surplus account, excluding paid-in surplus and the like, is largely the aggregation of past earnings, the use made of it in this respect is an indirect routing of earnings. The directors are here nominally exercising the power (noticed in the previous chapter) to purchase stock; but if they are actually using accumulated earnings for this purpose, they are deflecting, at will, the profit stream.

Another not unfamiliar capital structure includes a class A stock and a class B stock, the charter requiring that whenever a dividend is declared on class A, each share of class B must receive a dividend equal to a certain proportion of the dividend on each share of class A.

Here there is a still wider power of routing earnings, through the device of increasing or decreasing the number of outstanding shares of either class. A number of mechanisms, moreover, may be used in conjunction with that of parasitic classification. For one thing, power to withhold dividends can be used to pile up earnings in surplus account. This may operate to increase or depress the market price of either or both classes of stock at the same time. In the second place, the power to purchase stock of either class with surplus at once makes it possible to use the very strength acquired by accumulating earnings in surplus, so as to shift distribution of the remaining earnings. In the third place, the control of the directors over the price at which stock is to be issued, permits them to use their power to issue stock as a means of determining the ultimate recipients of the earnings. They may, for example, heavily increase the number of outstanding shares of class B stock; in which case the earnings, derived, perhaps largely from capital contributed by class A shareholders, will be divided with

---

[12] Under the doctrine of the non-cumulative preferred stock cases it seems to be held that there is no allocation of surplus to classes; and accordingly, that accumulated earnings of the corporation may be used for any purpose legally allowed in dealing with surplus. There would therefore seem to be no legal objection to using all of the cumulative earnings to buy in for retirement shares of either class. Where (as in the case supposed in the previous note) the classes participate depending on the number of shares,—that is, each share of class B receives a stated proportion of the dividend declared to the class A,—the differences might be minor. In a case where the participation is by classes—that is, where class A as a class receives an additional dividend of one-third of the amount declared out to class B *as a class*, the diminution of outstanding shares in class B might result in leaving only a few shares of such stock, which nevertheless were entitled to receive the entire participation of the class. This is the arrangement, for instance, in the Ward Baking Corp. class A stock. It is further complicated in that corporation by the fact that the preference of the class A is non-cumulative —the two devices used together giving an almost complete power to the Board of Directors.

class B, which may have contributed little or nothing—indeed, the complex classification of stock is not infrequently used to disguise the fact that a non-contributing group is obtaining a disproportionate share of the profits.

Stock dividends

A device apparently feasible under the law, but as yet not used to any great extent, is that of declaring stock dividends in connection with parasitic stock structures. Stock dividends may apparently be declared whenever the corporation has surplus which may be transferred to capital account to a degree sufficient to act as payment for the issue of additional shares. Shares, thus paid up, are then distributed ratably as a dividend. There seems to be no limitation on the class of stock which may be distributed as a stock dividend. If, therefore, a corporation has authorized but unissued preferred stock of no par value, carrying say a 6 per cent dividend—or, still more, if it has "blank" stock—there is no apparent reason why the directors may not transfer $1 of surplus to capital account in respect of each share of preferred stock which they propose to issue, and declare out such stock as a dividend to the class A common or the class B common in the cases supposed above. This would mean that either of these classes would acquire, not a present distribution of earnings, but a preferred claim on future earnings.

A variant on the same situation is the granting of "rights" to one class of stock to subscribe to additional shares of the same class or of another class where the effect is to vary the distribution of earnings between shares. This has already occurred, especially in the utility field; and in at least one case it reached the courts.[13] The General Gas and Electric Corporation did precisely this. Here the corporation had preferred stock outstanding; and also 300,000 shares of class A stock and 200,000 shares of class B. The class A stock was entitled to a non-cumulative dividend equal to $1.50 per year and the class B stock was then entitled to receive $1.50 per share per year; in case of further dividends class A and class B, share for share, were entitled to equal distribution. The corporation offered to the class A shareholders continuously rights to subscribe to additional class A stock at $25 per share; and to facilitate this operation granted each class A shareholder the right to use his cash dividends in purchase of such additional stock. It was, of course, obvious that by so doing additional

---

[13] *Bodell v. General Gas & Electric Company,* 132 Atlantic 442, 15 Del. Ch. 119 (1926).

capital was being secured for the corporation. But, out of the earnings derived from the capital paid in on the class A shares thus sold, the first $1.50 went to the A shares, and the balance to making more certain the dividend on the class B shares up to $1.50 per class B share, after which the earnings were to be divided equally. Paradoxically, the complainant in the case referred to was the holder of class B shares, who apparently did not realize how vigorously the system was working in his favor. Observing that the class A stock was selling in the open market at about 50, he objected to the directors selling such stock at 25 on "rights" in which he did not participate. The court held that the device adopted by the corporation was legitimate because it insured a steady flow of capital; and that the directors' judgment in adopting this means of raising such captial was reasonable. The directors were in fact holders of class B stock. Had the complainant been a little more mathematically minded, he might have realized that the ultimate result was to pile up a block of capital which presumably would earn money; and that the earnings on such capital would ultimately cause additional accruals to class B.[14]

Stock purchase warrants

Stock purchase warrants are, in ultimate analysis, claims on earnings; and the power (referred to in the previous chapter), to issue these at will and for any consideration deemed desirable, is necessarily a power to create, from time to time, conduits through which such earnings may flow from existing shareholders into other groups of shareholders.

Whenever the option price stated in the warrant as the figure for which the warrant holder can buy shares, is below the book or capital worth of the shares, the stock purchase warrant represents a potential dilution in capital or asset value. But since the warrant is, in theory at least, an option to buy stock at the price during the life of the option, irrespective of its asset value, the possibility is always contemplated that the directors may pile up earnings in the corporation. In that case, when the warrant is at length exercised and stock is issued at the option price, the stock will share not merely in capital value but in accumulated but undistributed earnings. Practically all corporations do endeavor to accumulate earnings in surplus account; it is con-

---

[14] It should be noted, however, that if the earnings per share on all shares outstanding, of both class A and class B were greater than $1.50 and also greater than could be expected from the capital obtained from each new class A share sold, then a class B share would suffer dilution by the issue of class A stock "rights" to the A holders alone.

sidered conservative business policy; this is, indeed, one of the factors leading an option holder to believe that the price of the shares of stock will so increase, that it will ultimately become profitable to exercise the warrant. What all this really comes to is that by paying a certain price today for the option, the warrant holder obtains the power at any time to pay a stated contribution to the corporation and thereby secure a *pro rata* interest not merely in capital assets but in future accumulations of earnings. By creating option warrants, the directors can thus create a set of claims on earnings accumulated in the future.

Whether and when a stock purchase warrant will ever be exercised remains a moot point. To date, the perpetual or long term warrants seem not to have been exercised to any great degree. Conceivably, when the corporation begins to pay dividends at a high rate, the fact that the warrant holders do not participate in such dividends may lead them to exercise their options. The American Telephone and Telegraph Co. convertible bonds issued in 1929 included what was virtually a "call" on American Telephone and Telegraph stock. When in 1930 the corporation announced the distribution of "rights" to subscribe to new stock having a large present value in the open market, this (among other factors) tended to induce the option holders to "convert" their bonds and exercise their call privilege.[15] This might be expected to be the case with a stock purchase warrant.

The result of exercising stock purchase warrants can only be to dilute earnings. Obviously, the warrant holder will not exercise his option unless the warrant price is below the market price of the shares. In other words, it is likely he will not be contributing equitably to the assets of the corporation, at least in relation to the share of earnings which the stock he receives against his option will entitle him to receive. Again, he is most likely to convert it at a time when the corporation needs his capital least—having enough on hand already—and instead of being able to employ it profitably, the added contribution that he makes when he pays the option price may well be worth nothing more to the corporation than the interest it can secure

[15] A tremendous amount of these bonds were actually "converted"; the market situation favored this. The stock obtainable by conversion was selling at a higher price than the bonds, though the two tended to move together. Naturally, when the stock price was higher than the bond price, a so-called "arbitrage" operation was possible. That is, it became possible to sell the stock short and buy the bonds for a higher price. The bonds could then be converted, thus obtaining the stock with which to satisfy the short commitment. This would happen whenever the price of a warrant was lower than the price of the stock minus the option price expressed in the warrant. Speculators know this; and in result, the warrant price practically never falls below this differential.

on it through its investment in a call loan or a high grade bond. Whereas the existing capital in the business may be earning 12 or 15 per cent, the incoming capital derived from the exercise of warrants may well be capable of earning at the moment only 3 or 4 per cent.

Stock purchase warrants may easily affect the power of the corporation to raise capital elsewhere. A stockholder in a corporation having, let us say, three times as many warrants outstanding as it has shares of stock, must always reckon on the possibility that the warrants will be exercised; and that the dilution may drastically cut down the book value of his shares. It will, in like measure, cut down his participation in earnings; and he has no reason to suppose that the earnings of the corporation will increase very much by reason of the exercise of the warrants and payment of the warrant price. Logically, the stock market should discount this possibility. To some extent, no doubt it does so; though it does not seem that this factor is adequately understood. When and as it is understood, certain avenues which corporations ordinarily have for financing probably will be impeded, if not blocked altogether. A share of stock in a concern which has not issued warrants should sell higher than a share of stock in one which has. It can accordingly obtain capital through the sale of its common stock with greater ease, thereby contributing considerably to its financial safety.

In the view of one of the writers, the present use of stock purchase warrants seems to be unsound finance. The basis, if any, on which they can be soundly issued has not yet been worked out. The market as yet has not been able to grapple with the exceedingly complicated problem of their valuation. The ultimate fate of corporate structures carrying a large proportion of stock purchase warrants, remains in doubt. Of course, where a corporation as a last resort is forced to issue warrants as fees to bankers, additional "sweetening" to make bonds more attractive, or otherwise, in order to get money which it needs to avoid disaster or serious trouble, the financing can be supported, on the ground that it is this or nothing. Corporations issuing warrants to any large degree on any other basis, however, probably are fairly open to the charge that they and their business advisers simply do not know what the effect of such financing will ultimately be.

The position of warrants as a claim on accumulated earnings, however, and the possibility that they achieve an immediate or ultimate dilution of earnings seems economically unquestionable.[16] The

---

[16] The position of warrants in the event that their terms are violated, is, however, extraordinarily weak. See Berle: "Studies in the Law of Corporation Finance,"

real problem is whether the long term or perpetual warrants now popular will ever be exercised, or whether they will be treated by the market as paper gambling counters supported by the reserve possibility that in an emergency they can be converted into actual values by transmutation into the stock.

Once issued, Directors have little reserve control over warrants. They do have, however, all of the control mentioned above over the asset value, and over the routing of earnings, in respect of the shares of stock into which the warrants may be transmuted through exercise of the option.

Control over accounting

The directors have another powerful weapon which may be combined with any or all of the foregoing. They have a large measure of control over the company's income account. So long as accounting standards are not hardened, and the law does not impose any specific canons, directors and their accountants may frame their figures, within limits, much as they choose. Railroads, banks and utilities are of course subject to stricter regulation in this regard; but industrial companies and holding companies are not. Where shares are classified; and where, by charter provisions, the respective claims on earnings of the various classes are dependent on the existence of earnings year by year, or for any specified periods of time (this is the case in the ordinary non-cumulative preferred stock), the directors may route the earnings by merely arranging that in certain years there shall be none, and in other years they shall be large. The methods of accounting by which this result can be achieved are various. Among the simplest are the charging or failing to deduct depreciation; charging to capital expenses which properly should be charged against income account; including non-recurrent profits as income though their real place is in surplus; and creation of "hidden reserves."

One of the reasons why the power of the directors in this regard is so wide lies in the fact that accountants themselves have as yet failed to work out a series of standard rules. The reason may be that in the nature of things strict rules are out of the question. A residual rule that there must be a good faith attempt to approximate the facts as the directors and their accountants believe them to be is perhaps as

---

Chapter 7. Reference may again be made to the two articles by Messrs. R. D. Garner and A. S. Forsythe, 4 Southern California Law Review 269, 375 (April and June, 1931).

close as either accountants or lawyers can now come. In result, however, securities like, say, participating preferred stock, or income bonds, whose yield is payable only if it is earned, year by year, are substantially meaningless unless they set up provisions definitely regulating the corporation's accounting. In fact, the more carefully drawn of such securities, where the design is really to protect the holders, include a definition of accounting methods.

Control through pyramid corporate structures

All the foregoing devices exist and are cumulated where the corporation has an involuted structure—that is, where it operates in whole or in part through one or more subsidiaries. In respect of each such subsidiary, the directors of the parent have and may exercise all the devices. Through controlled directors the parent has all of the powers of directors. It also has all of the powers of shareholders. A parent or holding corporation can, accordingly, perform all of the operations noted in the previous chapter and the present chapter, with respect to its subsidiaries and their assets and earnings. The "holding company," indeed, has a far wider latitude in this respect perhaps than any other corporation. This is one of the reasons why holding companies can always be looked upon with a certain amount of suspicion; and why the investing public has always felt somewhat helpless in their presence. Here the control of the parent's directors over the subsidiaries' machinery is absolute; even the information disclosed may be so blind as to be unintelligible. The possibility of inter-company transactions—that is, sale of the assets of one subsidiary to another subsidiary; the routing of profitable business to one subsidiary in preference to another; the concealment of losses or the creation of non-existent deficits, make possible an almost unlimited variation in the resulting income account. How far this power has been used, it is simply impossible to say. No information regarding the practice of some of the principal holding companies is yet available.[17]

Many holding companies are scrupulous not to take advantage of their powers. This is, for instance, the position of the American Telephone and Telegraph Company; of the Pennsylvania Company, and of a few other classic corporations. The newer railroad holding

[17] Litigation is now pending in connection with the Gillette Safety Razor Co., occasioned in part by the fact that this company transferred inventory to subsidiaries at a price yielding a paper profit, and reported such profits as "earnings." The subsidiaries of course ultimately showed a loss. The parent company's shares, however, had a brilliant stock market career for a time on the strength of the apparent earnings.

companies—for example, Pennroad and Alleghany—have not been in existence long enough to indicate whether their use of the power in connection with routing of income is fair or not. Ultimately, of course, both the investment market, the business community, and the good sense of those in control will demand conformity to a reasonable standard in this regard. To some degree it has been approximated already. In some fields considerable scepticism must still prevail.[18]

With control over earnings, as in the case of control over asset values, it is impossible to determine the use made of the power by directors, and by or at the instance of the "control." In comparison to the breadth of the power, the use of it seems to have been relatively small. Yet in recent months the numerous disclosures of corporate

[18] Every quality of a share of stock in favor of the management may be intensified in power where the corporate mechanism is reduplicated. In practice, this applies to shares of securities in corporations which, in turn, hold securities of other corporations. In such case, the shareholder having, for example, surmounted all of the legal obstacles between himself and his management, and having finally made his rights or privileges valid as against the property of his corporation, finds that he has merely achieved the status of a security holder in still another corporation, and once more must surmount all of the obstacles before he is able to trace his rights through to specific assets. Where the second corporation is dominated by the holding corporation, the management has thus two sets of powers over the corporate property, either or both of which it may use. All of the phenomena traced in chapter VI may thus occur in double form.

The holding company structure and the complications growing out of it, sometimes known as the "involution of corporate mechanisms" forms a study by itself. It is logical, however, to consider the existence of the added power here because of the wide use of the holding company. For instance, out of 573 corporations, securities of which were listed on the New York Stock Exchange and were active in 1928, 92 were holding companies pure and simple; 395 were holding and operating companies; and 86 were operating companies pure and simple. Thus in the overwhelming majority of instances, there was at least a double mechanism interposed between the public investor and at least some of the properties represented by his securities, with a consequent increase of the legal powers which could be called into play by the persons managing the corporations. Of the pure holding corporations, 69 were industrial, 21 were public utilities, 2 were railroads. Of the corporations which were both operating and holding companies 338 were industrials; 13 were public utilities; 44 were railroads.

Out of the list, of the 86 operating companies, 83 were industrial; 3 were public utilities; none were railroads.

The duplication of mechanism appears to have increased rapidly in recent years. Of the 92 holding companies mentioned above only 15 existed in 1910. Between 1913 and 1920, 23 companies were added to the list, while 54 were formed between 1921 and 1928.

Of the corporations which both operated and held, classification is not easy. In many cases the duplication of mechanism has, at the moment, little effect on the actual situation. In some cases the securities held are purely investments. In others they are the stocks of a small wholly owned subsidiary set up for purely internal purposes and amounting in practice only to a bookkeeping division of the corporation's assets, for tax purposes, convenience in operation, or some similar reason. But wherever the duplication exists there is a potential increase of

mismanagement in quarters where it was least suspected, suggest the probability that this power has been exercised to a greater extent than is apparent. Until recently, plentiful earnings made it possible to route ample income into interested quarters to satisfy even an avaricious "control," and still to pay dividends or create apparent values sufficient to satisfy the desires of all stockholders. The real test of such devices commonly comes at the close of a period of depression. In the period immediately following depressions, a large part of earnings are withheld in the corporate treasury; all classes of security holders usually recognize the necessity of this. As most of the devices here discussed came into wide use in the period between 1925 and 1929, their final incidence cannot be known for some years.[19]

---

the management power. Though not used at any given moment it can be called into play whenever desired. The small, wholly owned subsidiary, may at any time be used as a basis for business credit, thereby inserting a class of creditors whose rights are prior to the rights of the stockholders of the holding corporation; and indeed, their securities may be handled at any time so that even the prior lien creditors of the holding corporation are shifted from a senior to a junior position with respect to actual assets. A collateral bond issue of a holding company, secured by all of the stocks of the subsidiary corporations is junior even to an unsecured debt in the subsidiary corporation, since the holding corporation and its creditors can only avail themselves of the net equity in the subsidiary after its debts are paid.

As significant of the trend towards that corporate mechanism with the broadest powers to the management, it is interesting to note the steady trend towards the states having a loose incorporation law. Of the 92 holding corporations mentioned above 44 were organized in Delaware, all of them being formed since 1910. Indeed, of the 44 holding corporations now chartered in that state, 25 were incorporated there between the years 1925 and 1928. In the less liberal New York State 13 of the above holding companies were formed, 6 of them having been chartered between 1910 and 1920, while only 4 were formed since 1920. Ten of the holding companies were chartered in Maryland, one in 1920 and the remaining 9 between 1923 and 1928, presumably in large measure as a result of the looseness of the Maryland corporation law of 1923. New Jersey, a relatively popular state at the turn of the century shows only two of the holding company charters granted there since 1910; while Virginia shows 7 such charters.

Combined holding and operating corporations likewise show a steady trend towards Delaware. Of the whole list, 148 of the 573 corporations hold Delaware charters, most of them relatively recent; New York is second with 121, most of them relatively old; New Jersey third with 87, most of which grow out of the great merger period from 1898–1910.

A number of instances exist in which corporations have deserted the state of their first allegiance and have exchanged their charters for charters in states having a looser corporation act, notably Delaware,—that is, to a place where a greater range of corporate mechanism existed.

[19] As, for instance, in the *Wabash* case, *supra*, p. 173. Over a period of years the Wabash directors had withheld earnings, building up a substantial surplus. When they undertook to declare dividends on the common stock, the non-cumulative preferred stock became restive.

CHAPTER IV: POWER TO
ALTER THE ORIGINAL CONTRACT
RIGHTS OF SECURITY HOLDERS

ALL THE MECHANISMS set out in the previous two chapters—that is, powers to rearrange participation interests represented by shares of stock and powers to route earnings to one or more groups within the corporation, are qualified by a still wider power. This is the power to change the underlying contract by which participations in the assets and in the earnings have been regulated. Such a power in most instances differs from the powers previously examined. It must commonly be exercised by a group of shareholders, commonly a majority (and not infrequently a two-thirds majority) at least of the shares having voting power, and of the shares affected by the change. This means that it can not be exercised save through the proxy machinery. Further, a given "control" which may be quite sufficient to elect directors and thus dictate policies of business management, may still be unable to mobilize the necessary majority of votes to effect change in the contract rights of the parties, because not infrequently statutes require the vote of classes of stock which had not normally voted for directors, or a larger vote than a majority where the object of the vote is to amend a charter or effect a merger. The existence of "control" sufficient for ordinary purposes may not necessarily mean "control" sufficient to change the underlying contract; though in fact the two usually go together.

The change of the underlying contract is commonly affected as a financial matter in one of two ways: either by amendment of the certificate of incorporation or by merging the corporation with another enterprise. The latter term is a financial colloquialism covering any method by which the assets of two corporations are subjected to the same management.

Amendment of the corporate charter

A corporate charter determines, primarily, three subjects:

(a) The scope of the enterprise.
(b) The method of selecting a management—voting rights.
(c) The relative positions and rights of the participants.

There is a fundamental distinction between the first two and the third. The possible activities of the corporation, and the means by which its responsible directors are chosen, relate to the carrying on of operations. The last relates to the division of the property rights between the participants—a matter which may be closely tied in with operating policies (as where a continuous flow of new capital is required to keep the business healthy—a familiar situation in the public utility field) or it may be quite apart from any necessity of management, save as one group desires to gain an advantage at the expense of another group, all within the same corporation. This distinction the law has never fully grasped, though, as will appear, there is a vague tendency to treat changes in operations differently from changes in participations.

The authority to change the contract

An initial technical problem has to be cleared up. There are three distinct methods by which charters can be changed: (1) By direct legislation; (2) by a vote or decision of the corporation authorized by legislation enacted after the corporation was formed; and (3) by a vote or decision of the corporation permitted by the corporation law and charter from inception. Were it not for a point of constitutional law, the three methods would fall, for practical purposes, into the same class—as, indeed, they now do for practical purposes in many States.

A charter was originally conceived as a contract between the State and the corporation [1] and once made, the State could not constitutionally "impair the obligation" of such a contract,[2] even though the State was a party to it; unless the contract definitely reserved to the State the power to change, amend or repeal the charter, the fictitious creature was beyond control. The answer was an express reservation of the right to "alter, amend or repeal," legislated into substantially every charter since the *Dartmouth College* case.

[1] Ballantine: "Private Corporations" (1927) Sec. 270. Cook: "Corporations," Vol. II, Sec. 492 (5th Ed.) *Dartmouth College case,* 4 Wheat. (U. S.) 518.
[2] U. S. Constitution, Art. I, Sec. 10.

Prima facie, this reserve power left the State a free hand. But it presently became plain that a corporate charter was a more complex document than this simple expedient envisaged. The State granted privileges to the corporation; and it also had interests of its own to protect. These were the interests safeguarded by the "alteration, amendment and repeal" clause. Those provisions of the charter splitting the dividends between shareholders, whereby one group got a fixed, preferred dividend, and another got an unlimited junior dividend were obviously matters of private agreement in which the State had little, if any, interest. This led the United States Supreme Court to decide

> A contract between individuals or between a corporation and individuals is not subjected to the action of the legislature by the mere fact that it is embraced in a charter or an amendment to a charter, or results from a dealing had with reference to such an enactment. The state has power to revoke its own contracts where it has in making them reserved such right. But it has no power to impair the lawful contracts of its citizens, or even of corporations created by it. When such contracts relate to the rights of individuals and not to the powers of the corporation, any attempt to reserve such a power would be ineffectual. And a state constitution is no more effectual for such purpose than a statute.[3]

It did leave the state free to take back or change any peculiar concessions it might have granted,[4] or to revoke an exemption from taxes, but beyond that the problem of change or amendment rested in the hands of the corporate group itself, a result which, had it stopped there, would have been fair enough. Factually, a change in a corporate charter through direct legislation is extremely rare. The only area in which such tendencies are occasionally found in the usual business corporation has to do with methods of selecting a management—the State, for reasons for police policy finding it necessary to protect against certain practices. One such experiment was the Michigan Statute prescribing that all corporations must allow "cumulative" voting, to ensure representation of minorities. The legislation was upheld [5] Conceivably (perhaps, even, probably) States may some day take an enlarged view of their police power in handling corporations—perhaps in protecting security holders—and in that case the direct legisla-

---

[3] *Miller v. State of New York* (1872) 15 Wall. (U. S.) 478, 484. See also *Holyoke Co. v. Lyman,* (1872) 15 Wall. (U. S.) 500; *Garey v. St. Joe Mining Co.,* 32 Utah 497; *Zabriskie v. Hackensack & New York R. R. Co.* (1867) 18 N. J. Eq. 178.
[4] As, *e.g.,* a railroad right-of-way: *Greenwood v. Union Freight Co.,* (1881) 105 U. S. 13.
[5] *Looker v. Maynard,* (1900) 179 U. S. 46.

tive amendment will once more become a vivid issue in corporation law. At present, it is of historic importance only.

A second power to change proved more subtle. This consisted in legislation, passed after the corporation was in existence, conferring power on a group in the corporation (frequently a majority of the shareholders) to amend the corporation by their vote if they so desired. In cold logic there was not a great difference between this kind of a law and a law which directly and brutally changed the charter. If, for example, the charter provided for preferred stock, and left the matter so that no preference could be changed without unanimous consent of that class of shares, there is no large distance between an act of the legislature changing the preference by fiat, and an act giving a majority of the stockholders the privilege of changing the preference by amendment. In the one case the State introduces the new situation itself. In the other, the State concedes the right to a private group to create a new situation. The latter is, indeed, more violent than the former, since the private group will be actuated by personal motives, whereas the State (theoretically) would be governed by considerations of public welfare. Though the State is commonly held not to have power to change participation rights,[6] certain recent decisions uphold the constitutionality of legislation granting the privilege of changing the charter to a group within the corporation which previously did not have such power, and (very possibly) were specifically intended not to have it.[7] Both the cited cases proceeded on some vague theory that the State's interest in fostering business allowed the grant of rights to an intra-corporate group to change the agreement as against their associates, which the State itself probably did not have.

Whether this logic was wrong or not, the result was probably justified as a matter of economics. Early charters were incautiously drawn; unanimous votes were needed even for elementary changes; the experience with such votes was that they damaged shareholders through paralysis of the corporation quite as often as they protected against intra-corporate raids by one group on the rights of another. Both in finance and economics the ideal result would be to have the power in existence, and to use it providently for the best interests of all concerned; and accordingly, powers were presently legislated into substantially all incorporation acts permitting amendment of the charter by specified majorities of the shareholders.

[6] *Miller v. State of New York* (1872) 15 Wall. (U. S.) 478. *Zabriskie v. Hackensack & N. Y. R. R. Co.* (1867) 18 N. J. Eq. 178.
[7] *Davis v. Louisville Gas & Elec. Co.* (1928) 142 Atl. 654 (Del. Ch.); *Somerville v. St. Louis Mining & Milling Co.* (1912) 46 Mont. 268.

The third method of change involves amendment pursuant to some method set up and embodied in the charter—that is, by a mechanism which was accepted when the charter was drawn. This presented no constitutional difficulty; it could be considered as a part of the charter-contract, rather than an impairment of it. The main problem then was whether, with the existence of authority to change recognized, there were any limitations on the *use* of this power.

The legality of changes in contract rights

The power to change the corporate contract, once established, has been pushed to extreme lengths. So much so, indeed, that to an experienced investor the charter provisions carry only a small degree of weight, particularly where there is a mobilized, smooth-working control. Some of the major possibilities in the situation may be indicated here.

Changes in the scope of the enterprise

Save in one early case, where a single dissenter was allowed to block an amendment permitting a railroad to extend its originally stated railway line to a more distant point,[8] the Courts have almost from the first permitted amendments enlarging or changing the objects of the business, or the kind of operations [9]—a situation almost forced by the exigencies of a rapidly developing country, a revolution in industrial technique, and a virtual impossibility of predicting the shifts and turns in any business unit. One may question, however, whether this doctrine would extend to a situation where the shareholders quite specifically bargained for a share in an enterprise of limited scope,—bargained, for instance, for a true "investment trust"—and found the "control" amending the corporate charter so as to permit the corporation to become a holding company. But that case seems, as yet, not to have arisen.

Changes in the contribution exacted from shareholders

There is an even split of authority as to whether or not a majority may amend the charter so as to make shares, sold as full-paid and non-assessable, subject to further assessment. This, perhaps the most

[8] *Zabriskie v. Hackensack & N. Y. R. R. Co.* (1867) 18 N. J. Eq. 178.
[9] *Durfee v. Old Colony & Fall River R. R. Co.* (1862) 5 Allen (Mass.) 230.

drastic of amendments, shocks the commercial world most, and it is rarely resorted to. A Utah court held that the thing could not be done, and enjoined the amendment as an impairment of the obligation of contract,[10] laying hold of the circumstance that the legislature had not authorized this amendment to be passed until after the corporation was organized. Under exactly the same facts, however, a Montana Court decided that the amendment was valid,[11] remarking that

> the reserved power may be exercised, not only to alter the contract as it exists between the State and the Corporate entity, but as well to alter the contract existing between the corporation and its stockholders, and the stockholders *inter sese*,[12]

—completely overlooking the fact that it is one thing for the State to undertake alterations, and quite another for the State to endow private groups with that power—as had here been done. The dispute rests there; eastern States have not yet attempted anything quite so drastic.

Changes in relative position or risk as between participants

By a gentle series of gradations, the Courts have established the proposition that an amendment changing the relative position of the shareholder's stock in the capital structure is valid. So, an amendment was upheld creating an issue of preferred stock to be superimposed on the complainant's common stock,[13] though that Court had to distinguish an old New York case[14] involving somewhat similar facts, where the amendment was thrown out. There is, manifestly, a change in the relative hazards since a junior equity stock has more chance of both profit and loss than shares in a corporation having but one class of securities. A prior preferred stock can be superimposed upon a class of preferred stock which theretofore had the senior claim[15]; and an amendment retiring part of the preferred stock which was thereupon to be replaced by a huge bond issue was held valid.[16] In this class of case, of course, there is no direct change of right. The shareholder has what he always had. But it is subject to a new set of hazards.

[10] *Garey v. St. Joe Mining Co.*, (1907) 32 Utah 497. See also *Enterprise Ditch Co. v. Moffitt*, (1899) 58 Neb. 642.
[11] *Somerville v. St. Louis Mining & Milling Co.* (1912) 46 Mont. 268.
[12] *Ibid.*, at page 275.
[13] *Salt Lake Auto Co. v. Keith O'Brien Co.* (1914) 45 Utah 218. *Hinckley v. Schwarzschild Sulzberger Co., Inc.* (1905) 107 N. Y. A. D. 470.
[14] *Kent v. Quicksilver Mining Co.* (1879) 78 N. Y. 159.
[15] *Pronick v. Spirits Distributing Co.* (1899) 58 N. J. Eq. 97.
[16] *Berger v. U. S. Steel Co.* (1902) 63 N. J. Eq. 809.

A more nearly direct shift of right is reached in the type of amendment which changes par value stock into non-par shares. Such amendments are allowed [17] though the change eliminates one of the safeguards the shareholders had prior to the change, viz., the right to a fixed minimum contribution equal to par, from each new shareholder. Put differently, the change breaks down one protection against dilution, though no present cut in his participation rights may have taken place.

These cases have been assumed by the law to be authority for a more drastic kind of amendment—an amendment reducing the capital despite the fact that preferred shares are outstanding. Obviously such a reduction vastly increases the risk borne by such shares. Assume an investment company which is capitalized at $5,000,000 par value preferred and $5,000,000 represented by non-par common. An amendment reducing the capital from $10,000,000 to $6,000,000, but leaving the preferred in its original status, has in fact reduced the safeguard for both its dividend and its ultimate liquidation, since the surplus created can be distributed to the common holders, thereby decreasing the equity junior to the preferred issue. It is by no means clear that the authority cited justifies the conclusion.

Changes in participation rights

It is only a short step from an amendment in the charter changing the relative position of a share in the capital structure, to an absolute change in participation. Such, for instance, as the reduction in the right of a preferred stockholder to receive dividends from seven per cent to six per cent. Such a change nevertheless tends to shock the financial community because the incidence is more nearly obvious. Accordingly, Courts seem to have some difficulty in reaching the conclusion that the amendments should be permitted though in the great majority of cases the amendments are ultimately allowed to stand. The difference is less a matter of law than a matter of psychology on the part of Judges. Where it is desired, for example, to create a new issue of preferred stock ahead of an existing issue of common stock (the case in *Salt Lake Auto. Co. v. Keith O'Brien Co., supra*), the Courts are inclined to take the view that if the directors and their shareholders in their discretion believe this is a good way to raise capital, the problem ends there. Where, however, the amendment operates as a reduction of the participation of one group in favor of another, some kind of a case has to be made showing the necessity for the change. This is formal

[17] *Randle v. Winona Coal Co.* (1921) 206 Ala. 254.

rather than real since almost any group of corporate managers can make a case for necessity if they so desire. They can either indicate plans which they have or rely on business conditions in the industry which they are better able to estimate than a dissenting stockholder; or, if absolutely necessary, they can create a business situation from which there is no exit save by the proposed change in the rights of the shareholders.

In the common stock field, the leading case relates to a charter which provided for Class A and Class B Common Stock. The Class A Common was redeemable at $32.50 per share; was entitled to be paid $25.00 on liquidation in preference to Class B; and was entitled to receive a preferred dividend (non-cumulative) at the rate of $1.50 per share. After this dividend, Class B was entitled to receive dividends at the rate of $1.50 per share; and thereafter the directors were permitted to declare dividends at the rate of not more than 50 cents per share per annum to the holders of both Classes. If excess income was distributed thereafter, it must be distributed so that the holders of Class B shares should receive four times the dividend declared on the Class A.

The Standard Gas & Electric Company owned the great majority of the Class B shares which carried the sole voting rights. They proposed an amendment to the effect that, whenever Class A and Class B stock had each received dividends of $1.50 per share, all dividends should be declared share and share alike between the two Classes; and likewise the permission to redeem Class A stock at $32.50 per share was eliminated. Obviously, this cut down the participation of Class B stock. A dissenting holder of Class B filed a bill to restrain the passing of the amendment. The Court allowed the amendment, first pointing out that the Delaware Corporation Law permitted corporations to adopt amendments of the kind proposed; and second, that the terms were not unfair and inequitable because the corporate management insisted it was for the best interests of the corporation, permitting additional capital to be obtained by sale of its Class A stock; and because the overwhelming majority of the Class B shares (that is to say, the Standard Gas & Electric Company) were prepared to accept. The Court said accordingly that unless it could be shown that the Directors were not "acting in good faith," the amendment should be sustained.[18]

This is an extreme use of the power. It is to be noticed that the interests of the corporation are here placed above the interests of the participants. The enterprise might be benefited by this transaction, but

[18] *Davis v. Louisville Gas & Electric Co.* (Del. Ch. 1928) 142 Atl. 654.

no showing was made that the Class B would share the benefit, except as the consent of the bulk of Class B might tend to indicate that fact. Since it by no means follows that the interests of the holding company might not be better served in some other direction even though their Class B interest was cut down, the factual analysis by the court is obviously incomplete. In other words by ignoring the factor of "control" the court left out an essential element of the situation. The result is a decision which goes to extreme lengths in permitting an alteration of participations which quite frankly resulted in taking rights from one group and giving them to another, the only excuse being that the company might find use for additional capital.

It appears that financially the transaction ultimately worked out to the advantage of both classes of shareholders, though it is difficult to tell whether the amendment had anything to do with the result.

Alterations in preferences are more common; though it is to be noticed that here most courts demand a far higher showing of necessity than was required apparently in the *Davis* case. In one case, the dividend rate on first preferred stock was cut from 7% to 6%; and on the second preferred stock was cut by amendment from 6% to 2%. The amendment was enjoined by a New Jersey court; New Jersey courts being on the whole strict in such matters.[19] Nevertheless, even in that jurisdiction, an amendment cutting down a preferential dividend rate was allowed where the corporation was in difficulties; and the rearrangement was in order to permit the issue of additional stock which might help the company avoid a threatened insolvency.[20] The Federal Court reached the same result under substantially similar circumstances.[21]

Under this doctrine it would seem that almost any preference may be cut down. Obviously the right to a fixed preferential dividend is crucial; if this paramount contractual right can be altered without the consent of its holder, there is little ground for protecting lesser rights against change. Having gone as far as this, few further steps remain in the breakdown of the seemingly fixed contractual rights of stockholders.

There are two instances in which courts tend to draw the line.

[19] *Pronick v. Spirits Distributing Co.* (1899) 58 N. J. Eq. 97.
[20] *Windhurst v. Central Leather Company* (1930) 105 N. J. Eq. 621.
[21] *Yoakum v. Providence Biltmore Hotel Co.* (1927) 34 Fed. (2d) 533 (D. C. R. I.).
For a review of the various authorities see Kades "Constitutional and Equitable Limitations on the Power of the Majority to Amend Charters so as to Affect Shareholders' Interests in the Corporation"—76 Univ. of Pennsylvania Law Review 256 (December, 1928).

One is where a preferred stock carries a cumulative dividend; arrears of dividends have piled up and it is sought by amendment to wipe out these accumulated arrearages; the other, where a sinking fund is provided. In such cases, courts generally insist on a very strong state of facts before they will allow the amendment. New Jersey did allow one such amendment in *Windhurst v. Central Leather Company, (supra)* where there was a threatened insolvency. But even the loose Delaware Courts declined to sustain an amendment wiping out such arrearages; [22] and the Federal Courts had reached the same result in the *Providence Biltmore Hotel Co.* case. The New Jersey Courts normally decline to sanction such an amendment. [23]

The importance of the power to amend the corporate charter, which is prima facie unlimited, and only dubiously restrained by courts, (save in New Jersey and a bare minority of States following its lead) can hardly be overestimated in Corporation Finance. However oppressive an amendment may be, in nine cases out of ten a dissenting shareholder cannot afford the expense of starting a lawsuit. Scattered shareholders do not easily organize for mutual protection. Were they to do so the outcome of litigation would always be uncertain. The shareholder who does object is likely to be a professional "striker"; and if he wins a preliminary injunction, the next step is commonly for the corporation to pay to him or to his attorneys the blackmail demanded, whereupon the injunction is dissolved and the amendment goes through as scheduled. Most changes in contract positions proposed by amendments go through; and the management and control in practice rely on the possibility of using this power as a last resort where their corporation did not at the outset provide itself with a sufficient number of the mechanisms described in the previous two chapters; or where new mechanisms have been devised; or whether the original bargain no longer serves the present convenience or purposes of the "control." If put to their trumps a management can usually make a showing of "business exigency"; and if it is far-seeing it can set the stage to indicate such business exigency long in advance. A shareholder who objects must sustain the burden of proof of unfairness, in which case he is commonly at a hopeless disadvantage in coping with the "control" which has both the funds and the information of the corporation at its free disposal. As a result, the power of amendment of the corporate charter, though somewhat more difficult of use than the mechanisms previously described, remains the residual expedient of the "control"—an expedient often used with telling effect.

[22] *Morris v. American Public Utilities Co.* (1923) 14 Del. Ch. 136, 122 A. 696.
[23] *Lonsdale v. International Mercantile Marine Co.* (1927) 101 N. J. Eq. 554.

CHAPTER V: THE LEGAL POSITION

OF MANAGEMENT [1]

"MANAGEMENT" may be defined as that body of men who, in law, have formally assumed the duties of exercising domination over the corporate business and assets. It thus derives its position from a legal title of some sort. Universally, under the American system of law, managers consist of a board of directors and the senior officers of the corporation. The board of directors commonly secures its legal title to office through election by the stockholders or those of them who, under the corporate charter, are accorded a vote. This is not universal. In some States provision can legally be made for election of directors by bondholders and by employees.[2] But such permission is not usually availed of. Corporations having directors elected either by the employees or by bondholders, though by no means unknown, are rare indeed.

The law holds the management to certain standards of conduct. This is the legal link between ownership and management. As separation of ownership from management becomes factually greater, or is more thoroughly accomplished by legal devices, it becomes increasingly the only reason why expectations that corporate securities are

---

[1] The law of management has been elaborately explored by text-writers almost from the beginning of corporate history. See Morawetz: "Corporations," especially Section 519; H. H. Spellman: "A Treatise on the Principles of Law Governing Corporate Directors," (New York, 1931) which is the latest collection of substantially all of the decisions on the point and which is a good and authoritative statement of the liability. See also Cook on Corporations, Sections 643–666; 14A Corpus Juris, Pages 49–243 and especially Sections 1887–1893. This chapter is merely a concise summary of the rules as they bear on the problems envisaged in this book.

[2] See for instance General Corporation Law of Delaware, Section 29 (Paragraph 2)—Certificate of Incorporation may confer on holders of bonds or debentures whether or not secured, the power to vote in the same manner as the stockholders.

worth having, can be enforced by the shareholders. If the situation ever arises that a management is, in fact, not chosen by its security holders, and has no duties towards the security holders recognized at law or enforceable through legal means, then the security holder has a piece of paper representing a capital contribution, which is valuable only as the good nature or the good faith or the economic advantage of the men actually in charge of the corporate affairs lead them to make it so. We thus are led to conclude the strength of law in this regard is the only enforceable safeguard which a security owner really has.

The law governing the duties of a management towards security owners is perhaps the only section of corporate jurisprudence which has not undergone a sustained weakening process. To some extent, as will appear, it has been cut into by statutes and charter provisions of one or another kind. But, in the main, the rules of conduct applicable to managements were developed out of the common law and not out of statute; which may perhaps account for their development along lines which seem, to the detached observer, more healthy than those of the statutes. Humanly speaking, the common law, though often laggard, is both flexible and realistic; in the last analysis judges when presented with situations which seem to demand a remedy, will, if untrammeled by statute, usually attempt to find a solution.

The three main rules of conduct which the law has developed are: (1) a decent amount of attention to business; (2) fidelity to the interests of the corporation; (3) at least reasonable business prudence.

In applying these rules a distinction must be taken which invariably irritates the layman and is today, for the first time, giving some pause for thought for lawyers. This is the ancient metaphysical squabble between loyalty to the "corporation" and loyalty to the stockholders or security holders, as the case may be. The law sums up the three rules above mentioned by saying that the management stands in a "fiduciary" capacity towards the corporation. Since the corporation is a distinct legal identity, separate and apart from stockholders, it may become necessary to determine whether a director can be honest and faithful with regard to the whole corporation at the same time that he is taking a hostile position towards an individual shareholder. And on this a dispute is at present going forward in the law which has, as yet, reached no solution.[8] The general lines of it may be indicated here.

[8] It is a theory of A.A.B. that the dispute probably could be solved by a closer analysis of the relief asked.

Where a director violates his duties towards the corporation, say by causing the corporation to enter a transaction in which the director is personally

A director, let us say, owns property, and without disclosing that he owns it, induces the corporation to buy it at an unfair price. The corporation is thereby injured; it has paid for property more than it is worth and has done so owing to the influence of one of the very men who is supposed to forward its interests. Legally, the law condemns the action of this director and permits the corporation either to set aside the transaction making him give back the price he received and returning him his property; or to make him pay the damage which his corporation suffered.[4] It is plain that there has been a damage to the corporation as such; its treasury is impoverished by the over-price paid.

Let us suppose the same director, however, owning a block of shares of stock in the corporation. He knows that the corporation has just run into an unexpected stroke of good fortune—perhaps has struck an oil well on its land, many times increasing the present value of its assets. He finds another shareholder who does not know the good news and buys his stock from him. Presently the information comes out;

---

interested, a wrong is done to the corporation—it has paid for property or services more than they are worth. This damages the shareholders by reducing the corporate assets or earnings. When the Courts say that relief can only be had on behalf of the corporation, what is really meant is that relief for all of the individuals who have suffered loss can best be worked out by giving damages to the corporation. This repletes the corporate funds which automatically accrue to the shareholders. In this view the refusal of the law to consider the complaint of an individual shareholder ought to be taken not as a denial of his right to relief, but as a device of procedure to insure that the relief reaches all stockholders ratably.

Some cases raise situations where the directors have harmed the corporation, though there is no apparent loss to the corporation itself. The ill-fated Bank of United States did this when it organized an affiliate corporation whose stock was sold to the Bank of the United States shareholders, the directors and officers of the Bank of the United States retaining for themselves a large block of the affiliates' stock for which they paid little or nothing. The affiliate was designed to exploit opportunities open to the Bank. Since these opportunities did not appear as balance sheet items it was not easy to point out any definite damage to the Bank. Obviously, however, the Bank had not made profits which otherwise it might have made. This is one of the many phases of litigation still overhanging the liquidation of the Bank of United States in New York.

[4] *Aberdeen Railway Co. v. Blaikie Brothers* (House of Lords 1854) 1 Macqueen's App. Cas. 461. The rules of law have developed from various bases but they reach about the same result. One group of cases holds that where a director is interested the transaction is voidable without regard to fairness: this is the federal rule—*Wardell v. Railroad Co.* (1880) 103 U. S. 651; *Cleveland-Cliffs Iron Co. v. Arctic Iron Co.*, 261 Federal 15. To the same effect is *Robotham v. Prudential Insurance Co.* (1903) 64 N. J. Eq. 673; New York, *Jacobson v. Brooklyn Lumber Co.* (1906) 184 N. Y. 152; California, *San Diego Railway Co. v. Pacific Beach Co.* (1896) 112 Cal. 53. Other cases hold that the transaction will be upset if in fact unfair to the corporation—which means that the Court will substitute its

the stock rises in value to accord with the changed situation, and the director has a handsome profit on the operation. Here the corporation, as such, has not suffered a single item of loss. Nothing that the director did has changed its position in the slightest; a set of shares have changed hands, but its own balance sheet is not changed. Its assets are just as great. The director has made his profit, not at the expense of the corporation, but at the expense of one of the stockholders. As in the previous case, he has done this by taking advantage of his position as one of the managers of the corporation; in the former case as director he induced the corporation to purchase, in the latter case he used for his own benefit information which came to him strictly as a member of its board of directors. Yet in the second case a majority of decisions proceed on the theory that the director is a fiduciary for the corporation only; that he has no fiduciary obligations towards the stockholder; that he deals with the stockholder at arm's length as he would any outsider; and that he is entitled to keep his profit.[5] In

---

judgment for that of the Board of Directors; *Smith v. Wells Manufacturing Co.*, 148 Indiana 333 (1807); *General Investment Co. v. Bethlehem Steel Corporation*, 87 N. J. Eq. 234. The final rule in New York seems at length to have crystallized on the theory that if the transaction is unjust it will be upset; otherwise not. See *Globe Woolen Co. v. Utica Gas & Electric Co.*, 224 N. Y. 483 (1918). Judge Cardozo writing for the Court observed, "A trustee may not cling to contracts thus won unless their terms are fair and just." This case is interesting from another point of view since a dominant stockholder was involved and the question of "control" thus came up. The Court's remark "a dominating influence may be exerted in other ways than by a vote" is illuminating.

The question of interlocking directors has given a good deal of difficulty. Here, of course, a director owes a double loyalty. If the two corporations contract (this was the situation in the *Globe Woolen Co. v. Utica Gas & Electric Co.* case and the *Cleveland-Cliffs Iron Co. v. Arctic Iron Co.* case, above) the general rule is that the eventual contract may be voidable only if in fact it is unfair. An interesting note on this point is found in Canfield and Wormser's "Cases on Private Corporations," pages 464, 465. The only conclusion that can be drawn is that in fact, courts try to evaluate the situation, upsetting the transaction if it is obviously unfair and allowing it to stand where it is fair.

[5] *Carpenter v. Danforth*, 52 Barbour (N. Y.) 581; *Board of Commissioners v. Reynolds* (1873) 44 Indiana 509; *Strong v. Repide*, 213 U. S. 419 (1908), but in this case it was held that there were special circumstances which entitled the stockholders to relief since they had virtually appointed the offending director their individual agent. Contra: See *Oliver v. Oliver*, 118 Georgia 362 (1903) squarely holding that in purchase and sale of stock a director was liable to a stockholder where he had failed to communicate important information to that stockholder.

There is real confusion of thought here. The instinct of the Courts against permitting a stockholder to sue a director for the stockholder's individual loss was probably due to a fear of many actions and to the idea that relief should be worked out through the corporation. Thus where the New York Central Railroad Co. controlled the Board of Directors of the New York & Northern Rail-

other words, the director represents only an aggregate of the interests pooled under the corporate machinery; he has no duties to any of the participants.

To laymen this distinction is neither particularly plain nor particularly healthy.[6] That director was chosen presumably to represent the

---

road Co. and wrecked the latter (See *Farmers' Loan & Trust Co. v. New York & Northern Railway Co.*, 150 N. Y. 410—1896) by routing traffic over the New York Central line, and, despite an opinion unfavorable to its conduct, succeeded in getting control of the road by foreclosing second mortgage bonds which had been purchased for the purpose, a shareholder sued to recoup his personal losses. The Courts declined to permit him to recover insisting that the relief must be worked out through the corporation, *Niles v. New York Central Railroad Co.*, 176 N. Y. 119 (1903), the Court saying "True, that plaintiff has suffered a depreciation in the value of his stock as a result of the wrong, and in this respect the injury was personal to the holders of the stock. But every stockholder has suffered from the same wrong, and, if the plaintiff can maintain an action for the recovery of the damages sustained by him, every stockholder must be accorded the same right. The injury, however, resulting from the wrong was, as we have seen, to the corporation."

On the other hand, there are a whole set of injuries which may be done to the shareholder without reference to the corporation, for which the corporation has no cause of action and needs no remedy. Falsifying accounts so that the shareholder is led to pay a higher price than the stock is worth for instance; See *Ottinger v. Bennett*, 144 N. Y. App. Div. 525, affirmed 203 N. Y. 554 (1911); *Walsham v. Stainton*, 1 De Gex J. & S. 678 (1863), though that was a close corporation.

But the majority view in the cases holds that a director, while liable for fraud like any other individual, is not under any enhanced duties to the shareholders of his own company; see *Connolly v. Shannon*, 105 N. J. Eq. 155 (1929).

The result as against the individual shareholder is that the director has no duties which are not imposed on any other individual. If he harms the corporation presumably the corporation can recover; and the corporation can be made to recover by a minority stockholder.

[6] It would seem that the Director, along with his power, acquired a good deal of information, which might be extremely valuable on occasion. This information he acquires only in his capacity as a manager of the corporation. Ethically it would seem plain that the information and any advantage from it belonged to the shareholders rather than to the director personally.

Some corporations rigidly decline to permit anyone connected with the institution to speculate in stock of the corporation, so that this information may not be unconscionably availed of. Others go to the opposite extreme, having lists of individuals to whom important information is relayed in sufficient time to permit action.

Mr. Newton D. Baker is said to have declared at one time that a director ought not to be allowed to have stock holdings in a corporation he directs; the temptations were too great. The real difficulty probably lies with a lack of adequate system of payment to the corporate directors. The director's fee does not remotely compensate for successful and faithful management. Not unnaturally directors feel they are entitled to reap some profit. If capitalizing on information is the simplest mode afforded it is beyond human nature to expect that it will not be used. The ultimate solution would seem to be an honest and fully disclosed profit sharing scheme of some kind, such as that recently adopted by the Standard Oil Company of New Jersey.

interests of everybody; and to forward and protect them. It is of no interest to the shareholder that the director may be the ablest of individuals in managing the corporate business, if the use he makes of his ability is to deprive the stockholder individually of the fruits of his management. A minority of courts in the United States adopt the view that the director may not use his position to advantage himself against the interests of any of his shareholders; if he proposes to deal with them he must disclose what he knows, so that the stockholder is at least as able to deal intelligently as is the director himself.[7] The theory is that the information on which the director is acting is not the private property of the director, but is given to him for the benefit of everyone; in a word, that the director is a fiduciary for all of the individuals concerned as well as for the mythical corporate entity as a whole. With this latter view the writers agree; but it is not generally accepted. A compromise view, held by the Federal and some other courts, is to the effect that where the circumstances are peculiar, and special facts make it inequitable for the director to act at the expense of the stockholder, he may be held liable; and this view seems likely in the end to supersede the older law on the subject.[8] Yet at present, any fair statement of the law would have to be based on the theory that the fiduciary duties of the director were limited to the corporation; and that if, by reason of his position, he can without deception but equally without disclosure take advantage of a shareholder without depleting the corporate assets, he may do so.

Business men are not so clear about this distinction. It is probably generally true that managements do take advantage of the shareholders individually, particularly along the lines of purchase and sale of stock dictated by their fiduciary knowledge of the corporation's affairs.[9]

---

[7] *Oliver v. Oliver*, 118 Georgia 362; see for a discussion of the conflicting rules 14A Corpus Juris, page 128 (1896); Fletcher's Encyclopædia of Corporations, Volume 4, Section 2464.

[8] *Strong v. Repide*, 213 U. S. 419 (1908); *Stewart v. Harris*, 69 Kansas 498.

[9] One of the writers attended a conference at which the President of a corporation was working out plans for the redemption of the preferred stock of the corporation then selling at about $60. The redemption price was $110. The writer asked whether this should not be submitted at once to the Board of Directors. The President observed that he did not feel himself at liberty to do so until he could make public announcement of the redemption plans simultaneously with the Directors' meeting. Otherwise he feared certain of his Directors would go into the market and purchase all of the stock possible at a low price for the purpose of taking advantage of the higher redemption price. This perhaps accounts for Judge Gary's famous policy with the United States Steel Directors of insisting that notice of dividends should be sent out over the stock ticker before the meeting at which the dividend had been announced was adjourned.

There is no great disagreement about the ethics of the transaction. Managements engaged in this kind of business do not enjoy having it divulged. And when business men dislike to have their methods disclosed, even after the fact, it is usually sound to conclude that their ethical judgment is against it.

As yet this ethical feeling has not (save in the minority of States referred to above) injected itself into the law; and, at the moment, the stockholder as an individual, when coping with his management, must rely on the conscience of the men involved.

Starting then from the proposition that the fiduciary duty of the mangement is limited to the corporation, i.e., that they are pledged to adhere to standards of conduct which do not deplete the assets or earnings of the company—it will appear that the law has gone to great lengths to insure a clean standard—fidelity, industry and business sense on the part of the management. In the classic case on the subject Judge Allen of New York observed that "No principle is better settled than that a person having a duty to perform for others cannot act in the same matter for his own benefit" (*Abbott v. American Hard Rubber Co.*, 33 Barbour 578) and this rule, laid down in 1861, remains no less valid today. So, whenever a director finds his own interests in conflict with that of his corporation, it is his duty to exercise no influence on the corporation in the transaction; if he does so, he places himself in an exposed position which most men do not care to assume.

In like manner, a measure of ordinary business sense is required of managers; and directors or officers not having it, or possessing it and not exercising it, are liable personally for the resulting damages. Another rule in the common law, was set out in another old case, "One who voluntarily takes the position of director, and invites confidence in that relation undertakes, like a mandatory, with those whom he represents, or for whom he acts, that he possesses at least ordinary knowledge and skill, and that he will bring them to bear in the discharge of his duties," (Earl, J. in *Hun v. Cary*, 82 N. Y. 65, 1880), and this rule likewise remains in active force.[10] It took a little time for the

[10] In 1742 an English Lord Chancellor said of corporate directors "By accepting a trust of this sort, a person is obliged to execute it with fidelity and reasonable diligence; and it is no excuse to say that they had no benefit from it, but that it was merely honorary. . . ."

"If upon inquiry before the Master, there should appear to be a supine negligence in all of them, by which a gross complicated loss happens, I will never determine that they are not all guilty." (*The Charitable Corporation v. Sutton*, 2 Atk. 400); See *Briggs v. Spaulding*, 141 U. S. 132 (1890)—Fuller, C. J.—"It is perhaps unnecessary to attempt to define with precision the degree of care and prudence which directors must exercise in the performance of their duties. The

law to get over the idea that if a man acted in good faith and had not himself tried to defraud the corporation, he could not be held liable except for "gross" negligence or inattention to duty. But that hurdle was passed a full half century ago; and the rule today is unquestioned.[11] However honest he may be, he must be reasonably careful and reasonably able. It is true that as the law can find no definite standard of ability in business matters (this quality not being as yet the subject of accurate measurement), the best it can do is to leave to a jury in each case to decide whether the manager accused of incompetence was reasonably able. But after the fact, where the result has been catastrophic, juries are more likely to err on the severe than on the lenient side in dealing with the director attacked.[12]

---

degree of care required depends upon the subject to which it is to be applied, and each case has to be determined in view of all the circumstances. They are not insurers of the fidelity of the agents whom they have appointed, who are not their agents but the agents of the corporation; and they cannot be held responsible for losses resulting from the wrongful acts or omissions of other directors or agents, unless the loss is a consequence of their own neglect of duty, either for failure to supervise the business with attention or in neglecting to use proper care in the appointment of agents." See also *Gibbons v. Anderson* (1897) 80 Fed. 345; see also "Liability of the Inactive Corporate Director" 8 Columbia Law Review 18-26.

[11] The theory that directors were liable for only "gross negligence" and not for "slight negligence" was demolished by Mr. Justice Bradley, in *Railroad Co. v. Lockwood,* 17 Wall. 357, 382 (United States Supreme Court). Mr. Justice Bradley came to the conclusion that "negligence" means simply "failure to bestow the care and skill which the situation demands"; Chief Justice Fuller amplified this by saying that the degree of care to which directors are bound is that which ordinarily prudent and diligent men would exercise under similar circumstances.

Even in those days the argument that to require diligence of directors would prevent "gentlemen of property and means" from accepting directorships was put forward as a reason why the courts should be lenient. Of course, the answer was that if gentlemen of property and means did not propose to run the business with care they were not acceptable directors; and Chief Justice Fuller in the opinion quoted above so held.

There is a corollary to the rule. If damages are to be recovered from a director for not attending to his job "the plaintiff must accept the burden of showing that the performance of the defendant's duties would have avoided loss and what loss it would have avoided" (Learned Hand, J. in *Barnes v. Andrews,* 298 Fed. 614 (1924).) An interesting compilation of the historical source of material is contained in Canfield and Wormser's "Cases on Private Corporations" (Second Edition, Indianapolis, 1925—pages 449-451).

[12] These cases invariably are judged as a result of hindsight rather than foresight which presents a real difficulty. Of course, the test whether an action taken by the Directors was fair must be made as of the time when they acted. The dangers in the situation have led to the inclusion of clauses in corporate charters attempting to relieve Directors in large measure. Pullman Company's charter for example provides:

"*Thirteenth:* No contract or other transaction entered into by the Corporation shall be affected by the fact that any director of the Corporation in any

Similarly, perhaps as a variant from the preceding one, our manager must attend to his job. This disposes summarily of the inactive gentleman who has lent his name to the board of directors with the understanding that he would not take any real part in management. Mr. George Jay Gould found himself in this unhappy position by assuming office as director of the Commonwealth Trust Co. in 1902, with the distinct understanding that he was not expected to attend meetings or take active part in the company's affairs. Reckless operations by the active men in charge led the bank to collapse a few months later; and one of the stockholders sued Mr. Gould to make good the corporate losses. The court observed that what was required of a director for the reasonable exercise of his powers was a question of fact; and directed that the Trial Court ascertain whether as a matter of fact Mr. Gould's participation in the bank's affairs lived up to "reasonable care" under the particular circumstances. This apparently left the burden on Mr. Gould to prove that he had acted as a sensible bank director.[13]

This situation raises many nice questions of conduct. It is not always easy for directors who may have large affairs to remain wholly disinterested in the transaction of the corporation's business. Of late a situation has arisen with which the law has not yet attempted to cope. Where a single individual finds himself a director of two companies whose policies conflict, he may have some difficult choices to make. In strict ethics the business community regards it his duty to

---

way is interested in, or connected with, any party to such contract or transaction, or himself is a party to such contract or transaction, provided that such contract or transaction shall be approved by a majority of the directors present at the meeting of the Board or of the Committee authorizing or confirming such contract or transaction, which majority shall consist of directors not so interested or connected. Any contract, transaction or act of the Corporation or of the Board of Directors or any Committee, which shall be ratified by a majority of a quorum of the stockholders at any annual meeting, or at any special meeting called for such purpose, shall be as valid and as binding as though ratified by every stockholder of the Corporation."

This is a Delaware charter. A similar clause appears in the charter of the United Corporation. The charter of the Dodge Brothers Inc., a Maryland corporation, went even further, providing that a Director should not be liable for secret profits even though he had failed to disclose to his fellow Directors that he was interested in the transaction on which he voted. It is highly doubtful whether these clauses of absolution have any great effect when a case comes up. Similar clauses limiting the liability of trustees have been restricted in effect by the courts.

[13] *Kavanaugh v. Gould,* 223 N. Y. 103 (1918)—apparently the case was settled out of court afterward. What had happened was that the President of the Bank sank a large portion of the Bank's funds in the U. S. Ship Building Company whose bonds subsequently became valueless.

solve the situation according to the best business sense he may have. A still nicer feeling on the subject might lead him to resign from one of the two directorates. But the latter alternative may not be to the best interest of either of his corporations, since the very existence of a representative of a conflicting interest on the board of a competing or adverse company may supply a channel of communication by which the difficulty can ultimately be solved to the best advantage of both.[14] So far as the law can be worked out from analogous situations it would seem that his position is dangerous; and indeed, men try to avoid it. From a business point of view the result is the final test; if what he does on the whole makes for a sound development of both companies, the fact that he acts for two adverse interests at the same time is rather to his credit than otherwise.[15] The one ethical point on which every one is agreed is that the adverse interest, if any, must be disclosed. There appears to be a general feeling that where a man represents adverse interests without letting that fact be known, he has created a situation so dangerous as not to be tolerated in the business community.

There is, however, a range of neutral activity in which the management of a corporation, without acting adversely to the corporation, may nevertheless benefit itself. Control of the corporate assets may and not infrequently does permit a management to do favors for its friends without injuring the corporation. Thus, they can place the

---

[14] Such a situation came up in connection with the financing of the United States Steel Corporation. There the Steel Company floated a bond issue of $100,000,000 through J. P. Morgan & Co. Fifteen of the twenty-four members of the Board of Directors were members of the bankers' syndicate which Morgan got up to handle the issue. An injunction was granted by the trial court which was reversed on appeal, the court finding that the transaction was voidable but not void; that there was full disclosure; that the interconnecting directorships helped rather than hindered the contract and that it had been ratified anyhow. See *United States Steel Corporation v. Hodge*, 64 N. J. Eq. 807 (1903).

[15] The writers feel that the charge that directors are interested on both sides of the transaction is entirely too loosely made in the financial community. A director, especially if he is an important man financially, will have a dozen or more interests all going at once. In many cases the action taken by him in one corporation is necessarily more or less adverse to the interests of other corporations in which he may be interested. Yet, in a number of cases known to the writers, the directors have scrupulously ignored their own interests. The real problems arise where the director is an important factor in the "control" of two corporations at once. There, it would be almost beyond possibility for him not to consider the possibilities of both situations before casting a vote or inducing an action. Many directors are elected frankly because they have interests in other corporations whose activities may complement those of the corporation electing him. In other words, the corporations expect to transact business with each other or in the same field, to their mutual advantage; and the very duality of interest of the director is thus turned to the advantage of both.

corporation's funds in a bank friendly to them. If the bank is safe and if the terms on which the deposit account is arranged are those prevailing in an open and competitive market, there may be no injury to the corporation. Yet the directors themselves may have profited by the transaction since they have steered business towards their friends, and may themselves expect reciprocal favors later on.[16] This kind of problem is recurrent. The business community, on a purely realistic basis, appears to take the view that if the corporation is not hurt there can be no objection. Actually, the shareholders of the corporation may be adversely affected by this favoritism. Yet such injury to the stockholders is on the very periphery of the area of legal control. Development in this direction lies almost entirely in the future.

It was observed at the outset that management normally proceeded from the election of directors by all or some of the stockholders. But the increasing numbers of these, and their unorganized dispersion, almost necessarily implies a mediary group, analogous to a political "boss." Such groups have appeared; they are called by the financial community "control." And this extra-legal, or at least separate group, so far conditions management, that it deserves a separate analysis.

[16] Most Banks have two classes of directors. One class is made up of bankers. The other consists of business men who may be able because of their business affiliations to shift accounts and banking transactions towards the Bank. These connections are openly known and are perfectly well understood. The director himself gains power. But his corporation may obtain assistance through having "friends at court" in the Bank; and the Bank is strengthened by the connection with a business enterprise. The situation has its dangers but it also has its advantages; in the business view the advantages outweigh the dangers.

CHAPTER VI: THE LEGAL POSITION
OF "CONTROL" [1]

CORPORATE MANAGEMENT is at least an institution created by the law itself. Composed of directors and ordinary officers of the corporation, it has a status which the law itself prescribes. Evolution of the corporation, however, has developed a situation in which the dominant forces within the corporation are frequently not the directors or ordinary officers, but are individuals or controlling groups who have no necessary titular place in the corporate scheme. Nevertheless, their powers, for practical purposes, may be complete. With this problem the law has only just begun to cope; it is still incomplete; and it has to be considered rather as a framework to be filled in than as a set of settled rules.

[1] This chapter is designed to deal only with the legal position of "control" as bearing on the rights of shareholders of the controlled corporation.

Legally, a number of other questions arise, especially whether an outsider can hold the "control" individually responsible for the acts of the corporation. In a good many cases, where a group of individuals, or another corporation, completely dominate the affairs of a corporation, and so use it that it becomes substantially an agency or instrumentality of the controlling group or company, outsiders such as creditors, can ignore the existence of the control and sue the corporation directly. This is done by what is known as "piercing the veil of the corporate entity." For a discussion of this branch of the law, see: H. W. Ballantine, "Parent and Subsidiary Corporations," 14 Cal. Law Review, 15 (1925); and a recent treatise by Frederick J. Powell, "Parent and Subsidiary Corporations: Liability of a Parent Corporation for the Obligations of its Subsidiary" (Chicago, 1931), especially chapters II, III, IV and V, collecting the cases. A further study involving this element is being written by Bliss Ansnes, Esq., now of the staff of the Columbia Law School, scheduled to appear in 1932, covering among other things, problems of "control," but oriented especially towards the problems of merger, consolidation, and reorganization of railways. The usual form of "control" raising this question is the control by a parent corporation of a subsidiary through the ownership of a majority of its stock.

A brief sketch of the history of the subject is itself illuminating. The problem was first presented when the device of the voting trust came into being. On the corporate books, under the then rule of law, all that appeared were the names of three or four men who held all the stock.[2] By private instrument they had created themselves trustees for others who were the real owners, but who had no standing on the corporate books, and whose only relation was with the voting trustees. The three or four voting trustees, having an absolute power to elect and re-elect the Board of Directors, necessarily were able to tell the Directors substantially what they should or should not do. As far back as the "Shepaug Voting Trust Cases"[3] in 1890, a Connecticut court faced a situation in which a voting trustee had caused the directors to make the corporation enter into a set of construction contracts out of which the individuals named as a committee to direct the voting trustee how to vote expected to make a considerable individual profit. The committee members were, it seems, interested both in the construction company and in a competing railroad line which would derive profit from a resulting traffic distribution. The court held the transaction invalid, rescinded the contracts and gave the corporation relief. This case was relatively simple because certain of the committee were also corporate directors.

Very shortly thereafter, the law was faced with a situation in which the control was quite as complete but less obvious. This was where two or three shareholders had privately agreed among themselves to vote stock as might suit their best interests.[4] Here, the court

[2] Under the present law, in many states, voting trusts are required to enter into direct relationships with the corporation; see, for instance, Section 18 of the General Corporation Law of the State of Delaware, which requires deposit of the voting trust agreement in the principal office of the State of Delaware; Section 50 of the New York Stock Corporation Law, containing a similar provision; Maryland, Laws of 1929, Chapter 581 (Code of 1924, Article 23, Title "Corporations," Section 133). This, however, represents a later development in voting trust law. At that time, voting trust control was nominally, at least, unknown to the corporation, so far as the records were concerned.

[3] *Bostwick v. Chapman; Starbuck v. Mercantile Trust Co.,* 60 Conn. 553 (1890). The individuals involved were in fact, though not technically, voting trustees—being a committee named in the trust indenture and given the right to direct the trustee to vote for officers and directors of their choice.

[4] Such agreements, of course, nearly always occur in the small or "close" corporations; and still do among large stockholders of corporations. The difficulty is that such agreements are rarely formal, with one important exception. It is not unusual for a banking house which has floated a bond issue for a corporation to exact an agreement that during the life of the bonds, one or more representatives of the banking house will be elected to the Board of Directors. For legal purposes, an informal agreement would probably be subject to the same tests as a formal document; but in practice, it is as difficult to discover an agreement of this kind as in the case of political combinations.

was faced with a dilemma. The stockholder, being the absolute owner of his stock, might vote as he pleased. An ancient rule of law used to be that courts would not inquire into the motive in so doing—the reason probably being that courts feared to follow the tremendous range of questions which might be opened up if, in every election, the motive of each shareholder had to be inquired into. And yet, where the obvious result of the vote was to create a dummy board of directors which thereupon obeyed the controlling group, and followed the interests of the "control" rather than the interests of the corporation, something had to be done about it. In 1893, Mr. Taft, then Circuit Judge, had before him a contract between a company and a shareholder from which the shareholder expected to make a profit. Mr. Taft observed:

> The vice of such contracts is not that they do not represent the real relation between the parties, but that they are contracts made by a corporation with one who exercises such an undue influence over the directors, by reason of his relation to them as principal stockholder or otherwise, that it is inequitable and unconscionable for him by such influence to secure individual profit to himself at the expense of the corporation and its other stockholders and bondholders.[5]

This is the genesis of the doctrine known in the law as "the doctrine of dominant stockholder." It presently led to still more judicial cognizance of the institution of "control."

The great issue turned first on whether stockholders could agree among themselves to dominate the management. A New York court, in 1918, held that it was

> not illegal or against public policy for two or more stockholders owning a majority of the shares of stock to unite upon a course of corporate policy or action, or upon the officers whom they will elect. An ordinary agreement among a minority in number but a majority in shares, for the purpose of obtaining control of the corporation by the election of particular persons as directors, is not illegal. Shareholders have the right to combine their interests and voting powers to secure such control of the corporation and the adoption of an adhesion by it to a specific policy and course of business.[6]

[5] *Central Trust Company v. Bridges*, 57 Fed. 753, 766 (U. S. C. C. A., 1893). For a further discussion of the doctrine of "dominant stockholder," see Berle: "Studies in the Law of Corporation Finance; Non-Voting Stock and Bankers' Control."

[6] *Manson v. Curtis*, 223 N. Y. 313 (1918), Collin, J., writing for the Court. The Court cited a number of cases which do not altogether bear out the decision, though they indicate a trend of opinion in that direction: *Venner v. Chicago City Railway Co.*, 258 Ill. 523; *Thompson v. Thompson Carnation Co.*, 279 Ill. 54;

But it was one thing to say that stockholders were entitled to take control if they could get it, and another to give them complete latitude in exercising control. The same case threw out an agreement which contemplated the election of a board of directors and of a president who was in terms to be a figurehead.[7] If officers were elected by the "control," they were supposed to be free and independent, acting at all times in the best interests of the corporation.

The obvious difficulty was that it needs no agreement to make a director who is dependent on the will of one or two shareholders into a dummy. He is a dummy not because of a contract but because of his nature. First-rate men will never be dummies; third-rate men can never be prevented from being dummies where they are in fact dependent on the will of a small group, even though no precaution is taken by contract to make them so. And the same court, in the same year, faced a different situation in which the directors had duly caused a corporation to enter into a contract with a gas and electric corporation greatly to the benefit of the latter.[8] It developed that a large stockholder in the first corporation was also heavily interested in the utility company. He had not disclosed his interest in the utility company to the directors; and, although he was a director, he had declined to vote on the transaction. Plainly, however, the other directors were in his sphere of influence. Judge Cardozo upset the contract, remarking:

Palmbaum v. Magulsky, 217 Mass. 306, and held the agreement bad because it contained a clause prescribing that the management should be "nominal" only. Agreements by shareholders to vote together are normally legal: *Zeigler v. Lake St. El. Co.*, 69 Fed. 176; *Beitman v. Steiner*, 98 Ala. 241; *Smith v. San Francisco R. Co.*, 115 Cal. 584; *Brightman v. Bates*, 175 Mass. 105; *Kreissl v. Am. Distilling Co.*, 61 N. J. Eq. 5.

[7] The precise provision in the contract was as follows:

> "That any President of the Corporation to be thereafter elected should be only a nominal head as President, and be no more active in conducting the affairs of the corporation than the then President, Abel I. Culver, had been"

and that such President would not change, alter, molest or interfere with the plaintiff's method of managing the corporate business or interfere with the plaintiff as general manager.

In addition, it was agreed that the two parties to the contract should rename three directors and that they should mutually agree on a seventh director who should be disinterested. One of the parties agreed to sell a small part of his stock to the other so that the stockholdings should be even; he declined to do this, and thereupon elected a majority of the Board of Directors.

[8] *Manson v. Curtis, supra; Globe Woolen Co. v. Utica Gas & Electric Co.* (1918) 224 N. Y. 483.

A dominating influence may be exerted in other ways than by a vote and thereby formally took cognizance of the power of "control." The only conclusion which could be drawn was that where an individual or group had in fact exercised the power of management, they must be governed by the same standards of conduct as those applied to the formal management, even though they do not assume the title. A Federal district court, remarking that

authority may rest in *pais* (fact),[9]

held that a parent corporation which has dictated a course of action by a subsidiary, is both liable as manager and may even be held liable as a principal in the transaction. A Massachusetts court set up a rule that stockholders in voting for officers or otherwise on corporate affairs must exercise their influence honestly for the best interests of the whole body of shareholders—a rule which is rather a pious wish than an enforceable standard of conduct.[10] An Alabama court phrased it by insisting that in voting for directors, good faith and fair dealing was required—the vote must be in the honest interest of the whole body of stockholders [11]—again a standard not easily enforced.

Conversely, courts attempted to prohibit arrangements binding or influencing the directors in the direction of the controlling group. Mr. Victor Morawetz' summary of the rule to the effect that a director had no right to sell his influence in the management of a corporation, or to enter into any agreement by which his official action would be influenced or "controlled," states a rule with which most courts at present agree.[12] Indeed, a director cannot even for a consideration agree to resign.[13] Conversely, shareholders having "control" may not sell offices in the corporation.[14]

[9] *New York Trust Co. v. Bermuda-Atlantic S. S. Co.* (1913) 211 Fed. 989.

[10] *Guernsey v. Cook*, 120 Mass. 501. Two stockholders wished to sell part of their stock. They found a buyer who agreed to purchase if they in turn agreed to elect him a director and treasurer at a stipulated salary. The agreement was *held* void.

[11] *Holcomb v. Forsythe*, 216 Ala. 486.

[12] Morawetz: "Corporations," Volume I, Section 519. For a further discussion of this question, see "Sterilized Corporate Directors," 64 United States Law Review, page 281; *Jackson v. Hooper*, 76 N. J. Eq. 592; *Singers-Bigger v. Young*, 166 Fed. 82.

But agreements to give representation to certain interests are valid. See: *McQuade v. Stoneham*, 230 N. Y. App. Div. 57; *Manson v. Curtis, supra; Venner v. Chicago City Railway Co.*, 258 Ill. 523.

[13] *Forbes v. McDonald*, 54 Calif. 98; *Bosworth v. Allen*, 168 N. Y. 157.

[14] *Jones v. Williams*, 139 Mo. 1. But when stockholders sell their stock, they may validly agree to elect a Board of Directors, as directed by the incoming

Yet it is past denial that these rules can only hit the outward form of a process which is in fact more subtle. "Control" cannot be prohibited by law; and perhaps it would be as well not to try. All that can be governed legally, is the result of controlling action. Indeed, in large measure, courts have come to recognize this frankly. It is, for example, not illegal to agree to a new board of directors which shall be elected when a sale of the majority of the stock takes place; or to agree with certain interests that they shall be represented on the Board, though in each case it is obvious that the new Board, or the representative, will obey the wishes of its principal in the transaction.

"Control," on further analysis, may act in any one of three ways. First, it may influence or induce the directors in exercising the power of the corporation. Second, the "control" may, acting under its own legal right, perform certain corporate acts itself—such as, voting for directors, for amendments of the charter, or to ratify past acts of the directors. Third, the "control" may perform acts which nominally have nothing to do with the corporation, but which in fact gravely affect the fate of the enterprise. For instance, "control" may be sold.

The first of these types of exercise of power is fairly governed by legal theory. The doctrine that the individuals who actually induce management action are themselves liable as managers, subjects them to the fiduciary obligations which are imposed on the directors themselves.[15]

---

purchasers, and this agreement apparently is valid. See, *Freemont v. Stone*, 42 Barbour (N. Y.) 169, holding such an agreement invalid, but the law apparently is now settled otherwise in New York, by *Barnes v. Brown*, 80 N. Y. 527, in which the sellers agreed that they would elect a new Board upon the transfer, and the agreement was upheld.

[15] The rule was stated tersely by Mr. Justice Brandeis—*Southern Pacific Railway Co. v. Bogert*, 250 U. S. 483, 492. The Southern Pacific Company there contended that it should not be held liable as "control," because it did not directly dominate the affairs of the controlled corporation, but instead, exercised the power through the medium of a subsidiary corporation, the majority of whose stock it in turn owned. Mr. Brandeis said:

> "But the doctrine by which the holders of a majority of the stock of a corporation who dominate its affairs are held to act as trustees for the minority, does not rest upon such technical distinctions. It is the effect of control of the common property held and exercised, not the particular means by which or manner in which the control is exercised, that creates the fiduciary obligations."

The nature of the obligation he earlier stated (page 487) as follows:

> "The majority has the right to control; but when it does so, it occupies a fiduciary relation toward the minority, as much so as the corporation itself or its officers and directors,"

citing *Menier v. Hooper's Telegraph Works*, L. R. 9 Ch. App. 350, 354; *Farmers' Loan & Trust Co. v. New York & Northern Railway Co.*, 150 N. Y. 410 (the

The logic of this rule is sufficient to cover all situations; since by
hypothesis, wherever the management is in fact acting at the behest
of an identifiable "control," the "control" can be dealt with exactly as
though it were a manager.[16] The device used for "control" seems to be
immaterial—whether it be voting trust, domination by a stockholder, or
possibly even domination by a creditor. The difficulty lies in the fact
that the remedy afforded to the independent shareholder is hazardous
in the extreme. One case may serve as an illustration.[17] The New York
Central acquired control of the New York and Northern Railroad; and
likewise acquired a majority of its second mortgage bonds. It then diverted traffic; made the road unable to meet its obligations, defaulted
on the second mortgage bonds; and started foreclosure proceedings.
A stockholder intervened, and setting out the fraud in the transaction,
induced the New York Court of Appeals to reverse the decree of
foreclosure. Nevertheless,[18] the New York Central actually consummated a mortgage foreclosure sale, taking over the property. Thereupon, the stockholder brought suit against the New York Central for
the damage which he individually had suffered, because the value of
his stock had been virtually wiped out. The New York court correctly,
if cruelly, held that he had no recovery. He, individually, could not sue
for the wrong. The New York & Northern, as the corporation hurt,
must do that. Yet it was obvious that the New York & Northern was by
that time merely a shell in the hands of the New York Central. It
might, perhaps, have been compelled to sue its master, the New
York Central, for relief through the legal machinery which permits a
minority stockholder to bring such suit in the name of the corporation. But the victory would have been Pyrrhic; for any damages
recovered by the New York & Northern would have been at once at
the disposition of the New York Central, which, as majority stock-

---

famous case of the wreck of the New York & Northern by the New York Central
under the leadership of Mr. Chauncey Depew).

[16] Another way of stating the rule is that all officers of the corporation are prohibited from entering into any agreement or understanding by which their official
acts would be "influenced or controlled"; see *Thomas v. Matthews*, 94 Ohio State
32.

[17] *Farmers' Loan & Trust Company v. New York & Northern Railway*, 150 N. Y.
410 (1896).

[18] It does not appear from the record precisely how the New York Central succeeded in having a mortgage foreclosure sale held while an appeal from the decree
of foreclosure was being prosecuted. Probably, the complaining stockholder was
required to put up a bond of many million dollars to protect the trustee and its
real client, the New York Central Railroad, from damages. The average stockholder is, of course, unable to do this. Such are the difficulties with which a complaining stockholder has to cope; having a legal right, and even securing a court
decision, is not the same as being able to stop the process.

holder, and as principal creditor, could dominate the situation from almost every angle.[19]

The logic of the law does not fit the second group of problems referred to above—those arising where the "control" itself performs acts within the corporation—as for instance, casting a vote. We have had occasion to look at the pious wishes of courts like Massachusetts and Alabama. But a man's honest opinion of corporate interests is likely to be severely influenced by his own interests; for his opinions are pretty much his own property. The law could and did provide that a stockholder or the holder of any corporate right could not be hired to exercise that right; that is, that he could not sell his vote. Beyond that, courts were limited to attacking the result—probably the only possible position to be taken. Normally, where a group of share-holders pass a vote, courts do not interfere with the result on the theory that their self-interest has led them to agree upon the policy which to them seems likely to be most advantageous. But where the majority is made up of a compact group in control, and especially where it can be shown that this group stands presently to benefit by a given result, the presumption disappears.[20] Different courts reason out the result differently, though the effect seems to be the same. In New York, for example, the rule is that in regard to those matters which the stockholders are bound to determine,

> they occupy a trust relation as between themselves and the corporation, and are burdened and restricted by fiduciary obligations. Where a number of stockholders constitute themselves, or are by the law constituted, the managers of corporate affairs or interests, they stand in much the same attitude towards the other or minority stockholders that the direc-

---

[19] Conceivably, the shareholder might have obtained a receiver. At this point, however, his troubles would really begin. In the first place, the receiver is chosen by the court and not infrequently the question of political influence enters into his selection. Certainly at that period in judicial history, railroads freely brought influence to bear both in the selection of judges and in determining their acts afterward. Further, the receiver can do little without money. He might raise a loan through issuing receiver's certificates. But the New York Central in this litigation had as its financial representatives, Messrs. J. P. Morgan & Co., who were almost in a position at that time to dominate the money market. The complainant's counsel, Mr. James Coolidge Carter, was the then leader of the New York Bar, and he certainly had at his command every resource which the law could provide. But he was in the position of having to out-maneuver the most powerful financial antagonists in the country, not only legally but financially; and he simply was not in a position to do it.

[20] This is sometimes stated as a rule of law, by saying that where a transaction occurs to which the corporation is a party in which the controlling majority has a private interest or profit, the courts will scrutinize the transaction with extreme care: see *Pennsylvania Canal Co. v. Brown*, 229 Fed. 444; 235 Fed. 669, 242 U. S. 646, denying a writ of certiorari.

tors sustain generally towards all stockholders, and the law requires of them the utmost good faith. ° ° ° In taking corporate action under the statute, the stockholders are acting for the corporation and for each other, and they cannot use their corporate power in bad faith or for their individual advantage or purpose.[21]

A New Jersey court, having before it a merger, in which the Public Service Corporation of New Jersey voted a majority of the stock of five subsidiaries in favor of the merger (though the merger was obviously unfavorable to the interests of the shareholders), took occasion to observe:

> The merger is, in result, an appropriation of corporate property by a majority of stockholders, by force of numbers and the grace of the statute, and, while no valid legal obligation can be interposed on that score ° ° ° the agreement calls for careful scrutiny, and the burden is on the majority to show that the consideration is fair and equitable, and judgment, as to fairness, is not to be influenced by the heavy vote of approval as it otherwise would be if the vote were independent.[22]

The net effect of these cases, and decisions like them, is, legally, to change the burden of proof. A transaction supported by a majority of votes, accomplished by technically correct procedure, is normally presumed valid. Where the majority is obviously made up of a "control," and where it can be shown that the "control" stands to make a profit out of the result, the presumption disappears.

Again the logic is fair, but the application is extremely difficult; for the burden is placed on the protesting shareholder to work out all of the ramifications of possible interest which the "control" may have. If, for example, the "control" is a utility holding company, its real in-

---

[21] *Kavanaugh v. Kavanaugh Knitting Company,* 226 N. Y. 185 (1919). Circuit Judge Sanborn, considering the Federal rule—see *Wheeler v. Abilene National Bank Building Co.,* 159 Fed. 391,—observed: "The holder of a majority of the stock of a corporation has the power, by the election of biddable directors, and by the vote of his stock, to do everything the corporation can do. His power to control and direct the action of the corporation places him in its shoes, and constitutes him the actual, if not the technical, trustee for the holders of the minority of the stock. He draws to himself and uses all the powers of the corporation. In fact, he holds an irrevocable power of attorney from the minority stockholders to manage and to sell the property of the corporation for himself and for them. Times, places and notices of meetings of the directors and of meetings of stockholders become of secondary importance, because the presence, the vote, and the protest of holders of the minority of the stock are unavailing against the will of the whole of the majority. They can act and contract regarding the corporate property, they can preserve and protect their interests in it, only through him and through the courts." See also *Jones v. Missouri Edison Electric Co.,* 144 Fed. 765, especially page 771.

[22] *Outwater v. Public Service Corporation of New Jersey,* 143 Atl. 729 (1928).

terest may lie far removed from the corporation whose affairs are being examined; and its profit may turn on the fate of some far-away property or some undisclosed transaction of which an outside shareholder is hardly likely to find trace. Still more, an apparent business exigency can always be created calling for almost any course of action. All that is needed is skill in manipulating the corporate affairs.

With the third and last group of problems, the law has hardly attempted to deal. One case (the only case squarely on the point) much commented on in New York, is still pending of decision.[23] There, a small group of dominant stockholders in the Loew Theatre chain arranged to sell their stock to interests dominated by Mr. William Fox. The price they received was nearly double the current market price of the shares. The obvious reason for the terrific premium paid by Fox was that these shares carried "control." In a word, he was buying power and not stock. A minority stockholder sued to compel the Loew "control" to pay over to the corporation the premium over market price which they had received for their stock. A motion was made to dismiss the complaint on the ground that it did not state a cause of action. The New York trial judge (Cotillo) held that the complaint was adequate, but was put to curious shifts in reaching the result. He argued that certain of the "control" were also directors in the Loew corporation. They had a chance to sell stock at a very high price. The Loew corporation had authorized but unissued stock. Therefore, said Judge Cotillo, the directors were bound to give the chance to the Loew corporation to sell its authorized but unissued stock at the high price, instead of taking advantage of it themselves. This, of course, is pure legerdemain. Fox would not have bought authorized but unissued shares; there was no opportunity to the corporation. But it apparently involved too great a leap into the dark for the New York court to say that the power going with "control" is an asset which belongs only to the corporation; and that payment for that power, if it goes anywhere,

[23] *Stanton v. Schenck*, 252 N. Y. Supp. 172. The case was subsequently tried; determined in favor of the defendant; and was on appeal at date of writing.

The law has exhibited a certain sensitiveness where sales of control are concerned. For instance, an officer agreeing to assist others to remain in control through buying stock is held to have made an illegal contract. See *Carlisle v. Smith*, 234 Fed. 159. Directors who manipulate a subsidiary corporation into purchasing stock of the parent for the purpose of keeping themselves in control may be enjoined from carrying out the scheme: *Robotham v. Prudential Life Insurance Company*, 64 N. J. Eq. 673 (1903). In general, however, all prior cases have related to the use by officers of their powers or peculiar position to assist in procuring or maintaining "control." The law has seized on the fiduciary obligation of the officer as an instrument through which it may deal with "control." But the bulk of transactions take place where there is no such technical handle and where the "control" has to be considered as a thing apart.

THE LEGAL POSITION OF "CONTROL"   217

must go into the corporate treasury. The case has not yet been finally disposed of. Yet transactions for the sale of "control" are frequent in the financial district; and they are regarded as the private business only of the individuals and groups concerned. In effect, a position of "control" is a valuable piece of property to its holder, and so regarded; its value arises out of the ability which the holder has to dominate property which in equity belongs to others. And the law thus far has been unable to deal with the situation.

There remains a situation essential in the institution of "control" but as yet untouched by judicial decision. Where "control" is in the hands of the Board of Directors because stock is widely dispersed, and because the Directors are able to control the sending out of proxies year by year, it is evident that the relationship is still more subtle. On the one hand, the Directors are bound to use their powers as fiduciaries for the stockholders—this, in their quality as Directors. On the other hand, the proxies for the shareholders will cast the stockholder's vote at the meeting, as agents for the shareholders (a proxy is merely a power of attorney after all), and in this process they are acting for the shareholders. Since the proxy or agent is in legal theory a representative of the shareholders, while in fact he is an individual under the domination of the Board of Directors, there is almost inevitably a division of interest. Legally, the proxy is an agent for the shareholder; and necessarily under a duty of fidelity to him. Factually, he is a dummy for the management, and is expected to do as he is told. Indeed, proxies are often clerks in the management, perhaps assisted by the company's attorney. The vote when mobilized really represents the will of the Directors.

It would seem that the proxy or agent for the shareholder was under the same duty as the shareholder himself to cast a vote in all honesty for the best interests of the whole. It would further seem, that if he casts the vote under the influence of an interested party— say a Director—whether in the hope of gain or in the fear of losing his job, this might invalidate the vote. Particularly, this might be true where there was not a rival proxy committee in the field so that the shareholder was unable to register a choice. But no case has gone this far; and until the issue is squarely presented it is difficult to forecast the result which the courts may reach. It should be suggested, however, that on this line the law may afford possibilities for dealing with "control" through the proxy machinery which are not as yet envisaged by corporate officers and by the Bar.

What will be the development in the field of "control"? It is not easy to prophesy. There is, here, no line of analogous logic which may easily be laid hold of to permit a common law remedy. And there is no judicial machinery which can be made to fit the extremely delicate relationships on which "control" ordinarily turns. Nor is it possible to prevent outsiders from coveting the power given by "control"; from buying it for their own use. Economically, the problem is likely to change in form as corporations gradually increase in size and as stock distribution increases, to the point where the "control" is virtually in the hands of a self-perpetuating Board of Directors like that of United States Steel or American Telephone & Telegraph Company. But with this class of control, the public up to now has little quarrel; nor does it usually thresh out such problems in the courts. It is conceivable, therefore, that the problems of "control" here discussed may become academic within another generation. It is more likely that the law will deal, blunderingly, with each situation as it comes up on its individual merits; and most likely of all, the transactions by the "control," lying outside the technical sphere of corporation action, will remain outside the normal cognizance of the law.

CHAPTER VII: CORPORATE POWERS

AS POWERS IN TRUST

THE REVIEW of corporate powers over participations and income which has preceded, sufficiently indicates the rise of a power which is virtually new in the common law. This is in substance the power of confiscation of a part of the profit stream and even of the underlying corporate assets by means of purely private processes, without any test of public welfare or necessity. As they stand, these powers are nominally uncontrolled.

It requires little analysis to make plain the fact that private property, as understood in the capitalist system, is rapidly losing its original characteristics. Unless the law stops the wide open gap which the corporate mechanism has introduced, the entire system has to be revalued.

It is entirely possible and some students of the situation are beginning to contend, that the corporate profit stream in reality no longer is private property, and that claims on it must be adjusted by some test other than that of property right. The writers are unable to say that as a matter of law, this advanced view, however justifiable as a matter of sociology, has yet attained standing. It is rather the reflexion of a movement which is likely to take form in the future, than the statement of a present ordering of affairs. Further, there is a view of the law which, if ultimately taken, would fill the breach made in the rights of private property through the corporate form. It is the purpose of this chapter to state this theory, with full realization of the possibility that private property may one day cease to be the basic concept in terms of which the courts handle problems of large scale enterprise and that the corporate mechanism may prove the very means through which such modification is brought about. Until this modification does occur, however, the lawyer is forced to think in terms of private property; and his system of law, if complete, must be prepared to cope with the problems presented in the foregoing chapters.

A study of the powers like those which have been discussed above indicates the necessity of an underlying thesis in corporation law which could be applied to each and every power in the whole corporate galaxy. Succinctly stated, the thesis appears to be that all powers granted to a corporation or to the management of a corporation, or to any group within the corporation, whether derived from statute or charter or both, are necessarily and at all times exercisable only for the ratable benefit of all the shareholders as their interest appears. That, in consequence, the *use* of the power is subject to equitable limitation when the power has been exercised to the detriment of their interest, however absolute the grant of power may be in terms, and however correct the technical exercise of it may have been. That many of the rules nominally regulating certain specific uses of corporate powers are only outgrowths of this fundamental equitable limitation, and are consequently subject to be modified, discarded, or strengthened, when necessary in order to achieve such benefit and protect such interest; and that entirely new remedies may be worked out in substitution for or supplemental to existing remedies. And that, in every case, corporate action must be twice tested: first, by the technical rules having to do with the existence and proper exercise of the power; second, by equitable rules somewhat analogous to those which apply in favor of a *cestui que trust* to the trustee's exercise of wide powers granted to him in the instrument making him a fiduciary.

The question is not academic. Its solution in the sense suggested would give greater flexibility to corporate managements in certain respects. It would permit them, when the action is actually necessary or beneficial, to do things in the doing of which they are now unduly hampered by technical rules. But where no showing of benefit can be made, and where one group within the corporation is to be sacrificed for the benefit of another, it would, equally, circumscribe the use of certain apparently absolute powers. In this latter aspect it is noteworthy that for years corporate papers and general corporation laws have multiplied powers and made them increasingly absolute; that charters have to an increasing extent included immunity clauses and waivers of "rights." It seems not to have occurred to draftsmen that, through the very nature of the corporate entity, responsibility goes with power.

Stated thus broadly, the thesis can be supported only by an examination of the law governing every corporate power. As space does not permit this, five of the principal apparently "absolute" corporate powers are here examined. Examination of all other powers would, as far as the writers' studies have gone, lead to the same result; the five chosen cover a fair cross-section of the field.

A. The power to issue stock is at all times subject to the equitable limitation that such issue must be so accomplished as to protect the ratable interest of existing and prospective shareholders.

Among the rules developed are:

(1) The rule that the incoming shareholder must make a contribution which in good conscience entitles him to participate to the extent allowed by his shares.

The requirement that stock be paid for has two distinct bases in American law. One line of thought required that stock be paid for in order to supply a fund available for the protection of creditors. With this ideology we are not at present concerned.

The second line was definitely based on the theory that every shareholder had an interest in the payment made by every other shareholder upon the issuance of his stock.[1] Mathematically this is obvious; but it would by no means necessarily follow that the law would adopt the mathematical rule. Statutory provisions requiring payment for stock in cash or property afford no ground for an assumption as to which of the two lines of thought influenced the legislature. It was left to the courts first to interpret the statutes in this sense, and later to evolve the same result in the absence of statute and even in the face of provisions apparently granting to

---

[1] A clear statement of this rule is found in *Luther v. Luther Co.*, 118 Wis. 112, 123, 94 N. W. 69, 72 (1903), the court saying: "For the purposes of the present case, it is not necessary to consider the unissued stock otherwise than as mere property, over which the powers of the directors are the same as over any other assets of the corporation, namely, to sell to whom and at such prices as to them shall seem best for the corporation and all its stockholders, in the honest exercise of the discretion and trust vested in them. Even then, however, their duties with reference thereto are fiduciary; they are bound to act *uberrima fides* for all stockholders. To dispose of or manage property of the corporation to the end and for the purpose of giving to one part of their *cestuis que trustent* a benefit and advantage over, or at the expense of, another part, is breach of such duty, especially when the directors themselves belong to the specially benefited class." This case merely carried forward the line of thought marked out by the Massachusetts court in *Hayward v. Leeson*, 176 Mass. 310, 57 N. E. 656 (1900), that the fiduciary duty extends to present and prospective shareholders, a doctrine which in turn necessarily follows from the reasoning of the court in *Gray v. Portland Bank*, 3 Mass. 363 (1807).

corporate managements wide latitude as to what and how much consideration should be required to justify the issuing of stock. As long ago as 1876[2] a requirement by statute that all stocks should be subscribed for "in good faith" caused an Illinois court to hold that stock issued for a nominal consideration was void; and in this case the thrust of the decision was primarily the protection of other shareholders.

Almost at once, however, the question arose in a new form. Statutory provisions generally provided for the issue of stock for "property received." "Property" is a word so broad as to include almost every definable fragment of value capable of being transferred. In its wide sense under these provisions stock could be issued for a note of the subscriber (negotiable instruments being certainly personal property), goodwill, contracts for services to be rendered, and a whole range of intangible elements of a similar sort. Commonly these provisions were accompanied by the requirement that the par value of stock (prior to 1912 non-par stock was unknown), if not paid in cash, must be paid in by a transfer of "property." The courts were at once faced with the problem of determining whether *all* property could be so received; and if not, of distinguishing between types of property to be accepted and types to be rejected, and giving a reason for the distinction. Greater latitude was introduced at once because, while the measure of cash is always cash, property must be appraised, and there is great leeway for difference in valuation. The judicial reasoning on both questions is by no means clear in its groundwork; but on both issues the results, particularly in retrospect, are astonishingly plain. Thus, courts declared a note of the subscriber insufficient consideration,[3] except when it was adequately

[2] *People v. Sterling Mfg. Co.*, 82 Ill. 457 (1876), where the court's difficulty arose from the fact that the voting rights granted to the common stock were equal to those granted to the preferred, though the former invested only $50,000 and the latter $950,000. Of course, whenever the words "good faith" appear, the language in and of itself imports a certain fiduciary quality. In normal business transactions, the state of mind of the opposite party is not a factor; it is enough if there is actual consent without deceit.

[3] *Alabama Nat. Bank v. Halsey*, 109 Ala. 196, 19 So. 522 (1895); *Jones Drug Co. v. Williams*, 139 Miss. 170, 103 So. 810 (1925); *Southwestern Tank Co. v. Morrow*, 115 Okla. 97, 241 Pac. 1097 (1925); *Kanaman v. Gahagan*, 111 Tex. 170, 230 S. W. 141 (1921); see (1926) 10 Minn. L. Rev. 536; (1930) 39 Yale L. J. 706, 712. But it does not follow that a note so taken is necessarily unenforceable as against the maker, which has given rise to confusion in the result of these cases. See *Pacific Trust Co. v. Dorsey*, 72 Cal. 55, 12 Pac. 49 (1887); *Goodrich v. Reynolds, Wilder & Co.*, 31 Ill. 490 (1863); *German Mercantile Co. v. Wanner*, 25 N. D. 479, 142 N. W. 463 (1913); *Schiller Piano Co. v. Hyde*, 39 S. D. 74, 162 N. W. 937 (1917).

secured,[4] in which case the security element made the note "property" within the terms of the now judicially amended statutes. This was further defined in one case where the security was worthless stock, by throwing out even a secured note of the subscriber. What happened here was that the courts permitted the corporation to issue stock against one type of risk and declined to permit its issue against other types of risk. The obvious rationale of the decisions is that the former reasonably protected both creditors and stockholders; the latter did neither.

The question subsequently came up as to patents, obviously property, as remarked by one court, but

> There is no species of property the value of which is more uncertain than letters patent which secure to the patentee the exclusive right to manufacture the patented article. From the nature of the property, the real value of patents can only be determined after the invention is introduced and in use.[5]

Accordingly the quality of the property was referred back to the question of valuation; and in respect to patents this is generally the rule. It will be noticed that this is a less rigid rule, permitting more latitude, and permitting protection of the interests actually involved. A contract for the services of an outsider to help publish a history has been held not "property" within the meaning of these statutes.[6] Goodwill—well understood as property in other fields of law, and differing from tangible property only in that it is more difficult to reduce to definite appraisal—has been treated both ways; one case disallowed it completely;[7] others left the question open for the determination of the possibility of a demonstrable valuation.[8]

[4] See the discussion in *Sohland v. Baker*, 15 Del. Ch. 431, 141 Atl. 277 (1927). For a case in which the facts and the statute forced a decision that even a secured note was not property, see *Walz v. Oser*, 93 N. J. Eq. 280, 116 Atl. 16 (1922).

[5] *Insurance Press Co. v. Montauk Co.*, 103 App. Div. 472, 475, 93 N. Y. Supp. 134, 136–137 (1905).

[6] *Stevens v. Episcopal Church History Co.*, 140 App. Div. 570, 125 N. Y. Supp. 573 (1910). But see *Van Cott v. Van Brunt*, 82 N. Y. 535 (1880), where the work done had to be paid for in stock and such stock was issued in good faith. The issue was upheld even though the labor might not be worth the par value of the stock issued.

[7] *Coleman v. Booth*, 268 Mo. 64, 186 S. W. 1021 (1916), a case weakened by the fact that the circumstances raised the issue of probable fraud.

[8] This would seem to be the rule in New York. The case of *Gamble v. Queens County Water Co.*, 123 N. Y. 91, 25 N. E. 201 (1890), raised the problem of validity of issue of stock for water mains and connections in adjacent territory. Concededly, the cost of the property was less than the amount of stock issued. Yet its strategic location might very well give it a value to the issuing corporation

Once in the valuation field, judicial modification of liberty of action becomes even more striking. Both of the principal rules on the subject—the rule that stock may be issued for property at its "absolute value," as over and against the rule that stock may be issued for property upon such valuation as reasonable business men would approve under the circumstances [9]—merely give the courts the power to correct unconscionable issues of stock, whether they use the value of the consideration on the one hand or the directors' morals on the other as the primary test. The attempt to create a rule that the judgment "in good faith" of the board of directors shall be conclusive has received only minor support in the cases; [10] but these holdings necessarily force back even further upon the board of directors the decision as to what constitutes a fair and conscionable consideration for the issue.

In determining both the nature of the property for which stock may be issued, and the valuation at which property may be taken to justify the issue of stock, courts have consistently rejected apparently absolute tests set out by statute and carried forward by corporate charters, and have submitted (as they needs must) a test for the conduct of the corporate management. In practically every case this conduct is couched in terms of "good faith," except where the situation has been carried to the point in which apparently the courts thought that no group in "good faith" could justify its action.

---

in excess of cost. The New York Court of Appeals directed a new trial, instructing that this element be taken into consideration. The prospective earning power of the development—substantially goodwill in the modern understanding of that term—would appear thus to be recognized at least in connection with tangible property.

[9] See Dodd, "Stock Watering" (1930) 57 *et seq.*, 77. Dr. Dodd comes to the conclusion that there is no sharp distinction between the rules such as is commonly assumed by the bar, the fact being that courts starting from apparently opposite premises reach pretty much similar results.

[10] Among the cases in this sense are *Troup v. Horbach*, 53 Neb. 795, 74 N. W. 326 (1898); *Holcombe v. Trenton White City Co.*, 80 N. J. Eq. 122, 82 Atl. 618 (1912); *Van Cott v. Van Brunt*, 82 N. Y. 535 (1880); *American Tube & Iron Co. v. Hays*, 165 Pa. 489, 30 Atl. 936 (1895); *Kelley Bros. v. Fletcher*, 94 Tenn. 1, 28 S. W. 1099 (1894).

The majority rule requires that a value must be set on the property taken for stock such as would be approved by prudent and sensible business men under the circumstances, exclusive of visionary or speculative hopes. See *Detroit-Kentucky Coal Co. v. Bickett Coal & Coke Co.*, 251 Fed. 542 (C. C. A. 6th, 1910); *State Trust Co. v. Turner*, 111 Iowa 664, 82 N. W. 1029 (1900) (no statute involved); *Ryerson & Son v. Peden*, 303 Ill. 171, 135 N. E. 423 (1922); *Jones v. Bowman*, 181 Ky. 722, 205 S. W. 923 (1918); *Van Cleve v. Berkey*, 143 Mo. 109, 44 S. W. 743 (1897) (result reached without benefit of statute); *Gates, Adm'r v. Tippecanoe Stone Co.*, 57 Ohio St. 60, 48 N. E. 285 (1897) (without statutory test); *Cole v. Adams*, 92 Tex. 171, 46 S. W. 790 (1898).

The moment, however, that "good faith" is introduced in the picture the fiduciary principle is raised. The phrase implies good faith towards someone, arising out of some previous relation. The argument has never been made that directors "in good faith" would believe it desirable for one group of men (not otherwise contributing) to pay one-third the contribution to the corporate capital required from everyone else.[11] Nor would such an argument find much favor in any court. The "good faith" phrase is merely a shorthand way of saying that the directors must use their power to test the quality and appraise the value of the consideration offered for stock in such a manner that creditors and shareholders will not be hurt.

This is, in rough outline, the result of the cases down to the advent of non-par stock. With the appearance of this device legal concern for the protection of the creditors largely passed away.[12] There remained the proper protection of the interests of the other shareholders; and this consideration at once became paramount. Commencing with the decision that non-par stock could not be issued for nothing, as a bonus,[13] there ensued a decision holding that such stock must be issued at approximately equal prices at the same time to all concerned.[14] This decision was subsequently modified by the Circuit Court of Appeals into a rule that where there is an inequality of consideration exacted, reasons must appear justifying the board of directors in making the distinction.[15] And the test of justification was whether the amount of consideration required was or was not sufficient to operate as a protection to the remaining shareholders.

(2) The rule that after stock has been issued additional stock may be issued only (a) at a price or under circumstances which protect the equities of the existing shareholders or (b) in accordance with a scheme which permits the existing shareholders to protect their

---

[11] Conceivably, all of the parties might agree that one set of stockholders should pay less than another. See the discussion in *Welton v. Saffery*, [1897] A. C. 299 (H. L.), in which both the majority and the dissenting Law Lords agreed that there was nothing essentially impossible in such an agreement, but differed as to whether the text of the statute involved permitted it.

[12] *Johnson v. Louisville Trust Co.*, 293 Fed. 857, 862 (C. C. A. 6th, 1923), the court saying: "The generally, if not universally, accepted theory of the purpose of such statutes is that they are intended to do away with both the 'trust fund' and 'holding out' doctrines." The court approved Mr. Cook's remark that the whole theory of stock without par value is to let the buyer beware and let the creditor beware.

[13] *Stone v. Young*, 210 App. Div. 303, 206 N. Y. Supp. 95 (1924), the court saying that the no par stock statute is "no warrant for the gratuitous distribution."

[14] *Hodgman v. Atlantic Refining Co.*, 300 Fed. 590 (D. Del. 1924).

[15] *Atlantic Refining Co. v. Hodgman*, 13 F. (2d) 781 (C. C. A. 3d, 1926).

equities by subscribing for a ratable amount of the additional stock.

When the stock is without nominal or par value, there is usually direct authority, as clear as can be derived from words, permitting the directors of a corporation to issue stock as they see fit, when they see fit, and for any price they see fit. *Prima facie* this would appear to be an absolute power. Actually, however, courts have controlled this power almost from the time its implications became apparent. And there is manifestly no difference between the issue of non-par stock and the issue of stock having par value, except that in the latter case statutes and charters prescribe a minimum issue price (the par value) payable in a more or less restricted form (cash, property of approved quality, services actually rendered). The situation is approximately the same in both cases, however, barring only this statutory restriction.

Even statutory restrictions involving a minimum price upon the issue of par value stock have been swept away by the courts under circumstances in which it appeared that the position of the corporation did not permit the issue of par value stock for its par value,[16] but in these cases the courts required that it should be made to appear both that the stockholders had assented or were protected under all the circumstances, and that creditors would not be prejudiced. Faced even with an apparent restriction, the courts evolved an equitable principle to the effect that under the circumstances indicated the restriction could be ignored.

Early in the history of corporation law the equitable principle was developed that *prima facie* the directors, despite their power to issue stock, must so issue it that the stockholders would be given an opportunity to protect their equities by subscribing to ratable shares of new stock. This rule, evolved in 1807, in *Gray v. Portland Bank*,[17] probably was misunderstood by the bar and by courts generally. An examination of the facts in that case indicates that some members, at least, of the court did not undertake to lay down a piece of judicial legislation requiring the management to offer stock promiscuously to all shareholders. The court did hold that in that particular situation the issue of additional shares without permitting a shareholder to subscribe impaired his equity.[18] Judge Sewall observed that an in-

---

[16] *Handley v. Stutz,* 139 U. S. 417 (1891).

[17] 3 Mass. 363 (1807).

[18] It is noticeable that the court was preoccupied with working out a remedy. The preëmptive right was arrived at after the court had excluded the possibility of specific relief or of restoration of the stock, and had pointed out that the accumulated dividends were in the hands of third persons, and that the plaintiff had not paid for the stock anyhow. Judge Sewall thereupon came to the conclusion: "Upon the whole, I am of the opinion that the plaintiff's loss in this case

corporation for a bank was "a trust created with certain limitations and authorities, in which the corporation is the trustee for the management of the property, and each stockholder a *cestui que trust* according to his interest and shares," [19] and he went on to say that the power to the corporation was "not a power granted to the trustee to create another interest for the benefit of other persons than those concerned in the original trust, or for their benefit in any other proportions than those determined by their subsisting shares." [20] It followed that the power to increase the number of shares did not "abolish the security of the members first engaging in it in the beneficial interest and property they might acquire in the institution." The conclusion was that plaintiff's loss could be compensated by allowing him the market value of the shares he was entitled to at the time when he demanded his certificates, and they were refused to him. The thrust of the case was that, relying on equitable principles to find the right, the court used equal latitude in evolving a remedy compensating the particular plaintiff.

This was the nascence of the so-called preëmptive right. It would by no means follow that the preëmptive right should attach in every case. But the spirit of the last century sought specific and rigid rules, and built up the doctrine here laid down into a rule that all additional shares, whenever issued and whatever the circumstances, were always subject to a preëmptive right. Necessarily the very rigidity of the rule led to equally arbitrary exceptions. Some courts declined to attach the preëmptive right to previously authorized but unissued stock (obviously fearing that the first subscriber to the share of stock would promptly claim a preëmptive right to the entire balance of the issue); [21] courts declined to extend the right to treasury stock; [22]

---

will be compensated, by allowing him the market value of the shares he was entitled to at the time he demanded his certificates, and they were refused to him" (3 Mass. at 381), the theory being that at that time the plaintiff could have bought an equivalent number of shares in the open market.

[19] 3 Mass. at 379.

[20] *Ibid.*

[21] Such was the law in New York under the case of *Archer v. Hesse*, 164 App. Div. 493, 150 N. Y. Supp. 296 (1914), but the doctrine received a rude shock in *Dunlay v. Avenue M. Garage Co.*, 253 N. Y. 274 (1930), holding that authorized but unissued shares could be issued without preëmptive right only where it is "reasonably necessary to raise money to be used in the business of the corporation rather than the expansion of such business beyond the original limits." This is the kind of distinction which satisfies a meticulous jurist and drives a business man to distraction. Must I, says he, determine at my peril whether or not the money I expect to raise by selling stock is for "the business" of my corporation or "the expansion of such business"?

[22] *Borg v. International Silver Co.*, 11 F. (2d) 147 (C. C. A. 2d, 1925).

and the mistake of a New Jersey vice-chancellor who was pressed for a quick decision over a lunch hour led to the evolution of a third exception—the issue of stock for property.[23] None of these exceptions, perhaps, need have been labored as the courts evolving them seemed to think necessary. It would have been simpler to observe that the circumstances in respect to these particular transactions required no preëmptive right to protect adequately the interests of the existing shareholders. The case finally came up of an additional issue of preferred stock which could not by any possibility affect either the amount of the equity of existing shareholders or their proportionate voting control; the New Jersey court was forced to say that in such circumstances there was no reason for the rule and it thereupon disappeared.[24] Commentators on this situation, with varying degrees of emphasis but with considerable unanimity, have been forced to two conclusions: first, that the preëmptive right, while a rough and ready protection to common shareholders in a corporation having only a simple capital structure, did not fit many situations where there was a complex capital structure, and frequently was unnecessary even in the simpler cases; second, that the so-called preëmptive right was not a right at all, but a remedy—a remedy evolved out of equitable principles—and that unless a situation appeared calling for a remedy and requiring this particular remedy the right should not necessarily be assumed to exist.[25]

The only conclusion that can be drawn from the tangled history of preëmptive rights is that the doctrine arose from an attempt to impose an equitable limitation on an apparently absolute power of directors to issue stock; that it should never have hardened into a rigid rule of law, and that it should revert to its original status as a remedy, available in equity and possibly, by transposition, at law. But it should be

[23] *Meredith v. New Jersey Zinc & Iron Co.*, 55 N. J. Eq. 211, 37 Atl. 539 (1897). See the comment in Berle, Cases and Materials in the Law of Corporation Finance 344. Prof. A. H. Frey of Duke University first pointed out publicly the exceedingly dubious basis on which this exception was based in 38 Yale L. J. 563 (1929), and in drawing an early draft of the Restatement of the Law of Business Associations, he endeavored to eliminate the exception. The massed opposition of the corporate bar, however, compelled the recognition of an exception to the preëmptive right rule where stock is issued for property in later drafts. See also *Thom v. Baltimore Trust Co.*, 158 Md. 352, 148 Atl. 234 (1930).

[24] *General Investment Co. v. Bethlehem Steel Corp.*, 88 N. J. Eq. 237, 102 Atl. 252 (1917).

[25] Drinker, "Preëmptive Right of Shareholders" (1930) 43 Harv. L. Rev. 586; Dwight, "The Right of Stockholders to New Stock" (1908) 18 Yale L. J. 101; Frey, "Shareholders' Pre-emptive Rights" (1929) 38 Yale L. J. 563; Morawetz, "Preëmptive Right of Shareholders" (1928) 42 Harv. L. Rev. 186.

considered merely as one of many possible remedies—certainly not an exclusive one and not necessarily, though usually, the best one.

In cases where, by reason of the exceptions to the preëmptive right doctrine, no such right existed, courts have had no difficulty in applying equitable remedies of other sorts and kinds. Thus a Wisconsin court enjoined the issue of shares where the sole motive was to permit the directors to augment a rapidly melting majority; [26] a federal court insisted that a sale of treasury shares must be made either at public auction or at a price which demonstrably would maintain the equities of the existing shareholders.[27] Non-par stock without a preëmptive right was held to be of such nature that the price paid for it must adequately protect the existing equities.[28] At this point, however, courts ran into a familiar business situation. Not infrequently it is worthwhile to have a substantial shareholder even though equities are sacrificed to bring him in. Such was the case in *Atlantic Refining Co. v. Hodgman*,[29] and the situation being made plain, the court sanctioned a scheme by which existing equities of approximately $16 were sacrificed to permit the entrance of the Atlantic Refining Company on payment of $8 a share in view of the added strength which that company lent to the issuing corporation through its connections, its good will, and its business tactics. So, a Delaware court sanctioned the issue of non-par stock at $25 a share, though its market value was $40 a share, where it appeared that the stock was being offered preëmptively to existing shareholders and that the offer of such stock at a low price made it possible for the corporation to obtain a higher price for shares issued to outsiders with full knowledge of the facts.

The language of the Delaware court in connection with the issue of no par stock is interesting not merely as regards the issue of such stock, but for its bearing on the general thesis of this chapter. After pointing out the absolute authority which directors had to issue such stock at any price they deemed fit, the Chancellor said:

> The statute does not impose any restraint upon the apparently unbridled power of the directors. Whether equity will, in accordance with the principles which prompt it to restrain an abuse of powers granted in absolute terms, lay its restraining hand upon the directors in case

[26] *Luther v. Luther Co.*, 118 Wis. 112, 94 N. W. 69 (1903).
[27] *Borg v. International Silver Co.*, 2 F. (2d) 910 (S. D. N. Y. 1924). The history of the handling of the sale of this block of treasury stock is peculiarly interesting as an exercise of the equitable power to protect shareholders in the case of stock freed from the so-called technical rule of preëmptive right.
[28] *Atlantic Refining Co. v. Hodgman*, 13 F. (2d) 781 (C. C. A. 3d, 1926); *Bodell v. General Gas & Elec. Corp.*, 15 Del. Ch. 119, 132 Atl. 442 (1926).
[29] *Supra* note 28.

of an abuse of this absolute power, is another question which will be presently considered and answered in the affirmative. . . . Notwithstanding the absolute character of the language in which the power to the directors is expressed, it cannot be that a court of equity is powerless in proper cases to circumscribe it. The section requires the directors to fix the consideration. It certainly would be out of all reason to say that no court could review their action in fixing it.[30]

And the court went on to point out that directors stood in the situation of fiduciaries; and while not "trustees in the strict sense of the term, yet for convenience they have been described as such."

The foregoing is by no means a complete resumé of the limitations which courts have thrown around the issue of shares despite an apparently absolute power granted to the management. Enough has been said, however, to indicate the completeness with which the apparently absolute power has been circumscribed, and the principal lines of limitation which have been thrown around this power.

B. The power to declare or withhold dividends must be so used as to tend to the benefit not only of the corporation as a whole but also of all of its shareholders to the extent that this is possible.

Among the rules worked out are:

(1) The rule that dividends must be withheld only for a business reason: private or personal motives may not be indulged.

The statute and charter alike accord to the directors the power to declare dividends, and impose no limitation on them in so doing or declining so to do except (normally) that dividends may not be declared out of capital or (in most instances) where the capital is impaired. Beyond this their power is at least nominally absolute. Despite this, where dividends were withheld in a family corporation apparently because the father of the family decided that the shareholders who were other members of the family needed discipline, a court directed the declaration of dividends.[31] In another case, where the object of withholding dividends was to depress the price of stock in the market, presumably to enable the management or its friends to buy in such stock at a lower price (a process colloquially called "freezing out"), the court again intervened.[32] Where, also, the primary object of the transaction was to accumulate a large surplus ultimately available for objects which Mr. Henry Ford believed to be to the general good of the community, an order was made requiring the declaration of

---

[30] *Bodell v. General Gas & Elec. Corp., supra* note 28, at 128–9, 132 Atl. at 446.

[31] *Channon v. Channon Co.,* 218 Ill. App. 397 (1920).

[32] *Anderson v. Dyer,* 94 Minn. 30, 101 N. W. 1061 (1904).

dividends; [83] and generally, where dividends are "unreasonably with-held" courts have interfered to control the use of the power.[84]

(2) The rule that dividends may not be withheld so as to benefit one class of stock as against another class, save where there is a business situation requiring such action.

The rule stated in the caption has been the subject of contro-versy in recent years. Wherever the corporate charter includes in its financial structure non-cumulative stock or its equivalent (participat-ing preferred stocks form such equivalent in a great majority of in-stances) it is possible, by timing the dividend declarations properly, to withhold earnings and to use these for the purpose of building up surplus which subsequently falls to junior stock. A New Jersey court and two federal courts came to the conclusion that where dividends were earned, they must be either declared or set aside as a dividend credit to the stock which would have been entitled to such dividends had they been declared annually or periodically.[85] This doctrine must be regarded as shaken if not completely overset by the recent Supreme Court ruling in *Barclay v. Wabash R. R.*[86]

That decision does not go as far as is currently supposed, since the only *ratio decidendi* is that although non-cumulative dividends, earned but unpaid, have not been paid out to the non-cumulative pre-ferred shareholders, dividends may, nevertheless, be paid to the com-mon stock provided the non-cumulative dividend for the year in question has been declared and paid. The facts are worth a glance. The Wabash Railroad had issued non-cumulative preferred stock. Over a period of years the unpaid dividends on this stock amounted to some $16,000,000. Year by year the railroad had earned sufficient profits to pay these dividends had the directors elected to declare them. The directors did not do so, but converted the earnings into surplus. Finally, having paid the dividends on the non-cumulative stock in one year, they then undertook to inaugurate dividends on the common. A bill for an injunction was brought by a preferred shareholder; and the Supreme Court reversed a decision of the Circuit Court of Appeals granting the injunction. It is to be noticed, however, that the payment of dividends to the common stock in no way cut into the $16,000,000

[83] *Dodge v. Ford Motor Co.*, 204 Mich. 459, 170 N. W. 668 (1919).
[84] See *Wilson v. American Ice Co.*, 206 Fed. 736, 745 (D. N. J. 1913). The cases are collected in (1919) 14 C. J. §1235.
[85] *Bassett v. United States Cast Iron Pipe Co.*, 75 N. J. Eq. 539, 73 Atl. 514 (1909); *Collins v. Portland Elec. Power Co.*, 12 F (2d) 671 (C. C. A. 9th, 1926); *Barclay v. Wabash Ry.*, 30 F. (2d) 260 (C. C. A. 2d, 1929).
[86] 280 U. S. 197 (1930), rev'g *Barclay v. Wabash Ry.*, 30 F. (2d) 260 (C. C. A. 2d, 1929).

accumulated by withholding dividends on the cumulative preferred; the question remains open, therefore, as to the ultimate disposition of the surplus so created. Even assuming that the *Wabash* case would permit the distribution of this surplus to the common shareholders, as by a liquidation or in subsequent dividends, the Supreme Court above and the dissenting opinion by Judge Learned Hand below both indicated that where withholding the non-cumulative dividend was unreasonable, a preferred shareholder could bring his suit to compel the declaration of the dividends; and Judge Hand intimated that a design to withhold dividends on the one class of stock so as to benefit the junior stock would in and of itself (and nothing appearing to the contrary) be evidence showing unreasonableness.

It would seem, therefore, that by way of dictum at least, even the jurisdictions following the *Wabash* case have indicated a certain measure of equitable protection where the declaration of dividends is manipulated primarily with a view toward benefiting one class of stock as against another class, leaving latitude only where a business situation exists in which it may reasonably be said that the withholding of the dividend will ultimately work for the benefit of the corporation as a whole, and that the benefit will be spread with substantial equity over the various classes.

(3) The rule that there may be no discrimination between shareholders of the same class, and no discrimination between any shareholders except as provided in the charter.

This rule, whether worked out in equity or from a "presumed interpretation" of simple contract, is fundamental.[37] It requires no discussion here save to point out that it forms one of the standard safeguards in equity against the unreasonable manipulation of dividend policy.

> *C. The power to acquire stock in other corporations must be so used as to tend to the benefit of the corporation as a whole and may not be used to forward the enterprises of the managers as individuals or to subserve special interests within or without the corporation.*

The rule above stated is probably honored more in breach than in present practice, but there seems to be no reason to doubt its existence as a matter of law. The rule has a history which may be briefly sketched here. Leaving aside special restrictive statutes of which there are many, and assuming a full kit of statutory and charter powers to purchase stock, courts have, nevertheless, limited the use of this power

[37] Cases are collected in (1919) 14 C. J. §1236.

almost from the beginning of corporate history.[38] Thus it has been insisted that where one corporation purchases stock in another, such purchase must tend to forward the "primary" purpose of the corporation; as one court said,

> whether the purchase of stock in one corporation by another is *ultra vires* or not, must depend upon the purpose for which the purchase was made, and whether such purchase was, under all the circumstances, a necessary or reasonable means of carrying out the object for which the corporation was created, or one which under the statute it might accomplish.[39]

This would mean little if the "object" of the corporation could be ascertained by merely reading the "object clauses" in its charter. It seems plain, however, that in ordinary circumstances the situation is more complicated than that. For instance, although the Prudential Insurance Company certainly had power to purchase stock, where it proposed to buy a majority of the stock of the Fidelity Trust Company which already owned a majority of stock in the Prudential Insurance Company, and the result of the scheme was to create a situation in which the management could maintain itself perpetually in office, the court observed that the purchase was not for the purpose of making an investment (which the insurance company could do) but for the purpose of carrying out a scheme of corporate control of advantage to the management individually.[40] Accordingly, the transaction was enjoined. One may suggest that a so-called investment trust which used its funds for the purchase of share not primarily for investment but for the purpose of obtaining control of a corporation to the advantage of the managers of the investment trust, would come under the same condemnation.[41]

[38] The first line of limitation was that the mere existence of a corporation implied that its powers should be exercised and its capital extended through its own officers and employees and not indirectly through another corporation operated under its control. *Anglo-American Land Co. v. Lombard*, 132 Fed. 721, 736 (C. C. A. 8th, 1904); see also *People v. Chicago Gas Trust Co.*, 130 Ill. 268, 22 N. E. 798 (1889); *Elkins v. Camden & Atlantic R. R.*, 36 N. J. Eq. 5 (1882).

[39] *Hill v. Nisbet*, 100 Ind. 341, 349 (1884).

[40] *Robotham v. Prudential Ins. Co.*, 64 N. J. Eq. 673, 53 Atl. 842 (1902).

[41] This is a problem which should be a matter of general concern. Some billions of dollars have been acquired by so-called "investment trusts." The theory is that the investment trust managers or officers can supplant the individuals in the management of funds, with advantage to the latter by reason of the peculiar experience and information which the managers have. These rapidly turn up as devices by which the investment trust managers purchase actual or partial control of a series of unrelated corporations. Dillon, Read & Co. are said by this

Purchases of stock by one corporation in another commonly fall into two categories. In the one case the purchase does not involve control of the corporation whose stock is being purchased. In this situation normally the only problem is whether the purchase can fairly be treated as an investment by the purchasing corporation. The second category involves situations in which the purchasing corporation acquires control over a second corporation by buying a controlling block of its stock. Here the naked power to purchase is an insufficient justification. Transactions have been steadily enjoined unless the corporation can justify its purchase on the ground that the controlled corporation may furnish facilities or materials in carrying out its objects, or is engaged in substantially the same enterprise, or that the purchase aids the corporation in carrying on its business.[42] Failing such justification, the purchase is frequently enjoined.

The ground of prohibition is commonly called *"ultra vires."* At first blush this seems to be a long way from equitable limitation. Yet on closer analysis it develops that the words, *"ultra vires"* are here used in a sense quite different from that usually applied to the familiar phrase. The courts do not deny the "power" to make the purchase. What they say is that by reason of the *object,* the power is not well exercised. The only conclusion which can be drawn is that the courts have weighed the power in the light of the circumstances and have in certain cases declined to sanction its *use*—a position quite different from asserting that the power does not exist. The criteria adopted in cases where the purchasing corporation is buying control of another,

---

means to have obtained representation on the board of the Rock Island Railroad. It was charged that by this means Cyrus Eaton sought to control the Youngstown Sheet & Tube Co. These are two of many instances. There is no reason why a corporation may not agree with its shareholders not to use a power which the law accords it. There is, likewise, no reason why such agreement may not be spelt out from the circumstances under which stock was sold—this would be the case in many of the so-called "investment trust" stocks.

[42] Among the many cases may be cited: *Edwards v. International Pavement Co.,* 227 Mass. 206, 116 N. E. 266 (1917); *Fernald v. Ridlon Co.,* 246 Mass. 64, 140 N. E. 421 (1923); *Dittman v. Distilling Co. of America,* 54 Atl. 570 (N. J. Ch. 1903); *State v. Missouri Pac. Ry.,* 237 Mo. 338, 141 S. W. 643 (1911); *Ellerman v. Chicago Junction Ry.,* 49 N. J. Eq. 217, 23 Atl. 287 (1891). On the other hand, see: *Sumner v. Marcy,* Fed. Cas. No. 13,609 (D. Me. 1847); *Pauly v. Coronado Beach Co.,* 56 Fed. 428 (S. D. Cal. 1893); *Savings Bank v. Meriden Agency,* 24 Conn. 159 (1855); *Hunt v. Hauser Malting Co.,* 90 Minn. 282, 96 N. W. 85 (1903); *Bank of Commerce v. Hart,* 37 Neb. 197, 55 N. W. 631 (1893); *Nebraska Shirt Co. v. Horton,* 93 N. W. 225 (Neb. 1903). In these last cases, purchase of stock by a corporation in another corporation was enjoined, the theory being that the object of such purchase did not tend to fulfil or round out the primary objects of the buying corporation.

concern management issues in practically every case—a comparison of the purposes of the two corporations, an examination of the relation between them, an assessment of the motive with which the purchase is made. Unless a reasonable connection can be found between the purposes, and an advantage to the corporation arises from linking the two concerns, and the motive has been to benefit the corporation as a whole, the purchase stands a good chance of being thrown out, although the paper authority is on its face unlimited.[43]

Manifestly, we are only on the eve of a development of law in this respect. Of recent years aggregations of capital have been collected from the public sale of stock in corporations with paper powers which are broad enough to permit them to rove the world at will. These are nominally supposed to be "investment" or "trading" corporations. Presently, however, it develops that their funds have been so invested as to give control of one or more enterprises to the bankers managing the so-called investment or trading companies. In other words, the purpose of the corporation is investment; but the power to purchase stock has been used, not for investment purposes, but to forward the control of the managing group in extraneous fields. The "investment trust" has suddenly become a holding and management company. *Quaere* if this was the "object" of the corporation.

D. The reserved power of the corporation to amend its charter must be so exercised that the result will tend to benefit the corporation as a whole, and to distribute equitably the benefit or the sacrifice, as the case may be, between all groups in the corporation as their interests may appear.

Since the power to amend the charter or by-laws is normally conferred on a majority of shareholders, we are manifestly now dealing with a somewhat different group from that heretofore considered. In principle, however, this would seem to make little difference. A power in the one case exercised by the directors is here exercised by the

---

[43] The question remains open as to whether a corporation may not have as its primary purpose the use of its funds in a fashion analogous to a "blind pool." The older corporation statutes do not readily permit a corporation so to state its objects. The modern corporation form does permit precisely this. It would seem that the avowed object of the corporate management, particularly as announced to the public in the publicity surrounding the issue of its stock, might well indicate the "primary purposes" sought for in these cases.

In any case, a studied trend toward liberality in permitting purchases of stock in other corporations is noticeable. One reason for this seems to be that no field of business is necessarily disconnected from any other field under the prevailing circumstances; it would be a courageous court which would undertake to tell the directors of an enterprise that another area of business necessarily lay outside the scope of reasonable and profitable connection with their enterprise.

majority. There is a difference in one respect. The vote of shareholders would at least tend to create a presumption that the action
taken benefited all of such shareholders.[44] The presumption is apparently subject to be rebutted either by proof that the majority is a
compact group having interests adverse to the corporation as a whole
or to the other classes,[45] or, possibly, by the mere fact of adverse interests, though this last is not so clear. Ultimately courts may take judicial
notice of the "rubber-stamp" quality of most stockholders' votes.

In general, however, power granted to a majority must be regarded as standing on the same footing with power granted to the
management. While an individual shareholder normally is not required
to exercise his voting rights in a fiduciary capacity,[46] nevertheless the
power of a majority is subject to certain equitable limitations, which
appear to differ under varying states of fact. Thus, a majority composed of scattered shareholders, not actuated by a unifying interest,
nevertheless must not so exercise its power as to "confiscate" the rights
of the minority, nor so as to oppress them unreasonably.[47] The mere
power concentrated in the hands of, say, a parent corporation, or of
the management itself, appears to be tested by rules almost exactly
like those applicable to boards of directors. Where the majority power
is in fact exercised by or through the management or its control, courts
take cognizance of that fact.[48]

[44] See Berle, "Studies in the Law of Corporation Finance" (1928) ("Non-voting
Stock and Bankers' Control"). And the presumption would certainly not exist as
regards shares which did not vote. For instance, in the case of a vote of common
stockholders reducing capital and thereby reducing the "cushion" or security behind preferred shares, which did not vote on the reduction.

[45] The language of the court in *Davis v. Louisville Gas & Elec. Co.*, 142 Atl. 654
(Del. 1928), would seem to indicate this. The court, after remarking that where
a large majority of stockholders have voted for the change there is a presumption
of good faith, then examined where stock most hurt by the amendment was held,
and pointed out that since the management itself stood to be most prejudiced by
the change, the presumption of good faith would be difficult to rebut. But the
implication is plain that the presumption is rebuttable. One may feel, however,
that in the *Davis* case the court's examination of the facts was hardly adequate.
A public utility holding company (the majority holder in the *Davis* case) might
well have an interest in sacrificing both its own and the minority interests in one
company in order thereby to forward the interests of a quite different company.

[46] *North-West Trans. Co. v. Beatty*, [1887] 12 A. C. (P. C.) 589; *Camden &
Atlantic R. R. v. Elkins*, 37 N. J. Eq. 273 (1883) (but *quaere* whether this case
would be decided in the same manner today).

[47] *New Haven & Darby R. R. v. Chapman*, 38 Conn. 56 (1871); *Perkins v.
Coffin*, 84 Conn. 275, 79 Atl. 1070 (1911); *Lonsdale Corp. v. International Mer-
cantile Marine Co.*, 101 N. J. Eq. 554, 139 Atl. 50 (1927); *Kent v. Quicksilver
Mining Co.*, 78 N. Y. 159 (1879).

[48] *Central Trust Co. v. Bridges*, 57 Fed. 753 (C. C. A. 6th, 1893); *Kavanaugh v.
Kavanaugh Knitting Co.*, 226 N. Y. 185, 123 N. E. 148 (1919). The same rule in

To the principle of equitable control of the power to amend the certificate of incorporation, there seems to be not a single exception in any American jurisdiction. The stringency of the control varies. In substantially all states it is held that no amendment of the certificate of incorporation can interfere with certain specific rights. The principal example of this is the right of a holder of cumulative preferred stock to be protected against any amendment which disturbs accrued unpaid cumulative dividends.[49] This is familiarly spoken of as a "vested right," though the phrase states a conclusion rather than an argument. As a matter of strict English, the right to have unpaid cumulative dividends charged as a preference against the net assets of the corporation, seems not different in kind from the right to receive a preference on liquidation up to a stated amount. As such, the former would seem to be as subject to amendment as the latter under a reserved power to alter "preferences." Nevertheless, practically every case on the subject prohibits an amendment modifying accrued cumulative dividends, substantially on the theory that to do so is an oppression of the preferred shareholder.

Certain states, notably New Jersey, enlarge this area of "vested rights." [50] A majority of jurisdictions appear to permit the amendment upon a showing that the business interests of the corporation, including the class of stock whose preferences are affected, require the change. Even Delaware, the loosest of jurisdictions, suggests, *obiter*, that if a showing can be made that the majority is acting adversely to the minority, primarily to benefit itself as against the minority, without corresponding compensation through business strength or otherwise to all concerned, an injunction will issue.[51] This process of advantage to one group at the expense of another is usually described under the loose and somewhat misleading term "fraud"; but the meaning seems plain.

The majority of amendments, even those cutting down specific contract rights such as the right to a fixed dividend, the right to a

---

a different form appears in *Farmers' Loan & Trust Co. v. New York & Northern Ry.*, 150 N. Y. 410, 44 N. E. 1043 (1896). See also *Outwater v. Public Serv. Corp. of New Jersey, infra* note 56.

[49] *Yoakum v. Providence Biltmore Hotel Co.*, 34 F. (2d) 533 (D. R. I. 1929); *Morris v. American Pub. Util. Co.*, 14 Del. Ch. 136, 122 Atl. 696 (1923); *Lonsdale v. International Mercantile Marine Co.*, 101 N. J. Eq. 554, 139 Atl. 50 (1927). But even this right was questioned in *Windhurst v. Central Leather Co.*, 101 N. J. Eq. 543, 138 Atl. 772 (1927), where the corporation was in such bad condition that failure to modify such rights might have been disastrous.

[50] *Lonsdale v. International Mercantile Marine Co., supra* note 49.

[51] *Davis v. Louisville Gas & Elec. Co.*, 142 Atl. 654 (Del. Ch. 1928).

fixed preference in assets, and the right to a stated participation, are commonly sustained; but no court seems to have based its decision on the naked power to amend. In every case, the equities have been examined, the business situation considered, and the reasoning upholding the amendment has been grounded on the theory that the amendment was under the peculiar circumstances equitable for all concerned. There may be dispute on the facts; there certainly is ground for believing that few dissenting stockholders are in a position to cope with the management (which commonly represents the majority) in a battle to determine where the business interests of the group as a whole really lie. But it can not be said that the results lend any color to the proposition that an absolute right to amend the charter has ever been recognized despite the plain power granted by statute and carried forward by appropriate provision in the certificate of incorporation.

> E. *The power to transfer the corporate enterprise to another enterprise by merger, exchange of stock, sale of assets or otherwise, may be exercised only in such a manner that the respective interests of the shareholders of all classes are respectively recognized and substantially protected.*

Substantially all corporate statutes today grant to corporations created under them the power to unite with other enterprises or to transfer their activities to other corporations. Various mechanisms are provided to this end. The old power to merge and consolidate is historic; the power to lease all of the assets followed; today, the result is more often obtained by a sale of the assets to the acquiring entity in return for an assumption of all liabilities and for a block of stock, which stock is in turn distributed to the stockholders of the transferring corporation. Another method is the individual transfer by shareholders of their stock in exchange for stock of the acquiring corporation, or in exchange for stock of a holding company, the process becoming complete when a controlling majority of the shares of stock has been so exchanged. Financial jargon lumps all these processes, as well as other more recondite methods, under the loose word "merger."

This power was not inherent in a corporation; historically, it could be exercised only by unanimous consent.[52] Under an early decision, the power to sell the assets, for example, did not include the power to take stock of another corporation in compensation and to force this stock down the throats of the old shareholders; but the ground of the decision was lack of power, not misuse of power.[53] The

---

[52] See Ballantine, "Corporations" (1928) 594–95.
[53] *International & Great Northern R. R. v. Bremond*, 53 Tex. 96 (1880).

modern statute, however, contains such authority, and the modern corporate charter carries forward the authority by inserting an appropriate provision suggesting corporate action by which the authority may be exercised.

In its earlier phases, it was thought that the validity of a merger was tested by power only—a decision flatly contrary to the thesis of this chapter. A federal court once remarked that where a sale of assets had taken place and the proceedings conformed to the organic law, it did not matter "that the majority were actuated by dishonorable or even corrupt motives, so long as their acts were legitimate. In equity, as at law, a fraudulent intent is not the subject of judicial cognizance unless accompanied by a wrongful act." [54] Subsequent decisions, however, have obliterated this doctrine. Thus in *Windhurst v. Central Leather Co.*,[55] the court remarked: "Every case must to some extent stand on its own facts as they are affected by the principles and doctrines of equity," a decision which sets out substantially the doctrine of the modern cases. So, where a corporation owned properties leased to a public service corporation,[56] the corporate income being the lease rental, and the lessee corporation acquired a majority of the stock of the lessor and then attempted to force a sale of the assets in consideration of preferred stock of the lessee corporation, the transaction was enjoined since in substance the rights of the stockholders of the lessor were being reduced from a first charge on the property of the lessee by way of rental, to a junior charge in the form of preferred dividends. The court made an added point of the fact that the preferred stock was redeemable in three years, so that the transaction amounted to an option by the lessee corporation to buy out its lessor. In that case, the court did not even require a showing of actual fraud; and, after conceding that the merger agreement was "in legal form," remarked, "The agreement calls for careful judicial scrutiny, and the burden is on the majority to show that the consideration is fair and equitable, and judgment, as to fairness, is not to be influenced by the heavy vote of approval, as it otherwise would be if the vote were independent." [57] The last remark was, of course occasioned by the fact that the majority stock voting in favor of the transaction was owned by the lessee cor-

[54] *Ervin v. Oregon Ry. & Nav. Co.*, 20 Fed. 577, 580 (C. C. S. D. N. Y 1844), aff'd, 27 Fed. 625 (C. C. S. D. N. Y. 1886). The quotation belies the actual decision; the court ultimately held the transaction inequitable, and charged the new corporation's assets with a lien in favor of complainants.

[55] 101 N. J. Eq. 543, 138 Atl. 772 (1927).

[56] *Outwater v. Public Serv. Corp. of New Jersey*, 103 N. J. Eq. 461, 143 Atl. 729 (1928).

[57] *Ibid.* at 464, 143 Atl. at 730.

poration which benefited from it. An earlier case, *Jones v. Missouri Edison Elec. Co.*,[58] dealt with a merger, likewise carried out in scrupulous accord with the legal requirements, in which the equities of the shareholders of one of the merging corporations were tremendously diluted. Here, the merger was an accomplished fact and the eggs could not be unscrambled. The appellate court remanded the case to the court below with instructions to work out appropriate relief, and pointed out that the directors were in substance trustees for shareholders, that a majority having control was in much the same position, and that a dilution of the equity of the minority was a breach of trust. The court took occasion to say: "The fraud or breach of trust of one who occupies a fiduciary relation while in the exercise of a lawful power is as fatal in equity to the resultant act or contract as the absence of the power." [59]

In a New York case, *Colby v. Equitable Trust Co.*,[60] the court faced a situation in which there was a dilution of the stock in one of the merging corporations. On examination, however, the business situation indicated that that corporation had been running a losing race and was facing an uninviting future. The court, taking these facts into consideration, came to the conclusion that the merger was not "so unfair and unconscionable . . . that a court of equity should interfere and prevent its consummation." There are many similar cases. Though an equitable limitation was applied in favor of *pro rata* control when additional stock was issued, the fact that proportionate control is diluted by a process of merger seems not to be persuasive.[61] Whether this is because courts today take a more realistic view and recognize *pro rata* control as not being worth very much, or because its loss is not a sufficient consideration to over-balance the business interests involved, does not appear; but few students of corporate problems will quarrel with the conclusion.

Though by no means complete, the foregoing substantially summarizes the position of courts in regard to the power to consummate a merger. In Pennsylvania an archaic rule requires that no merger be consummated unless the shareholder is given an option to be paid out in cash,[62] but generally the equitable limitation seems undisputed;

[58] 135 Fed. 153 (E. D. Mo. 1905), aff'd. 144 Fed. 765 (C. C. A. 8th, 1906).
[59] 144 Fed. at 771.
[60] 124 App. Div. 262, 108 N. Y. Supp. 978 (1908).
[61] *Mayfield v. Alton Ry., Gas & Elec. Co.*, 198 Ill. 528, 65 N. E. 100 (1902).
[62] *Laumann v. Lebanon Valley R. R.*, 30 Pa. St. 42 (1858); *Petry v. Harwood Elec. Co.*, 280 Pa. 142, 124 Atl. 302 (1924).

and even under the Pennsylvania rule it would appear that the courts involved were struggling for an automatic right compensating the shareholder for his loss of position, much as the Massachusetts court in *Gray v. Portland Bank* struggled for such a right.

It is singular that no generalization has been attempted covering equitable control over situations where statute and charter have granted apparently clear powers to act. Yet such a generalization is not difficult to find. By contract shareholders may distribute rights and participations *inter sese*. They may grant to one of their number a senior preferred position and to another a junior position; they may divide or limit rights in assets, or the immediate participations in earnings as they agree. These are individual agreements among themselves. But where powers are conceded to the management or to any group to act for the corporation as a whole, the obvious, if tacit, assumption is that these powers are intended to be used only on behalf of all. They are distinctly not intended to be granted for the purpose of benefiting one set of participants as against another. To do so would be to violate every intendment of the whole corporate situation. While incidental variations in individual participations, or in class participations may take place as the powers are used, the powers themselves are designed to forward the ends of all, not to forward the ends of some and defeat the ends of others.

In this respect, corporation law is substantially at the stage in which equity was when it faced the situation of a trustee who had been granted apparently absolute powers in his deed of trust. So far as the law and the language went, the power *was* absolute; the trustee could do as he pleased; could perhaps trade with himself irrespective of his adverse interests; could, perhaps, sell the trust assets at an unfairly low price. Yet to permit untrammeled exercise of these powers would be to violate the whole underlying concept of the trust institution. It was possible to argue under the old and rigid corporation laws that the statute had carefully laid down the lines of corporate action, and that wherever a power was not to be exercised, the statute had itself declined to grant the ability to act. Modern statutes and charters admit no such interpretation. The statute is in substance a permission to the trustees to claim any powers they choose, within very few limits. This very liberty negatives the assumption that the state through its statute has undertaken to say that all powers, however exercised, must be considered to be properly exercised. Courts, accordingly, have been substantially forced to the conclusion here expressed: namely, that no power, however absolute in terms, is absolute in fact; that every power is subject to the essential equitable limitations.

In this concept, corporation law becomes in substance a branch of the law of trusts. The rules of application are less rigorous, since the business situation demands greater flexibility than the trust situation. Probably the requirements as to motive and clean-mindedness on the part of the persons exercising the powers are substantially similar. The requirements of exactitude in apportioning or assessing ratable differences must yield to the necessary approximations which business entails. But the fundamental requirements follow similar lines.

As a conclusion, it necessarily follows that:

First: Whenever a corporate power is exercised, its existence must be ascertained and the technical correctness of its use must be checked; but its use must also be judged in relation to the existing facts with a view toward discovering whether under all the circumstances the result fairly protects the interests of the shareholders.

Second: Many of the apparently rigid rules protecting shareholders, as, for example, the rule creating pre-emptive rights, are in reality not "rights" but equitable remedies, to be used, molded, or discarded as the equities of the case may require.

Third: New remedies may be worked out and applied by the courts in each case, depending on the circumstances. For example, to protect the rights of a non-cumulative preferred stockholder whose dividend should be withheld for business purposes but should be retained for him for purposes of equitable treatment, a court might require the declaration of the dividend in stock or scrip. The powers of courts of equity in this regard are as broad as may be necessary to adjust and maintain the relative participations of the various classes of shareholders.

Fourth: No form of words inserted in a corporate charter can deny or defeat this fundamental equitable control. To do so would be to defeat the very object and nature of the corporation itself.

It is believed that this theory may fairly be derived from the existing cases; and that it may fairly be said to represent a major premise of the courts in dealing with corporation cases. But mere theory does not meet the existing situation. The difficulty is less with theory than with application. It would require an expert and courageous court to apply this theory to most of the corporate problems reaching litigation. For this reason, it cannot be reckoned on as a solution of the major difficulties in the problem. It does indicate, however, that the common law has at its command tools adequate to meet the situation in sufficiently competent hands. The indefiniteness of its application, and the extreme expense and difficulty of litigation, still leave the stockholder virtually helpless. In fact, if not in law, at the moment we are thrown back on the obvious conclusion that a stockholder's right lies in the expectation of fair dealing rather than in the ability to enforce a series of supposed legal claims.

IT FOLLOWS from all of the foregoing that the shareholder in the modern corporate situation has surrendered a set of definite rights for a set of indefinite expectations. The whole effect of the growth of powers of directors and "control" has been steadily to diminish the number of things on which a shareholder can count; the number of demands which he can make with any assurance that they must be satisfied.

The stockholder is therefore left as a matter of law with little more than the loose expectation that a group of men, under a nominal duty to run the enterprise for his benefit and that of others like him, will actually observe this obligation. In almost no particular is he in a position to demand that they do or refrain from doing any given thing. Only in extreme cases will their judgment as to what is or is not to his interest be interfered with. And they have acquired under the corporate charter power to do many things which by no possibility can be considered in his interest—whether or not they can be considered in the interest of the enterprise as a whole.

As a result, we have reached a condition in which the individual interest of the shareholder is definitely made subservient to the will of a controlling group of managers even though the capital of the enterprise is made up out of the aggregated contributions of perhaps many thousands of individuals. The legal doctrine that the judgment of the directors must prevail as to the best interests of the enterprise, is in fact tantamount to saying that in any given instance the interests of the individual may be sacrificed to the economic exigencies of the enterprise as a whole, the interpretation of the board of directors as to what constitutes an economic exigency being practically final.

This doctrine is significant. It has been employed heretofore primarily in connection with the political state. A sovereign can and does subordinate the interest of the individual to its own purpose, though its power to do so may be limited by self-denying ordinances such as are contained in the Bill of Rights in the American Constitution. The peculiarity of the corporate form is that it subjects economic rights, heretofore known as property rights, to such exigencies in a peculiar and drastic degree and for far more limited ends.

The only example of a similar subjection of the economic interests of the individual to those of a group which appears to the writers as being at all comparable, is that contained in the communist system. Though the communist ideology differs and the communist application is more drastic, the principle seems similar. As a qualification on what has been known as private property in Anglo-American law, this corporate development represents a far greater approach toward communist modalities than appears anywhere else in our system. It is an odd paradox that a corporate board of directors and a communist committee of commissars should so nearly meet in a common contention. The communist thinks of the community in terms of a state; the corporation director thinks of it in terms of an enterprise; and though this difference between the two may well lead to a radical divergence in results, it still remains true that the corporation director who would subordinate the interests of the individual stockholder to those of the group more nearly resembles the communist in mode of thought than he does the protagonist of private property.

The shift of powers from the individual to the controlling management combined with the shift from the interests of the individual to those of the group have so changed the position of the stockholder that the current conception with regard to him must be radically revised. Conceived originally as a quasi-partner, manager and entrepreneur, with definite rights in and to property used in the enterprise and to the profits of that enterprise as they accrued, he has now reached an entirely different status. He has, it is true, a series of legal rights, but these are weakened in varying degree (depending upon the completeness with which the corporation has embodied in its structure the modern devices) by the text of the contract to which the stockholder is bound. His power to participate in management has, in large measure, been lost to him, and has become vested in the "control." He becomes simply a supplier of capital on terms less definite than those customarily given or demanded by bondholders; and the thinking about his position must be qualified by the realization that he is, in a highly modified sense, not dissimilar in kind from the bondholder or lender of money. This similarity is heightened as the typical bondholder comes to rely increasingly on the success of a going enterprise and less on items of its property (whether mortgaged to him or not) which may, and usually do, become almost valueless if the enterprise is discontinued. Both the change in the form of many new bond contracts, and the evolution of receivership and reorganization practice have led to a situation in which many bondholders, though still somewhat stronger as far as their legal position is concerned, can no longer make effective the absolute rights which would appear from the lettering on their bonds or the covenants contained in the underlying indentures.

Though the law still maintains the conception of a sharp dividing line recognizing the bondholder as a lender of capital and the stockholder as a quasi-partner in the enterprise, economically the positions of the two have drawn together. Consequently, security holders may be regarded as a hierarchy of individuals all of whom have supplied capital to the enterprise, and all of whom expect a return from it. These expectations are based, *prima facie*—upon their legal rights—that is to say, upon the words of the contract. The bondholder expects his coupons regularly paid and his principal paid at maturity; the preferred stockholder, his cumulative or non-cumulative dividend, which, however, may be passed or omitted from time to time, but in the case of the former will in theory ultimately be paid out of the profits; the common stockholder expects a participation in all of the profits of the corporation, as and when they are distributed, and after the needs of the senior securities have been met.

In practice, the bondholder, for all his legal rights, has not a legal machinery enabling him in fact to collect his interest or his principal. What he has is a mechanism by which he can, through the machinery of a bondholders' committee, so affect the management of the corporation that so long as it is able, it will fulfill his expectations. But the reorganization he may compel, rarely if ever results in the literal fulfillment of the bond. The preferred stockholder has a weaker position, but he may, either by the terms of his contract, or because of certain legal rules, be able to prevent the management from accomplishing something which it desires to do—as, for instance, the payment of common dividends—until he is satisfied. The common stockholder has the weakest position of all. His expectation is based weakly on the fact that, if any common stockholder is treated well by way of distribution, all must be treated alike including himself; and that if the management is unfaithful to its trust he may, in extreme cases, either revolt, thereby changing the management, or through legal steps materially upset the situation.

Only one general protection beside the power of active revolt remains to guarantee a measure of equitable treatment to the several classes of security holders. The enterprise may need new capital. The management must, therefore, maintain a situation in which additional capital is forthcoming. We have already seen how dependent on new capital the growing quasi-public corporation is. Though the large corporations which we examined in Book I reinvested a very much larger proportion of their earnings than did other corporations, such reinvestment only furnished a quarter of their growth. The bulk of their growth came almost entirely from new issues of stock or other securities. This need for new capital sets a very definite limit on the extent to which those in control can abuse the suppliers of capital. The expectations of bondholders, preferred stockholders, or common shareholders must all be satisfied to some degree if an enterprise is to grow. How adequate a protection this is, however, depends on factors that are wholly beyond the investor's control: the state of the industry, the position of the particular corporation; and the attitude of the management.

The net result of stripping the stockholder of virtually all his power within the corporation is to throw him upon an agency lying outside the corporation itself—the public market. It is to the market that most security holders look both for an appraisal of the expectations on their security, and by curious paradox, for their chance of realizing them. A shareholder who possesses common stock in the expectation that it will ultimately pay large dividends, though in fact it is paying none, would, nevertheless, regard his expectations as reasonably satisfied if the price of his stock were to mount steadily so that he could realize his expectation by sale of his security for cash through the machinery of a public market.

Virtually all security holders have two major expectations. They expect or hope to receive distributions as and when made, which combined with an increase in market value will constitute a return on the capital they have supplied during their tenure of holding. They also expect that at some point they will be able to secure a return of that capital, either by repayment from the corporation or by the resale of their security to someone else, (commonly the latter), releasing to them personally the capital thus supplied, increased or decreased, as the case may be. In other words, they have, in a somewhat modified sense, the old expectation which a bondholder had, viz., that he would receive interest during the life of his obligation and repayment of principal at maturity, but as we pass from senior to junior securities in the hierarchy, the certainty and definiteness of period in receiving return becomes increasingly obscure; and the date of repayment, with the release of capital, ceases to turn on any act of the corporation and becomes involved in an operation of resale.

Further, the so-called "return" on capital apparently no longer needs to be current. An investor will frequently be satisfied with a current rate of cash dividends by no means compensating him for his capital, provided he thinks there will be appreciation in market value, presumably as a result of earnings not distributed. This appreciation, supplementary to the current return, would work out as a deferred return on the capital invested. This places the junior security holder still further at the mercy of the management, which can thus retain in the enterprise accumulated profits, and forces him into the public markets to which he is bound to look for realizing his appreciation.

The need for the market arises in large measure out of the difference between the time for which the capital is needed by enterprise and the period for which the investor desires to tie up his wealth. Today, the life of the investment as such is either long, or indefinite, or perhaps perpetual, and the public investor cannot accordingly count on the release of his capital through repayment. On the contrary, few investors under normal conditions buy stock in a company in the expectation that the company will be liquidated in the near future. The operation of supplying capital has a double aspect. To the enterprise, capital must be contributed for one period, or perhaps in perpetuity; but the investor's needs may require that the capital supplied by him be repayable or at least recoverable by him at some period which perhaps he cannot foresee. The gap must be supplied by the public markets. For this reason, the appraisal of the various expectations under a mechanism which permits the immediate turning of the expectations into cash, becomes a focal point in the corporate system of today.

One of the recognized functions of modern finance has been to make mobile the wealth otherwise locked up. In other words, to permit the use for ready exchange or as security for loans of properties otherwise not available for either purpose. For example, a man may be the owner of a gold mine in Alaska, worth many millions of dollars, and yet he may starve to death in the streets of Chicago, unless some method can be devised by which his properties can be used as collateral for a loan, or may be exchanged for cash or commodities. Throughout the entire history of finance there is apparent a constant struggle so to arrange matters that values anywhere may be made available anywhere. This involves two subsidiary processes: the first being a method for assigning recognized value to property; and the second, the devising of instrumentalities by which participations representing an interest in such properties may be created and made salable more or less universally. From the days when Roman Merchants arranged to discount drafts against wheat on the Alexandrian triremes plying between Egypt and the Tiber so that the wheat afloat could be readily converted into money at Rome, to the present time, when a share of stock may be turned into cash at any one of many points throughout the financial world, the demand for liquidity or mobility of value has been constantly apparent.

Mobility decreases, in general, as the size of the unit of property sought to be made liquid increases. The cheap or low priced unit moves swiftly and easily. The high priced unit moves with greater difficulty. Consequently, the first problem in securing mobility is that of dividing bodies of value into fractions. If the property is an integral whole it cannot be physically divided. Goods like wheat or sugar, which can be split into units at will and sold in small quantities, are apt to be liquid the world over; property like a factory or a mine which cannot be cut up, is rarely sold. To divide such properties into participations involves the creation of a mechanism, by which their management and integral quality is undisturbed, despite the transfer from hand to hand of relatively low-priced participations in them. This has been accomplished by the aid of the corporate device and, at least in part, accounts for the popularity of the so-called "share of stock."

With this increased liquidity have come corresponding changes in the whole property relationship. These result from two characteristics. First, the relationship of the so-called owner to the property is itself shifted. Second, the machinery by which liquidity is created—in our case the public market—itself introduces a set of elements which in and of themselves affect values.

The owner of non-liquid property is, in a sense, married to it. It contributes certain factors to his life, and enters into the fixed perspective of his landscape. If, for example, it be a small business, a farm, or a little mill, he lives with it, works at it, builds his life at least partly around it with an agent or some human mechanism devised to run it in his absence. These are the bases of association and interests, of desires, ambitions, fears, troubles. At the same time, the quality of responsibility is always present. It is never possible, save with the irresponsible, the spendthrift, or the disabled, to decline decisions. As one financier put it pithily, "If the horse lives the owner must feed it; if he lets it die he must at least bury it." Physically the owner cannot absent himself very much; he must either be on the ground, or be close enough so that by communication, (however long the range) his people on the ground can keep in touch with him. To some extent, non-liquid property immobilizes the owner by its own immobility.

At the same time such property is in turn immobilized by the necessity that it should have an attentive owner whose activity is indispensable to its continued usefulness. Only as the energy or resources of an owner are spent in feeding a horse or tilling a farm are they capable of rendering a service to him. So long, then, as a property requires a contribution by its owner in order to yield service it will tend to be immobile. For property to be easily passed from hand to hand, the individual relation of the owner to it must necessarily play little part. It cannot be dependent for its continued value upon his activity. Consequently, to translate property into liquid form the first requisite is that it demand as little as possible of its owner,—the most liquid form, cash demanding nothing save the minor necessity of safe-keeping. Thus if property is to become a liquid it must not only be separated from responsibility but it must become impersonal—like Iago's purse: " 'twas mine, 'tis his, and hath been slave to thousands."

The separation of ownership from management and control in the corporate system has performed this essential step in securing liquidity. It is the management and "control" which is now wedded to the physical property. The owner has no direct personal relation to it and no responsibility toward it. The management is more or less permanent, directing the physical property which remains intact while the participation privileges of ownership are split into innumerable parts—"shares of stock"—which glide from hand to hand, irresponsible and impersonal.

More, however, is necessary. To make property truly liquid it must be not only divisible, movable and impersonal, but some machinery must exist to assign to it an acceptable value. What is a share of stock "worth"? However fluid and impersonal a piece of property may be it will not pass in exchange or serve as a basis for credit unless some method exists by which value can be assigned to it. The liquidity of property thus turns upon the determination of a market price and the mechanism for such price-determining is the open market. Curious as it may seem, the fact appears to be that liquid property, at least under the corporate system, obtains a set of values in exchange, represented by market prices, which are not immediately dependent upon, or at least only obliquely connected with, the underlying values of the properties themselves. Two forms of property appear, one above the other, related but not the same. At the bottom is the physical property itself, still immobile, still there, still demanding the service of human beings, managers, and operators. Related to this is a set of tokens, passing from hand to hand, liquid to a degree, requiring little or no human attention, which attain an actual value in exchange or market price only in part dependent upon the underlying property. Into it enter elements which are not normally admitted to be elements in the value of the latter. The tokens may, for instance, represent in their value an appraisal of the supposed ability of the particular management interposed between the properties and the owners. A first-rate manager would not increase the values of the properties were they to be sold; but he will cause an increase in value of tokens representing that property. A poor management will have an opposite result. Speculative activity may cause the tokens to have a temporarily abnormal market price. Or the price may be the result of purely artificial manipulation.

Most striking of all, a liquid token acquires a value purely and simply because of its liquidity. Property in non-liquid form is worth one price. Property represented by liquid tokens is worth another price, which may be higher or lower as the bulk of the community demands this liquid quality or avoids it. The privilege of being able to borrow upon property at once, or the ability to turn it into cash on twenty-four hours' notice may in itself be worth paying for and thereby enhance the value of the token. Or the very sensitiveness of the value of liquid property to unreasoned surges of popular fear may detract from its value.

Finally, as the token becomes more and more separated from the physical properties through the interposition of managements and their endowment with legal power which can be traced through to the physical assets, the *"jus disponendi"* over the physical property ceases to be in the owner of the token. His real right of disposition is a right of disposition over the token itself, over any returns which may be distributed to him, and over the proceeds of its sale. He has, in fact, exchanged control for liquidity. It is thus plain that the concept of a share of stock must now be vigorously changed. No longer can it be regarded, from the point of view of the investor as primarily a *pro rata* share in an asset fund, or as a continuing, *pro rata* participation in earnings. It is true that legally, both the underlying assets (to a small extent) and the participation in earnings (*to a far greater extent*) *are supposed to measure the legal right of a shareholder* and exercise their influence over its actual value. But the factual concept must be not what these legal participations and rights are, but what expectation the shareholder has of their being fulfilled in the form of distributions and what appraisal an open market will make of these expectations. Tersely, the shareholder has a piece of paper with an open market value, and as holder of this paper may receive from time to time, at the pleasure of the management, periodic distributions. He is forced to measure his participation, not in assets, but in a market quotation; and this market quotation "discounts" or appraises the exception of distributions.

This idea does not accord either with the popular or the legal concept of a shareholder. Economically, however, it seems inescapable. A set of legal rights which can hardly be enforced, constituting claims on an economic operation from which the individual shareholder is separated by so many barriers, present an appearance of satisfactory legal relationships to the enterprise, which in practice have little significance to the individual investor. The various incidental rights—voting, preëmptive rights in new stock issues, and the like, discussed in this Book, all affect and enter into this open market appraisal. Save as they are likely to do so, they are of little interest to the investor. Economically, the various so-called "legal rights" or the economic pressures which may lead a management to do well by its stockholders, in and of themselves are merely uncertain expectations in the hands of the individual. Aggregated, interpreted by a public market, and appraised in a security exchange, they do have a concrete and measurable value; and it is to this value that the shareholder must and in fact does address himself. His thinking is colored by it; and in large measure the corporate security system is based on it.

BOOK THREE

*Property in the Stock Markets: Security
exchanges as appraisers
and liquidators* *

* This book, describing property in the stock markets, became the foundation for
the Federal legislation begun in 1933 and further developed later, regulating stock
markets and the rights of security holders which prevailed in 1968. These laws are
popularly referred to as the "Securities and Exchange Acts." They are collected in
U.S. Code Annotated, Title 15, Chapter 2A and 2B, and lawyers cite them as
15 USCA, §77 and §78. They have been further amplified by regulations of the
Securities and Exchange Commission, and by an immense number of decisions of
the United States courts and of the Securities and Exchange Commission.

The doctrines stated in Chapters Three and Four of this book indicated the
state of the common law existing in 1932, together with suggestions for its extension
by judicial decision. Though a generation has passed, they are still apposite.

The Securities and Exchange laws, the regulations and decisions thereunder,
and the practice of stock markets and bankers have carried to reality, and in some
cases have gone beyond, the conceptions expressed in this book.—A. A. B.

CHAPTER I: THE FUNCTION OF

THE PUBLIC MARKET

THE PUBLIC security markets are one of the economic enigmas of the present system; they, like other markets, have only recently become the focus for intensive economic research. Much of the purely economic analysis is not germane to our present problem; most of it has not reached a point permitting definite conclusion. The law likewise has hardly touched the central problem. All that can be done here is to indicate certain major lines of significance in connection with that body of problems surrounding the power which corporate management and control has over the economic position of the prospective or actual security holder. At this point digression must be made heavily into the realm of theory. Even the legal material, which is exceedingly scant, becomes so meaningless as hardly to justify citation, since almost without exception it ignores the central function of the public market, save to recognize its existence as a means by which securities can be converted into cash.[1]

[1] The law of the stock market (aside from brokerage questions) is scanty in the extreme. It may be summarized briefly as follows:

1. In England (and possibly in the United States) the market is a medium through which representations may be made to the public. Thus in an English case, a company listed its shares on the London Stock Exchange and in connection with its application to list made certain representations which were false. Subsequently, a purchaser bought stock on the Exchange claiming to rely on the facts stated in the listing application. He was allowed to recover. Pollock, C. B., in the Court of Exchequer remarked "all persons buying shares on the Stock Exchange must be considered as persons to whom it was contemplated that the representation would be made." See *Bedford v. Bagshaw*, (Court of Exchequer, 1859, 4 H. & M. 538, 29 L. J. Ex. 59, 157 English reprint 951).

The American cases have not gone as far; though where an American corporation announced a dividend when it had not surplus sufficient to justify such a dividend, a purchaser in the open market was allowed to recover against the directors on the ground that, through the medium of the public market, a false

Security markets are of all gradations, though the underlying idea is always the same. They are meeting places for buyers and sellers. In fact, however, they are more than this. They are points at which there are always purchasers prepared to buy at some price and sellers prepared to sell at some price. In other words, a security market contemplates that at all times there shall be stock offered for sale at a price and purchasers ready to take, at a price,

---

representation had been circulated. The stock in question was that of the American Ice Company; and it seems to have been actively traded in. See *Ottinger v. Bennett*, 144 New York App. Div. 525 (1911), affirmed 203 New York 554 (1911) by the Court of Appeals.

2. For some purposes, the Stock Exchange is recognized as a method by which stockholders' rights can be easily translated into cash. This makes it possible for courts to approve policies which might otherwise be held inequitable.

For instance, where a corporation sold its properties taking shares of stock in exchange, a suit was brought to upset the transaction on the ground that a corporation should sell for cash, otherwise it was merely putting its own property outside the control of its own officers. The Court dismissed the suit, on the particular ground that the shares of stock received in exchange for the property were actively traded in on the Stock Exchange and that accordingly they should be regarded in much the same light as cash. The Supreme Court of the United States, while approving the rule that a corporation cannot hand over its property to another corporation said "But it has been suggested that this rule, also, should be subject to the exception that, when stock which has an established market value is taken in exchange for corporation property, it should be treated as the equivalent of money, and that a sale otherwise valid should be sustained. Noyes, Incorporate Relations, Sec. 120, and cases cited. We approve the soundness of such an exception. It would be a reproach to the law to invalidate a sale otherwise valid, because not made for money, when it is made for stock which a stockholder receiving it may at once, in the New York or other general market, convert into an adequate cash consideration for what his holdings were in the corporate property." See *Geddes v. Anaconda Copper Mining Co.*, 254 U. S. 590–598 (1921). The selling corporation in that case was known as the "Alice Company," and it transferred its property for stock in the Anaconda Copper Mining Company. The Supreme Court took occasion to say "that it is, of course, public knowledge that there was a wide and general market for Anaconda stock"; presumably basing this on the quotation of that stock on the Stock Exchange.

When the Southern Pacific Railroad was compelled to divest itself of its oil properties, it did so by declaring a stock dividend to its shareholders payable in stock of a newly organized oil company which received the oil properties. In order, however, to obtain such stock, every shareholder was obliged to pay $15 per share—the dividend thus consisting, in effect, of a right to subscribe to stock of the new oil company. Venner brought a suit to enjoin, alleging that if the oil properties on segregation belonged to the shareholders of the Southern Pacific Railroad, they should not be obliged to pay in order to secure such properties. The Court approved the transaction and it was upheld on appeal by the Circuit Court of Appeals on the ground that no hardship was involved. If the Southern Pacific Railroad shareholders were unable to pay the stipulated amount to secure the stock of the new oil company, they did not lose their property inasmuch as the rights were actively traded in upon the New York Stock Exchange; and the shareholder could, by selling, make himself whole. The Court took occasion to remark "Courts may take judicial notice of facts of common knowledge and of well-known

stock which might be offered. When either of these requisites ceases to exist there is no market. The process must be continuous—i.e., the exigency must never arise when there is a buyer with no seller or a seller with no buyer.

At the lowest end of the scale are the so-called "private" or "made" markets. They are maintained by a single investment banking house which constantly draws in buyers and sellers. These commonly

---

financial conditions. We are entitled to take notice of the marketability of certain stocks and the practical equivalence of such stocks to cash; and after the action taken by directors of the Southern Company, giving to its stockholders the right to acquire one share of the new stock for each share of the Southern Company stock held by him upon payment of $15, or, if he preferred, the right to assign to another his privilege of purchase, those rights to the public knowledge have been dealt with on the New York Stock Exchange and the New York curb, and have enjoyed a broad and active market. If a stockholder did not desire to take advantage of his right to acquire the new stock, he had a market where he could realize upon his right and in effect receive his proportionate distributive share of the assets transferred to the Oil Company." *Venner v. Southern Pacific Company,* 279 Federal 832, U. S. C. C. A. 2nd Circuit, 1922.

A very similar situation came up when the Reading Railroad was ordered to divest itself of its coal properties. In this case also the plan was adopted of offering stock in the new company organized to receive the coal properties, to shareholders of the Reading Company upon payment by them of $2.00 per share. Chief Justice Taft decided that this was in substance a liquidation of the assets of the Reading Company, and in passing on one phase of the case, took occasion to say "We come now to the issue upon which these appeals were brought here. It concerns the respective rights of the common stockholders and the preferred stockholders in the assets of the Reading Company. They all, under the plan, will receive the benefit of the difference between the real value of the privilege of disposing of their distributive certificates of interest in stock in the new Coal Company, and the payment of $2, or such other sum as may be fixed, per share held by them of the Reading Company stock. Such difference has already been the subject of sale and quotation on the market in New York, and has varied from $11 to $20. This might have been expected, in view of the disparity between par of the capital stock of the Reading Coal Company and the far greater actual value of its properties. The disparity shows that while the transfer of certificates of interest in the new Coal Company stock is denominated a sale, it is only a distribution of the surplus or assets of the Reading Company to its stockholders."

3. Certain other collateral aspects have been touched upon. For instance, the fact that non-par stock sells on an Exchange at a given price is *prime facie* an argument why the similar stock should not be sold at a less price by the Corporation. See *Bodell v. General Gas & Electric Company,* 15 Del. Ch. 119 (Court of Chancery, Delaware 1926).—where stock was sold at $25 when it had a market price of $45. The Court supported the transaction, however, because the market price was in part directly due to the fact that the shareholders received "rights" to subscribe to new stock at $25. The Court observed that this was the result of skillful marketing operations by bankers and that in a sense the corporation was lifting itself by its own bootstraps.

Likewise, in *Continental Insurance Company v. United States,* 259 U. S. 156, the Court permitted the statement made by the company in listing its preferred shares on the New York Stock Exchange to be used as strong evidence of the real interpretation to be placed on the certificate of incorporation.

exist in respect of some one security only, the familiar phrase being that "the market for the security is 'made' by" such and such a house. Where a security is not listed on an Exchange, it is frequently sold under some kind of promise of liquidity; the investment banking house sponsoring the issue will usually undertake this responsibility for a time at least.

The combination of a great number of such situations gives rise to what is known as an "over the counter" market.

Then come the exchanges. Of these there are all sorts, from local exchanges in towns not situated in the financial centers to the great markets of the United States, the New York Curb and the New York Stock Exchange. The mechanics of these exchanges are well understood and it would serve no purpose to go into them here. The better established the exchange, the more scrupulously it endeavors to assure a situation in which there is a "free" market—i.e., that there shall be willing buyers at a price and willing sellers at a price, and an adequate floating supply of the security available for purchase or sale to satisfy the normal requirements of both.

The so-called "listing requirements" or assurances which the investment bankers and the corporation whose securities are listed are obliged to give were originally designed primarily for this purpose. In their embryonic stages they required merely that there be a stated minimum number of shareholders before the stock was eligible to listing. Out of these have grown the elaborate safeguards thrown around the entire open market situation by the great exchanges—requirements which tend to grow progressively more lax as one deals with the less well established or weaker security markets.

One of the primary functions of these markets has been from the first to secure ready convertibility of securities into cash—"liquidity" as financiers say—hence the requirement that there be a constant supply of both buyers and sellers. This object has never been abandoned and remains the dominant motive in the entire machinery. But liquidity is itself only a relative term. A security may be exceedingly liquid at $\frac{1}{10}$ of its worth [2] in the sense that at that price plenty of people are prepared to buy it. It may be absolutely immobile at ten times such worth, in the sense that nobody is prepared to pay that price or that for technical reasons—such as a "corner"—the holders do not propose to sell.

Some theory had to be worked out by which "liquidity" did not mean merely that someone was prepared to buy if the price were

[2] Based, say on capitalizing its current dividend or interest, and duly corrected for the possibility that such dividend or interest will increase, decrease or cease.

slaughtered beyond reason. In a word, a respectable open market appraisal, based on a compromise between the opinions of willing buyers and willing sellers was what was actually required.

Appraisal necessarily turns on information. If the open market view was to approximate a judgment of worth, it became essential that some material for such judgment should be provided. The private market in an unsystematic way contemplated this through the various disclosures of facts concerning the security by the banker "making" the market. The exchanges went to far greater lengths. All of them require a statement of certain facts if the security is listed. The more respectable exchanges, at least in recent yars, have required a certain amount of continuous disclosure by the corporation; such material permitting an appraisal. Unofficially the market has collected around itself a tremendous mechanism for collection and dissemination of facts. These are made available through the standard publications (Poor's, Moody's, Standard Statistics) and at more frequent intervals through the standard financial chronicles (as the Commercial and Financial Chronicle, Annalist, Dun's Review); and in still more transitory form, through the financial pages of the daily newspapers and certain papers which specialize in such matters (Wall Street Journal, New York Commercial); and from moment to moment, through the various ticker services. These, and many more besides, constantly pour into the market a running narrative of facts, figures, amounts, opinion, and information of all sorts, which does or is thought to bear upon values of the securities traded in. Naturally much of what is disclosed is not necessarily true; and much of what is true never reaches the market; the ideal situation—that of constant running disclosure of all information bearing on value being of course necessarily unattainable. It can, however, be approximated; and it certainly is true that the mechanisms of dissemination are so well developed that any facts bearing on values can become common market property almost instantaneously.

The obvious corollary, likewise insisted upon in all the public exchanges, and, to some extent, observed in the private markets, is that the prices agreed upon between buyers and sellers shall be recorded and be made public. If liquidity is desired, the sale price of yesterday, or of an hour ago or of ten seconds ago all become important; in fact, each of these recorded prices is a statement of the open market cash equivalent of that particular security at that particular minute. It is easy to argue, of course, that such a record is not accurate as an appraisal of worth; it may merely reflect a seller in distress and a bargain-hunting buyer. Or it may reflect a buyer who has sold short and is being squeezed by a pool operator. In theory, however, over a period of time these situations correct themselves, the running result being supposed to represent the concensus of the market stimates of the price at which the security should sell. It is not surprising, therefore, to find that exchanges penalize severely trades made by persons within their control not reported; and that, in like manner, they are apt to be agitated when an artificial movement unduly depresses or unduly raises the price of the security. They do not, however, feel called upon to interfere under the prevailing system of ethics unless there is no longer a "free" market—unless there are no longer sufficient persons having stock for sale who are willing to sell it on the one hand or so long as there are *bona fide* bids on the other. Stock exchanges provide no machinery for taking care of the latter situation, the theory being that if a security has any worth someone will be prepared to buy it, granted that it is well enough distributed and well enough known. On the only occasions in recent history when the situation actually developed in which no one was willing to bid anything for a security, (the panic market of November, 1929, and the bond market in December, 1931, and January 1932) an unofficial "bankers' consortium" itself stepped in and supplied bids; and at the same time brought influence to bear on everyone possible who might be interested to make a bid of some kind for those securities in which temporarily no buyers appeared.

In the converse situation—i.e., where buyers who have sold short wish to purchase securities to cover commitments, and some person or group to whom these unhappy persons are committed holds all the stock, the exchange machinery has developed an official procedure. Its first step is to require all of its members—necessarily brokers—to disclose their own and their customers' positions, in the security in question. This indicates who is long, and short, in what amounts, and who is withholding the supply of stock. From such information it becomes apparent whether or not there is a sufficient supply of the security to permit a "free market." If it is ascertained that a free market exists, the exchange authorities stand aside; it is no affair of theirs if the owners of stock demand an unreasonable price for it so long as there are enough of them to make it clear that the result represents a real difference between their appraisal of the security values, and the appraisals put on the stock by the would-be buyers. But if they are of opinion that in fact there is not a "free market" and that the price demanded for the stock by the holders really represents a species of blackmail levied on the unhappy "short," they may strike the stock from the exchange list, and themselves order a settlement of all outstanding commitments at a price deemed fair under the circumstances.

Both these situations are abnormal and unusual, occurring at relatively long intervals. The former implies a panic of some sort; the latter implies a "corner." Between these, however, there is, in all conscience, room enough for fluctuation. Artificial movements both unduly depressing the price of securities and unduly raising them are perfectly possible, and indeed are of frequent occurrence. But in theory these turn on the creation by the manipulators of a situation in which a considerable number of people actually believe that the stock is worth considerably more or considerably less than what might, aside from their activities, be the fair appraisal figure. And those governing the security markets have never undertaken to regulate the state of mind of the people who trade in them. So long as the result is freely arrived at, they regard their task as done.

There is another type of manipulation amounting neither to a panic nor a corner, of which an exchange may take cognizance and with which the New York Stock Exchange particularly does intend to deal. This is manipulation based on action by the company tending to obscure or prevent a true appraisal of the security. It cannot be said that the activities of the New York Exchange have gone the whole way in taking care of such situation. It is almost impossible that the Exchange should have done so, in view of the extreme difficulty of handling these questions. In as sensitive a field as stock exchange prices, the greatest caution has to be observed and the achievements of the Exchange are among the most hopeful accomplishments of our entire financial system. Year by year, the Exchange has developed a series of rules, always widening in scope, and all tending towards the elimination of a situation in which a true market appraisal cannot be obtained.

Thus, the Exchange insists on a prompt report to it of impending changes in capital structure. If a dividend has been declared, it must be immediately reported. If a stock split-up or a stock dividend is declared, this must also be reported as soon as formally determined upon. In certain other fields, less obvious but clearly important, the Exchange takes a hand. Thus, its authorities decline to permit corporations to declare regular stock dividends (for instance, 2 per cent in stock payable quarterly) unless these represent actual transfers of earnings to capital account—the theory apparently being to prevent giving to stock an apparent dividend status to which its earnings do not entitle it. Quarterly statements of earnings and balance sheets have been required since 1916 from corporations whose securities were listed subsequent to that time. Investment trusts are required not merely to do this but to disclose their actual portfolios. This trend is constantly extending; the direction is towards an increasingly full and increasingly prompt disclosure of information leading the open market to appraise the stock with full knowledge of the facts, applying for that purpose of course any standard of appraisal which the market thinks proper.

Out of this mechanism primarily designed to secure liquidity and resulting in apparatus permitting an open market appraisal through the operation of buyers and sellers and a free market, the security markets have evolved a totally different function. They serve as a yardstick by which security values are measured not only in respect of the floating supply but also in respect of tremendous immobile holdings throughout the country. This measurement of value, coupled with liquidity, makes securities available as a basis of credit or exchange; and at the same time it measures their monetary worth for these purposes. A stockholder in Akron, Ohio, may be able to borrow $80 per share on stock having a current quotation in New York for $110, despite the fact that neither he nor the lender has the slightest intention (barring accidents) of selling the stock. If the market value drops from $110 to $50 in New York, the banker feels that his loan is insecure, and he demands its repayment or its guarantee by additional security. A small business man in Peoria, Illinois, with 500 shares of stock currently quoted on the New York Exchange at 250 considers himself moderately well off, and, perhaps, obtains credit from the butcher, the baker, the candlestick maker, and the local department store, on the theory that he is well to do. The stock drops to 100, and he no longer considers himself provided for. He changes his standard of living; he neither seeks nor is accorded credit to the same extent.

There is at present no possible method of ascertaining the precise incidence of this situation; all that can be stated with certainty is that it is less far reaching than is sometimes supposed, but more pervasive than was believed up to the disturbances of November, 1929. While it is true that the values accorded to securities on the faith of market quotations are only "paper" and perhaps ought not to be invested with any great amount of significance, nevertheless they do enter into the calculations of many people, both directly and indirectly, and have in consequence a widespread effect on the economics of the community. The community has learned to count on the yardstick measures which security markets provide and to assume that securities can be converted into cash at or near the prices thus indicated.

The result is that a basis for the extension of credit has been created or at any rate amplified on the faith of the market machinery. So long as the machinery is running smoothly, and supplies real open market appraisals, this is probably safe enough. Business situations change, it is true; and sometimes rapidly; but usually less rapidly than do market prices; the fluctuations in securities, if accurately appraised, would tend to be relatively moderate, though still substantial, changing as the underlying corporate affairs change. No one pretends that the business situation changed between October 30, 1929 and November 15, 1929, with a suddenness comparable to the swift change in security prices which then occurred. It may, indeed, have changed previously; or the drop in securities may itself have caused the change. The point is that the two changes were not necessarily either synchronous or proportionate. The open market appraisals on the first date may have been too high; and the fluctuation represented the trades between inaccurate appraisals rather than an actual appraisal of an actual change in the industrial situation. Yet the effect was considerably to decrease the worth of certain securities as a basis for credit or for exchange; and the consequences approximated those which occur when a savings bank fails.

It may be said, therefore, in summary, that the security markets have acquired three functions.

The first is that of maintaining a meeting place and facilities for trading by bringing together a constant stream of buyers and sellers. This involves the maintenance of a "free market."

Second, the security markets supply a continuous measure of worth, making the securities useful as a basis of credit or exchange throughout the country at a figure based roughly on the market price in the Exchange. This involves the availability of an adequate supply of information on which to base an appraisal.

Third, these markets afford the only substantial means by which an investor can withdraw his capital either for other capital employment, or for personal expenditures. The market is the paying teller's window. The amount payable will vary daily; but there is virtually no other means of securing any amount; or, at least, all other means are dependent on the existence of the market. In brief, the market performs the function of providing liquidity for securities.

In combination these factors have so largely entered into the economic life of the country that their importance can hardly be overestimated. The economic laws of liquidity (if there be any) and even the experience in that field, have never adequately been worked out. They remain among the great and pressing problems in our economy.

CHAPTER II: FLOTATION AND

BANKERS' DISCLOSURE

FLOTATION IS THE PROCESS by which securities are introduced to the public markets.

The process commonly begins with the publication by the banker, or possibly by the corporation itself (usually, the former), of a statement commonly known as the "brokers' circular" containing a summary description of the security offered. The name arises from the fact that the statement commonly is embodied in the folder or circular, widely distributed among brokers and salesmen of securities. Simultaneously, this circular or an extract from it is commonly published in the leading financial journals.

Nominally, there is a fixed date of flotation; on that date the circular is published in the papers. In fact, preliminary drafts or advance copies are likely to have been circulated by the originating banker to persons who may be large buyers, or who may assist in selling; these are in theory confidential.

The circular may relate to securities actually in existence and ready for immediate sale. It may, however, and frequently does relate to securities yet to be issued, and in that case it states that the securities are for sale on a "when, as, and if issued basis," which means merely that orders may be now placed for such securities, payment to take place against delivery. Not infrequently also, though the securities are not in existence, they are represented by "interim receipts" which, for purposes of the public market take the place of and are traded in as though they were the actual securities in question (this is notably true in the case of bonds). Both in fact and in legal effect they are quite different; but as in ordinary course they are replaced within a relatively short period of time by the securities themselves, their effect is merely that of a device permitting the trading in a security prior to the time of its actual creation, or at all events of its actual delivery to the buyer. For market purposes they may be regarded as the security itself.[1]

The brokers' circular may be regarded as the most important document in the early market history of a security. It serves a double function. It is the prospectus designed to attract buyers for the security. It is also the bankers' disclosure of information upon which the market is expected to appraise the securities. As will appear, it is the first in a long line of informative statements on which such appraisals are made and readjusted throughout the entire career of the security in the public market. It is probably more significant than any subsequent piece of information given to the market, since it appears at a time when the corporation in question and the bankers or promoting group are probably the sole possessors of facts permitting an accurate appraisal of the security.

It becomes necessary, therefore, to consider this intermediary phase of the career of a security in the market in two aspects: first, the relation of the bankers' disclosure towards buyers who purchase the security on the faith of the representations contained in the disclosure, and second, the relation of the disclosure towards persons who do not depend upon the circular itself, but who buy in the open market on the faith of a market appraisal, which, in turn, depends on the disclosure so made.

Bankers' disclosure to a purchaser. The circular is commonly the joint product of the banker and the officials of the corporation whose securities are being sold; the banker and his attorneys commonly have the dominating voice in its draftsmanship. Customarily it is drawn in the office of the banker or his lawyers; presented for revision to the corporate officials; drafted and redrafted with a view to accuracy, putting the best foot forward, creating a proper market effect, and diminishing, so far as possible, the responsibility of everyone concerned in the flotation. There are many types of circulars; three rough classifications being discernible.

The first type may be called a full disclosure; it sets out the name of the corporation, the particular security offered for sale; the general financial plan of organization of the corporation, its capitalization, etc.; the corporate assets; a history, more or less complete, of the corporate earnings. The purpose for which the money is being raised by the sale of the issue (which is commonly extremely indefinite as, "to purchase such and such properties and for other corporate purposes");

[1] See Berle: "Cases and Materials in the Law of Corporation Finance" (Chicago 1930) pp. 737–750.

the scope of the business corporation, perhaps also its management and board of directors; the price of the shares and, most important of all, the signature of the sponsoring bankers. The completeness of the information may, of course, vary: but in this type, what is really aimed at is a picture of the corporate activities, and of the place of this financing in the general scheme.

The second type approximates the first, but it does not purport to give a full history of the corporation, confining its disclosure to the position of the security offered. This is commonly true of prior lien securities, in which the aim is merely to suggest that the security is amply protected both by assets and by earnings. The theory here is apparently that the junior issues are of little concern to the buyer—an assumption which is more or less true, but probably less true than is generally believed. Use is perhaps most frequently made of this type in connection with the railway financing, notably prior mortgage bonds, equipment trust certificates, and the like.

The third type discloses very little save the particular rights of the security offered. Use is frequently made of this short form method in floating the complex securities of public utility companies; it is not a persuasive method; and can only be employed by corporations well known to the market.

In the case of an original issue of securities of a corporation just making its bow in a public market, the first type is almost essential. The second two methods may be employed with increasing success as the corporation's record becomes familiar.

The legal rules affecting the bankers' disclosure to a purchaser divide themselves into two main categories. The first question has to do with the responsibility of the banker. The second relates to the responsibility of the corporation. Certain intricacies, which seem unwarrantable to the layman, wind themselves into the law; and have to be considered here, technical though they may appear. They may be entered most easily through the legal door of liability for false representation.

At law, one is liable for the damages occasioned by him when he has made a representation of fact which is false, and known to him to be false, and made with intent that the opposite party should act upon it, and he has so acted and has been damaged. This is sometimes known as the action of "deceit." When a bankers' circular is put out and finds its way into the hands of a purchaser who buys securities, there is no question but that it is made with intent to induce action; and that the buyer in purchasing his securities has acted on the faith of the circular. Assuming that subsequently the security declines in price, the damage is obvious and ascertainable. The banker's responsibility thus turns on the three first elements of deceit, viz., the question whether the representation was made by him; whether it was false; and whether he knew it was false. None of these questions are as simple as would at first blush appear. There is also the question as to whether the representation was one of "fact," since the law does not normally impose this responsibility in respect of a representation of "opinion" or in respect of something to be done in the future. The answers to these questions so far limit the legal responsibility for "deceit" that no intelligent lawyer normally brings this kind of action. He has an alternative, that of "rescission," of which more later. For the moment we will confine ourselves to the technical remedy of "deceit."

The first question has to do with whether the representation was made by the banker at all. Bankers have steadily attempted to avoid being in the position of making statements on their own behalf. This is the reason for the common announcement of a broker's circular with a statement, "Mr. John Smith, president of the corporation, summarizes his letter to us as follows:" the intent being to throw the circular into a form of representation to the bankers by the corporation. Were this accepted it would eliminate the responsibility of the banker, and throw all liability back on the corporation itself. To the non-legal mind a glance into the inner workings of the banking office at the time the circular is drawn up would eliminate this as a technical obstacle at once. Not infrequently the letter of the president of the corporation to the banker, summarized in the circular, is drawn by the banker on the faith of researches made by the banker, whipped into shape by his attorneys, and sent over to the president for signature. Further, it is not difficult to point to the fact that the banker has assumed a relationship to the corporation so intimate that the two can almost be regarded together in fixing the liability. To the lawyer this is not so simple. But there is a well recognized doctrine that liability for false statements cannot be avoided merely by attributing them to the authority of someone else. A banker commonly attempts still further to limit his liability by closing his circular with a statement to the effect that, anything contained in the circular, though taken from sources believed to be reliable, is not guaranteed by the banker, or perhaps is not construed as a representation by him. The classic house in this field, J. P. Morgan & Co., has steadily refused to make use of this artifice, assuming full responsibility for the statements made; and there is no doubt that this is not only the best financial practice, but that the saving or "hedge" clause used by other bankers probably fails of its effect. While the corporation may make the statement the banker assumes the responsibility of repeating it. Further, the courts probably will now take judicial notice of the fact that a banker claims to examine the corporate history and business with extreme care; that the circular commonly represents the result of his researches; and that the information is presumed to be that of the banker in any event.

The next problem from the lawyer's point of view is whether or not the representation is known to the banker to be false. This is always a difficult matter to prove, since it turns on demonstrating the state of mind of the banker. The law relieves somewhat from the rigor of this requirement, however, by considering that statements recklessly made will be treated in the same manner as statements known to be false; also, that a direct affirmation of knowledge, when no knowledge exists, amounts to a representation that the banker knew whereof he spoke—in itself a misrepresentation. The real twilight zone appears when statements are made in a broker's circular which the banker actually believes to be true, but whose falsity would have been discovered had care actually been used. The New York doctrine holds that the issuer of the circular must actually have known the representation to be false, and he is not liable where he was merely negligent; [2] and this is probably the law, though certain earlier cases at one time gave rise to a different theory. So far as technical deceit is concerned, it would seem at present that a banking firm escapes liability provided it did not know, and that a purchaser cannot set up the fact that by a use of reasonable care the banker would have known that a misrepresentation existed in the circular.

There remains the question, what is a representation of fact? As to this, courts tend to enlarge the technical English existing in the circular. A representation that "application will be made to list these securities on the New York Stock Exchange" is in terms of a statement of something to happen in the future, and would seem not to be a representation of present fact. Yet it has been held to be an ample representation both that the corporation intended to list such securities on the Exchange; and that the circumstances were such that they could be listed; [3] so that when it appeared both that no intention to list existed and that they could not perhaps be listed in any event, a purchaser was allowed to recover on the technical ground that a lie had been told him. This rule probably will be extended to other representations, such as the familiar one that "the financial structure of the company at the close of this financing will be" thus and so,

[2] *Reno v. Bull*, 226 N. Y. 546 (1919).

[3] *Seneca Wire & Mfg. Co. v. A. B. Leach & Co.*, 247 N. Y. 1 (1928).

which may fairly be considered as a representation that matters have already been so arranged that on completion of the issue, the corporate structure can be made to conform with the description given.

But the great question in this area has to do with the price. In a sense, no disclosure can be either complete or accurate, since the ponderables and imponderables all combine into one picture, not susceptible of being accurately reduced to words. The estimate of all the facts, important and unimportant, salient and obscure, demonstrable and otherwise, finds a summation in the banker's own appraisal of the worth of the security, which is, of course, embodied in the price at which he offers it. Can it be said that the price is a representation of value? If a banker offered stock at $100 per share when in fact it is worth less when appraised by the market standards of the day, has he told a lie with intent to deceive? On this the law is still in the making; but there is some reason to believe that the result will hold the banker to some accountability in this regard. The law has always made a distinction between a sale by one purporting to be an expert in the value of the thing sold and sales made by a mere outsider. Thus, if a passerby finds a jewel and offers it for sale at $1,000 as and for a diamond but claiming no special knowledge of it, he is not held to have represented that he knew its value to be that of the price asked. Tiffany doing the same thing, would probably be dealt with under a different rule; as an expert in jewels, that house offering a jewel for sale as a diamond and for a thousand dollars would impliedly at least represent that they knew it to be a diamond and that its value was in the vicinity of the price asked. A banker is an expert in securities and presumably an expert in the security offered; falling in this respect more nearly in line with Tiffany than with the bystander. In at least one recent case, it was held that a syndicate who recommended the purchase of securities at a price on the ground that they were a good investment had in fact made a representation that the securities were fairly worth the price and this proving to be false, gave rise to an action by the buyer.

The trouble with this situation of course rests in the difficulty of defining "worth." In a violent market, securities may be appraised by the general public as worth far more than the sounder judgment of a quieter time would apprehend. Is the banker to be guided by the standards of a speculatively crazed market, and make the appraisal accordingly? Or must he abide by the better economic judgment of his own expert staff? If the former, he may be consciously taking advantage of a temporary phase of folly; if the latter, he will find that a security offered by him at $100 is traded in tomorrow at $150, outsiders having reaped the profit which his own sense of ethics declined to permit him to accept. It is not an easy question; and in any case it is difficult to see that the courts will hold the banker to a higher standard than that prevalent in the market at the time. From the strictly financial point of view it may be to the advantage of a banker to offer securities at a time when in the estimation of the banker the market will pay an unduly high price for them. The risk of a subsequent decline in market price, with distress to his customers and impaired prestige to the banker may be more than outweighed by the profits to be made in the process. The self-interest of the banker cannot be depended upon to fill the gap which the law fails to close.

We have been dealing with the action of deceit. Unfortunately, this action is made immensely difficult by the requirement that the plaintiff prove the conscious knowledge of falsity on the part of the banker. The law has developed an easier remedy, known as "rescission," the theory of which is that the buyer of securities tenders them back to the seller, and requests his money back. This action, taken over from equity procedure, offers a considerably wider latitude. It is subject to one important limitation: the person seeking redress by this means must actually have bought from the person who circulated the false statement about the security, whereas an action of deceit can be brought by a buyer at second, third or fourth hand. The purchaser must have bought his securities upon a misrepresentation of fact; and on discovering misrepresentation he must demand that the bargain be called off, and both parties restored to their previous situation. It is enough that the representation be false even though innocent. Further, the concealment or non-disclosure of a material fact permits this action; and it is enough that the buyer acted on the faith of a misrepresentation even though it were made by someone other than the party from whom he bought.

Here the fact that the banker honestly believed a statement which turns out to be untrue is no protection; and this is particularly true where with reasonable care he might have ascertained its falsity. Likewise, the far more difficult situation where there has been failure to disclose a fact material to the situation, affords ground for relief. While the force of this liability is limited, inasmuch as only the sale by banker to customer can be rescinded, and not sales made in open market after the banker has initially disposed of the securities, nevertheless the liability, even so limited, is a fairly effective check against actual misstatement though not against concealment. In general, it is the opinion of the writers, that statements contained in brokers' circulars are generally the truth. It is by no means so clear that they are the whole truth and the thing not stated may be far more important than the thing stated.

Certain difficult areas furnish a twilight zone. In one instance which never reached the courts the stock in a corporation was sold and a history of earnings was given. The earnings were good for the previous few years; and for the first six months of the year in which the stock was offered for sale. The fact was not disclosed that in the subsequent six months a catastrophic decline in earnings had taken place. The year was not finished, so that a purchaser would not normally have expected disclosure of this fact. Yet the promoting group must have realized that the picture created by the circular was entirely false. The truth was stated; but the determinative factor of the situation did not appear. Is this a non-disclosure sufficient to permit rescission?

Again, the use of "averages" may serve to conceal a latent vice of first importance. A statement, for example, "that the average income during the past five years" has been thus and so, may hide the fact that the income is steadily declining. Accountants of the highest grade decline to certify to such statements; first-rate bankers do not, in general, countenance them. The use of this method has materially declined of recent years largely due to the influence of accountants; but enough of it still goes on to raise questions whether the law should not itself take cognizance of the situation.

It is fairly supposable that the right of rescission will be extended to cover cases in which there has been manipulation of this sort. It is not so clear that they will form misrepresentations sufficient to justify the bare action of deceit. But it must always be remembered that in dealing with rescission a plaintiff can make a case by pointing out that the seller painted a picture sufficient to create a mistaken belief in the mind of the buyer as to the nature of the thing he bought. The increasing liberality of courts in handling the right of rescission forms the principal legal stimulus to accuracy in connection with bankers' disclosures.

Accountancy plays a great part at this point, as indeed, elsewhere, in the market career of the security. It is customary for bankers to rely in making up their statements on accountants' reports, and the integrity of the accountant and the soundness of his method are the greatest single safeguard to the public investor and to the market in general. But rules of accounting are not as yet fully recognized rules of law in this field; though it is obvious that the development of the law of corporation finance makes almost mandatory the legal sanction of good accounting practice. In fact, the failure of the law to recognize accounting standards is probably due to the lack of agreement among accountants; but year by year certain tenets are forged out, finding their way into the body of standard accounting practice and ultimately into the law.[4] In general the problem revolves around securing a method of accounting which will give an approximately accurate picture of the situation.

Taking as one illustration, the possibility of accounting manipulation for the purpose of showing an abnormal profit, we find among the the methods which can be used the following:

(1) Manipulation of inventory values: Either there may be a gradually increasing inflation of inventory values up to the date of flotation, (which implies long standing plan to deceive) or there may be an inflation of value just at the time of flotation. The latter is more common, and is the less easily hidden, since a sudden increase in ratio of profit tends to put the examiner on guard. The above is well known.

(2) On reorganization, where revaluation of property shows large increases in plant and buildings subject to depreciation, it is not uncommon to cite the profits of prior years, charged with depreciation only on the low values preceding reorganization, although after reorganization the depreciation charge must be increased to provide for the increased value placed on the assets.

The best practice among public accountants is to revise prior years' accounts to show depreciation as it would have been if the revised asset values had been the basis, or, if the client refuses this, to state that the prior years' profits have been charged with depreciation on the basis of the former valuation of assets. Unfortunately this is not always done, the lower rate being allowed to stand without comment.

(3) Issue of bonds together with stock or stock warrants, the bonds bearing a low rate of interest and the stock or warrants being used to enable the seller to dispose of the bonds. Thus, in a recent case, a company sold bonds bearing 4½% interest, with warrants to buy common stock very cheaply. The profit and loss account would be charged with 4½% interest, whereas 6½ would have been a normal rate; and capital stock would be sold too cheaply, the company taking up as liability on this stock only the amount actually received. This is quite common, but not often so gross as the case referred to above. There is always an element of opinion, as to what was received for the bonds and what for the rights or stock.

(4) Other assets over-valued. One of the plans used to overstate profits is peculiar to motion picture distributors, although illustrative of a principle.

Negatives are produced, say, by "A Negative Co." It does not have

[4] See: Berle and Fisher (F. S., Jr.), "Elements of the Law of Business Accounting" (1932) 32 Columbia Law Review 573.

money, but borrows from "A Distributory Co.," with an agreement that
when the picture is finished the "Distributing Co." shall retain 40% of
the rentals to cover expenses, and set aside 60% to be credited against
the debt of "A Producer Co." Unless this 60% suffices to repay the
distributor he has no further recourse.

Now let a picture be a relatively poor one; the 60% has not been
sufficient to cover half the debt; it may be that future earnings will
still be insufficient to cover the remaining half. Part of this "Advance
to Producers" is irrecoverable. It is common practice to let the balance
stand as an asset, claiming possible future income, etc., and the auditor
is constantly fighting to cut out this overvaluation. It is easily seen that
this, without any effort, but solely by reason of failure to take any
trouble in the matter, results in inflating profits gradually over a period
of years unless a halt takes place by reason of intelligent audit or for
other reasons. A glance at the balance sheets of motion picture distributors will show the enormous proportions of these "advances to
producers."

(5) Charging direct to surplus items that should go to profit
account.

It is usual with some companies to charge direct to surplus items
of expense that are said to be applicable to prior periods. Then, having
accounts, perhaps certified, of those prior years, they may use the
figures for the prior years as they were first made up. This has been
done; it is said by some accountants that the best practice for auditors
is to insist that no item of a character that would indicate its place in
any profit and loss account be permitted to reach the surplus without
passing through the profit account.

(6) Eliminating so-called "non-recurring expenses."

Many enterprises are subject to non-recurring expenses; at the
same time each period is likely to have some non-recurring expense.
Such expenses as strike expenses, fire losses, damage by flood, special
allowances on contracts, are often classed as non-recurring. These are
sometimes eliminated from profit accounts, on the plea that their elimination gives a more correct picture of future probabilities.

(7) Crowding of sales into last period. Many classes of business
have sales "for Spring delivery," "for fall season," etc., which may be
delivered in advance at the option of seller, but with extra credit given.
In case sales are prematurely entered the effect is threefold: Sales,
and therefore profits, are increased; the balance sheet is improved by
the substitution of accounts receivable for inventory; and the trend of
sales is shown to be upward.

(8) Plain falsification of records.

Capable accountants of a high degree of integrity will catch these
situations as they arise, and will usually make the necessary corrections
before permitting the use of their name in connection with a broker's

circular. It does not follow, however, that the law would regard manipulations of the type here illustrated as constituting either a fraudulent misstatement of fact or a concealment of a material element in the situation. But it appears to the writers that courts distinctly tend to apply, in one form or another, the better rules of accounting practice; and it is fairly to be expected that these, as accountants themselves reduce them to a recognized body of standards, will find their place in the legal system.

In summary, it may be stated that: (1) Everything which appears in the banker's circular must be accurate. If a statement known to be false appears the banker is liable to a technical action of deceit despite any safeguard clauses or verbal devices employed. If the inaccuracy is unknown, there is a fair chance the banker will be obliged to take back the securities and return the money in an action of rescission.

(2) Representations that something will happen in the future may not be made unless the banker is virtually prepared to guarantee that the thing will be done within a reasonable time. The banker's statement is apparently held to imply both an intent that the thing shall be done and reasonable likelihood that the thing can and will be done.

(3) The price at which the banker issues the security, accompanied by a recommendation of the purchase at that price, may be held to be a direct representation that the security is worth the price asked, based on the market standards of the time. Should the security turn out not to be worth that amount, an action in deceit (if the worthlessness is known) or in rescission (if the banker innocently over-valued) may well result. This is a new tendency in the law; and is by no means well defined, though there appears to be a trend in that direction.

(4) In determining the truth or falsity of a financial fact the financial community holds the banker to a standard of decent accounting; these standards are not yet embodied in the law, though there is some reason to believe that they will ultimately find their place in the legal system.

The relationship of disclosure to the market. Heretofore we have been dealing with the relationship between the banker and the customer who purchases securities from him. But the disclosure is directed at a larger target. On the faith of it, trading takes place in the chosen market—over the counter, the New York Curb, the New York Stock Exchange, as the case may be—and the market transactions will largely depend on an appraisal of the situation as disclosed by the banker's circular. At the moment the market has no other material to go upon save its estimate of the men concerned, the ability of the banking house, and, perhaps, the state of the industry engaged in by the issuing corporation.

The disclosure is here cross-checked where the stock is at the same time introduced to a respectable Exchange, notably the New York Stock Exchange, whose Listing Committee requires a most elaborate and painstaking disclosure of the material facts in connection with the corporation, which is subjected to a searching analysis by the committee prior to the admittance of the stock to trading. The Exchange appears to adopt the theory that a disclosure must be made frankly and in terms "to the market," though it appears in a document formally known as "an application to list." The listing application is consequently an elaboration of the banker's circular; and must be consistent with it. Almost invariably however, it contains additional facts of considerable interest.

The New York Stock Exchange peculiarly insists on certain independent expert data; notably the opinion of independent counsel as to the legality of the organization, authorization, issue, and validity of the securities; the report of a qualified engineer covering the physical condition of the property at a recent date; and is now discussing the requirement that independent accounting reports and engineers' reports, on the responsibility of the accountants and the engineers be likewise filed. In addition, requirements are made assuring that there is sufficient distribution of stock to create a "free market." In a word, the distinct aim is to provide the market with sufficient information permitting appraisal of the security, and to assure the existence of a sufficient number of buyers and sellers so that the appraisal will find free reflection in the day-to-day market prices.

It is commonly supposed that the law takes no cognizance of the relationship between the issuing corporation and the bankers, and the open market. To a large extent this is true; but the question has arisen from time to time and has been dealt with in a manner indicating both that a legal relationship has been created and that reciprocal rates and audits have been set up which the courts will enforce in case of necessity. As long ago as 1859 an English court (*Bedford v. Bagshaw*) [5] permitted a purchaser in the open market to recover his damages from the director of a corporation, where he had purchased stock in the open market and the information contained in the application to list on the London Stock Exchange proved false. He had not himself acted on the information; but the market had; and he had purchased at market—i. e., on an appraisal based on a false representation by the

[5] Court of Exchequer, 1859. 29 L. J. Ex. 59.

issuers of the securities. There is no reason to believe that this rule is not even now law in England. Again, even in America, where a security was issued and a statement was made that application would be made "to list on the New York Stock Exchange" it was held that this statement implied a particular quality in the security, and that where the security did not have this quality, the purchaser had not secured the thing he believed he was buying, and could accordingly rescind the transaction.[6] It is probable that a further relationship can be worked out. It is not the banker but the corporation that makes application to list its shares. It frequently does so, nevertheless, under the sponsorship of a banker. Where a corporation creates a situation in the open market tending to give a false value to the stock, (a subject to be discussed in the following chapter) the law has in various situations intervened to declare a liability.

The fact appears to be that the market price of the security is in large measure a reflection of the market situation on that security; and the knowledge of the individual has little to do with the subject. The market, as a whole, makes an appraisal; by accepting this appraisal, the buyer or the seller in substance accepts the result of this information. Where the corporation or the bankers have themselves created the premises on which a false appraisal is based, it is by no means impossible that the law will ultimately consider the remedies both of rescission and deceit adequate. In fact, a representation made in a broker's circular is intended as much to induce public participation through the normal markets as it is to induce the direct purchase of the securities from the issuing banker, though the latter is of course the immediate motive. A purchase made in the open market on the faith of such a circular may easily be construed by the law of tomorrow as an action directly induced the corporation and the banker, the law granting the remedies accordingly in deceit and in rescission, as may be appropriate.

It cannot be said that the law is in a satisfactory state either in connection with the direct relationship of the buyer and the banker to the corporation, or with respect to the relationship between the buyer who relies on the information in an open market transaction. On the other hand, the business standards imposed in the New York market at least tend towards a situation far healthier than has prevailed for a considerable period of time. Reputable bankers observe a high degree of integrity in making their disclosures; and their sins in this regard tend to be rather of omission than of commission.

The public investor does not greatly concern himself with legal

[6] *Seneca Wire Co. v. A. B. Leach & Co.*, 247 N. Y. 1 (1928).

technicalities. What he asks is the services of the banker as an expert, and what he expects to get is a security which in the honest and competent opinion of the banker is worth the price paid. His judgment will be based on the pragmatic question whether or not, over a period of years, he makes or loses money. In bold relief he really imposes on the banker merely the liability to sell securities at a price which, all things considered, is fair, and which will, if it does not advance, at least not decline. In part he bases his judgment on the facts disclosed to him at the time of flotation. Still more, however, he relies upon the ability of the investment banker. The banker knows of this reliance, but he considers himself as a merchant rather than as representative of investors. The law has discovered no formula reducing this reliance to legal rights and liabilities. In endeavoring to work out the question through rules of deceit and rescission, and similar remedies, it is of course harking back to the historical analogy of rights and liabilities as between vendors and purchasers of goods. By treating the banker as an expert in a particular class of wares, some progress has been made; but until the law occupies in some manner the field opened by the relationship of the banker and the issuing corporation to the public market in general, the gap is left open.

CHAPTER III: DISCLOSURE
BY THE CORPORATION TO
THE MARKET

THE BANKER'S DISCLOSURE on flotation of a security gives to the market data designed to permit an appraisal of the security at once. This is merely the first of a series of disclosures which will be made so long as the corporation avails itself of the machinery of public exchanges. The banker thereafter drops out of the picture and, save in special circumstances, subsequent disclosures are made on the responsibility of the corporation itself.

Such disclosures take a number of forms. In order of importance they appear to be: (1) periodic statements of condition, (balance sheets and peculiarly income accounts); (2) extraordinary statements of condition and announcements, commonly in connection with a proposed development of considerable importance in the corporate affairs, as new financing, merger, reorganization, etc.; (3) extraordinary statements by the officers of a corporation commonly issued under peculiar circumstances—as, for instance, where there is a "corner" in the stock, or a bear raid leading to panic or the like, the corporate officials feeling it desirable to protect the shareholders against some abnormal situation; (4) information made available to brokerage or banking houses and designed by the corporation to be used by such houses in connection with market operations in the security; (5) information made available to standard financial publications or manuals; (6) occasional information made available without signature to financial periodicals.

All of these relate to information which the corporation itself has and which would not otherwise be easily or accurately discovered by the market. The information must, of course, be correlated with the general information regarding the trade or industry available at the time; a correlation which is made with varying degrees of accuracy and inaccuracy by the multitude of people who operate in and about the market, usually in connection with speculative activities.

It is interesting to note how little relation this variety of disclosure bears to the disclosures required by law. Various states have different requirements; but no state requires disclosure of the facts considered usual in the normal open market situation.

At law, this situation is roughly as follows:

(a) The corporate documents are a matter of public record in the office of the Secretary of State of the state of incorporation. This, of course, is not disclosure. It does, however, enable an interested party to secure the information; and, to some extent, charters are summarized in the financial manuals. On the whole, these summaries observe a high degree of accuracy, though in a complex corporate structure their effect is difficult to work out.

(b) In practically every state the corporation is obliged to keep on file at its principal office and open for inspection, a list of its stockholders and their holdings. This list is available only to shareholders; and the information does not usually circulate freely in the market.

(c) Practically every state contemplates an annual meeting of shareholders at which time something in the nature of an annual report is customary. Small or privately owned corporations may dispense with this without serious penalty; quasi-public corporations, which are formally administered, invariably observe the requirement. Inasmuch as exceedingly few shareholders attend the meetings and are commonly represented by their proxies who are individuals appointed by the management, disclosure made at an annual meeting not only does not reach the stockholders in general, but it may not reach the market unless it is embodied in a formal report distributed and published. Such distribution and publication seems not to be required in most states, though certain jurisdictions, notably Ohio, require the sending of such report.

(d) In certain jurisdictions the filing of an annual balance sheet is required. Massachusetts is the outstanding example of this; the formal balance sheet lodged in the Office of the Secretary of State becomes then a matter of public record, and when the corporation is generally known in the market, the information almost invariably reaches the public through the medium of the newspapers' statistical services, etc.

(e) A considerable number of states require the filing annually of the names of the board of directors and officers of the corporation.

It will be noticed that in dealing with corporate information the underlying assumption is that such information must be considered as a private matter, of interest only to its shareholders; and even in that regard limits in the extreme the information which the corporate management must make available, even to its own shareholders.

There are no legal requirements necessitating disclosure of information to creditors such as bondholders. These must acquire their knowledge of affairs either from the public information voluntarily made available by the corporation, or, at second hand to the shareholders. On the other hand, the banker who has floated an issue of bonds or notes, commonly assures to himself, in his arrangement with the corporation, the right to a continuous flow of information; and a reputable banker will make this information available to the market, at least to a considerable extent.

The New York Stock Exchange, pursuing a considerably more pragmatic policy than that of the corporation acts, insists on periodic statements; and these requirements largely account for the continuous flow of information actually reaching the market referred to above. In addition, in certain classes of corporations the Exchange has made still more vigorous requirements, notably its insistence that "investment trusts" shall publish their portfolios or lists of securities held. The New York Curb imposes a far less stringent set of requirements; though even these are considerably more elaborate than any legal requirements outstanding. Unlisted securities, availing themselves of an over-the-counter market, are subject to no requirements; the practice varies widely with the standards of the various managements.

Certain classes of corporations are subject to legal requirements by reason of the nature of their business. Railroads are obliged to make public (1) holdings of their twenty largest shareholders; (2) monthly income statements; (3) annual balance sheets; and the railroads actually publish, at short intervals, statements covering their business, notably car loadings and traffic movement. Operating public utilities are subject to a heterogeneous mass of requirements which differ in each state. These rules do not apply to public utility holding companies which are thus freed from any obligation in the matter.

In general it may be said that disclosure of the quality necessary to permit a market to appraise a security is required only by the New York Stock Exchange, and by the Interstate Commerce Commission in respect of railroads, and aside from that disclosure is voluntary.

It cannot be said that disclosures of the kind required furnish all of the information needed for an accurate appraisal. The formulation of such requirements would probably be impossible, since the important data in any given industry or in any given corporation may not only be different from that in any other industry or concern, but may itself change in importance from time to time. Pending negotiations for a merger may be of the highest importance in working out a market appraisal of stock, or of bonds; but there may be every reason why the information should not be made public. Again, the market tends to appraise on the basis of probabilities in a constant effort to anticipate the result of the fact, when arrived at; and it is not easy, if indeed, it is possible at all, to disclose anything other than that which has actually occurred. So long as a development, even of major importance, rests merely on the state of mind of the directors, the danger of making a statement about it is obvious.

Disclosure to the market after flotation raises many of the problems suggested in the previous chapter. There is, however, a distinct difference. The banker's disclosure on original issue is made with the primary purpose of inducing a customer to purchase a security from him or from his associates in the selling group. There is no question that it is intended to induce action. Disclosures made to the market, however, in theory are merely informative. If made with the intention of inducing action, they may easily be improper from a strictly ethical point of view, save where the circumstances are peculiar; since it is not the business of the management to create market movements. But it is conceivable that at any given time the management may find its position such as to dictate an exactly contrary policy. For instance, when a stock falls rapidly without reason, and the management is aware that this is due to some strictly manipulative operation, it may conceivably be the ethical duty of the management to issue a statement of fact, designed to prevent shareholders from selling their securities at an unreasonably low value. Again, if in the management's view the market appraisal is unfair, whether too high or too low, it is not impossible to suppose that a management might think it well to issue a statement for the purpose of creating a market appraisal more nearly in accordance with the facts. The Manhattan Electrical Supply Co. management issued a statement designed to prevent a further rise of the stock during the existence of a technical corner a few years ago; the managements of the Continental Baking Corporation and of Anaconda Copper Co. have issued statements designed to prevent sales of their stock at a time when they considered a disastrous fall in market values of these stocks unwarranted in view of the actual situation. In the normal case a management is supposed to be disclosing merely the facts of the situation, leaving the market to work out its own salvation, and interfering only when a somewhat obviously manipulative move is under way.

Is there any legal relationship giving rise to rights and liabilities as between the security holder and the management in respect of the information supplied? This problem has not been solved in the courts; and a discussion of it must necessarily be academic. Certain indications, however, tend to the belief that the law cannot remain entirely silent.

Granting the economic thesis that a share of stock is primarily a capitalized expectation, valued by an open market appraisal of the situation existing in the corporation and the industry, and granting further that it is reasonably foreseeable (as it certainly is) that appraisals will vary with the information given out, it is not difficult to suppose that the management of a corporation will be liable (a) for wilful misstatement of fact designed to induce action on the part of anyone buying or selling in the market; (b) perhaps also on account of a negligent misstatement of fact not designed to induce action in the market but resulting in a material fluctuation; (c) possibly, for a failure to disclose a material fact leading to a faulty appraisal. Leaving aside for a moment the knotty question as to what is a "statement of fact," the argument will proceed on the theory that the statements made by the management have a necessary, obvious, and foreseeable effect upon the open market appraisal; that the corporation has, in availing itself of the open market, contemplated action on such information; and that if it wilfully or negligently causes damage in connection with such action through wilful or negligent misstatement or concealment of material facts, it is liable in damages. Certainly, the financial community, though it cannot impose a liability for damages, passes judgment on a management in no uncertain terms in such a situation.

The difficulties are many. Where these is a wilful misstatement the difficulty is not great, provided the misstatement was in respect of a fact which can be demonstrated to affect the appraisal. For example, if a corporation consciously over-stated its income leading to a rise in the value of the shares, a buyer on the faith of such valuation should have no greater difficulty in recovering on the English theory set forth in *Bedford v. Bagshaw*. A negligent misstatement raises more difficulties; but the probability is they could be solved through the legal fiction that directors are presumed to know the facts in connection with their corporation; and are thus held to know the truth of the information they put out in any event. In other words, they could not claim innocence in dealing with a subject as to which they were the sole possessors of the information.

Non-disclosure, however, raises extreme difficulties. The first difficulty is one of time. A corporation can hardly issue to the market a slow cinema of all of its activities. Factual changes will take place from day to day. No sound rule could hold the corporate management to summarizing each occurrence and issuing it to the public press or to the market. On the other hand, certain major facts can be announced at once. If, for example, a corporation has decided to double its dividend, there is little, if any excuse for concealing this information for any period of time; the seller, during that period is acting in ignorance of a fact which has not been disclosed to him and which would materially change both his and the market's appraisal, if it were known. In one instance of recent occurrence, a corporation agreed that it would offer to exchange its shares for those of another. It was understood that this offer was to be made to all shareholders of the second corporation a few days later. The latter shares were selling at about 96; the shares offered in exchange, at 160 or thereabouts. Had the existence of the agreement been made known, the market appraisal would at once have brought the value of the shares of the first corporation and the shares of the second into line. In fact, the offer was disclosed to certain persons who not unnaturally purchased all of the readily obtainable stock of the latter corporation, and exchanged it for stock of the former corporation, securing a tremendous arbitrage profit. When, a few days later, the offer was made known to everyone, certain individuals had reaped a rich harvest. The management of the second corporation here apparently failed to disclose a material fact; and the individuals who sold their stock at a market appraisal made in ignorance of the fact quite conceivably might claim redress.

Remains the question, discussed in the previous chapter, as to what is a "fact." Little can be added to the observation made above. In a philosophical sense nothing is a "fact"; even a balance sheet or income statement is a reflection of the state of mind of the persons issuing it. Again, the problem is posed whether rules of accounting must not ultimately become rules of law in this connection.

In any event it would seem that the rules must be limited to facts peculiar to the corporation. Declaration of war in Europe, for example, might at once change the picture with regard to an American steel company; and the company might have advance knowledge of the fact; but a European war is not the affair of the steel company; and it is not at present considered either ethical or desirable to require the management to make such a disclosure. On the other hand, a tremendous order making large profits certain for the coming year would be a fact peculiarly within the knowledge of the company.

When a fact has sufficient materiality to require disclosure, raises still other nice questions. The large order above referred to might be merely one of a series of similar incidents in the corporate business, strengthening the position of the corporation to be sure, but not materially affecting the open market appraisal; on the other hand, it might be such as to change the entire outlook. It is probable that, save in the simplest and clearest situations, the law will not and cannot intervene. Were it to do so, the whole conduct of business might be thrown constantly into the courts.

As nearly as the writers can summarize, the standards to be approximated are that certain extraordinary facts should be the subject of immediate disclosure. These are: (1) sale of an integral asset; (2) declaration of dividends of any kind or class; (3) change in the capital structure; (4) a firm offer for the purchase or exchange of securities outstanding. But this list by no means implies that there may not be other special circumstances requiring immediate disclosure. On the other hand, any development in the law must contemplate at least the possibility of a legal privilege in the management permitting them to withhold information where in their honest judgment it is for the best interests of all concerned; and as to this the honesty and good faith of the management should be conclusive. In practice, honesty and good faith are frequently tested by ascertaining whether or not the management or friends and connections of it have made arrangements to profit by the disclosure or non-disclosure. Good faith will hardly be evoked where the management can be found to have profited. Bad faith will probably be difficult to prove where in fact no such profit has been made.

This appears to the writers to be the probable trend both of the law and of the business standards. The exact application must necessarily turn on the facts of each case and peculiarly on the nature of the business. For example, the situation in an "investment trust" or trading corporation which permits an accurate summation of the market prices of its assets justifies the imposition of a severer rule regarding disclosures in connection with these companies than would be either possible or desirable in the case of a manufacturing company whose activities turn on far more imponderable elements. It does, however, seem fair to say that the use of the open market machinery implies an obligation on the management both to make periodic disclosures and to make disclosures of extraordinary facts from time to time.

We have been unable to discover any legal obligation upon the management to intervene in special situations in order to induce market action. It is extremely dangerous for a management to make disclosures with the direct object of inducing market action. To do so may imply either the highest ethical intent of the managers, or the most sordid motives of personal gain; and the action induced may turn out profitable or unprofitable for the individual security owners, or for the business in general, depending on a variety of circumstances which the management certainly cannot be expected to control. What can be required is good faith, and probably nothing more. The intelligence and fidelity of those charged with the administration of the corporate affairs must determine their policy; the law certainly could not do so; and to compel a corporation or its individual directors to assume the responsibility of revising an appraisal either upwards or downwards is to place upon them an impossible burden. If they elect to do so, and act in reasonable good faith the current legal view is that they are protected; if they elect not to do so, the law does not interfere. First-rate managements, though they have difficulty in solving such problems, do not find them insuperable; but the law is not now in a position to lay down a standard to which they could safely conform; and accordingly could hardly impose a liability where they have acted in their honest discretion as to what seems best for all concerned.

THE PROBLEM of open market operations reaches its most acute stage when the corporate officers are themselves trading; or when the corporation or an affiliate of it is itself buying or selling.

A director or member of the corporate management necessarily has a tremendous advantage in speculating in the securities of his corporation. He has access to information not available to the market; he may well have reason to know that the open market appraisal is either too low or too high; and by appropriate purchases or sales he can enrich himself. This necessarily puts him in a position directly adverse to the shareholders of the corporation. He would be buying from stockholders who ought not to sell. He would be selling at a time when the stock is not worth the price he is asking incoming shareholders to pay for it, and he would be doing this on the basis of information which he has acquired, not individually, but in his capacity as a manager of the corporation and which accordingly belongs in equity to the body of shareholders as a whole.

The cognate situation arises when the corporation itself buys and sells its own shares. Legally it has power to do this, at least to the extent of its surplus. Apparently, though the cases have not yet so held, paid-in surplus may be used to purchase shares of the corporation's own stock. This operates in two ways. It may affect the open market price or quotation of the shares as a whole; and also it may yield profits (or losses, as the case may be) to the corporation which ultimately affect the values applicable to the outstanding shares. At the worst the corporation may maintain a "pegged" or artificial price for its stock.

Since the assumption of a shareholder and the theory of the open market is that there is the appraisal of a free association of buyers and sellers, the intervention either of the management, with its peculiar information, or of the corporation, with its ability to use some of the corporate assets for that purpose, materially impairs both the accuracy of the open market appraisal, and the supposed liquidity of the securities. Both situations must be considered.

Directors and officers as buyers and sellers of stock

No figures are available, and indeed in the nature of things information could hardly be secured, as to the extent of trading operations of corporate officers in their own stock. It is known that certain companies, usually under the dominance of some strong individual, decline to permit anyone connected with the concern, whether as director or as employee to conduct speculative operations in the corporate stock. On the other hand, it is certain that this is not the general practice; and that many directors feel perfectly free to buy and sell, though there is a certain squeamishness about disclosing their operations.

The law has had occasion to deal with this situation, the authorities dividing sharply. Once more legal metaphysics have been invoked. One group of states, comprising the majority and following the lead of New York, took the view that a director might trade in the market in securities of his corporation exactly as might any other individual; and that he was under no obligation to disclose any special information which he might have. If he were informed of some peculiarly advantageous development in advance of the shareholder, he might purchase stock without disclosing this information; if he knew of some unfavorable turn he might sell stock without announcing the reason. Since this placed a director who nominally represented the interests of stockholders in a position necessarily adverse to them, it was necessary to invoke some logistic reasoning to justify the result. The time honored distinction between the "corporation" and the individual shareholders was brought in for this purpose. In the leading case in New York [1] the courts adopted the view that directors were trustees and fiduciaries for the corporation only; but as the corporation was a separate entity from the stockholders, they were under no duty to the stockholders as individuals. Since buying and selling stock from or to a shareholder was a transaction between individuals, the director was under no duty to the shareholder to disclose his information, or to avoid placing himself in an obviously adverse position.

[1] *Carpenter v. Danforth*, 52 Barbour, 581 (New York 1868).

The succinct statement really was made by Judge Sutherland, who observed:

> There is . . . a certain trust relation between the shareholders and the directors of a corporation; but the trust put in the directors usually extends, and I must assume that in this case it extended only to the management of the general affairs of the corporation with a view to dividends or profits; and, therefore, that the trust relation between the plaintiff and the defendant, Danforth, extended no farther. . . . The plaintiff's stock was not the subject of trust between them, nor had the trust relation between them any connection with the plaintiff's stock, except so far as the good or bad management of the general affairs of a corporation by its directors, indirectly affects the value of its stock.

A series of cases comprising the weight of authority in America follows this rule.

It can only be pointed out that this ignores the function of the security market, and particularly the economic fact that the investor of today must look to the market as the means by which his capital is ultimately repaid to him. The corporation makes use of the market machinery in lieu of a definite promise of repayment, or a time of liquidation. This fact, far less important in 1868 when the rule was laid down, has become paramount today; and to say that directors can ignore market values simply begs the question.

A precisely contrary rule has been reached in a minority of jurisdictions. In certain southern and western states, notably Georgia and Kansas, the courts have adopted a square rule that a director trading in the market must disclose the material facts which he knows, otherwise a shareholder selling to him or buying from him may hold the director liable for the damages suffered. The theory is that any information which the director has is held by him solely as trustee for all of the shareholders including him whose stock is being bought or sold; that in buying or selling the shareholder is entitled to the benefit of such information; and that the director cannot use such information for his own individual benefits. Judge Lamar, taking square issue with the old New York rule quoted the above and said precisely:

> It is a matter of common knowledge that the market value of shares rises and falls, not only because of an increase or decrease in tangible property, but by reason of real or contemplated action on the part of managing officers; declaring or passing dividends; the making of fortunate or unfortunate contracts; the loss or gain of property in dispute; profitable or disadvantageous sales or leases. And to say that a director who has been placed where he himself may raise or depress the value of the stock, or in a position where he first knows of facts

which may produce that result, may take advantage thereof, and buy from or sell to one whom he is directly representing, without making a full disclosure and putting the stockholder on an equality of knowledge as to these facts, would offer a premium for faithless silence, and give a reward for the suppression of truth, . . .

and the metaphysical point that the director had no fiduciary relation towards stockholders as individuals was accordingly rejected.

An intermediate rule exists in the Federal courts and in a few other states. The United States Supreme Court adopted the reasoning of Judge Sutherland in New York; but qualified it by saying that special facts might take a case out of the rule. Among the special facts so recognized are cases where the director or officer has been made an agent of the corporation to sell its property, or to secure offers for its assets or the like. The reasoning underlying this rule is not particularly clear; in substance the result is that although the liability of the director is not set up, yet where a case arises involving too great hardship, the court may be induced to intervene.

Debate as to the desirability of the rule is perhaps profitless. Opinion seems to be divided among business men themselves, some holding that the making of incidental profits from trading in the stock of his corporation is one of the ways by which a director gets paid; others, that it should not be permitted save under extraordinary circumstances. It would seem that the real solution of the problem lies, not in prohibitions upon the directors, but in imposing rules requiring general disclosure by the corporation of all material facts tending to change open market appraisals. The practice of the United States Steel Company during the life of Judge Gary was to declare dividends at a meeting of the board of directors, and to make announcement before any director was allowed to leave the room—the disclosure following so quickly upon the action that no individual could take advantage of the information. So complete or prompt a disclosure could not, of course, be possible in all cases; but it is certain that a far greater degree of information could be vouchsafed to the stockholders or to the market in general than is often done. Information once granted to the market is available to everyone, whether or not individually communicated to him. While a director trading with a shareholder through the medium of a stock exchange could not greet him face to face and disclose to him information, and while a corporation can hardly be expected to send daily bulletins to all its stockholders' lists, the machinery of the stock and news tickers, and the distribution of information throughout the market has reached a point making it possible to discount or revise market appraisals almost instantaneously. As the standards of disclosure of corporate affairs become more exacting, the problem of the directors and managers in the market will become increasingly less important.

The "control" being as yet relatively unconsidered by the law save in certain rare instances, has not yet achieved legal recognition in open market operations. To the extent that courts do not permit free trading by directors without disclosure, the requirements are fastened upon him as an officer of the corporation by virtue of his peculiar office. It would seem, for all that appears at present, that a man who held no titular office but dominated the corporation through some "control" machinery, would be freed from any restriction.

Any survey of the problem of open securities markets reveals the existence of a great void, both in economic and legal theory. Whether because securities markets have only recently attained the dominant position they now hold, or because the problem has proved unduly complex, neither branch of theory seems to have thoroughly attacked the problem. The law is perhaps excusable in this regard, since it can never do more than make effective the conclusions of the community. Indications are not wanting that a focus of interest in the open market problem is now being reached. We should expect the next decade to be filled with attempts to deal with this question. Undoubtedly more can be done with existing financial machinery than has yet been accomplished. The New York Stock Exchange makes slow but steady progress in an endeavor to provide a continuous basis for appraisal of securities available to everyone. Legislation, of varying degrees of wisdom, is being constantly proposed. A real difficulty lies in the fact that in the securities markets, as in the case of commodity markets, the economic analysis is embryonic; there is no centralized mechanism of control analogous to the Federal Reserve Bank in the banking field; and the law can merely pick up occasional instances of specific unethical conduct.

And yet, it is plain that the whole future of the present system is inextricably bound to the successful functioning of the securities markets. If the apparent liquidity provided by the stock markets were eliminated, the history of industrial capitalism would probably take a new direction. Were it realized that capital invested in securities is at least potentially "frozen," financing would become more difficult and the size of industrial combinations might be considerably limited. Correspondingly, banking credits, standards of living and the habits of the community might conceivably change. As far as can be observed now, the direction of thought appears to be towards preserving liquidity; buttressing the stock markets; and increasing their importance as a responsible financial mechanism.

BOOK FOUR

Reorientation of Enterprise: Effects of the corporate system on fundamental economic concepts

CHAPTER I: THE TRADITIONAL

LOGIC OF PROPERTY

THE SHIFTING relationships of property and enterprise in American industry here described, raise in sharp relief certain legal, economic, and social questions which must now be squarely faced. Of these the greatest is the question in whose interests should the great quasi-public corporations (now representing such a large proportion of industrial wealth) be operated. This problem really asks in a different form the question, who should receive the profits of industry?

It is traditional that a corporation should be run for the benefit of its owners, the stockholders, and that to them should go any profits which are distributed.[1] We now know, however, that a controlling group may hold the power to divert profits into their own pockets. There is no longer any certainty that a corporation will in fact be run primarily in the interests of the stockholders.[2] The extensive separation of ownership and control, and the strengthening of the powers of control, raise a new situation calling for a decision whether social and legal pressure should be applied in an effort to insure corporate operation primarily in the interests of the "owners" or whether such pressure shall be applied in the interests of some other or wider group.

The lawyer answers this question in no uncertain terms by applying to the quasi-public corporation the traditional logic of property. The common law, extended to meet the new situation, logically

[1] Bonus schemes are usually undertaken with an aim of *increasing* the profit remaining and available to be distributed as dividends. For this reason they must, in general, be regarded as a cost to the stockholders rather than as a sharing or distribution of profit.

[2] While there are other possible groups,—the employees, the consumers, etc., in whose interest a corporation might be run, discussion of them can best be delayed.

demands the award of the entire profit to the security holders, and in particular to the stockholders. According to this logic a corporation should be operated primarily in their interests.

The legal argument is largely historical; but it has been built up through a series of phases which make this conclusion inevitable. From earliest times the owner of property has been entitled to the full use or disposal of his property,[a] and in these rights the owner has been protected by law. Since the use of industrial property consists primarily of an effort to increase its value—to make a profit— the owner of such property, in being entitled to its full use, has been entitled to all accretions to its value—to all the profits which it could be made to earn. In so far as he had to pay for the services of other men or other property in order to accomplish this increase in value, these payments operated as deductions; the profit remaining to him was the difference between the added value and the cost of securing these services. To this difference, however, the owner has traditionally been entitled. The state and the law have sought to protect him in this right.

From earliest times, also, the stockholder in the corporation has posed both as the owner of the corporation and the owner of its assets. He was removed slightly from legal ownership in the assets in that he did not have legal "title" to them—that was vested in the corporation; but collectively the stockholders, through their participations were entitled to the whole of corporate assets and to the whole of any corporate profits which could be made. The corporation was theirs, to be operated for their benefit.

In the development of the corporation, constantly widening powers over the management of the enterprise have been delegated to groups within the corporation. At first these powers concerned mainly the technical (profit-making) activity of the enterprise. Later, powers were delegated which had to do with the distribution of profits and interests among the security holders. With the separation of ownership and control, these powers developed to a stage permitting those in control of a corporation to use them against the interests of ownership. Since powers of control and management were created by law, in some measure this appeared to legalize the diversion of profit into the hands of the controlling group.

Following the traditional logic of property, however, it is clear that these powers are not absolute. They are, rather, powers in trust. The controlling group is, in form at least, managing and controlling a corporation for the benefit of the owners. While insertions might be

[a] Except as impaired by the exercise of police power by the state.

made in corporation statutes and in corporate charters apparently giving power which could be used against the interests of the owners, these were, in the light of the common law, only grants of power to the controlling group, the better to operate the corporation in the interests of its owners. The very multiplication of absolute powers, including power to shift interests in the corporate assets and profits from security holders to those in control threw into bold relief the tacit (but by no means fictitious) understanding that all these powers were designed for the benefit of the corporation as a whole, and not for the individual enrichment of the management or control. While the law fumbled in application of this principle, and developed through a series of rules, sometimes inconsistent and often not clear in application, not a single case on record denies the ultimate trusteeship of the controlling group, nor even faintly implies that such a group may use its power for its individual advantage. Fact-situations can be "rigged" whereby the individual profit of this group is made to appear an advantage to the corporation as a whole; advantage may be taken of emergencies in which the management and control present the security-holding group with the alternative of permitting profit to the "control" on the one hand or inviting disaster on the other. Sometimes the courts, shielding themselves behind a consideration of the advantage to the "corporation as a whole," have overlooked the fact that apparent advantage to the mythical corporate entity may mean staggering loss to its separate owners; and that it is often necessary to trace *what group within the corporation* receives the ultimate advantage. Despite these situations, in many of which the controlling group is able, first, to seize a portion of the corporate profits and, second, to hold them against legal attack, the theory of the law seems clear. All the powers granted to management and control are powers in trust.

Tracing this doctrine back into the womb of equity, whence it sprang, the foundation becomes plain. Wherever one man or a group of men entrusted another man or group with the management of property, the second group became fiduciaries. As such they were obliged to act conscionably, which meant in fidelity to the interests of the persons whose wealth they had undertaken to handle. In this respect, the corporation stands on precisely the same footing as the common-law trust. Since the business problems connected with trusts were relatively restricted, a series of fairly accurate regulations could be worked out by the equity courts constraining the trustee to certain standards of conduct. The corporation, which carried on any and every kind of business, raised a set of problems of conduct infinitely more varied, and calling for expert business judgment which courts were not equipped to render. Fixed standards of conduct, therefore, became impossible of development in the corporate situation; such rigid standards as were worked out, (for instance, the standard that no stock must be issued unless first offered preëmptively to existing shareholders) became arbitrary or inapplicable in the complex corporate structure of today. But though definite rules could not be laid down, the courts have maintained a supervisory jurisdiction; the fundamental principle of equitable control remains unimpaired; and the only question is how it should be applied in each case. Inability to answer these questions has given ample latitude to the control to absorb a portion of the corporate profits. This does not mean, however, that the law concedes them a right to such absorption. It merely means that legal machinery may not be sufficiently developed to accomplish a remedy.

Underlying all this is the ancient preoccupation of the common law with the rights of property. Primarily, the common law did not undertake to set up ideal schemes of government. It aimed to protect men in their own. Only where the property interests conflicted with some very obvious public policy did the law interfere. Its primary design was protecting individual attributes of individual men,—their right to property, to free motion and locomotion, to protection of individual relationships entered into between them. In this aspect the corporation was merely one more bit of machinery by which the property of individuals was managed by other individuals; and the corporate management took its place in the picture alongside of agents, trustees, ship captains, partners, joint adventurers, and other fiduciaries. As the power of the corporate management has increased, and as the control of the individual has sunk into the background, the tendency of the law has been to stiffen its assertion of the rights of the security holder. The thing that it has not been able to stiffen has been its regulation of the conduct of the business by the corporate management. And this omission has resulted, not from lack of logical justification, but from lack of ability to handle the problems involved. The management of an enterprise is, by nature, a task which courts can not assume; and the various devices by which management and control have absorbed a portion of the profit-stream have been so intimately related to the business conduct of an enterprise, that the courts seem to have felt not only reluctant to interfere, but positively afraid to do so.

The result accordingly is that the profits of the enterprise, so far as the law is concerned, belong to the security holders *in toto*. Division of these profits among the various groups of security holders is a matter of private agreement, but they, between them, have the complete right to all of the profits which the corporation has made. Not only that: they are entitled to those profits which the management in reasonable exercise of its powers ought to make. They have further a right that no one shall become a security holder except upon a suitable contribution to the corporate assets—that is, that the security holding group shall be a group of persons who have committed actual property to the administration of the management and control of the corporation.

Such is the view which the law has developed by extending to the new situation the traditional logic of property. The control group is not in a position openly to combat this logic. Constant appeals are made both to this ideology and to its legal basis when corporations go into the market seeking capital. The expectation of the entire profit is the precise lure used to induce investment in corporate enterprises. The possibilities of the situation are continuously stressed by investment bankers who, in turn, act for the corporate management and control when the latter are bidding for the public investor's savings. Whatever their private views or actual practice, the control groups within corporations have estopped themselves from maintaining any other view. The legal hypothesis has been too much the basis of the financial structure of today.

Yet, while this conclusion may result inevitably when the traditional logic of property is applied to the new situation, are we justified in applying this logic? In the past, the ownership of business enterprise, the only form of property with which we are here concerned, has always, at least in theory, involved two attributes, first the risking of previously collected wealth in profit-seeking enterprise; and, second, the ultimate management of and responsibility for that enterprise. But in the modern corporation, these two attributes of ownership no longer attach to the same individual or group. The stockholder has surrendered control over his wealth. He has become a supplier of capital, a risk-taker pure and simple, while ultimate responsibility and authority are exercised by directors and "control." One traditional attribute of ownership is attached to stock ownership; the other attribute is attached to corporate control. Must we not, therefore, recognize that we are no longer dealing with property in the old sense? Does the traditional logic of property still apply? Because an owner who also exercises control over his wealth is protected in the full receipt of the advantages derived from it, must it *necessarily* follow that an owner who has surrendered control of his wealth should likewise be protected to the full? May not this sur-render have so essentially changed his relation to his wealth as to have changed the logic applicable to his interest in that wealth? An answer to this question cannot be found in the law itself. It must be sought in the economic and social background of law.

CHAPTER II: THE TRADITIONAL
LOGIC OF PROFITS

THE ECONOMIST, approaching the problems growing out of the shifting relationship of property and enterprise which we have examined, must start from a different background and with a set of interests differing essentially from those of the law. His interest is not primarily in the protection of man in his own, but in the production and distribution of what man desires. He is preoccupied, not with the rights of property, but with the production of wealth and distribution of income. To him property rights are attributes which may be attached to wealth by society and he regards them and their protection, not as the inalienable right of the individual or as an end in themselves, but as a means to a socially desirable end,[1] namely, "a plentiful revenue and subsistence" for the people.

The socially beneficent results to be derived from the protection of property are supposed to arise, not from the wealth itself, but from the efforts to acquire wealth. A long line of economists have developed what might be called the traditional logic of profits. They have held that, in striving to acquire wealth, that is, in seeking profits, the individual would, perhaps unconsciously, satisfy the wants of others. By carrying on enterprise he would employ his energy and wealth in such a way as to obtain more wealth.[2] In this effort, he would tend

[1] Adam Smith treated property as a "natural right" (following the teachings of Locke) and its protection as a "law of nature." At the same time he analyzed the beneficent results which might be expected to flow from making actual conditions conform to this "law of nature," i.e., from protecting property. The Nineteenth Century has seen the atrophy of the idea of "natural law" and the shift of emphasis to the advantages of the protection of property. See Adam Smith, "Wealth of Nations," Book I, Chap. X, Pt. II.

[2] Since this study is concerned with property rights in the instruments of production, we need not here consider the process of acquiring wealth in the form of wages and salaries or in the form of interest.

to make for profit those things which were in most demand. Competition among countless producers could be relied upon in general to maintain profits within reasonable limits while temporarily excessive profits in any one line of production would induce an increase of activity in that line with a consequent drop of profits to more reasonable levels. At the same time it was supposed that the business man's effort to increase his profits would, in general, result in more economical use of the factors of production, each enterprise having to compete with others for the available economic resources. Therefore, it has been argued that by protecting each man in the possession of his wealth and in the possession of any profits he could make from its use, society would encourage enterprise and thereby facilitate the production and distribution of goods desired by the community at reasonable prices with economic use of labor, capital, and business enterprise. By protecting property rights in the instruments of production, the acquisitive interests of man could thus be more effectively harnessed to the benefit of the community.

It must be seen that under the condition just described, profits act as a return for the performance of two separate functions. First, they act as an inducement to the individual to risk his wealth in enterprise, and, second, they act as a spur, driving him to exercise his utmost skill in making his enterprise profitable.[3] In the case of a private enterprise the distinction between these two functions does not assume importance. The owner of a private business receives any profits made and performs the functions not only of risk-taking but of ultimate management as well.[4] It may be that in the past when industry was in the main carried on by a multitude of small private enterprises the community, through protecting property, has induced a large volume of risk-taking and a vigorous conduct of industry in exchange for the profits derived therefrom.

In the modern corporation, with its separation of ownership and control, these two functions of risk and control are, in the main, performed by two different groups of people. Where such a separation is complete one group of individuals, the security holders and in particular the stockholders, performs the function of risk-takers and

[3] These two functions have been recognized in the current literature on profits. Some writers have maintained that profits are primarily a return for the taking of risk while others have maintained that they are primarily a return for exercising business judgment and enterprise. See S. H. Nerlove, "Recent Writings on Profits," The Journal of Business of the University of Chicago, Vol. II (1929), p. 363.

[4] Even though he employs a manager to carry on the immediate activities of the business, his desire for profits presumably induces him to select the most efficient manager available and to require of him a high standard of performance.

suppliers of capital, while a separate group exercises control and ultimate management. In such a case, if profits are to be received only by the security holders, as the traditional logic of property would require, how can they perform both of their traditional economic roles? Are no profits to go to those who exercise control and in whose hands the efficient operation of enterprise ultimately rests?

It is clear that the function of capital supplying and risk-taking must be performed and that the security holder must be compensated if an enterprise is to raise new capital and expand its activity just as the workers must be paid enough to insure the continued supplying of labor and the taking of the risks involved in that labor and in the life based on it. But what if profits can be made more than sufficient to keep the security holders satisfied, more than sufficient to induce new capital to come into the enterprise? [5] Where is the social advantage in setting aside for the security holder, profits in an amount greater than is sufficient to insure the continued supplying of capital and taking of risk? The prospect of additional profits cannot act as a spur on the security holder to make him *operate* the enterprise with more vigor in a way to serve the wants of the community, since he is no longer in control. Such extra profits if given to the security holders would seem to perform no useful economic function.

Furthermore, if all profits are earmarked for the security holder, where is the inducement for those in control to manage the enterprise efficiently? When none of the profits are to be received by them, why should they exert themselves beyond the amount necessary to maintain a reasonably satisfied group of stockholders? *If* the profit motive is the powerful incentive to action which it is supposed to be, and *if* the community is best served when each enterprise is operated with the aim of making the maximum profit, would there not be great social advantage in encouraging the control to seize for themselves any profits over and above the amount necessary as a satisfactory return to capital? Would not the prospect of this surplus profit act as an incentive to more efficient management by those in control? Certainly, one cannot escape the conclusion that if profits have any influence as a motivating force, any surplus which can be made over a satisfactory return to the investor would be better employed when held out as an incentive to action by control than when handed over to the "owners" who have surrendered control.

[5] "Profits sufficient to keep the security holders satisfied," etc., is a vague expression and not easily defined. In practice, however, it is not necessarily so vague. Dissatisfaction among stockholders is presumably not important if it does not make itself known; and inability to raise new capital with ease is likely to be all too evident to a controlling group.

This conclusion is somewhat modified by the fact that the separation of ownership and control has not yet become complete. While a large body of stockholders are not in a position to exercise any degree of control over the affairs of their corporation,[6] those actually in control are usually stockholders though in many cases owning but a very small proportion of the total stock. It may be that the prospect of receiving one or two per cent of the total added profit which could be produced by their own more vigorous activity would be sufficient inducement to produce the most efficient operation of which the controlling group are capable. It remains true, however, that profits over enough to keep the remaining stockholders satisfied and to make possible the raising of new capital would still involve an economically wasteful disposal. Only the one or two per cent of profits going to the controlling group would perform both roles traditionally performed by profits.

The traditional logic of profits, when thus applied to the modern corporation, would indicate that *if profits must be disturbed either to the owners or to the control,* only a fair return to capital should be distributed to the "owners"; while the remainder should go to the control as an inducement to the most efficient ultimate management. The corporation would thus be operated financially in the interests of control, the stockholders becoming merely the recipients of the wages of capital.

This conclusion runs directly counter to the conclusion reached by applying the traditional logic of property to precisely the same situation—and is equally suspect.

[6] Except under the most unusual conditions as for instance in case of a proxy fight, when the bulk of the stockholders play the role of the populace supporting or refusing to support a palace revolution.

CHAPTER III: THE INADEQUACY
OF TRADITIONAL THEORY

WHEN SUCH divergent results are obtained by the application of the logic of two major social disciplines to a new fact situation, we must push our inquiry still further back into the assumptions and concepts of those disciplines.

Underlying the thinking of economists, lawyers and business men during the last century and a half has been the picture of economic life so skillfully painted by Adam Smith. Within his treatise on the "Wealth of Nations" are contained the fundamental concepts which run through most modern thought. Though adjustments in his picture have been made by later writers to account for new conditions, the whole has been painted in the colors which he supplied. Private property, private enterprise, individual initiative, the profit motive, wealth, competition,—these are the concepts which he employed in describing the economy of his time and by means of which he sought to show that the pecuniary self-interest of each individual, if given free play, would lead to the optimum satisfaction of human wants. Most writers of the Nineteenth Century built on these logical foundations, and current economic literature is, in large measure, cast in such terms.

Yet these terms have ceased to be accurate, and therefore tend to mislead in describing modern enterprise as carried on by the great corporations. Though both the terms and the concepts remain, they are inapplicable to a dominant area in American economic organization. New terms, connoting changed relationships, become necessary.

When Adam Smith talked of "enterprise" he had in mind as the typical unit the small individual business in which the owner, perhaps with the aid of a few apprentices or workers, labored to produce goods for market or to carry on commerce. Very emphatically he repudiated the stock corporation as a business mechanism, hold-ing that dispersed ownership made efficient operation impossible. "The directors of such companies . . . ," he pointed out, "being the managers rather of other people's money than of their own, it can-not well be expected that they should watch over it with the same anxious vigilance with which the partners in a private copartnery fre-quently watch over their own. Like the stewards of a rich man, they are apt to consider attention to small matters as not for their master's honour, and very easily give themselves a dispensation from having it. Negligence and profusion, therefore, must always prevail, more or less, in the management of the affairs of such a company. It is upon this account that joint stock companies for foreign trade [at the time he was writing the only important manifestation of the corpora-tion outside of banks, insurance companies, and water or canal com-panies] have seldom been able to maintain the competition against private adventurers. They have, accordingly, very seldom succeeded without an exclusive privilege, and frequently have not succeeded with one. Without an exclusive privilege they have commonly mis-managed the trade. With an exclusive privilege they have both mis-managed and confined it." [1]

Yet when we speak of business enterprise today, we must have in mind primarily these very units which seemed to Adam Smith not to fit into the principles which he was laying down for the con-duct of economic activity. How then can we apply the concepts of Adam Smith in discussing our modern economy?

Let us consider each of these concepts in turn.

Private property

To Adam Smith and to his followers, private property was a unity involving possession. He assumed that ownership and control were combined. Today, in the modern corporation, this unity has been broken. *Passive property,*—specifically, shares of stock or bonds,—gives its possessors an interest in an enterprise but gives them practically no control over it, and involve no responsibility. *Active property,*—plant, good will, organization, and so forth which make up the actual enterprise,—is controlled by individuals who, almost invariably, have only minor ownership interests in it. In terms of relationships, the present situation can be described as including:—(1) "passive prop-erty," consisting of a set of relationships between an individual and

[1] Adam Smith, "The Wealth of Nations." Everyman's Library edition, Vol. II, p. 229.

an enterprise, involving rights of the individual toward the enterprise but almost no effective powers over it; and (2) "active property," consisting of a set of relationships under which an individual or set of individuals hold powers over an enterprise but have almost no duties in respect to it which can be effectively enforced. When active and passive property relationships attach to the same individual or group, we have private property as conceived by the older economists. When they attach to different individuals, private property in the instruments of production disappears. Private property in the share of stock still continues, since the owner possesses the share and has power to dispose of it, but his share of stock is only a token representing a bundle of ill-protected rights and expectations. It is the possession of this token which can be transferred, a transfer which has little if any influence on the instruments of production. Whether possession of active property,—power of control over an enterprise, apart from ownership,—will ever be looked upon as private property which can belong to and be disposed of by its possessor is a problem of the future, and no prediction can be made with respect to it.[2] Whatever the answer, it is clear that in dealing with the modern corporation we are not dealing with the old type of private property. Our description of modern economy, in so far as it deals with the quasi-public corporation, must be in terms of the two forms of property, active and passive, which for the most part lie in different hands.

Wealth

In a similar way, the concept "wealth" has been changed and divided. To Adam Smith, wealth was composed of tangible things,—wheat and land and buildings, ships and merchandise,—and for most people wealth is still thought of in physical terms. Yet in connection with the modern corporation, two essentially different types of wealth exist. To the holder of passive property, the stockholder, wealth consists, not of tangible goods,—factories, railroad stations, machinery,—but of a bundle of expectations which have a market value and which, if held, may bring him income and, if sold in the market, may give him power to obtain some other form of wealth. To the possessor of active property,—the "control"—wealth means a great enterprise which he dominates, an enterprise whose value is for the most part composed of the organized relationship of tangible properties, the existence of a

[2] Such would be the case, for instance, if by custom the position of director became hereditary and this custom were given legal sanction.

functioning organization of workers and the existence of a functioning body of consumers.[3] Instead of having control over a body of
tangible wealth with an easily ascertainable market value, the group
in control of a large modern corporation is astride an organism which
has little value except as it continues to function, and for which
there is no ready market. Thus, side by side, these two forms of
wealth exist:—on the one hand passive wealth,—liquid, impersonal
and involving no responsibility, passing from hand to hand and constantly appraised in the market place; and on the other hand, active
wealth,—great, functioning organisms dependent for their lives on
their security holders, their workers and consumers, but most of all
on their mainspring,—"control." The two forms of wealth are not
different aspects of the same thing, but are essentially and functionally
distinct.

Private enterprise

Again, to Adam Smith, private enterprise meant an individual or few
partners actively engaged and relying in large part on their own labor
or their immediate direction. Today we have tens and hundreds of
thousands of owners, of workers and of consumers combined in single enterprises. These great associations are so different from the
small, privately owned enterprises of the past as to make the concept
of private enterprise an ineffective instrument of analysis. It must be
replaced with the concept of corporate enterprise, enterprise which
is the organized activity of vast bodies of individuals, workers, consumers and suppliers of capital, under the leadership of the dictators
of industry, "control."

Individual initiative

As private enterprise disappears with increasing size, so also does
individual initiative. The idea that an army operates on the basis of
"rugged individualism" would be ludicrous. Equally so is the same
idea with respect to the modern corporation. Group activity, the
coördinating of the different steps in production, the extreme division

[3] The concept of the consumer as a functioning part of a great enterprise is one
which may at first be difficult to grasp. Yet, just as a body of members is essential
to the continued existence of a club, so a body of consumers is essential to the
continued existence of an enterprise. In each case the members or consumers are
an integral part of the association or enterprise. In each case membership is obtained at a cost and for the purpose of obtaining the benefits. The advertising
slogan, "Join the Pepsodent Family," is perhaps unintended recognition of this fact.

of labor in large scale enterprise necessarily imply not individualism but coöperation and the acceptance of authority almost to the point of autocracy. Only to the extent that any worker seeks advancement within an organization is there room for individual initiative,—an initiative which can be exercised only within the narrow range of function he is called on to perform. At the very pinnacle of the hierarchy of organization in a great corporation, there alone, can individual initiative have a measure of free play. Yet even there a limit is set by the willingness and ability of subordinates to carry out the will of their superiors. In modern industry, individual liberty is necessarily curbed.

The profit motive

Even the motivation of individual activity has changed its aspect. For Adam Smith and his followers, it was possible to abstract one motive, the desire for personal profit, from all the motives driving men to action and to make this the key to man's economic activity. They could conclude that, where true private enterprise existed, personal profit was an effective and socially beneficent motivating force. Yet we have already seen how the profit motive has become distorted in the modern corporation. To the extent that profits induce the risking of capital by investors, they play their customary role. But if the courts, following the traditional logic of property, seek to insure that all profits reach or be held for the security owners, they prevent profits from reaching the very group of men whose action is most important to the efficient conduct of enterprise. Only as profits are diverted into the pockets of control do they, in a measure, perform their second function.

Nor is it clear that even if surplus profits were held out as an incentive to control they would be as effective an instrument as the logic of profits assumes. Presumably the motivating influence of any such huge surplus profits as a modern corporation might be made to produce would be subject to diminishing returns. Certainly it is doubtful if the prospect of a second million dollars of income (and the surplus profits might often amount to much larger sums) would induce activity equal to that induced by the prospect of the first million or even the first hundred thousand. Profits in such terms bear little relation to those envisaged by earlier writers.

Just what motives are effective today, in so far as control is concerned, must be a matter of conjecture. But it is probable that more could be learned regarding them by studying the motives of an

Alexander the Great, seeking new worlds to conquer, than by considering the motives of a petty tradesman of the days of Adam Smith.

Competition

Finally, when Adam Smith championed competition as the great regulator of industry, he had in mind units so small that fixed capital and overhead costs played a role so insignificant that costs were in large measure determinate and so numerous that no single unit held an important position in the market. Today competition in markets dominated by a few great enterprises has come to be more often either cut-throat and destructive or so inactive as to make monopoly or duopoly conditions prevail. Competition between a small number of units each involving an organization so complex that costs have become indeterminate does not satisfy the condition assumed by earlier economists, nor does it appear likely to be as effective a regulator of industry and of profits as they had assumed.

In each of the situations to which these fundamental concepts refer, the Modern Corporation has wrought such a change as to make the concepts inapplicable.[4] New concepts must be forged and a new picture of economic relationships created. It is with this in mind that at the opening of this volume the modern corporation was posed as a major social institution; and its development was envisaged in terms of revolution.

[4] It is frequently suggested that economic activity has become vastly more complex under modern conditions. Yet it is strange that the concentration of the bulk of industry into a few large units has not simplified rather than complicated the economic process. It is worth suggesting that the apparent complexity may arise in part from the effort to analyze the process in terms of concepts which no longer apply.

CHAPTER IV: THE NEW

CONCEPT OF THE

CORPORATION

MOST FUNDAMENTAL TO the new picture of economic life must be a new concept of business enterprise as concentrated in the corporate organization. In some measure a concept is already emerging. Over a decade ago, Walther Rathenau wrote concerning the German counterpart of our great corporation:

"No one is a permanent owner. The composition of the thousandfold complex which functions as lord of the undertaking is in a state of flux. . . . This condition of things signifies that ownership has been depersonalized. . . . The depersonalization of ownership simultaneously implies the objectification of the thing owned. The claims to ownership are subdivided in such a fashion, and are so mobile, that the enterprise assumes an independent life, as if it belonged to no one; it takes an objective existence, such as in earlier days was embodied only in state and church, in a municipal corporation, in the life of a guild or a religious order. . . . The depersonalization of ownership, the objectification of enterprise, the detachment of property from the possessor, leads to a point where the enterprise becomes transformed into an institution which resembles the state in character." [1]

The institution here envisaged calls for analysis, not in terms of business enterprise but in terms of social organization. On the one hand, it involves a concentration of power in the economic field comparable to the concentration of religious power in the mediaeval church or of political power in the national state. On the other hand,

[1] "Von Kommenden Dingen," Berlin, 1918, trans. by E. & C. Paul, ("In Days to Come"), London, 1921, pp. 120, 121.

it involves the interrelation of a wide diversity of economic interests,—those of the "owners" who supply capital, those of the workers who "create," those of the consumers who give value to the products of enterprise, and above all those of the control who wield power.

Such a great concentration of power and such a diversity of interest raise the long-fought issue of power and its regulation—of interest and its protection. A constant warfare has existed between the individuals wielding power, in whatever form, and the subjects of that power. Just as there is a continuous desire for power, so also there is a continuous desire to make that power the servant of the bulk of the individuals it affects. The long struggles for the reform of the Catholic Church and for the development of constitutional law in the states are phases of this phenomenon. Absolute power is useful in building the organization. More slow, but equally sure is the development of social pressure demanding that the power shall be used for the benefit of all concerned. This pressure, constant in ecclesiastical and political history, is already making its appearance in many guises in the economic field.

Observable throughout the world, and in varying degrees of intensity, is this insistence that power in economic organization shall be subjected to the same tests of public benefit which have been applied in their turn to power otherwise located. In its most extreme aspect this is exhibited in the communist movement, which in its purest form is an insistence that *all* of the powers and privileges of property, shall be used only in the common interest. In less extreme forms of socialist dogma, transfer of economic powers to the state for public service is demanded. In the strictly capitalist countries, and particularly in time of depression, demands are constantly put forward that the men controlling the great economic organisms be made to accept responsibility for the well-being of those who are subject to the organization, whether workers, investors, or consumers. In a sense the difference in all of these demands lies only in degree. In proportion as an economic organism grows in strength and its power is concentrated in a few hands, the possessor of power is more easily located, and the demand for responsible power becomes increasingly direct.

How will this demand be made effective? To answer this question would be to foresee the history of the next century. We can here only consider and appraise certain of the more important lines of possible development.

By tradition, a corporation "belongs" to its shareholders, or, in a wider sense, to its security holders, and theirs is the only interest to be recognized as the object of corporate activity. Following this tradition, and without regard for the changed character of ownership, it would be possible to apply in the interests of the *passive* property owner the doctrine of strict property rights, the analysis of which has been presented above in the chapter on Corporate Powers as Powers in Trust. By the application of this doctrine, the group in control of a corporation would be placed in a position of trusteeship in which it would be called on to operate or arrange for the operation of the corporation for the *sole* benefit of the security owners despite the fact that the latter have ceased to have power over or to accept responsibility for the *active* property in which they have an interest. Were this course followed, the bulk of American industry might soon be operated by trustees for the sole benefit of inactive and irresponsible security owners.

In direct opposition to the above doctrine of strict property rights is the view, apparently held by the great corporation lawyers and by certain students of the field, that corporate development has created a new set of relationships, giving to the groups in control powers which are absolute and not limited by any implied obligation with respect to their use. This logic leads to drastic conclusions. For instance, if, by reason of these new relationships, the men in control of a corporation can operate it in their own interests, and can divert a portion of the asset fund of income stream to their own uses, such is their privilege. Under this view, since the new powers have been acquired on a quasi-contractual basis, the security holders have agreed in advance to any losses which they may suffer by reason of such use. The result is, briefly, that the existence of the legal and economic relationships giving rise to these powers must be frankly recognized as a modification of the principle of private property.

If these were the only alternatives, the former would appear to be the lesser of two evils. Changed corporate relationships have unquestionably involved an essential alteration in the character of property. But such modifications have hitherto been brought about largely on the principle that might makes right. Choice between strengthening the rights of passive property owners, or leaving a set of uncurbed powers in the hands of control therefore resolves itself into a purely realistic evaluation of different results. We might elect the relative certainty and safety of a trust relationship in favor of a particular group within the corporation, accompanied by a possible diminution of enterprise. Or we may grant the controlling group free rein, with the corresponding danger of a corporate oligarchy coupled with the probability of an era of corporate plundering.

A third possibility exists, however. On the one hand, the owners of passive property, by surrendering control and responsibility over the active property, have surrendered the right that the corporation should be operated in their sole interest,—they have released the community from the obligation to protect them to the full extent implied in the doctrine of strict property rights. At the same time, the controlling groups, by means of the extension of corporate powers, have in their own interest broken the bars of tradition which require that the corporation be operated solely for the benefit of the owners of passive property. Eliminating the sole interest of the passive owner, however, does not necessarily lay a basis for the alternative claim that the new powers should be used in the interest of the controlling groups. The latter have not presented, in acts or words any acceptable defense of the proposition that these powers should be so used. No tradition supports that proposition. The control groups have, rather, cleared the way for the claims of a group far wider than either the owners or the control. They have placed the community in a position to demand that the modern corporation serve not alone the owners or the control but all society.

This third alternative offers a wholly new concept of corporate activity. Neither the claims of ownership nor those of control can stand against the paramount interests of the community. The present claims of both contending parties now in the field have been weakened by the developments described in this book. It remains only for the claims of the community to be put forward with clarity and force. Rigid enforcement of property rights as a temporary protection against plundering by control would not stand in the way of the modification of these rights in the interest of other groups. When a convincing system of community obligations is worked out and is generally accepted, in that moment the passive property right of today must yield before the larger interests of society. Should the corporate leaders, for example, set forth a program comprising fair wages, security to employees, reasonable service to their public, and stabilization of business, all of which would divert a portion of the profits from the owners of passive property, and should the community generally accept such a scheme as a logical and human solution of industrial difficulties, the interests of passive property owners would have to give way. Courts would almost of necessity be forced to recognize the result, justifying it by whatever of the many legal theories they might choose. It is conceivable,—indeed it seems almost essential if the corporate system is to survive,—that the "control" of the great corporations should develop into a purely neutral technocracy, balancing a variety of claims by various groups in the community and assigning to each a portion of the income stream on the basis of public policy rather than private cupidity.

In still larger view, the modern corporation may be regarded not simply as one form of social organization but potentially (if not yet actually) as the dominant institution of the modern world. In every age, the major concentration of power has been based upon the dominant interest of that age. The strong man has, in his time, striven to be cardinal or pope, prince or cabinet minister, bank president or partner in the House of Morgan. During the Middle Ages, the Church, exercising spiritual power, dominated Europe and gave to it a unity at a time when both political and economic power were diffused. With the rise of the modern state, political power, concentrated into a few large units, challenged the spiritual interest as the strongest bond of human society. Out of the long struggle between church and state which followed, the state emerged victorious; nationalist politics superseded religion as the basis of the major unifying organization of the western world. Economic power still remained diffused.

The rise of the modern corporation has brought a concentration of economic power which can compete on equal terms with the modern state—economic power versus political power, each strong in its own field. The state seeks in some aspects to regulate the corporation, while the corporation, steadily becoming more powerful, makes every effort to avoid such regulation. Where its own interests are concerned, it even attempts to dominate the state. The future may see the economic organism, now typified by the corporation, not only on an equal plane with the state, but possibly even superseding it as the dominant form of social organization. The law of corporations, accordingly, might well be considered as a potential constitutional law for the new economic state, while business practice is increasingly assuming the aspect of economic statesmanship.

APPENDIXES

APPENDIX A: *Size of Corporations Represented by Stock Listed and Active on the New York Stock Exchange* [1]

573 independent corporations

Gross assets	Number of corpora-tions	Gross assets	Number of corpora-tions
Under $10 million	100	$100–$200 million	49
$10–20 million	115	200–300 million	22
20–30 million	70	300–400 million	18
30–40 million	56	400–500 million	7
40–50 million	31	500–600 million	12
50–60 million	21	600–700 million	4
60–70 million	16	700–800 million	3
70–80 million	17	800–900 million	4
80–90 million	10	900–1000 million	
90–100 million	7	Over billion	11
Total under $100 million	443	Grand total	573

[1] Derived from Commercial and Financial Chronicle, vol. 128, No. 3324 (March 9, 1929), pp. 1514–1523 and Moody's Railroad, Public Utility and Industrial Manuals for 1928 and 1929.

APPENDIX B: *Comparison of Savings of Large Corporations and All Corporations*

Calendar year	Savings			Proportion of profits saved	
	By all non-financial corpora-tions [1] in million dollars	By 200 largest corpora-tions [2] (esti-mated) in million dollars	Ratio of savings of 200 largest to savings of all corpo-rations in per cent	By all non-financial corpora-tions [3] in per cent	By 108 identical corpora-tions included in largest 200 [4] in per cent
1922	1,747	555	31.8	33.7	33.8
1923	2,528	889	35.1	37.8	41.5
1924	1,575	839	53.2	26.6	37.5
1925	2,957	1,011	34.2	36.3	39.9
1926	2,335	1,290	55.3	28.2	42.2
1927	1,115	1,164	104.5 [5]	14.8	35.2
Total for 6 years	12,257	5,748	46.9	29.4	38.5

[1] Derived from Statistics of Income for respective years by deducting cash dividends paid by all non-financial corporations from net profits after taxes of all non-financial corporations.

[2] Estimated on the basis of savings by 108 identical corporations which were included in the list of the 200 largest at one time or another during the period. The savings of the 200 corporations were assumed to bear the same relation to the savings by the sample as the gross assets of the two groups.

[3] Ratio of savings to net profits after taxes for all non-financial corporations as reported in Statistics of Income for the respective years.

[4] For 108 identical companies (39 railroads, 31 public utilities and 38 industrials), included at one time or another between 1922 and 1927 in the list of the 200 largest corporations, information was obtained from Moody's Railroad, Public Utility, and Industrial Manuals, covering net income available for dividends and cash dividends paid. Any loss reported was treated as negative income. Savings were reckoned as net income less cash dividends.

[5] Savings can become negative—as where more is paid out by way of dividends than is taken in by way of profit.

APPENDIX C: *Proportion of Total New Issues of Corporate Securities Offered by 200 Largest Corporations or Their Subsidiaries* [1]

(*In millions of dollars*)

4 months of year	Total by all non-financial corporations	Total by 200 largest corporations [2]	Proportion by 200 largest corporations
1922	$ 502.4	$ 300.8	$59.8
1923	735.5	469.5	63.8
1924	1,004.8	740.6	73.8
1925	867.6	552.0	63.6
1926	1,249.9	782.5	62.6
1927	1,552.0	1,159.6	74.7
Total	$5,912.2	$4,005.2	$67.7

[1] Compilation covering March, June, September and December of each year, derived from the Commercial and Financial Chronicle.

[2] Assuming 90 per cent of refunding to have been done by these companies.

APPENDIX D: *Mergers of Big Companies* [1] *1922–1929*

Companies on list of 200 largest companies at some time during period which have been acquired by another company on the list.

Year	Company acquired	Acquiring company	Assets of company acquired at about the time of acquisition (million dollars)
1919	None		
1920	Associated Oil Co.	Pacific Oil Co.	$ 68.1
1921	Midwest Refining Co.	Standard Oil Co. of Ind.	85.9
1922	Lackawanna Steel Co.	Bethlehem Steel Corp.	89.6
1923	Toledo, St. Louis & West. Rd. Co.	N. Y., Chi. & St. L. R. R. Co.	59.5
	Chile Copper Co.	Anaconda Copper M. Co.	151.4
	Midvale Steel & Ordnance Co.	Bethlehem Steel Corp.	285.4
	Morris & Co.	Armour & Co.	95.0
	Steel & Tube Co. of America	Youngstown Sh. & T. Co.	94.0
	Utah Copper Co.	Kennecott Copper Corp.	66.0
1924	Carolina, Clinchfield & O. Ry. Co.	Atl. Coast Line R. R. Co.	78.7
	Internat. Gr. Northern Ry. Co.	Mo. Pac. R. R. Co.	77.5
	Chicago Elevated Rys. Co.	Commonwealth Ed. Co.	97.4
1925	Kansas City, Mex. & Or. Ry. Co.	At., To. & S. Fe. Ry. Co.	88.0
	Alabama Power Co.	Southeastern Pr. & Lt. Co.	86.0
	New Orleans Public Serv. Co.	Electric Pr. & Lt. Corp.	69.3
	Ohio Fuel Supply Co.	Columbia Gas & El. Corp.	78.9
	Utah Securities Corp.	Electric Pr. & Lt. Corp.	100.0 [2]
	Western Power Corp.	North American Co.	96.4
	Magnolia Petroleum Co.	Standard Oil Co. of N. Y.	212.8
	Pan Am. Pet. & Trans. Co.	Standard Oil Co. of Ind.	179.5
1926	Penn. Electric Co.	Ass. Gas & Elec. Co.	88.1
	Standard Power & Lt. Corp.	Ass. Gas & Elec. Co.	300.0 [2]
	United Rys. Investment Co.	Standard Gas & Elec. Co.	250.0 [2]
	Pacific Oil Co.	Standard Oil Co. of Calif.	181.0
	General Petroleum Corp.	Standard Oil Co. of N. Y.	102.0
	Pacific Petroleum Co.	Standard Oil Co. of Calif.	95.3
1927	Georgia Ry. & Power Co.	Southeastern Pr. & Lt. Co.	76.5
	San Joaquin Light & Power Co.	Western Power Corp.	75.0

APPENDIX D: *Mergers of Big Companies* [1] *1922–1929 (Continued)*

Year	Company acquired	Acquiring company	Assets of company acquired at about the time of acquisition (million dollars)
1928	Northwestern Pacific Rd. Co.	At., To. & S. Fe Ry. Co.	70.0
	Pere Marquette Ry. Co.	Alleghany Corp.	157.0
	Texas & Pacific Ry. Co.	Missouri Pac. R. R. Co.	140.0
	American Light & Traction Co.	United Lt. & Pr. Co.	128.5 [2]
	Brooklyn Edison Co.	Cons. Gas Co. of N. Y.	153.3
	Mackay Companies	Internat. Tel. & Tel. Co.	93.4
	Montana Power Co.	American Pr. & Lt. Co.	106.0
	National Electric Power Co.	Mid. West Utilities Co.	123.0
	National Public Service Corp.	Nat. Electric Power Co.	174.7
	Philadelphia Electric Co.	United Gas Imp. Co.	278.4
	Puget Sound Power & Light Co.	Eng. Public Service Co.	122.2
1928	California Petroleum Corp.	Texas Corp.	102.2
	Dodge Bros. Inc.	Chrysler Corp.	131.5
1929	General Gas & Electric Corp.	Ass. Gas & Elec. Co.	$175.0
	Massachusetts Gas Companies	Koppers Co.	89.6
	Mohawk Hudson Power Corp.	Niagara Hudson Pr. Corp.	190.0 [2]
	New England Power Assoc.	Internat. Pap. & Pr. Co.	216.8
	Northeastern Power Corp.	Niagara Hudson Pr. Corp.	131.4
	Penn-Ohio Edison Co.	Com. & So. Pr. Corp.	153.3
	Southeastern Power & Lt. Co.	Com. & So. Pr. Corp.	507.2
	Greene Cananea Copper Co.	Anaconda Cop. M. Co.	56.2

[1] Merger is used here to refer to the acquisition of control of one company by another involving either a consolidation of properties or simply stock control.

[2] Estimated.

APPENDIX E: *Partial List of Industrial Mergers in Which One of the Largest 200 Companies Acquired a Company Not on List but Large (1928–1929)*

Company acquired	Assets approximately at time of merger in million dollars	Acquiring company
Grasselli Chemical Co.	$56.7	E. I. DuPont de Nemours
Pierce-Arrow Motor Car Co.	24.0	Studebaker Corp.
Columbia Steel Corp.	34.0	United States Steel Corp.
Trumbull Steel Co.	51.2	Republic Iron & Steel Co.
Texon Oil & Land Co.	26.6	Marland Oil Co.
Continental Oil Co.	81.0	Marland Oil Co.
Hood Rubber Co.	35.7	Goodrich Tire & Rubber Co.
Pacific Public Service Co.	25.0	Standard Oil Co. of Calif.
Chase Cos. Inc.	29.9	Kennecott Copper Corp.
Lehigh & Wilkes Barre Coal Co.	63.1	Glen Alden Coal Co.
Standard Sanitary Mfg. Co.	55.0	American Radiator Co.
Shredded Wheat Co.	12.8	National Biscuit Co.
Creole Petroleum Corp.	50.0 [1]	Standard Oil of N. J.
Keith-Albee-Orpheum Corp.	84.3	Radio Corp. of America
Victor Talking Machine Co.	68.3	Radio Corp. of America
Hartmann Corp.	26.4	Montgomery Ward & Co.

[1] Estimated.

APPENDIX F: *Companies on List of Largest 200 in 1919 and Not on List of Largest in 1928* [1]

	Gross assets on or about Dec. 31 (in million dollars)	
	1919	1928
23 merged with a larger company		
Carolina, Clinchfield & Ohio Railway Co.	$ 68.2	
Kansas City, Mexico & Orient Railroad Co.	81.1	
Northwestern Pacific Railway Co.	72.6	
Pere Marquette Railway Co.	136.4	
Texas & Pacific Railway Co.	132.1	
Toledo, St. Louis & Western Railroad Co.	59.5	
Chicago Elevated Railways Co.	98.8	
Mackay Companies	93.3	
Montana Power Co.	98.8	
Philadelphia Electric Co.	92.7	
Puget Sound Power & Light Co.	89.7	
United Railways Investment Co.	247.0 [2]	
Western Power Corp.	57.3	
Associated Oil Co.	68.1	
Chile Copper Co.	153.5	
Lackawanna Steel Co.	95.4	
Magnolia Petroleum Company	182.0	
Midvale Steel & Ordnance Co.	280.1	
Midwest Refining Company	85.9	
Morris & Company	114.0	
Pan American Petroleum & Transport Co.	58.1	
Steel & Tube Co. of America	91.9	
Utah Copper Co.	79.3	
7 too small in 1928 to be on list but showing growth since 1919		
Buffalo, Rochester & Pittsburgh Railway Co.	63.2	65.8
Allis-Chalmers Mfg. Co.	61.0	64.0
Baldwin Locomotive Works	64.9	71.3
Cudahy Packing Co.	71.0	82.5
International Nickel Co. [10]	64.6	95.9
Lehigh Coal & Navigation Co.	76.0	79.3
Packard Motor Car Co.	63.0	75.1

APPENDIX F: *Companies on List of Largest 200 in 1919 and Not on List of Largest in 1928* [1] (*Continued*)

	Gross assets on or about Dec. 31 (in million dollars)	
	1919	1928
8 showing loss in assets since 1919 but not suffering reorganization		
Spring Valley Water Co.	76.2	75.3
American Agricultural Chemical Co.	110.7	76.9
Atlantic Gulf and West Indies S. S. Lines	120.8	69.8
Colorado Fuel & Iron Co.	82.5	80.0
Great Northern Iron Ore Properties (*wasting assets*)	98.5	42.9
Greene Cananea Copper Co.	61.0	57.5
Libby, McNeill & Libby	67.7	57.5
U. S. Smelting, Refining & Mining Co.	90.9	78.7
4 reorganized but still essentially intact		
Minneapolis & St. Louis Railroad Co.	$ 80.1	94.5
Calumet & Hecla Mining Co. [3]	100.0 [2]	59.3
Central Leather Co. [4]	146.8	46.4
Virginia-Carolina Chemical Company [5]	114.6	38.6
5 property essentially broken up		
Chicago Utilities Co. [6]	63.7	
Detroit United Ry. Co. [6]	63.8	less than 40.0
New York Railways Co. [7]	90.6	less than 34.4
American Cotton Oil Co. [8]	62.8	
Pierce Oil Corp. [9]	60.3	

[1] Derived from Moody's Railroad, Public Utilities, and Industrial Manuals or Standard Corporation Records.

[2] Estimated.

[3] Consolidated with other companies in 1923 to give Calumet & Hecla Consolidated Copper Co.

[4] Reorganized in 1927 as United States Leather Co.

[5] Reorganized in 1926 as Virginia-Carolina Chemical Corp.

[6] Liquidated.

[7] Reorganized elements acquired by Fifth Ave. Coach Co. which is ultimately controlled by the Omnibus Corporation.

[8] Parts of property acquired by Gold Dust Co.

[9] Part of assets transferred to Pierce Petroleum Corp.

[10] Assets transferred to a foreign corporation, but for present purposes classed as above.

APPENDIX G: *Stockholders of 44 Companies Not Included in Largest 200—Arranged According to Size of Company* [1] *(1928)*

Gross assets in millions	Company	Stockholders 1928
79.0	U. S. Smelting & Refining	14,971
78.1	Barnsdall Corporation	5,982
72.9	Willys-Overland	18,800
70.7	Westinghouse Air Brake	10,000
69.0	Continental Baking	20,469
62.1	Allis-Chalmers	4,056
61.0	Packard Motor Car	7,000
60.4	Maine Central Railroad	2,411
57.6	Quaker Oats	5,560
56.2	Green Cananea Copper	8,350
55.2	Pressed Steel Car	6,600
51.1	American Ice	3,653
47.7	General Asphalt	1,527–1927
45.3	Great Northern Iron Ore Properties	7,456–1927
44.8	Continental Can	6,100
43.5	Inspiration Consolidated Copper	9,394
40.0	South Porto Rico Sugar Co.	2,916
37.3	General Foods	4,665
36.4	Continental Motors Corporation	11,105–19
36.4	International Business Machines Corp.	2,880
33.5	Reo Motor Car	9,200
33.1	Congoleum-Nairn	4,200
31.5	White Eagle Oil & Refining Co.	3,435
29.9	Mergenthaler Linotype	3,887
29.7	Atlas Powder Co.	3,763
28.9	American Ship Building Co.	1,485
28.6	Texas Gulf Sulphur	11,500
28.4	Worthington Pump & Machinery	3,544
28.1	Burns Bros.	500–1926
28.0	Stewart-Warner Corporation	8,000
27.6	American International Corporation	2,610–1927
27.5	Certain-Teed Products Corporation	3,769
26.4	Hartmann Corporation	5,000–1927
23.3	Cluett, Peabody & Co.	2,227
23.3	Julius Kayser	1,300
20.1	Union Bag & Paper Corporation	1,278

APPENDIX G: *Stockholders of 44 Companies Not Included in Largest 200—Arranged According to Size of Company* [1] *(1928) (Continued)*

Gross assets in millions	Company	Stockholders 1928
19.4	American Bank Note	4,090
19.1	Simms Petroleum	2,075
17.1	Mathieson Alkali Works	974
14.2	Lima Locomotive Works	1,480
12.9	Motor Wheel Corporation	3,387
10.6	American Bosch Magneto Corporation	2,222
7.3	Reynolds Spring Co.	2,540
6.2	Jewel Tea Co.	1,101—1926

[1] Information derived from Standard Corporation Records, 1929.

APPENDIX H: *Stockholders of Thirty-one Large Corporations* [1]

Number of shareholders

Name of company	1900	1910	1913	1917	1920	1923	1928
Am. Car and Foundry	7,747	9,912	10,402	9,223	13,229	16,090	17,152
Am. Locomotive	1,700	8,198	8,578	8,490	9,957	10,596	19,359
Am. Smelting and Refining	3,398	9,464	10,459	12,244	15,237	18,583	15,040
Am. Sugar Refining	10,816	19,551	18,149	19,758	22,311	26,781	22,276
Du Pont Powder	809	2,050	2,697	6,592	11,624	14,141	21,248
General Asphalt	2,089	2,294	2,184	2,112	1,879	2,383	1,527
General Electric	2,900	9,486	12,271	12,950	17,338	36,008	51,882
Great Northern Iron Ore	3,762	4,419	4,685	4,855	6,747	9,313	7,456
International Paper	2,245	4,096	3,929	4,509	3,903	4,522	23,767
Procter and Gamble	1,098	1,606	1,881	2,448	9,157	11,392	37,000
Standard Oil of New Jersey	3,832	5,847	6,104	7,351	8,074	51,070	62,317
Swift and Co.	3,400	18,000	20,000	20,000	35,000	46,000	47,000
Union Bag and Paper	1,950	2,250	2,800	1,592	1,856	2,263	1,278
United Fruit	971	6,181	7,641	9,653	11,849	20,469	26,219
United Shoe Machinery	4,500	7,400	8,366	6,547	8,762	10,935	18,051
U. S. Rubber	3,000	3,500	12,846	17,419	20,866	34,024	26,057
U. S. Steel Corp.	54,016	94,934	123,891	131,210	176,310	179,090	154,243
	108,233	209,188	256,883	276,953	374,099	493,660	551,872

[1] Data derived from Warshow, *op. cit.*, for 1900–1923, and from Annual Reports, Moody's Manuals, Standard Corporation Records and news clippings for 1928.

APPENDIX H: *Stockholders of Thirty-one Large Corporations* [1] *(Continued)*

Name of company	Number of shareholders						
	1900	1910	1913	1917	1920	1923	1928
American Telephone & Telegraph Co.	7,535	40,381	55,983	86,699	139,448	281,149	454,596
Brooklyn Union Gas	1,313	1,593	1,646	1,834	1,985	1,879	2,841
Commonwealth Edison	1,255	1,780	2,045	4,582	11,580	34,526	40,000
Western Union	9,134	12,731	12,790	20,434	23,911	26,276	26,234
	19,237	56,485	72,464	113,549	176,924	343,830	523,671
Atlantic Coast Line	702	2,278	2,727	3,404	4,422	5,162	4,212
Chesapeake and Ohio	1,145	2,268	6,281	6,103	8,111	13,010	6,885
Chicago and North Western	4,907	8,023	11,111	13,735	19,383	21,555	16,948
Delaware, Lackawanna and Western	1,896	1,699	1,959	2,615	3,276	6,650	7,957
Great Northern	1,690	16,298	19,540	26,716	40,195	44,523	43,741
Illinois Central	7,025	9,790	10,776	10,302	12,870	19,470	21,147
New York, New Haven & Hartford	9,521	17,573	26,240	25,343	25,272	24,983	27,267
Pennsylvania	51,543	65,283	88,586	100,038	133,068	144,228	157,650
Reading	6,388	5,781	6,624	8,397	9,701	11,687	9,844
Union Pacific	14,256	20,282	26,761	33,875	47,339	51,022	47,932
	99,073	149,275	200,605	230,528	303,637	342,290	343,583
Book Stockholders 31 Companies	226,543	414,948	529,952	621,030	854,660	1,179,780	1,419,126
Total Book Stockholders excl. American Telephone & Telegraph Co.	219,008	374,567	473,969	534,331	715,212	898,631	964,530

[1] Data derived from Warshow, *op. cit.*, for 1900–1923, and from Annual Reports, Moody's Manuals, Standard Corporation Records and news clipping for 1928.

APPENDIX I: *Stock Sales Made by Public Utilities to Customers* *
(1914–1929)

Year	Number of additional companies adopting customer ownership plan [1]	Sales made [1]	Shares of stock sold [1]	Value of sales [2]
1914	7	4,044	92,310	
1915	3	4,357	57,130	
1916	4	3,681	38,183	
1917	8	8,242	82,007	
1918	7	5,186	42,388	
1919	12	19,872	194,021	
1920	34	53,063	454,139	$ 43,000,000
1921	37	118,544	830,222	80,000,000
1922	49	156,725	1,450,707	130,000,000
1923	24	279,186	1,806,300	175,000,000
1924	23	294,467	2,478,165	254,000,000
1925	18	236,043	2,926,271	297,000,000
1926	2	248,867	2,686,187	236,000,000
1927	18	249,491	3,581,206	263,000,000
1928	5	227,961 [3]	2,081,071	181,000,000 [3]
1929		280,600 [4]	2,432,550 [4]	153,436,000 [4]
1930		217,000 [4]	2,030,000 [4]	135,000,000 [4]

* In the compilation of these statistics, each separate purchase of stocks has been recorded by many of the reporting companies as being the acquisition of an additional "stockholder." There are possibilities of duplications, arising from: (a) repeat purchases of stock of the same company by the same individual; (b) the purchase of stock in two or more companies by the same individual; (c) in addition, the situation is further complicated by the purchase of stocks by customers from other sources than through the company's office.

[1] National Electric Light Association, Serial Report of Customer Ownership Committee 1928–29, p. 4.

[2] Electrical World, vol. xciii, no. 1, p. 27.

[3] *Ibid.*, vol. xcv, p. 67.

[4] *Ibid.*, vol. xcvii, p. 73. Figures for 1930 are preliminary estimates based on figures for ten months.

APPENDIX J: *The Increase of Employee Stock Purchase Plans in the United States*

Year	No. of companies instituting stock purchase plans [1]
1900 or earlier	5
1901–1905	13
1906–1910	14
1911	1
1912	7
1913	7
1914	6
1915	7
1916	10
1917	11
1918	8
1919	24
1920	46
1921	35
1922	17
1923	51
1924	29
1925	29
1926	13
1927	4
No information	49

[1] Compiled from appendix of National Industrial Conference Board, "Employee Stock Purchase Plans in the United States," N. Y. 1928.

APPENDIX K: *An Estimate of the Number of Individuals Owning Stock in the United States at the Close of 1927*

An estimate of the number of individuals owning stock in the United States must, at best, be very approximate. This is true, primarily, because a very great increase in the number of stockholders could be made without seriously affecting the ownership of the bulk of corporate shares. If the ownership of stock had been shifted so that one per cent of all dividends paid to individuals in 1927 had been shifted from a few individuals to persons who owned no stock so that each new stockholder received an average of $47 [1] in dividends, a million new stockholders would have been created. Such small stockholdings are by no means uncommon. In 1924, 37 per cent [2] of the stockholders of the American Telephone and Telegraph Company owned five shares or less and received less than $46 in dividends from this Company, probably averaging less than $25.

In seeking to arrive at some notion of the number of individuals who owned stock in 1927 three facts stand out:

First, only 516,029 individuals with incomes over $5,000 reported the receipt of dividends. This group received 78.9 per cent [3] of all dividends paid to individuals.

Second, 10.3 per cent of all dividends were reported by the 3,187,950 individuals reporting incomes under $5,000, though the number of stockholders included is not known.

Third, the remaining 10.8 per cent of dividends must, presumably, have been received by foreigners or by individuals not filing income tax returns.

It is not possible to estimate accurately the number of stockholders reporting incomes under $5,000, but it is possible to set extreme limits to the probable number. Only 56.6 per cent of the individuals reporting incomes over $5,000 reported receiving dividends. If the proportion was the same for individuals reporting incomes under $5,000, there would have been only 1,800,000 [4] receivers of dividends included in the 3,187,950 filing returns. In this lower income group, however, a very much smaller proportion of income was reported as derived from property ownership and a larger proportion from personal exertion than was the case in the upper brackets. It is, therefore, reasonable to suppose that the proportion of stockholders in the lower group was very much smaller than the proportion of stockholders among individuals reporting an income of $5,000 or more and we may accept the figure of 1,800,000 as a probable maximum.

While there is no statistical basis for arriving at the minimum figure for the number of stockholders in this group, it is highly unlikely that the average

[1] $4,765,700,000 of dividends were reported as paid by corporations and not received by other corporations in 1927. Statistics of Income, 1927, pages 312–313.
[2] American Telephone & Telegraph Company Annual Report, 1925, pages 33–34.
[3] Statistics of Income, 1927, pp. 4, 8, and 10.
[4] 3,187,950 × 56.6%.

stockholder with an income under $5,000 and filing a tax return received $1,000 in dividends as his income from this source. If we use this figure as representing an improbably high average holding and divide the amount of dividends received by the group by this average, we would have a figure of 500,000 stockholders as the minimum number of stockholders included. We will, therefore, be safe in saying that between 1,800,000 and 500,000 stockholders received an income of less than $5,000 and filed income tax returns.

We have thus far accounted for 89.2 per cent of all dividends, 78.9 per cent going to individuals reporting incomes over $5,000 and 10.3 per cent going to individuals reporting incomes under $5,000. This leaves 10.8 per cent or $510,000,000 of dividends unaccounted for. Part of this amount must have been received by foreigners or foreign corporations. In the study covering over 4,000 corporations representing one-eighth of all corporate stocks, the Federal Trade Commission found 1.6 [5] per cent of the stocks was owned by foreign holders in 1922. If we apply this figure to the dividends paid out by all corporations,[6] this would account for $103,000,000 dividends, leaving $407,000,000 which must, in the main, have been received by individuals not required to file income tax returns. This includes single individuals of incomes under $1,500 and husbands and wives living together and having a combined income of less than $3,500.

Very little basis is available for estimating the number of stockholders in this third portion. If the average holding in this group yielded dividends amounting to $500, the group would be composed of 800,000 stockholders. If the average holding yielded only $80, indicating an average investment of a little more than $1,000, the group would be composed of 5,000,000 stockholders. It is probable that the group includes a large number of individuals who received their main income from investments, stocks and bonds, and it is the author's belief that the existence of this latter group would bring the average dividend return to considerably more than $80. These two figures are given as probably the extreme limits. The third group would thus include the number of stockholders between 800,000 and 5,000,000.

Two additional facts are available in helping to estimate the number of stockholders. The National Industrial Conference Board found 806,068 employee stockholders or subscribers in 1927 with total holdings amounting to $1,045,150,410. Since this figure was believed to report the "great bulk of employee owned stock," [7] we may safely set 1,000,000 stockholders as the maximum number of employees who owned stock obtained through the stock purchase plan of the companies for which they worked, and $1,125,000,000 as the maximum amount of stock so owned.

The second fact—the number of customer owners—can only be a rough approximation. By 1927, 1,681,768 separate sales had been made to public

[5] Federal Trade Commission, National Wealth & Income, page 150, based on Table 82.
[6] $6,423,796,271 (Statistics of Income, 1927, page 313) $\times$ 1.6% gives $103,000,000.
[7] National Industrial Conference Board—*Op. cit.,* pp. 35–36.

utility customers, involving $1,478,000,000 worth of stock. As these sales frequently involved duplication,[8] and as the individuals purchasing in earlier years frequently disposed of their securities before 1927, we may roughly fix the number of customer owners as 1,000,000 with a volume of stock of $1,500,000,000. This estimate must be considered as only very approximate.

Taking these two classes alone, and assuming that the duplication between them is nil, we should have 2,000,000 stockholders owning stock worth $2,750,000,000. With a yield of 6 per cent, this would give the average stockholder $83 in dividends; but many employee stockholders and a large number of customer owners must also own stock in other corporations, so that the average dividends received by these two groups of individuals from all classes would be considerably higher.

One more fact can assist in making an estimate of the number of stockholders. This is an estimate of the number of stockholders of record; that is, the number of individual names on the stock record books of all corporations regardless of duplication. This has been estimated on the basis of separate data at a figure in the vicinity of 18,000,000 for 1927, though it may be as high as 20,000,000 or as low as 16,000,000.[9] If every stockholder owned stock in only one corporation, the total number of stockholders would, therefore, be approximately 18,000,000. Since most stockholders own stock of more than one company, the number of stockholders would be very much less. If the average holder owned stocks of four companies, the total number of stockholders would presumably be approximately 4,500,000.

With these three sets of facts in mind, it is possible to form a very rough opinion as to the number of individuals owning stock. The figures are brought together in the table below:

| | | Number of individuals owning stock | |
		Maximum	Minimum
I	*Stockholders with income over $5,000*	500,000	500,000
	Stockholders with income under $5,000 and filing tax returns	1,800,000	500,000
	Stockholders with income under $5,000 and filing no tax returns	5,000,000	800,000
	Total stockholders	7,300,000	1,800,000
II	*Employee and Customer Stockholders*	2,000,000	
III	*Estimated Stockholders of Record*	18,000,000	

[8] The Electrical World reports that in one case of a sale to customers by a public utility in 1929 "out of a total of 5,344 sales, 2,541 were sales to new customer owners," that is, in only 48 per cent of the sales was the customer buying for the first time and, thereby, adding to the number of book stockholders. Electrical World, vol. XCV, No. 1 (Jan. 4, 1930), p. 75.

[9] See "Diffusion of Stock Ownership in the U. S., *loc. cit.*, p. 565.

On the basis of income tax statistics, the minimum number of stockholders is 1,800,000 while the maximum is 7,300,000. The minimum appears to be much too low since there are presumably in the vicinity of 2,000,000 employee and customer stockholders. At the other extreme, if we compare the maximum figure of 7,300,000 individual stockholders with the estimate of stockholders of record, the acceptance of both figures would mean that the average individual stockholder owned stocks of only two and one-half companies. The extensive diversification of securities which has occurred in recent years would suggest the probability that the average stockholder owns stock in more than two and one-half companies, making the maximum estimate too high. It seems probable, therefore, that the number of individuals who owned stock in 1927 was between 4,000,000 and 6,000,000.

For 1929 no estimate has been made. However, the number of persons owning stock was certainly not less in 1929 than in 1927. It was probably somewhat more. For purposes of indicating the distribution of stock ownership in 1929, the outside limits have been roughly placed at 4,000,000 and 7,000,000 persons. See pages 59–60.

As of January 1, 1968, the number of individual stockholders in the United States has been estimated at between twenty-two and twenty-three million. The estimate is that of the New York Stock Exchange based on a sampling study made by its experts. It indicates that the number of stockholders in the United States has multiplied five times since 1932.

But in addition, wide diffusion of ownership has taken place through another route. Private pension trust funds, designed to pay old age pensions and other benefits to workers, have enormously increased; their total holdings may now amount to $85 billions. Nearly one-half of these funds are invested in common stocks. The beneficiaries of these funds probably number in excess of thirty million individuals. These thus have a stake in the market values of the common stocks held by their funds. Probably many of these beneficiaries of funds are also holders of common stocks; one cannot simply add the number of trust fund beneficiaries to the stock market figure of twenty-two millions-plus stockholders comprised in the New York Stock Exchange estimate. Even discounting duplication, nevertheless it is obvious that a substantial percentage of Americans probably ascending to 25% or more of the American population (without counting their families) hold directly or indirectly an interest in the stocks of American corporations.

APPENDIX L: *Proportion of Property in Corporate Securities Based on Estate Tax Returns*

Property of 8,079 estates of resident decedents for which returns were filed in 1928, divided so as to show proportion of property from which an income could be derived in each of the three main fields—Real Estate, Government Securities, and Corporation Securities. Derived from Statistics of Income, 1927, p. 48.

Real Estate	$ 610.6 mil.	
Mortgages, notes, cash, etc.[1]	385.3 mil.	
Attributable to Real Estate	$ 995.9 mil.	33.2%
Government Securities	$ 247.4 mil.	8.3%
Capital stock in corporations	$1,516.9 mil.	
All other bonds [1]	239.4 mil.	
	$1,756.3 mil.	58.5%
Total of Real Estate & Government or Corporate		
Securities	$2,999.6 mil.	100.0%
Insurance [2]	103.2 mil.	
Jointly owned property [2]	60.8 mil.	
Property from an estate [2] *taxed within 5 yrs.*	83.1 mil.	
Power of appointment [4]	18.3 mil.	
Transfers made within [5] *2 yr. prior to death*	87.0 mil.	
Miscellaneous [6]	151.0 mil.	
	$ 503.4 mil.	
Total estates reported	$3,503.0 mil.	

[1] In "Mortgages, Notes, Cash, etc.," the mortgages are almost certainly on real estate, the notes may be and the cash cannot be. "All other bonds" includes all corporate bonds but also may include bonds of foreign governments. The cash and the bonds of foreign governments will in some measure cancel each other and there is no reason to believe that either is large and that the final percentages are seriously in error as a result of their inclusion in so far as Real Estate and Corporate Securities are concerned. Government Securities are, of course, minimized by this procedure to a small extent.

[2] Insurance cannot be allocated to either of the three groups but if the property of the insurance company were divided into the three groups it would undoubtedly approximate the distribution of the decedent's assets and for this reason and also because of its small total no serious error should arise from its exclusion. The same applies to the item "Property from an estate taxed within five years."

[3] Jointly owned property is undoubtedly a larger part real estate than the estate as a whole but being small can be disregarded.

[4] Power of appointment is too small to be distributed, especially as it does not lend itself to classification.

[5] Transfers made within two years prior to death are not property of the decedents' estate except for taxation purposes and can be disregarded.

[6] Miscellaneous is presumably not property from which an income is derived (in the commercial sense).

APPENDIX M: *Main Fields of Investment*

Real estate and improvements, corporate securities, and government securities 1922

		Value in billions
1	Agricultural Real Estate and Improvements [1]	$ 53.0
2	Residential Real Estate and Improvements [2]	48.0
3	Business Real Estate and Improvements [2]	24.0
4	Total Real Estate (1, 2 and 3)	$125.0
5	Real Estate and Improvements of corporations engaged in trade [8]	3.4
6	Real Estate and Improvements of financial corporations including real estate holding companies [2]	8.9
7	Total Real Estate held by corporations (5 + 6)	12.3
8	Total Real Estate held by Individuals (4 − 7)	$112.7
9	Wealth (book value), other than securities, represented by corporate securities [4]	102.4
10	Government Securities held by non-financial corporations [5]	2.7
11	Total Wealth represented by Corporate Securities (9 + 10)	$105.1
12	Federal Government interest bearing securities [6]	22.7
13	Local Government securities [7]	7.2
14	Total Government securities (12 + 13)	$ 29.9

[1] National Wealth and Income, p. 29, footnote 1.

[2] Estimated from figures contained in National Wealth and Income, F. T. C., pp. 28 and 29:

Town and city dwellings, furniture and personal effects "probably is not less than ¼ of total wealth." Total wealth $353.0 bil.	
One-quarter of total wealth	$88.2 bil.
Furniture and personal effects	39.8 bil.
Town and City dwellings	$48.4 bil.
Business and residential real estate	$72.0 bil.
Business Real Estate	24.0 bil.

[8] Statistics of Income, 1922, p. 41. Since for corporations engaged in both trade and finance, the equipment apart from their buildings is negligible, no great error results from regarding "Real Estate, buildings, and equipment" as equivalent to "Real Estate and Improvements."

[4] National Wealth and Income, F. T. C., p. 134.

[5] In 1927 the total Government securities held by corporations amounted to $9,780 mil. from which interest of $500.8 mil. was received. (Stat. of Income, 1927, pp.

APPENDIX M: *Main Fields of Investment* (*Continued*)

Real estate and improvements, corporate securities, and government securities 1922
(*Continued*)

		Value in billions
15	*Government securities held by non-financial corporations* [8]	$ 2.7
16	*Total Investment in Government securities by individuals* [9] (*14 − 15*)	$ 27.2
17	*Total investment opportunity* (*8, 11 and 16*)	$245.0
18	*Ratio of Real Estate to Total investment opportunity* (*8 ÷ 17*)	46.0%
19	*Ratio of Corporate to Total investment opportunity* (*11 ÷ 17*)	43.0%
20	*Ratio of Government to Total investment opportunity* (*16 ÷ 17*)	11.0%

372 and 312.) Applying this ratio to the $139.0 mil. of interest on government securities received by non-financial corporations in 1922 (Statistics of Income, 1922, p. 19) gives $2,700 mil. of government securities held by corporations.

[6] Annual Report of the Secretary of Treasury, 1929, p. 467.

[7] Total local government debt in 1920 was estimated as $6,200 mil. by the National Bureau of Economic Research. The average increase in debt was approximately $500 mil. a year for 1919 and 1920. Nat. Bureau of Economic Research, Income in the U. S., Vol. II, p. 262. Adding at this rate for two years would give $7,200 mil. (6,200 + 2 × 500) as the local government debt in 1922.

[8] In 1927 the total Government securities held by corporations amounted to $9,780 mil. from which interest of $500.8 mil. was received. (Stat. of Income, 1927, pp. 372 and 312.) Applying this ratio to the $139.0 mil. of interest on government securities received by non-financial corporations in 1922 (Statistics of Income, 1922, p. 19) gives $2,700 mil. of government securities held by corporations.

[9] Directly or via banks, etc.

APPENDIX N: *Income from Property*

All individuals reporting income for 1922 and 1927

NOTE: (1) *Figures for 1922 and 1927 are not strictly comparable since the exemption limits were lower in 1922, giving a larger proportion of small incomes.* (2) *The figures for government securities are very rough approximations.*

		1922 in millions	1927 in millions
1	Dividends on stocks of Dom. Corporations	$2,664.2 [1]	$4,254.8 [2]
2	Interest from corporate securities	760.0 [3a]	910.0 [3d]
3	Income from corporate securities (1 + 2)	$3,424.2	$5,424.8
4	Interest and investment income other than that derived from Corporate and Government sources	$ 978.6 [4a]	$1,116.9 [4b]
5	Rent and Royalties	1,224.9 [1]	1,302.2 [3]
6	Income from Real Estate, etc. (4 + 5)	$2,203.5	$2,419.1
7	Interest paid by Federal Government on Public Debt	989.5 [5]	787.8 [5]
8	Interest from Local Government Securities	327.0 [6]	650.0 [7]
9	Total interest from Government Securities (7 + 8)	$1,316.5	$1,437.8
10	Interest from Government Securities received by Corporations	394.0 [8]	500.8 [9]
11	Income from Government Securities (9 − 10)	$ 922.5	$ 937.0
12	Estimated interest received from Government Securities by individuals filing income tax returns	$ 692.0 [10]	$ 700.0 [10]
13	Total income from property exclusive of capital net gain from sale of real estate or securities and exclusive of income from fiduciaries (3, 6 and 12)	$6,319.7	$8,643.9
14	Ratio of income from corporate securities to total income from property (3 ÷ 13)	54.2%	62.8%
15	Ratio of income from Real Estate to total income from property (6 ÷ 13)	34.8%	28.1%
16	Ratio of income from Government Securities to total income from property (12 ÷ 13)	11.0%	8.1%

[1] Statistics of Income, 1922, p. 9.

[2] Statistics of Income, 1927, p. 8.

[3] (a) In 1922 the bond and mortgage indebtedness of all corporations amounted to $22.7 bil. (Statistics of Income, 1922, p. 41.) Assuming a rate of interest of 4½

APPENDIX N: *Income from Property (Continued)*

All individuals reporting income over $5,000 in 1922 and 1927

NOTE: (1) *Figures for 1922 and 1927 are comparable.* (2) *Figures for Government securities are very rough approximations.*

		1922 in millions	1927 in millions
1	Dividends on stocks of Dom. Corporations	$2,173.5 [1]	$3,761.9 [2]
2	Interest from corporate securities	380.0 [ab]	580.0 [ac]
3	Income from corporate securities (1 + 2)	2,553.5	4,341.9
4	Interest and investment income other than corporate government	470.0 [4c]	721.0 [4d]
5	Rents and Royalties	482.2 [1]	644.3 [2]
6	Income from Real Estate, etc. (4 + 5)	952.2	1,365.3
7	Interest from Government Securities [11]	340.0	450.0
8	Total income from property exclusive of capital net gain from sale of real estate or securities and exclusive of income from fiduciaries (3, 6 and 7)	3,845.7	6,157.2
9	Ratio of income from corporate securities to total income from property (3 ÷ 8)	66.4%	70.5%
10	Ratio of income from Real Estate, etc., to total income from property (6 ÷ 8)	24.8%	22.1%
11	Ratio of income from Government Securities to total income from property (7 ÷ 8)	8.8%	7.3%

per cent this would yield $1,020 mil. Though part of this was undoubtedly received by corporations, it is probable that at least ¾ or $760.0 mil. was received by individuals. (In 1927 ¼ of all dividends paid by corporations were received by corporations, Statistics of Income, 1927, pp. 312 and 313.)

(b) Individuals with incomes over $5,000 reported incomes from "interest and investment income" of $850.9 mil. or 49% of this type of income reported. Attributing 49% of interest received from corporations by individuals to this group gives $760.0 mil. × 49% or $380.0 mil. interest received by individuals with incomes over $5,000 from corporations in 1922.

(c) In 1927 bond and mortgage indebtedness of all corporations amounted to $34.7 bil. (Statistics of Income, 1927, p. 372) giving, at 4½%, $1,560 mil. interest. Assuming the same proportions as above $1,560 × ¾ × 49% or $580 mil. going to individuals with incomes over $5,000.

(d) If the ratio of interest received from corporations to all interest,

$$\frac{\$585.0 \text{ mil.}[2]}{1,301.0 \text{ mil.}[2]} = 45\%,$$

by individuals with incomes over $5,000 is applied to interest received by all individuals reporting, it gives $2,026.9 mil. × 45% = $910.0 mil. received from corporations.

[4] (a) The income received by all individuals from interest and investment in 1922 was $1,738.6 mil.[1] Subtracting the $760.0 mil. of interest from corporate securities derived above (3a) gives $978.6 mil. received from other sources.

(b) The income received by all individuals from interest and investment in 1927 was $2,026.8 mil.[2] Subtracting the $910.0 mil. of interest from corporate securities derived above (3d) gives $1,116.9 mil. received from other sources.

(c) Individuals with incomes over $5,000 received interest and investment income in 1922 of $850.0 mil.[1] Substantially the $380.0 mil. of interest from corporate securities derived above (3b) gives $470.0 mil. received from other sources.

(d) Individuals with incomes over $5,000 received interest and investment income in 1927 of $1,301 mil.[2] Substantially the $580.0 mil. of interest from corporate securities derived above (3c) gives $721.0 mil. received from other sources.

[5] Annual Report of the Secretary of the Treasury, June 30, 1929, p. 407.

[6] Total interest paid on local government debt in 1920 was estimated as $282 mil. by the National Bureau of Economic Research. The average increase in debt was approximately $500 mil. a year for 1919 and 1920 adding $22½ mil. to interest payments. Estimate for 1922 on the basis of the same rate of growth would be 327 (282 + 2 × 22½). National Bureau of Economic Research, Income in the U. S., Vol. II, p. 262.

[7] Method same as in (6).

[8] Statistics of Income, 1922, p. 19.

[9] Statistics of Income, 1927, p. 312.

[10] Arbitrarily taken as ¾ of all income from government securities.

[11] In 1922 49% and in 1927 64% of reported interest and investment income was received by individuals reporting incomes over $5,000. Applying these ratios to the estimated income from Government securities gives $340.0 mil. for 1922 and $450.0 mil. for 1927 as received by individuals reporting incomes of over $5,000.

APPENDIX O: *American Telephone & Telegraph Company*

20 *largest stockholders* [1] (1928)

Name of holder	1928 shares held	Per cent of stock out- standing	1927 shares held	1926 shares held
Sun Life Assurance Co.	76,711	.69%	76,711	65,752
George F. Baker (Director, 1928)	53,522	.48%	40,022	34,161
Northern Finance Corp.	50,064	.45%	50,064	42,912
A. Iselin & Co.	46,566	.42%	40,708	28,261
Bell Tel. Secur. Co., Inc.	32,160	.29%	50,456	51,538
D. Talman Waters	31,391	.28%	31,391	27,621
Kidder, Peabody & Co.	22,935	.21%	25,284	25,400
Paine, Webber & Co.	22,723	.21%	26,022	18,054
J. Capel & Co., London	21,711	.20%	23,408	12,999
Frank H. Pierson	21,000	.19%	21,000	18,000
F. J. Kennedy, Boston	20,083	.18%	15,083	unknown
Hurley & Co.	19,541	.18%	unknown	unknown
Admin. Van Andeelen der A. T. & T. Co., Amstrdm.	18,110	.16%	16,192	9,662
Lee, Higginson & Co.	15,591	.14%	14,698	14,295
Est. Mrs. A. M. Harkness	15,017	.14%	15,017	15,017
Edward S. Harkness	10,373	.09%	unknown	unknown
Theodore E. Parker	10,000	.09%	10,000	9,000
The Kennedy Co., Boston	10,000	.09%	10,000	8,000
Eddy & Co.	9,157	.08%	unknown	unknown
U. S. Trust Co. of N. Y.	8,833	.08%	8,783	8,584
Total of 20 Largest Hold- ings	515,488			
Shares Outstanding	11,040,284 [2]			
Per cent held by 20 Larg- est Stockholders	4.6%			

[1] New York Times, April 4, 1928.
[2] Standard Corporation Records, 1929.

APPENDIX P: *United States Steel Corporation*

20 largest stockholders [1] (*1928*)

Name of holder	Preferred shares held	Common shares held	Total shares	Per cent of stock outstanding
J. W. David & Co.	21,250	73,225	94,475	.88%
G. F. Baker (Director, 1928)	500	77,000	77,500	.72%
Newborg & Co.	1,215	46,892	48,107	.45%
Lawrence C. Phipps	5,000	42,000	47,000	.44%
J. S. Bache & Co.	44	44,603	44,647	.42%
Hornblower & Weeks	416	39,958	40,374	.38%
E. F. Hutton & Co.	413	39,958	40,371	.38%
M. C. Taylor (Director, 1928)	0	40,100	40,100	.37%
Harris, Winthrop & Co.	633	39,219	39,852	.37%
Eddy & Co.	19,646	6,915	26,561	.25%
Shearson, Hammill & Co.	2,655	23,087	25,742	.24%
Lake H. Cutter	0	24,293	24,293	.23%
Louchheim, Minton & Co.	0	24,242	24,242	.23%
George Singer	8,860	14,000	22,860	.21%
Logan & Bryan	0	18,682	18,682	.17%
Josephthal & Co.	48	18,318	18,366	.17%
C. D. Halsey & Co.	5	15,982	15,987	.15%
Frank R. Bacon	0	15,000	15,000	.14%
Charles D. Barney & Co.	155	14,544	14,699	.14%
Laidlaw & Co.	156	14,264	14,420	.13%
Total (20 Stockholders)	60,996	632,282	693,278	
Shares Outstanding [2]	3,602,811	7,116,235	10,719,046	
Per cent held by largest 20 holders	1.7%	8.8%	6.4%	

[1] New York Times, April 17, 1928.
[2] Standard Corporation Records, 1929.

STATISTICAL APPENDIX TO REVISED EDITION

By Gardiner C. Means

THIS REVISED EDITION of *The Modern Corporation and Private Property* gives an opportunity to examine the criticisms which have been made of the statistical estimates it contains and to review developments in the years since its initial publication in 1932.

There was much criticism of the figures given on the concentration of economic power. The key figure attacked was one indicating that at the end of 1929 the 200 largest non-financial corporations controlled 49.2 per cent of the assets of all non-financial corporations.[1] We said that this was a crude estimate and suggested that the true figure probably lay somewhere between 45 and 53 per cent. Critics held that nothing like half of the assets of all non-financial corporations were controlled by the largest 200. However, in 1938 a very careful study was made using the actual income-tax returns of the corporations filed with the Treasury Department, and the conclusion reached for essentially the same concepts was that the 200 largest non-financial corporations controlled 49.4 per cent of the total assets of all such corporations. The closeness of the two estimates was fortuitous, but the more precise estimate made it clear that the cruder estimate was not misleading.

A second criticism concerned the figures showing increased concentration from 1909 to 1929. It was not directed at the actual figures, but, rather, contended that concentration was greater around 1900 than in 1937.[2] This argument was supported by estimates of the 1900 con-

[1] Page 33. The term "non-banking corporations" was used to exclude banks, insurance companies, et cetera. In later discussions the more precise term "non-financial corporations" has been used, adopting the classification employed by the Treasury Department in *Statistics of Income.*

[2] Warren G. Nutter, *The Extent of Enterprise Monopoly in the United States, 1899–1939*, Chicago, 1951.

centration, *industry by industry,* based on informed guesses by John Moody and others, by some piecemeal statistical data from the census, and by the critic's own subjective evaluation and estimates, industry by industry, for 1937.

These estimates have not stood up under professional examination.[3] Quite apart from the general uncertainty due to the subjective element in the estimates, one single subjective decision reverses the conclusion reached. The Nutter study assumes that around 1899 railroading was concentrated but would not have been concentrated in 1937 if it had not been regulated. This is a highly subjective classification, and, in addition, if regulation enters in the classification there is ample evidence that it has slowed concentration, not accelerated it. If railroading had been treated alike in both periods, either as concentrated or not concentrated, the study would have shown an increase in concentration from 1900 to 1937. By one of the critic's concentration measures, concentration would have increased from 19 per cent around 1900 to 33 per cent in 1937. Furthermore, even if the estimates of concentration, industry by industry, were acceptable, the technique of combining them could not throw any light on over-all concentration because many companies operate in several industries. The rigorous application of the anti-trust acts after the turn of the century limited combination within industries but did not prevent conglomerate merging, which certainly went on. The combination of industry-by-industry figures of concentration could not possibly reflect the concentration arising from this source.

No one questions that toward the end of the nineteenth century there was a great wave of mergers, culminating in the formation of United States Steel in 1901. Then many of the poorly designed combinations failed or were broken up by government action, as in the case of Standard Oil, and the economy may have become less concentrated. Just how much this merger movement contributed to the corporate revolution with which *The Modern Corporation* is concerned will probably never be known with any degree of certainty. But no one has suggested that there was a high degree of concentration before

[3] See Stanley Lebergott, "Has Monopoly Increased," *Review of Economics and Statistics,* November, 1953. Also see *Hearings before the Subcommittee on Antitrust and Monopoly of the Committee on the Judiciary,* United States Senate, Eighty-eighth Congress, "Economic Concentration," Part I, Appendix 4, pp. 343–352, in which there appears a critique of the Nutter estimates and a reply by Nutter, and a controversy between M. A. Adelman and the staff of the Senate committee over Adelman's use of the Nutter figures. Adelman presented the Nutter figures in testimony before the committee on September 10, 1964, without meeting or even mentioning the potent Lebergott criticism.

this merger movement, and no evidence has been presented that the increase in concentration from 1909 to 1929 shown in *The Modern Corporation* did not take place.

Criticism was also leveled at the use of corporate *assets* as the primary measure of concentration. Some argued that sales or value-added or employment should have been the basis of measurement. But here again it is clear that for an analysis concerned with *property,* the appropriate measure of concentration is the property controlled by the corporations. While other measures of concentration are more appropriate for other purposes, concentration of control over the instruments of production would seem to have the most general application, and this is measured by assets.

Criticism developed, too, of the calculations showing what would happen if the trends of concentration from 1909 to 1929 were to continue for another 20 to 40 years. These projections showed 70 to 85 per cent of corporate activity carried on by 200 corporations in 1950 and all activity carried on by 200 giants by 1970. Some critics have treated these projections as forecasts and have claimed that we were "proved wrong by events." Yet it was clearly indicated that these projections were not forecasts. The only forecast made was that "the great corporation, already of tremendous importance today, will become increasingly important in the future" (p. 42).

What events have actually shown is that the New Deal policies broke the swift upward trend toward concentration. The Holding Company Act forced the breakup of some of the big utility systems and inhibited the rapid growth of others. Railroad regulatory policy slowed the merging of railroads; only in recent years have important railroad mergers been taking place. Government policy also slowed the merging of manufacturing companies; in the case of aluminum, the government by its action created competition where there was formerly monopoly. And the Securities Exchange Act brought greater order and greater probity into the issuance of the securities of the large corporations. As will be shown below, the process of concentration has continued, but not at the earlier rate.

A quite different kind of criticism developed concerning the companies included. It was contended that the railroads and public utilities should not have been included in the estimates of concentration because these corporations were regulated by government. If *The Modern Corporation* had been concerned with concentration *in relation to markets* this might have been a valid criticism. But the book was concerned with the economy as a whole and most specifically with property relationships and the separation of ownership and control. In a subsequent book by the present writer, *The Structure of the American Economy*, which included a concern with concentration in relation to markets, concentration ratios were given for the first time on the relation of the largest four and largest eight companies, industry by industry. Such figures or figures for concentration in the non-regulated part of the economy alone would have been irrelevant to a book on the corporation and private property.

Since the figures on concentration in *The Modern Corporation* have withstood the critics and the figures on the dispersion of stock ownership and on the separation of ownership and control have not received serious challenge, one can say that on the whole the statistical aspects of *The Modern Corporation* have stood up well.

But what is the present situation with respect to concentration, with respect to the dispersion of stock ownership, and with respect to the separation of ownership and control? What has happened in the years since *The Modern Corporation* was published?

A great deal of information on the big corporations has become available in recent years. *Fortune* Magazine has published a list of the 500 biggest industrial corporations for a number of years and also publishes similar lists for the transportation, utility, merchandising, and banking fields. But no one has repeated the 1929 study based on direct access to Treasury returns or made a study of concentration of assets compared with the 1929 figures. The difficulty arises partly from the incomplete consolidation of controlled corporations in the published figures and partly from the necessity of removing the double counting when a corporation owns the stocks of other corporations it does not control. Unless adjustments are made for these, the resulting estimates will not be comparable with the earlier figures.

In the area of manufacturing alone there is no problem. The present writer presented to the Senate Committee on Anti-Trust and Monopoly estimates of concentration for 1962 which were as nearly comparable to those for 1929 as available statistics made possible.[4] The list of the hundred largest manufacturing corporations in 1962 is given in Table I, with their total assets and their net capital assets. This list is substantially the same as the list of the 100 largest by assets in the *Fortune* compilation, and the total assets given are the same except where footnotes indicate a difference. In the case of the Getty Oil Companies and Kaiser Industries, corporations subject to majority control have been combined, though they may have been listed sepa-

---

[4] *Hearings before the Subcommittee on Antitrust and Monopoly of the Committee on the Judiciary,* United States Senate, Eighty-eighth Congress, "Economic Concentration," Part I, pp. 16–19, 281–283, 301.

rately in the *Fortune* list; for Kaiser Aluminum and Chemical and Richfield Oil, which are jointly controlled by two companies already on the list, the assets are treated as controlled by the 100 largest. These were the procedures employed in the 1929 compilations.

The assets controlled by the 100 largest manufacturing corporations in 1962 are compared with the assets of all manufacturing cor-

TABLE I: *The 100 Largest Manufacturing Corporations in 1962 Measured by Size of Assets*

Asset rank	Company	Total assets (in millions)	Net capital assets (in millions)
1	Standard Oil (New Jersey)	$11,487.7	$6,875.7
2	General Motors	10,239.5	2,884.1
3	Ford Motor	5,416.5	2,140.2
4	United States Steel	5,059.7	2,820.1
5	Gulf Oil	4,243.6	2,458.7
6	Texaco	4,165.8	2,551.7
7	Socony Mobil Oil	4,136.5	2,253.1
8	Standard Oil (California)	3,353.1	2,273.5
9	Standard Oil (Indiana)	3,108.9	2,172.3
10	E. I. DuPont	3,095.7	984.7
11	General Electric [1]	3,047.6	712.9
12	Bethlehem Steel	2,212.2	978.9
13	International Business Machines	2,112.3	960.4
14	Shell Oil	1,989.1	1,281.4
15	Western Electric [1]	1,970.1	888.0
16	Union Carbide	1,791.7	958.5
17	Phillips Petroleum	1,735.3	1,084.0
18	Getty Oil Companies [2]	1,591.7	1,093.1
19	Westinghouse Electric [1]	1,547.6	367.8
20	International Harvester	1,527.2	424.5
21	Chrysler Corp.	1,525.0	398.9
22	Sinclair Oil	1,515.3	961.0
23	Cities Service	1,505.8	882.3
24	Aluminum Co. of America	1,377.8	821.1
25	Monsanto Chemical	1,324.9	769.9
26	Continental Oil	1,241.1	752.2
27	Goodyear Tire & Rubber	1,286.3	422.8
28	Anaconda	1,163.8	704.3

TABLE I: *The 100 Largest Manufacturing Corporations in 1962 Measured by Size of Assets (Continued)*

Asset rank	Company	Total assets (in millions)	Net capital assets (in millions)
29	*Republic Steel*	1,131.6	644.7
30	*Eastman Kodak*	1,102.6	367.8
31	*Radio Corp. of America* [1]	1,091.9	264.4
32	*Procter & Gamble*	1,090.4	414.4
33	*Reynolds Tobacco*	1,080.7	145.6
34	*International Paper*	1,038.0	583.9
35	*Allied Chemical*	1,022.4	678.0
36	*Dow Chemical*	1,021.5	577.9
37	*Reynolds Metals*	1,002.1	565.5
38	*Armco Steel*	995.0	464.4
39	*Boeing* [1]	964.0	114.9
40	*American Can*	958.7	524.8
41	*International Telephone & Telegraph (manufacturing)* [4]	950.8	206.2
42	*Firestone Tire & Rubber*	931.0	302.9
43	*Sperry Rand* [1]	914.1	251.2
44	*Atlantic Refining*	908.3	664.9
45	*National Steel*	902.5	564.4
46	*Olin Mathieson*	878.3	398.2
47	*Lockheed Aircraft*	857.4	94.3
48	*Inland Steel*	853.8	490.9
49	*Sun Oil*	844.7	549.2
50	*American Tobacco*	839.5	65.2
51	*Kennecott Copper*	831.0	434.1
52	*Jones & Laughlin*	829.8	540.6
53	*Continental Can*	806.8	486.4
54	*Union Oil of California*	796.9	502.1
55	*National Dairy Products*	774.3	326.6
56	*Youngstown Sheet & Tube*	772.7	376.0
57	*Brunswick*	768.3	59.0
58	*North American Aviation* [1]	765.9	106.7
59	*Kaiser Industries* [5]	761.6	355.1
60	*W. R. Grace*	722.2	326.7
61	*General Dynamics* [1]	696.2	170.8
62	*American Cyanamid*	695.9	311.6
63	*U. S. Rubber*	686.1	202.9

Asset rank	Company	Total assets (in millions)	Net capital assets (in millions)
64	*United Aircraft* [1]	670.9	134.9
65	*Burlington Industries*	667.2	252.7
66	*Singer Manufacturing Co.*	648.0	88.4
67	*B. F. Goodrich*	647.7	218.4
68	*John Deere*	643.2	119.7
69	*Pure Oil*	642.5	432.7
70	*National Distillers & Chemical*	642.4	216.2
71	*Weyerhaeuser*	639.9	409.0
72	*Caterpillar Tractor*	638.0	260.0
73	*Pittsburgh Plate Glass*	637.7	308.7
74	*Crown Zellerbach*	621.6	368.3
75	*Marathon Oil*	610.8	422.2
76	*General Foods*	602.3	193.2
77	*Swift & Co.*	593.4	242.7
78	*Sunray DX Oil*	592.9	408.5
79	*St. Regis Paper*	585.2	284.6
80	*Minnesota Mining & Manufacturing*	573.3	217.3
81	*Martin-Marietta* [1]	566.3	241.4
82	*General Telephone & Electronics (manufacturing)* [6]	548.1	157.4
83	*Owens-Illinois Glass*	529.2	255.6
84	*Allis-Chalmers* [1]	517.4	129.1
85	*Corn Products*	503.6	204.1
86	*Borden*	502.7	208.7
87	*General Tire & Rubber*	502.4	137.0
88	*Seagrams (United States)*	488.7	81.2
89	*American Smelting & Refining*	477.1	148.5
90	*Georgia Pacific*	477.0	167.3
91	*Borg-Warner*	469.0	131.9
92	*Schenley Industries*	461.4	39.4
93	*Celanese*	456.4	182.8
94	*National Cash Register*	452.6	123.4
95	*Coca-Cola*	452.0	145.1
96	*General American Transportation*	450.3	341.0
97	*Phelps Dodge*	445.9	143.1
98	*Kimberly-Clark*	443.7	237.7

TABLE I: *The 100 Largest Manufacturing Corporations in 1962 Measured by Size of Assets (Continued)*

Asset rank	Company	Total assets (in millions)	Net capital assets (in millions)
99	*National Lead*	438.6	145.2
100	*Armour*	436.1	145.4
	Total, 100 largest	136,234.3	62,951.2
	Add jointly controlled big corporations:		
	Kaiser Aluminum & Chemical [7]	729.6	491.0
	Richfield Oil [8]	404.6	294.9
	Adjusted total, 100 largest	137,368.5	63,737.1
	All manufacturing [3]	291,222.0	114,589.0
	Ratio (in per cent)	47.2	55.6

[1] Assets reported in Moody's Industrials, with adjustment for reported progress payments on government contracts (credited by company as a deduction from inventory value). Procedure follows FTC/SEC reporting practice.

[2] Consolidated assets (less equities of each company in the others) of Getty Oil Co., Mission Corp., Mission Development Co., Tidewater Oil Co., and Skelly Oil Co.

[3] Revised figure for total assets and net capital assets supplied by the Federal Trade Commission.

[4] I. T. & T. assets, excluding telecommunications, derived from company's 1962 Annual Report. Company reports breakdown based on net current assets (i.e., current assets less current liabilities). Consolidated current liabilities have been prorated between manufacturing and telecommunication on the following bases: bank loans and long-term debt maturing within 1 year, on the basis of the ratio between net property in manufacturing and that in telecommunications; accounts payable, on the basis of the ratio between manufacturing and telecommunications inventories; accrued taxes, on the basis of the ratio between manufacturing and telecommunications net incomes.

[5] Kaiser Industries and Kaiser Steel (79.3 per cent of voting stock, Dec. 31, 1962, held by Kaiser Industries) consolidated.

[6] General Telephone & Electronics Co., assets of manufacturing subsidiaries only, as reported in company prospectus for debenture issue, dated Mar. 1, 1963.

[7] More than 50 per cent of Kaiser Aluminum & Chemical Co. voting stock held by 2 other firms among the 100 largest: Kaiser Industries (42.2 per cent) and Kennecott Copper Co. (12.6 per cent). Book values of Kaiser and Kennecott holdings subtracted from total assets of firm.

[8] More than 50 per cent of Richfield Oil Corp. voting stock held by 2 firms among the 100 largest: Sinclair (30.2 per cent) and Cities Service Co. (31.0 per cent). Book values of Sinclair and Cities Service holdings subtracted from total assets of firm.

SOURCE: "Moody's Industrial Manual." As reported in Moody's except as footnoted. Total assets includes tax anticipation securities, following the FTC/SEC practice.

porations in Table II, with the adjustments necessary to eliminate the double counting of assets and make the two sets of figures comparable. According to these estimates, the 100 largest manufacturing corpora-

TABLE II: *Adjusted Assets of the 100 Largest Manufacturing Corporations in 1962 and the Assets of All Manufacturing Corporations*

100 largest corporations	Total assets (in billions)	Net capital assets (in billions)
Assets partly consolidated (from table I)	$137.3	$ 63.7
Estimated investments in other corporations [1]	6.5	
Assets exclusive of investments in other corporations	130.8	63.7
Estimated investments in legally controlled corporations not consolidated in published balance sheets ($6,500,000,000 × 43 per cent) [2]	2.8	
Estimated investments in legally controlled domestic corporations not consolidated in published balance sheets as carried on corporate books ($2,800,000,000 × 40 per cent) [3]	1.1	
Estimated equity represented by investments in unconsolidated domestic subsidiaries ($1,100,000,000 × 3) [4]	3.3	
Estimated total equity of unconsolidated domestic subsidiaries ($3,300,000,000 ÷ 80 per cent) [5]	4.2	
Estimated total assets of legally controlled domestic corporations not consolidated in published balance sheets ($4,200,000,000 × 163 per cent) ($6,800,000,000 × ratio of $63,700,000,000 to $130,800,000,000) [6]	6.8	3.3 [7]
Assets of 100 largest corporations including unconsolidated domestic subsidiaries	137.6	67.0
All manufacturing corporations:		
Assets partly consolidated (from table I)	291.0	114.6
Estimated investments in other corporations [8]	10.2	
Assets exclusive of investments in other corporations	280.8	114.6

TABLE II: *Adjusted Assets of the 100 Largest Manufacturing Corporations in 1962 and the Assets of All Manufacturing Corporations (Continued)*

100 largest corporations	Total assets (in billions)	Net capital assets (in billions)
Ratio of consolidated assets of 100 largest to all manufacturing corporations (in per cent)	49.0	58.4
82 corporations	46.3	

[1] Compiled from *Moody's Manuals*.

[2] Estimate based on a sample of 30 of the 100 largest corporations covering half their combined assets and reporting investments in legally controlled subsidiaries. The ratio of investments in subsidiaries to total investments (43 per cent) was applied to the total investments of $6,500,000,000.

[3] Assumes 40 per cent of estimated investments in legally controlled but unconsolidated subsidiaries is in domestic subsidiaries.

[4] Estimate based on a sample of 9 large companies which report both the value of their investments in unconsolidated subsidiaries as carried on their books and the equity or market value of these investments. For 3, the average ratio of equity to value of investments as carried in the books was 3.11 to 1; for 5, the average market value to value on the books was 3.33 to 1. In the above estimate, the equity interest was assumed to be 3 times the value of the investments as carried on the books.

[5] Assumes average of 80 per cent of equity interest in unconsolidated subsidiaries is controlled by parent (directly or indirectly).

[6] Estimate derived by applying the ratio (163 per cent) of total assets to stockholders' equity for all manufacturing corporations with assets under $250,000,000 as reported for December 1962 in *Quarterly Financial Report, op. cit.*, 4th quarter 1963, pp. 28–32 to estimated equity in unconsolidated domestic subsidiaries.

[7] Applies same ratio of net capital assets to assets exclusive of stockholdings for subsidiaries as for parents (48 per cent).

[8] Includes the $6,500,000,000 of investments by the 100 largest corporations in other corporations and, for the investments of smaller corporations in other corporations, assumes such investments bore the same relation to assets exclusive of, such investments that investments by the 100 largest corporations in corporations other than those legally controlled bore to their consolidated assets exclusive of such investments.

tions controlled 49.0 per cent of the total assets of all manufacturing corporations and 58.4 per cent of their net capital assets.

The corresponding estimates for manufacturing concentration for 1929 are given in Table III. They indicate that the 100 largest manufacturing corporations controlled approximately 40 per cent of corporate manufacturing assets in 1929 and 44 per cent of net capital assets.

Thus, if concentration is measured by total assets, manufacturing concentration has increased in the 33-year period from 40 per cent to

TABLE III: *Manufacturing Concentration in 1929*

	Total assets exclusive of securities	Net capital assets
82 largest manufacturing corporations [1]	$23.6 billion	$11.8 billion
18 next-largest manufacturing corporations [2]	1.8	.7
100 largest manufacturing corporations	$25.4 billion	$12.5 billion
All manufacturing corporations [1]	$63.6 billion	$28.5 billion
Ratio	40.0%	44.0%

[1] Senate Testimony, *op. cit.*, p. 301.

[2] Estimated on the assumption that the next-largest 18 corporations had an average of $100 million total assets (excluding securities) and $40 million of net capital assets. Both of these assumptions are generous, making the estimates of concentration perhaps .1 or .2 per cent too high.

49 per cent, and if measured by net capital assets, from 44 per cent to 58 per cent.

The increase in manufacturing concentration in recent years is confirmed by estimates made from time to time by the Federal Trade Commission. None of these estimates goes back to 1929, and they all underestimate the actual degree of concentration, partly because consolidation is incomplete and partly because no adjustment is made for the duplication of assets and similar matters. But the estimates are consistent with each other and show clear evidence of an increase in manufacturing concentration since 1950. This series is given in Table IV and shows a rise in concentration from 40.2 per cent of manufacturing corporation assets held by the largest 100 in 1950 to 45.7 per cent in 1962. When non-corporate manufacturing assets are included, the rate of increase is slightly higher, because a smaller proportion of manufacturing assets remains unincorporated. Census figures for concentration based on value-added for all manufacturing enterprises are indicated in Chart I for 1947–1963. There can be little doubt that manufacturing as a whole became more concentrated in the 15 years from 1950 to 1965 and also in the 36 years from 1929 to 1965.

Just what happened in manufacturing from 1929 to 1947 is not so clear. There was a sharp increase in concentration from 1929 to 1933 as smaller enterprises disappeared or were merged with larger and as the working capital of both large and small companies was dissipated. A part of this trend was reversed with economic recovery, and the

TABLE IV: *Comparison of Total Assets Held by the 100 Largest Manufacturing Corporations with Assets Held by All Manufacturing Corporations and All Manufacturing Enterprise*

	1950	1962
100 largest manufacturing corporations	$ 55.4 billion	$133.0 billion
All manufacturing corporations	$137.7 billion	$291.0 billion
Ratio	40.2%	45.7%
100 largest manufacturing corporations	$ 55.4 billion	$133.0 billion
All manufacturing enterprise	$143.4 billion	$295.7 billion
Ratio	38.6%	45.0%

SOURCE: Testimony by Willard F. Mueller, Senate Anti-trust and Monopoly Hearings, *op. cit.*, pp. 120 and 121.

CHART I: *Share of Value Added by Manufacture Accounted for by 200 Largest Manufacturing Companies, 1947–1963*

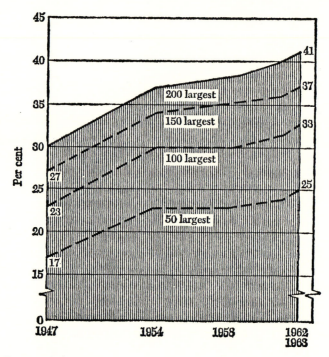

SOURCE: *Bureau of the Census*

war years do not appear to have brought any great change in manufacturing concentration. The net change from 1929 to 1950 appears to have been an increase in concentration in manufacturing from the 40 per cent of 1929 to around 43 per cent in 1950.[5]

No adequate estimates are available for the change in concentration for non-financial corporations as a whole since 1929. One can make estimates of change in recent years from Treasury compilations, but one cannot tie these in with 1929 figures without going back of the Treasury figures to individual corporations in order to combine the assets of legally controlled subsidiaries.

The Statistics of Income for corporations does not compile corporate figures by a specified number of corporations, but by all corporations with assets over an arbitrary figure. For successive years, the number of big corporations grouped together varies, so that it is difficult to trace changing concentration from the figures. Fortunately, the number of big corporations grouped together in 1950 and in 1965 is almost identical. In 1950, all corporations with assets over $100 million were compiled, giving 360 big non-financial corporations. In 1965, all corporations with $250 million assets were compiled, giving 367 big non-financial corporations. By adding seven corporations, assumed to have $90 million assets each to the 1950 list, the total number for each year can be made the same and no significant error is introduced. The results of such a comparison are given in Table V, with similar comparisons for manufacturing, public utilities (including transport), and trade. They show a marked increase in concentration. Of course, the degree of consolidation of balance sheets might have changed significantly in the 15-year period, but this seems unlikely. Apart from this possibility, the increase in concentration would seem to be established for the period, not only for non-financial corporations taken as a whole, but also for each of the three sub-groups.

It should be recognized that those Treasury figures grossly understate the actual degree of concentration. They would have to be adjusted for under-consolidation and for duplication of assets and similar

[5] One author, M. A. Adelman, "The Measurement of Industrial Concentration," *The Review of Economics and Statistics*, Vol. XXXIII, No. 4 (Nov. 1951), p. 287, sought to establish that there was an actual decline in concentration from 1931 to 1947, but the techniques of analysis were so patently faulty and the mathematical errors so frequent (16 out of 51 mathematical operations) that the results are not worth discussion here. See also Gardiner C. Means, "Thoughts on Concentration," *1962 Proceedings of the Business and Economic Statistics Section*, American Statistical Association, pp. 123–125, in which the weakness of the Adelman analysis was examined.

TABLE v: *Change in Concentration 1950–1965 Derived from Statistics of Income (in billions)*

Non-financial Corporations

	Assets of 367 largest	Assets of all	Ratio
1950 [1]	$134.9	$299.8	44.7%
1965	364.3	771.3	47.2%

Manufacturing Corporations

	Assets of 195 largest	Assets of all	Ratio
1950 [2]	$ 65.1	$141.6	46.0%
1965	195.6	372.6	52.5%

Public Utilities (including transportation)

	Assets of 128 largest	Assets of all	Ratio
1950 [3]	$ 58.4	$ 79.2	73.6%
1965	143.7	187.4	76.7%

Trade

	Assets of 25 largest	Assets of all	Ratio
1950 [4]	$ 6.3	$ 51.8	73.6%
1965	18.0	126.9	76.7%

SOURCE: *Statistics of Income (Corporations)* 1950 and preliminary for 1965 except as noted.

[1] Seven corporations added to largest with average assets assumed to be $90 million.

[2] Twenty-five corporations added to largest with average assets assumed to be $80 million.

[3] Fifteen corporations deducted from largest with average assets assumed to be $100 million.

[4] Two corporations deducted from largest with average assets assumed to be $100 million.

matters. For example, the assets controlled by the 100 largest manufacturing corporations in 1962 arrived at directly, in Table II, amounted to $137.6 billion, while the Treasury reported 141 manufacturing corporations with assets over $250 million each, and yet this group had combined assets of only $139.1 billion. Clearly some of the 141 must have been controlled by others in the group or smaller corporations must have been controlled by the 100 largest and their assets not consolidated with those of the latter.

For the period from 1929 to 1950, there is no present basis for saying whether there was an increase in concentration for non-financial corporations taken as a whole. The increase in manufacturing from 1929 to 1962 is clear. The increase for non-financial and the three subgroups after 1950 is highly probable. Also it is established that there was a very considerable increase in over-all concentration from 1929 to 1933, clearly in large part a depression phenomenon, which was presumably reversed between 1933 and 1939. There is little evidence that World War II changed the degree of concentration significantly. Only a careful repetition of the 1929 study can establish the changes in concentration between 1929 and 1950. Working with the available statistics makes me believe that there was not too much change in over-all concentration, though what there was was probably upward. A careful repetition of the earlier study would almost certainly find for the period 1929 to 1962 or 1965 a substantial increase, though not at anything like the rate of the 1920's.

There has been little, if any, criticism of the estimates of ownership dispersion given in *The Modern Corporation,* and there is little doubt that the dispersion has continued. Below is a comparison of the number of stockholders of the three largest 1929 corporations in 1929 and in 1966.

	Number of Stockholders	
	Dec. 31, 1929	*Dec. 31, 1966*
American Telephone and Telegraph Co.	469,801	3,080,000
Pennsylvania Railroad	196,119	96,284
United States Steel Corporation	120,918	346,411
Total Stockholders of Record	786,838	3,522,695

If figures for the ownership of the 200 largest non-financial corporations were available they would probably far exceed today the estimate of

TABLE VI: *The 200 Largest Non-financial Corporations Classified by Type of Ultimate Control, 1929 and 1963*

	1929			1963		
Type of Control	Num-ber	Assets (in mil-lions)	Per cent of assets	Num-ber	Assets (in mil-lions)	Per cent of assets
Private Ownership	12	3,367	4	None	0	0
Majority Ownership	10	1,542	2	5	3,307	1
Minority Control	46½	11,223	14	18	28,248	11
Legal Device	41	17,565	22	8	8,765	3
Management Control	88½	47,108	58	169	224,377	85
In Receivership	2	269	°	None	0	0
	200	81,073	100	200	264,697	100

° Less than one half of one per cent.

SOURCE: For 1929, this volume, pp. 106 and 107. For 1963, "Ownership and Control in the 200 Largest Non-financial Corporations, 1929 and 1963," by Robert J. Larner, The American Economic Review, Vol. LVI, No. 4, Part 1 (Sept. 1966), pp. 781 and 782.

18 million book stockholders of *all* corporations in 1928 (page 56). And if one could trace the beneficial interest of the big corporations through the intricacies of investment trust and investment companies, the dispersion of financial interest in the big corporations would be shown to be even more widespread.

Estimates of the separation of ownership and control in the 200 largest corporations provided the third set of economic data in *The Modern Corporation*. By good fortune a recent study has duplicated the 1929 analysis for 1963, making only one significant change in concept.[6] The one exception is that the dividing line between minority control and management control was shifted from around a 20 per cent stock interest to a 10 per cent stock interest. If the 10 per cent dividing line had been used for 1929, the management control group would have been somewhat smaller in that year. The results of this new study are given in Table VI, showing the number and proportion of the 200 largest which were classed according to the degree of sepa-

[6] Robert J. Larner, "Ownership and Control in the 200 Largest Non-financial Corporations, 1929 and 1963," *The American Economic Review*, Vol. LVI, No. 4, Part 1 (Sept. 1966), p. 777*ff*.

ration between ownership and control in 1929 and in 1963 and the assets controlled. According to this table, there were no cases of private ownership (80 per cent or more closely controlled) and only 5 out of the 200 corporations were controlled through a majority stock control, so that majority control had declined from 22 in 1929 to only 5 in 1963. At the other end of the scale, the number classed as "management control" increased from 88 to 169, or nearly double. Thus nearly 85 per cent of the 200 largest had reached that end condition toward which *The Modern Corporation* suggested the corporate revolution was moving, the virtually complete separation of ownership and control. When attention is given to the assets controlled, the importance of majority control or better is even less, with only $1\frac{1}{4}$ per cent of the assets of the 200 corporations controlled in this fashion compared with 6 per cent in 1929. In the same period, management control had expanded from 58 per cent of assets to 85 per cent.

It is clearly apparent that the three trends of economic development envisaged in the original edition of *The Modern Corporation* have continued: the concentration of economic power, the dispersion of ownership, and the separation of ownership and control.

TABLES AND INDEX

Abbott v. American Hard Rubber Co., 130, 131, 202

Aberdeen Railway Co. v. Blaikie Brothers, 198

Alabama Nat. Bank v. Halsey, 222

American Macaroni Corp. v. Saumer, 144

American Tube & Iron Co. v. Hays, 224

Anderson v. Dyer, 230

Anglo-American Land Co. v. Lombard, 233

Archer v. Hesse, 134, 163, 227

Atlantic Refining Co. v. Hodgman, 146, 225, 229

B. & C. Electrical Const. Co. v. Oeven, 144

Bank of Commerce v. Hart, 234

Barclay v. Wabash Ry., 172, 231, 232

Barnes v. Andrews, 203

Barnes v. Brown, 212

Bassett v. U. S. Cast Iron Pipe Co., 172, 231

Bedford v. Bagshaw, 255, 275, 282

Beitman v. Steiner, 210

Bent v. Underdown, 144

Berger v. U. S. Steel Co., 191

Board of Commissioners v. Reynolds, 199

Bodell v. General Gas & Electric Corp., 146, 178, 229, 230, 257

Borg v. International Silver Co., 159, 227, 229

Bostwick v. Chapman, 208

Bosworth v. Allen, 211

Bridgewater Navigation Co. case, 148

Briggs v. Spaulding, 202

Brightman v. Bates, 210

Camden v. Stewart, 143

Camden & Atlantic R. R. v. Elkins, 236

Carlisle v. Smith, 216

Carpenter v. Danforth, 199, 287

Central Trust Co. v. Bridges, 209, 236

Channon v. Channon Co., 230

Cleveland-Cliffs Iron Co. v. Arctic Iron Co., 198, 199

Coddington v. Conaday, 144

Colby v. Equitable Trust Co., 240

Cole v. Adams, 224

Coleman v. Booth, 149, 223

Collins v. Portland Elec. Power Co., 231

Connolly v. Shannon, 200

Continental Insurance Co. v. U. S., 257

Crandall v. Lincoln, 149

Dartmouth College case, 136, 187

Davenport v. Lines, 124

Davis v. Louisville Gas & Electric Co., 125, 137, 138, 146, 169, 189, 193, 194, 236, 237

Deadwood First Nat. Bank v. Gustin Minerva Cons. Min. Co., 144

Detroit-Kentucky Coal Co. v. Bickett Coal & Coke Co., 224

Dittman v. Distilling Co. of America, 234

Dodge v. Ford Motor Co., 172, 231

Dominguez Land Corp. v. Dougherty, 149

Donald v. American Smelting & Refining Co., 158

Drewry-Hughes Co. v. Throckmorton, 148

Dunlay v. Avenue M. Garage & Repair Co., 134, 163, 227

Durfee v. Old Colony & Fall River R. R. Co., 190

Edwards v. International Pavement Co., 234

Elkins v. Camden & Atlantic R. R., 233

Ellerman v. Chicago Junction Ry., 234

Enterprise Ditch Co. v. Moffitt, 191

Equitable Life Assurance Society v. Union Pacific R. R. Co., 151

Ervin v. Oregon Ry. & Nav. Co., 239

Espuela Land & Cattle Co. case, 148

Farmers' Loan & Trust Co. v. N. Y. & Northern Ry. Co., 200, 212, 213, 237

Farwell v. Great Western Telegraph Co., 132

Fernald v. Ridlon Co., 234

Floyd v. State, 123

Forbes v. McDonald, 211

Fraser & Chalmers case, 148

Freeman v. Hatfield, 144

Freemont v. Stone, 212

Furlong v. Johnson, 144

Gamble v. Queens County Water Co., 143, 223

Garey et al. v. St. Joe Mining Co., 121, 137, 188, 191

Gates, Adm'r v. Tippecanoe Stone Co., 224

Geddes v. Anaconda Copper Mining Co., 256

General Investment Co. v. Bethlehem Steel Corp., 161, 199, 228

German Mercantile Co. v. Wanner, 222

Gibbons v. Anderson, 203

Globe Woolen Co. v. Utica Gas & Elec. Co., 199, 210

Goodrich v. Reynolds, Wilder & Co., 222

Grausman v. Porto Rican American Tobacco Co., 175

Gray v. Portland Bank, 124, 133, 221, 226, 241

Greenwood v. Union Freight Co., 137, 188

Guernsey v. Cook, 211

Hamlin v. Continental Trust Co., 148

Handley v. Stutz, 144, 226

Hayward v. Leeson, 221

Herbert v. Duryea, 143, 144

Hill v. Nisbet, 233

Hinckley v. Schwarzschild Sulzberger Co., Inc., 191

Hodgman v. Atlantic Refining Co., 225

Holcomb v. Forsythe, 211

Holcombe v. Trenton White City Co., 224

Hollander v. Heaslip, 144

Holyoke Co. v. Lyman, 188

Hood Rubber Co. v. Commonwealth, 152

Hopgoods v. Lusch, 144

Hoyt v. E. I. Du Pont de Nemours Powder Co., 151

Hun v. Cary, 202

Hunt v. Hauser Malting Co., 234

Hunter v. Roberts, Thorp & Co., 172

Insurance Press Co. v. Montauk Co., 223

International & Great Northern R. R. v. Bremond, 238

Jackson v. Hooper, 211
Jacobson v. Brooklyn Lumber Co., 198
Johnson v. Louisville Trust Co., 146, 225
Johnson v. Tenn. Oil Co., 144
Jones v. Bowman, 224
Jones v. Concord & Montreal R. Co., 161
Jones v. Missouri Edison Electric Co., 158, 215, 240
Jones v. Williams, 211
Jones Drug Co. v. Williams, 222
Joslin v. Boston & Maine R. R., 173

Kanaman v. Gahagan, 222
Kavanaugh v. Gould, 204
Kavanaugh v. Kavanaugh Knitting Co., 215, 236
Kelley v. Killian, 143
Kelley Bros. v. Fletcher, 224
Kent v. Quicksilver Mining Co., 191, 236
Kreissl v. Am. Distilling Co.. 210

Laumann v. Lebanon Valley R. R., 240
Lloyd v. Pennsylvania Electric Vehicle Co., 148
Lonsdale v. International Mercantile Marine Co., 138, 195, 236, 237
Looker v. Maynard, 188
Lothrop v. Goudeau, 144
Luther v. Luther Co., 159, 221, 229

McQuade v. Stoneham, 211
Macon etc. R. R. Co. v. Mason, 131
Manson v. Curtis, 209, 210, 211
Marrow v. Peterborough Water Co., 148
Mayfield v. Alton Ry. Gas & Elec. Co., 240
Menier v. Hooper's Telegraph Works, 212
Merchants Insurance Co. v. Schroeder, 149

Meredith v. New Jersey Zinc & Iron Co., 134, 228
Miller v. State of N. Y., 188, 189
Moran v. U. S. Cast Iron Pipe Co., 172
Morgan v. Bon Bon, 144
Morris v. American Public Utilities Co., 138, 195, 237

National Telegraph Co. case, 148
Nebraska Shirt Co. v. Horton, 234
New Haven & Darby R. R. v. Chapman, 236
N. Y. L. E. & W. R. R. Co. v. Nickals, 172
New York Trust Co. v. Bermuda-Atlantic S. S. Co., 211
Niles v. N. Y. Central Rd. Co., 200
North-West Trans. Co. v. Beatty, 236
Norwich v. Southern Ry. Co., 175

Oliver v. Oliver, 199, 201
Olympia Theatres v. Commonwealth, 152
Orpheum Theatre & Realty Co. v. Brokerage Co., 122
Ottinger v. Bennett, 200, 256
Outwater v. Public Service Corp. of N. J., 157, 215, 237, 239

Pacific Trust Co. v. Dorsey, 222
Palmbaum v. Magulsky, 210
Pauly v. Coronado Beach Co., 234
Pennsylvania Canal Co. v. Brown, 214
People v. Ballard, 131
People v. Chicago Gas Trust Co., 233
People v. New York Building-Loan Banking Co., 148
People v. Railway Comm., 144
People v. Sterling Mfg. Co., 222
People ex rel. Recess Exporting & Importing Corp. v. Hugo, 148
Perkins v. Coffin, 236
Petry v. Harwood Elec. Co., 240
Philips v. Wickham, 129
Pronick v. Spirits Distributing Co., 191, 194

Railroad Co. v. Lockwood, 203

Randle v. Winona Coal Co., 192

Reno v. Bull, 268

Robotham v. Prudential Life Insurance Co., 198, 216, 233

Ryerson & Son v. Peden, 224

Salt Lake Auto Co. v. Keith O'Brien Co., 191, 192

San Diego Railway Co. v. Pacific Beach Co., 198

Savings Bank v. Meriden Agency, 234

Schiller Piano Co. v. Hyde, 222

Scoville v. Thayer, 143, 144

Seneca Wire & Mfg. Co. v. A. B. Leach & Co., 268, 276

Shepaug Voting Trust cases, 208

Sherman v. S. K. D. Oil Co., 123

Singers-Bigger v. Young, 211

Small v. Sullivan, 151

Smith v. San Francisco R. Co., 210

Smith v. Wells Manufacturing Co., 199

Sohland v. Baker, 223

Somerville v. St. Louis Mining & Milling Co., 137, 189, 191

Southern Pacific Ry. Co. v. Bogert, 212

Southwestern Tank Co. v. Morrow, 222

Stanton v. Schenck, 216

Starbuck v. Mercantile Trust Co., 208

State v. Missouri Pac. Ry., 234

State Trust Co. v. Turner, 224

Stevens v. The Episcopal Church History Co., 143, 144, 223

Stewart v. Harris, 201

Stone v. Young, 143, 225

Strong v. Repide, 199, 201

Sumner v. Marcy, 234

Taylor v. Hutton, 129

The Charitable Corp. v. Sutton, 202

Thom v. Baltimore Trust Co., 134, 228

Thomas v. Matthews, 213

Thomas Branch & Co. v. Riverside & Dan River Cotton Mills, 161

Thompson v. Thompson Carnation Co., 209

Tomlinson v. Jessup, 137

Tracy v. Yates, 144

Troup v. Horbach, 224

Trust Co. v. Turner, 132

U. S. Steel Corp. v. Hodge, 205

Utica Fire Alarm Telegraph Co. v. Waggoner Watchman Co., 144

Van Cleve v. Berkey, 224

Van Cott v. Van Brunt, 223, 224

Venner v. Chicago City Ry. Co., 209, 211

Venner v. Southern Pacific Co., 257

Wabash Railroad v. Barclay, 173, 185

Wall v. Utah Copper Co., 134

Walsham v. Stainton, 200

Walz v. Oser, 223

Wardell v. Railroad Co., 198

Welton v. Saffery, 143, 225

Wheeler v. Abilene National Bank Building Co., 215

Whittenberg v. Federal Mining and Smelting Co., 149

Williams v. Renshaw, 148

Wilson v. American Ice Co., 231

Windhurst v. Central Leather Co., 194, 195, 237, 239

Yoakum v. Providence Biltmore Hotel Co., 138, 194, 195, 237

Zabriskie v. Hackensack & N. Y. R. R. Co., 122, 137, 188, 189, 190

Zeigler v. Lake St. El. Co., 210

Alabama Power Co., 320

Alleghany Corp., 25, 69, 70, 88, 90, 101, 102, 184, 321

Allied Chemical & Dye Corp., 20, 85, 103, 108, 348

Allis-Chalmers Manufacturing Co., 323, 325, 349

Aluminum Company of America, 7, 23, 27, 86, 347

American & Foreign Power Co., 166

American Agricultural Chem. Co., 324

American Bank Note Co., 326

American Bosch Magneto Corp., 326

American Can Co., 22, 27, 104, 348

American Car & Foundry Co., 19, 22, 104, 327

American Commonwealths Power Corp., 23, 88

American Cotton Oil Co., 324

American Cyanamid Co., 348

American Gas & Electric Co., 24, 91

American Ice Co., 256, 325

American International Corp., 325

American Light & Traction Co., 321

American Linseed Co., 173

American Locomotive Co., 19, 22, 91, 104, 327

American Power & Light Co., 24, 321

American Radiator & Standard Sanitary Corp., 22, 27, 104, 322

American Rolling Mill Co., 23, 103

American Ship Building Co., 325

American Smelting & Refining Co., 21, 23, 103, 327, 349

American Sugar Refining Co., 21, 104, 327

American Super-power Corp., 91

American Tel. & Tel. Co., ix, xiii, xxi, 6, 12, 23, 30–31, 45, 47, 52, 54, 55, 80, 99, 134, 161, 180, 183, 218, 328, 331, 341, 357

American Tobacco Co., 21, 89, 348

American Water Works & Elec. Co., 23, 88

American Woolen Co., 26, 27, 104

Anaconda Copper Mining Co., 23, 104, 256, 281, 320, 321, 347

Appleton Co., 12

Armco Steel Corp., 348

Armour & Co. of Ill., 21, 27, 104, 174, 320, 350

Associated Gas & Elec. Co., 24, 86, 88, 169, 175, 320, 321

Associated Oil Co., 320, 323

Associated Telephone Utilities Co., 23, 103

Atchison, Topeka & Santa Fe Ry. Co., 25, 48, 98, 320, 321

Atlantic Coast Line Co., 90

Atlantic Coast Line Rd. Co., 25, 90, 320, 328

Atlantic, Gulf & West Indies S. S. Lines, 324

Atlantic Refining Co., 20, 93, 229, 348

Atlas Powder Co., 325

Auburn Automobile Co., 153

Bache (J. S.) & Co., 342

Baldwin Locomotive Works, 19, 22, 104, 323

Baltimore & Ohio Rd. Co., 25, 48, 91, 95, 98, 101

Bank of United States, 198

Barney (C. D.) & Co., 342

Barnsdall Corp., 325

Bell Telephone Securities Co., 341

Bethlehem Steel Corp., 23, 82, 104, 320, 347

Blair & Co., Inc., 93

Boeing Co., 348

Boott Co., 12

Borden Co., 21, 104, 349

Borg-Warner International Corp., 349

Boston & Maine Rd. Co., 26, 95

Boston Elevated Ry. Co., 26, 48, 99

Boston Manufacturing Co., 12

Brooklyn Edison Co., 321

Brooklyn-Manhattan Transit Co., 26, 104

Brooklyn Union Gas Co., 24, 91, 328

Brunswick Corp., 348

Buffalo, Rochester & Pittsburgh Ry. Co., 323

Burlington Industries, Inc., 349

Burns Bros. Inc., 325

California Petroleum Corp., 321

Calumet & Hecla Consol. Copper Co., 324

Calumet & Hecla Mining Co., 324

Capel (J.) & Co., 79, 341

Carolina, Clinchfield & Ohio Ry. Co., 320, 323

Caterpillar Tractor Co., 349

Celanese Corp., 349

Central Leather Co., 324

Central Public Service Co., 24, 95

Central States Elec. Corp., 92, 153

Certain-Teed Products Corp., 325

Chase Cos. Inc., 322

Chesapeake and Ohio Ry. Co., 70, 71, 328

Chesapeake Corp., 70, 71

Chicago & Alton Rd. Co., 25, 101, 115

Chicago & Eastern Illinois Ry. Co., 25, 90

Chicago & North Western Ry. Co., 25, 98, 328

Chicago & St. Louis Rd. Co., 101

Chicago, Burlington & Quincy Rd. Co., 25, 102

Chicago Elevated Rys. Co., 320, 323

Chicago Great Western Rd. Co., 25, 90

Chicago, Milwaukee, St. Paul & Pacific Rd. Co., 25, 48, 98, 102

Chicago Rys. Co., 26, 101

Chicago, Rock Island & Pacific Ry. Co., 25, 97, 115

Chicago Union Station Co., 25, 102

Chicago Utilities Co., 324

Childs Co., 82

Chile Copper Co., 320, 323

Chrysler Corp., 19, 22, 71, 104, 321, 347

Cities Service Co., 24, 72, 88, 347, 350

Cliffs Corp., 23, 89

Cluett, Peabody & Co., 325

Coca-Cola Co., 349

Colorado Fuel & Iron Co., 324

Columbia Gas & Electric Corp., 24, 91, 320

Columbia Steel Corp., 322

Commonwealth and Southern Corp., 25, 91, 321

Commonwealth Edison Co., 24, 91, 96, 320, 328

Commonwealth Trust Co., 204

ComSat, xiii, xiv

Congoleum-Nairn, Inc., 325

Consolidated Gas Co. of New York, 24, 48, 100, 321

Consolidated Gas, Elec. Lt. & Power Co. of Baltimore, 24, 83, 104
Consolidation Coal Co., 21, 93
Continental Baking Corp., 174, 281, 325
Continental Can Co., 325, 348
Continental Motors Corp., 325
Continental Oil Co., 20, 103, 322, 347
Corn Products Refining Co., 20, 103, 349
Corporation Securities Co. of Chicago, 91, 92, 93
Crane Co., 22, 27, 87
Creole Petroleum Corp., 322
Crown Zellerbach Corp., 23, 27, 89, 349
Crucible Steel Co. of America, 23, 103
Cuban Cane Prod. Co., 21, 103
Cudahy Packing Co., 323
Curtis & Sanger, 99

David (J. W.) & Co., 342
Davis (J. W.) & Co., 99
Day (R. L.) & Co., 99
Deere & Co., 22, 28, 87
Deere (John) Intercontinental Ltd., 349
Delaware & Hudson Co., 25, 48, 98
Delaware, Lackawanna & Western Rd. Co., 25, 90, 328
Denver & Rio Grande Western Rd. Co., 25, 70, 102
Detroit Edison Co., 24, 92
Detroit United Ry. Co., 324
Dillon Read & Co., 71, 87, 233–234
Dodge Brothers, Inc., 71, 128, 204, 321
Doherty (H. L.) & Co., 72
Dow Chemical Co., 348
Drug, Inc., 22, 104
Duke Power Co., 24, 87
Du Pont de Nemours & Co., 20, 85, 93, 322, 347
Du Pont Powder Co., 327

Eastern Gas & Fuel Associates, 24, 87

Eastman Kodak Co., 20, 28, 104, 348
Eddy & Co., 341, 342
Edison Elec. Ill. Co. of Boston, 24, 104
Electric Bond & Share Co., 24, 49, 91, 92, 100
Electric Power & Light Corp., 24, 92, 320
Electric Securities Corp., 100
Engineers Public Service Co., 321
Equitable Office Building, Inc., 16
Erie Rd. Co., 25, 70, 90, 127, 175

Fahnestock & Co., 79
Fidelity Trust Co., 233
Fifth Ave. Coach Co., 324
Firestone Tire & Rubber Co., 19, 26, 104, 348
Florida East Coast Ry. Co., 25, 51, 86
Ford Motor Co., 7, 19, 22, 51, 86, 347
Fox Film Corp., 74
Fox Theatre Corp., 28, 74
French (Fred F.) Co., 154

General American Trans. Corp., 349
General Asphalt Co., 325, 327
General Baking Co., 174
General Dynamics Corp., 348
General Electric Co., 22, 27, 48, 96, 100, 327, 347
General Foods Corp., 325, 349
General Gas & Electric Corp., 178, 321
General Motors Corp., 19, 22, 27, 75, 93, 347
General Petroleum Corp., 320
General Securities Corp., 69, 70
General Telephone & Electronics Corp., 349, 350
General Theatre Equipment, Inc., 20, 89, 94
General Tire & Rubber Co., 349
Georgia Pacific Corp., 349
Georgia Ry. & Power Co., 320
Getty Oil Cos., 346, 347, 350

Gillette Safety Razor Co., 183
Girard Trust Co., 79
Glen Alden Coal Co., 21, 103, 322
Gold Dust Co., 324
Goodrich (B. F.) Co., 19, 26, 104, 349
Goodyear Tire & Rubber Co., 19, 26, 93, 322, 347
Grace (W. R.) Co., 348
Grasselli Chemical Co., 322
Great Atlantic & Pacific Tea Co., 22, 27, 86
Great Northern Iron Ore Properties, 324, 325, 327
Great Northern Ry. Co., 25, 48, 98, 102, 328
Greene Cananea Copper Co., 321, 324, 325
Gulf Oil Corp., 20, 86, 347

Halsey (C. D.) & Co., 342
Hamilton Co., 12
Harris, Upham & Co., 79
Harris, Winthrop & Co., 342
Hartmann Corp., 322, 325
Haygart Corp., 79
Hocking Valley Ry. Co., 70, 71
Home Insurance Co., 79, 98
Hood Rubber Co., 322
Hornblower & Weeks, 342
Hudson Manhattan Rd. Co., 26, 103
Hurley & Co., 341
Hutton (E. F.) & Co., 342

Illinois Central Rd. Co., 26, 90, 328
Inland Steel Co., 23, 94, 348
Inspiration Consolidated Copper Co., 325
Insull Utility Investments, Inc., 91, 92, 93
Interborough Rapid Transit Co., 26, 73, 88
International Business Machines Corp., 325, 347
International Great Northern Ry. Co., 320
International Harvester Co., 22, 28, 104, 347

International Match Corp., 20, 89
International Mercantile Marine Co., 27, 103
International Nickel Co., 323
International Paper & Power Co., 23, 104, 321
International Paper Co., 27, 327, 348
International Shoe Co., 21, 27, 103
International Telephone & Telegraph Corp., 23, 104, 321, 348, 350
Iselin (A.) & Co., 341

Jewel Tea Co., 326
Johnson & Co., 100
Jones & Laughlin Steel Corp., 23, 86, 348
Josephthal & Co., 342

Kaiser Aluminum & Chem. Co., 347, 350
Kaiser Industries, 346, 348, 350
Kaiser Steel Co., 350
Kansas City, Mexico & Orient Ry. Co., 320, 323
Kansas City Southern Ry. Co., 25, 90
Kayser (Julius) & Co., 325
Keith-Albee-Orpheum Corp., 322
Kennecott Copper Corp., 23, 104, 320, 322, 348, 350
Kennedy Co., 341
Kidder, Peabody & Co., 341
Kimberly-Clark Corp., 349
Koppers Co., 21, 51, 86, 321
Kresge (S. S.) Co., 22, 103
Kuhn, Loeb & Co., 79

Lackawanna Steel Co., 320, 323
Laidlaw & Co., 342
Lee, Higginson & Co., 341
Lehigh & Wilkes-Barre Coal Co., 322
Lehigh Coal & Navigation Co., 323
Lehigh Valley Rd. Co., 26, 95
Libby, McNeill & Libby, 324
Liggett & Myers Tobacco Co., 21, 89
Lima Locomotive Works, 326

Lockheed Aircraft Corp., 348
Lodenberg, Thalman & Co., 98
Loew's, Inc., 20, 94
Logan & Bryan, 342
Lone Star Gas Corp., 24, 87
Long-Bell Lumber Corp., 22, 103
Lorillard (P.) Co., 21, 104
Louchheim, Minton & Co., 342
Lowell Co., 12

Mackay Cos., 321, 323
Macy (R. H.) & Co., 22, 87
Magnolia Petroleum Co., 320, 323
Maine Central Rd. Co., 325
Manhattan Electrical Supply Co., 281
Marathon Oil Co., Inc., 349
Marland Oil Co., 322; see Continental Oil Co.
Marshall Field & Co., 22, 87
Martin-Marietta Corp., 349
Massachusetts Co., 12
Massachusetts Gas Cos., 321
Mathieson Alkali Works, 326
Mergenthaler Linotype Co., 325
Merrimack Co., 12
Middlesex Co., 12
Middle West Utilities Co., 24, 92, 93, 96, 321
Midland United Co., 24, 96
Midvale Steel & Ordnance Co., 320, 323
Midwest Refining Co., 320, 323
Minneapolis & St. Louis Rd. Co., 324
Minnesota & Ontario Paper Co., 23, 86
Minnesota Mining & Mfg. Co., 349
Mission Corp., 350
Mission Development Co., 350
Missouri-Kansas-Texas Rd. Co., 23, 48, 98
Missouri Pacific Rd. Co., 70, 320, 321
Mohawk Hudson Power Corp., 321
Monsanto Chemical Co., 347
Montana Power Co., 321, 323
Montgomery Ward & Co., 22, 104, 322

Morgan (J. P.) & Co., 205, 214, 267
Morgan, Turner & Co., 100
Morris & Co., 320, 323
Motor Wheel Corp., 326
Mountain States Telephone & Telegraph Co., 31

National Biscuit Co., 21, 27, 104, 322
National Cash Register Co., 349
National City Bank, 159
National City Co., 159
National Dairy Products Co. (& Corp.), 21, 105, 348
National Distillers & Chem. Corp., 349
National Electric Power Co., 321
National Lead Co., 23, 103, 350
National Power & Light Co., 24, 92
National Public Service Corp., 321
National Steel Corp., 23, 86, 348
Newborg & Co., 342
New England Gas & Electric Assoc., 24, 86
New England Power Assoc., 321
New England Telephone & Telegraph Co., 31
New Orleans Public Service Co., 320
New York & Northern Rd. Co., 199–200, 213
New York Central Rd. Co., 13, 26, 95, 98, 127, 199–200, 213
New York, Chicago & St. Louis Rd. Co., 25, 70, 90, 101, 320
New York Investors, Inc., 90
New York, New Haven & Hartford Rd. Co., 26, 49, 95, 97, 115, 328
New York Railways Co., 324
Niagara Hudson Power Corp., 25, 92, 321
Norfolk & Western Ry. Co., 26, 49, 90
North American Aviation, Inc., 348
North American Co., 24, 92, 96, 153, 320
North American Light & Power Co., 24, 96
Northeastern Power Corp., 321
Northern Finance Corp., 341

Northern Pacific Ry. Co., 25, 48, 99, 102

Northwestern Pacific Ry. Co., 321, 323

Ohio Fuel Supply Co., 320

Ohio Oil Co., 20, 103

Olin Mathieson Chem. Corp., 348

Omnibus Corp., 324

Owens-Illinois Glass Co., 349

Pacific Gas & Elec. Co., 24, 92

Pacific Lighting Corp., 24, 92

Pacific Oil Co., 320

Pacific Petroleum Co., 320

Pacific Public Service Co., 322

Pacific Telephone & Telegraph Co., 31

Packard Motor Car Co., 323, 325

Paine, Webber & Co., 341

Pan American Petroleum & Transport Co., 320, 323

Paramount Publix Corp., 20, 27, 103

Penn-Ohio Edison Co., 321

Pennroad Corp., 73, 95, 97, 184

Pennsylvania Electric Co., 320

Pennsylvania Rd. Co., 18, 26, 47, 48, 52, 54, 55, 73, 78, 79, 80, 90, 91, 95, 97, 99, 102, 183, 328, 357

Pennsylvania Rd. Employees Provident & Loan Assoc., 79, 99

Peoples Gas, Light & Coke Co., 24, 92, 96

Pere Marquette Ry. Co., 70, 115, 321, 323

Petroleum Corp. of America, 94, 97

Phelps Dodge Corp., 23, 87, 349

Philadelphia & Reading Coal & Iron Corp., 21, 105

Philadelphia Electric Co., 321, 323

Philadelphia Rapid Transit Co., 26, 88

Phillips Petroleum Co., 20, 103, 347

Pierce (A. E.) & Co., 95

Pierce-Arrow Motor Car Co., 322

Pierce Oil Corp., 324

Pierce Petroleum Corp., 324

Pittsburgh Coal Co., 21, 103

Pittsburgh Plate Glass Co., 21, 103, 349

Prairie Oil & Gas Co., 20, 94

Prairie Pipe Line Co., 20, 97

Pressed Steel Car Co., 325

Procter & Gamble Co., 21, 103, 327, 348

Prudential Insurance Co., 233

Public Service Co. of Northern Illinois, 24, 93, 96

Public Service Corp. of New Jersey, 25, 96, 157, 158, 215

Public Utility Holding Co., 95

Puget Sound Power & Light Co., 321, 323

Pullman, Inc., 19, 27, 105, 203–204

Pure Oil Co., 20, 105, 349

Quaker Oats Co., 325

Radio Corp. of America, 20, 27, 96, 322, 348

Railway & Bus Associates, 24, 86

Reading Co., 25, 95, 257, 328

Reo Motor Car Co., 325

Republic Iron & Steel Co., 23, 103, 322

Republic Steel Corp., 348

Reynolds Metals Co., 348

Reynolds Spring Co., 326

Reynolds (R. J.) Tobacco Co., 21, 89, 348

Richfield Oil Co. of California, 20, 105, 347

Richfield Oil Corp., 350

Rock Island Rd., 234

Rubber Securities Corp., 85

Sagg-Harbor Wharf Co., 125

St. Louis-San Francisco Ry. Co., 26, 97, 99, 115

St. Louis Southwestern Ry. Co., 26, 90

St. Regis Paper Co., 349

San Joaquin Light & Power Co., 320

Schenley Industries, 349

Seaboard Air Line Ry. Co., 26, 87

Seagrams (U. S.), 349

Sears, Roebuck & Co., 22, 105

Shearson, Hammill & Co., 342

Shell Oil Co., 347

Shell Union Oil Corp., 20, 89

Shenandoah Corp., 128, 153

Shredded Wheat Co., 322

Simms Petroleum Co., 326

Sinclair Consolidated Oil Corp., 20, 102, 105

Sinclair Crude Oil Purchasing Co., 20, 102

Sinclair Oil Corp., 347, 350

Singer Manufacturing Co., 22, 27, 87, 349

Skelly Oil Co., 350

Socony Mobil Oil Co., 347

Solvay American Investment Corp., 85, 108

Solvay & Co. of Belgium, 85

Southeastern Power & Light Co., 320, 321

Southern California Edison Co., 24, 104

Southern Pacific Co., 26, 48, 99, 256–257

Southern Ry. Co., 26, 48, 99, 175

South Porto Rico Sugar Co., 325

Sperry Rand Corp., 348

Speyer & Co., 99

Spokane, Portland & Seattle Ry. Co., 25, 102

Spring Valley Water Co., 324

Standard Gas & Electric Co., 72, 193, 320

Standard Oil Co., 344

Standard Oil Co. of California, 20, 103, 320, 322, 347

Standard Oil Co. of Indiana, 6, 20, 75, 76–78, 94, 102, 320, 347

Standard Oil Co. of New Jersey, 20, 94, 200, 322, 327, 347

Standard Oil Co. of New York, 20, 94, 320

Standard Power & Light Corp., 320

Standard Sanitary Mfg. Co., 322

Steel & Tube Co. of America, 320, 323

Sterling Securities Corp., 79

Stewart-Warner Corp., 325

Stone & Webster, Inc., 24, 103

Studebaker Corp., 19, 22, 105, 322

Submarine Armour Co., 122

Suffolk Co., 12

Sun Life Assurance Co., 99, 100, 341

Sun Oil Co., 348

Sunray DX Oil Co., 349

Swift & Co., 21, 27, 105, 327, 349

Texaco, Inc., 347

Texas & Pacific Ry. Co., 321, 323

Texas Corp., 20, 105, 321

Texas Gulf Sulphur Co., 325

Texon Oil & Land Co., 322

Third Avenue Ry. Co., 27, 103

Tide Water Associated Oil Co., 20, 94

Tidewater Oil Co., 350

Toledo, St. Louis & Western Rd. Co., 320, 323

Travelers Insurance Co., 79

Tremont Co., 12

Tri-Utilities Corp., 24, 88

Trumbull Steel Co., 322

Union & United Tobacco Corp., 145

Union Bag & Paper Corp., 325, 327

Union Carbide & Carbon Corp., 21, 105

Union Carbide Corp., 347

Union Oil Associates, 20, 89

Union Oil of Calif., 348

Union Pacific Rd. Co., 26, 48, 90, 98, 99, 328

United Aircraft, 349

United Cigar Stores of America, see United Stores Corp.

United Corp., 91, 92, 93, 96, 100, 145, 147, 204

United Drug Co., 27

United Fruit Co., 21, 105, 327

United Gas Improvement Co., 25, 91, 93, 96, 321

United Light & Power Co., 25, 88, 321

United Rys. & Elec. Co. of Baltimore, 27, 103

United Rys. Investment Co., 320, 323

United Shoe Machinery Co., 22, 105, 327

United States Electric Power Corp., 25, 88

United States Leather Co., 324

United States Realty & Improvement Co., 26, 103

United States Rubber Co., 19, 26, 85, 94, 327, 348

United States Ship Building Co., 204

United States Smelting, Refining & Mining Co., 324, 325

United States Steel Corp., 18, 23, 47, 52, 54, 55, 80, 81, 100, 201, 205, 218, 289, 322, 327, 342, 344, 347, 357

United States Trust Co. of N. Y., 341

United Stores Corp., 22, 28, 89

Utah Copper Co., 320, 323

Utah Securities Corp., 320

Utilities Power & Light Corp., 25, 88

Vacuum Oil Co., 20, 94

Vaness Co., 70

Victor Talking Machine Co., 322

Virginia-Carolina Chemical Co., 324

Virginian Ry. Co., 26, 51, 86

Wabash Ry. Co., 26, 49, 91, 95

Ward Baking Corp., 174, 177

Warner Bros. Pictures, Inc., 20, 28, 103

Western Electric Co., 45, 347

Western Maryland Ry. Co., 25, 49, 91

Western Pacific Rd. Corp., 26, 91, 102

Western Power Corp., 320, 323

Western Union Telegraph Co., 23, 48, 100, 328

Westinghouse Air Brake Co., 325

Westinghouse Electric & Manufacturing Co., 22, 27, 96, 105

Westinghouse Electric Corp., 347

Weyerhaeuser Co., 349

Wheeling & Lake Erie Ry. Co., 25, 70, 101

Wheeling Steel Corp., 23, 103

White Eagle Oil & Refining Co., 325

Willys-Overland Co., 325

Wilson & Co., 21, 27, 105

Woolworth (F. W.) & Co., 22, 105

Worthington Pump & Machinery Corp., 325

Youngstown Sheet & Tube Co., 23, 82, 83, 105, 234, 320, 348

accounting
    control over, 182–183
    importance of, 271–274
active property, xxvi, 249–251, 304–305
Alabama, 127, 211, 214
amendments to charter, 130, 187–195
    power to amend, 235–238
appraisal, in market, 261–263, 275–277, 290
Arizona, 127

bankers' disclosure
    to a purchaser, 264–274
    to the market, 274–277
bankers' responsibility, 266–277
"blank" stock, 143, 167–169, 178
bondholders, position of, 245–246
bonds, convertible, 143, 180
    at the option of company, 143
brokers' circular, 264–268

California, 127
capital
    changed nature of, xxii, 45–46
    changes in, 190–191
    contributions, 123, 131
    effect of need for, 247
    legal meaning of, 149–150
    need for, 62
capital structure, 123
    power to change, 137–138

capitalism, xxxv–xxxviii, 310
    collective, viii–x
Catholic Church, 82, 310
certificate of incorporation, see charter
charter, 121–122, 129–131, 142, 169–170, 186–195, 235–238
    amendments, 130, 187–195
    changes in
        by corporate action, 188–191
        by direct legislation, 189
    early conception of, 187–188
    power to amend, 235–238
classified shares, 156
communism, xxxv, 245, 310
competition, 308
    change in character of, 45
concentration, ix, xxix–xxx, 14–16, 343–359
Connecticut, 126, 127
consolidation, 238
contract, corporate, 121–122, 129, 142, 169–170, 187–195
    rights, 186–195
        power to alter, 186–195
contributions of capital, 123, 131–132, 190–191
    changes in, 190–191
    equitable, 131–132
control, 6, 66–116, 207–218
    adverse interests of, 207–209
    as fiduciary, 212–213

control (Cont.)
  as management, 212–213
  definition of, 113–114
  democratic, 83
  interests of, 113–116
  joint, 83, 95–97, 102, 111
  legal position of, 207–218
  majority, 6, 67–68, 87, 358, 359
  management, 6, 78–84, 98–100, 104–105, 109, 358, 359
  manner of
    almost complete ownership, 67, 86
    legal device, 69–75, 88–89, 108, 109
    non-voting stock, 71–72
    pyramiding, 69–71
    vote-weighted stock, 72
    voting trust, 72–74
  methods of classification, 84–85, 108–109
  minority, 6, 75–78, 90–94, 103, 109, 358
  private, 67, 86, 358, 359
  separation from ownership, xxx, xxxv, 65–111, 358–359
  type in largest companies, 84–111
control fight, 76–78, 82
convertible bonds, 143, 180
  at option of company, 143
corner, 258, 260–261, 281
corporate
  contract, 121–122, 128, 142, 169–170, 187–188
  enterprise, 9, 306, 313
  entity, 120–121, 197–201, 286–287, 293
  income tax, xvi
  revolution, xxx–xxxv, 5, 64, 359
  system, viii, 9–10, 66
  wealth, 29
corporation
  close, ix
  disclosure by, 278–285
  finance, 8
  large
    growth of, 33–37

corporation, large (Cont.)
    probability of survival, 43–44
    relative growth, 35–40
    relative importance, 29–32
    significance of growth, 41–42
    type of control, 84–111
    ubiquitous character, 19, 27–29
    ways of growth, 42–44
  limits on activity, 122–124
  new concept of, 309–313
  quasi-public, 9
creditors, 143
cumulative preferred stock, 237
cumulative voting, 188
customer ownership, 56–58

deceit, 266–267
Delaware, 127, 134, 139, 155, 162, 165, 168, 193, 195, 229, 237
democratic control, 83
dilution, 142–163, 179–180
directors
  adverse interests of, 204–206
  as fiduciaries, 197–206
  dummy, 210–211
  interlocking, 204–205
  negligence of, 202–203
  obligations to stockholders, 198–202
  powers of, 126, 141–185
    automatic check on, 163
    limitation of, 146
  speculation by, 286–290
  stockholdings of, 80–81
disclosure
  by bankers, 265–277
  by corporations, 278–285
  failure to disclose, 282–283
discrimination between shareholders, 232
dispersion of ownership, 47–65, 359
dividends, power to declare, 135–136, 171–185, 230–232
dominant stockholder, doctrine of, 209
dummy directors, 210–211

earnings, power over, 171–185, 230–232
Eaton, Cyrus S., 82, 234
employee stock ownership, 58
enterprise
  corporate, 9–10, 306, 313
  private, 8–9, 306
entity, corporate, 120–121, 197–201, 286–287, 293
equitable contribution of capital, 131–132
exchanges, *see* markets

false representation, 266–267
Federal Communications Commission, xiii
Federal Reserve Bank, 290
Federal Trade Commission, 36, 37, 51, 353
feudal system, 8–9
fictitious market value, 152
fiduciaries, 230
  directors as, 197–206
fiduciary principle, 197–206, 225
flotation, 264, 277
Ford, Henry, 230

Georgia, 288
good faith, *see* fiduciary principle

"hidden reserves," 182
holding companies, 84–85, 183–185, 190, 345
Holmes, Justice O. W., 173

Illinois, 127, 222
incorporation laws, general, 126–128, 130
Indiana, 126
individual initiative, 306
industrial revolution, 5, 112
inflation, xxxii–xxxiii
information, 258–285
  on prices, 259–260
  required by law, 279–280
  sources of, 259–260
institutional economic revolution, xxv–xxvi

interests
  adverse, 204–208
  of control, 207–208
  of directors, 204–206
  of owners, 113–115
  ratable, 221–230
interim receipts, 264
interlocking directors, 204–205
Interstate Commerce Commission, 280
investment, opportunities for, 61–64
investment trusts, 159, 190, 284

joint control, 83, 95–97, 102, 111

Kansas, 288

lease, 238
legal control, 69–75, 88–89
legal device, 69–75, 88–89, 108, 358
legal position of
  control, 207–218
  management, 196–206
  stockholder, 244–252
liquidity, xxi, 249–251, 258–261, 263
listing requirements, 258
listing statement, 275
logic of
  profits, 299–302
  property, 293–298

Maine, 127
majority control, 6, 67–68, 87
management
  control, xvi–xix, 6, 78–84, 98–100, 104–105, 109
  defined, 112, 196
  in the market, 286–290
  legal position of, 196–206
  revolt, 76–78, 82
  rules of conduct, 197
  self-perpetuating, 82, 116
  stockholdings by, 50–53
manipulation, 261, 272
market value, fictitious, 152

markets
  dependence of stockholder on, 247–248
  free, 260–262, 275
  functions of, 248–263, 275–277
    appraisal, 261–263, 275–277
    liquidity, 249–251, 258–261, 263
    meeting place, 258–263
    "over the counter," 258
    private, 257–258
    public, 258–263
Maryland, 126, 127, 166
Massachusetts, 126, 127, 211, 214, 241, 279
mergers, xxx, 157–158, 238–242, 320–322, 344–345
Michigan, 188
minimum-wage legislation, xvi
minority, 108, 188
  control, 6, 75–78, 90–94, 103
misstatements, 281–282
Montana, 191
mutual funds, xx

National Electric Light Association, 56
National Industrial Conference Board, 32, 40, 58, 332
national wealth, 29
New Jersey, 126, 127, 138, 166, 194–195, 215, 228, 231, 237
New York, 126, 127, 146, 153, 155, 163, 166, 191, 209–210, 214, 287–289
New York Curb Exchange, 7, 29, 72, 258, 274, 280
New York Stock Exchange, 29, 51, 72, 145, 153–154, 256, 257, 258, 261–262, 274, 275, 280
  listing committee, 275
non-cumulative preferred stock, 172–175, 231–232
  dividends on, 172–174
non-disclosure, 282–283
non-par stock, 133, 145–146, 153, 156, 225, 229
non-voting stock, 71–72, 84, 130–131

open market, 275
  appraisal, 159, 261–262, 281
option warrants, 139, 143, 164–167, 179–182
ownership, 47–65, 78–80, 112–115
  beneficial, xv, 9
  by directors, 80–82
  changed character of, viii, 64–65
  customer, 56–58
  defined, 112–114
  dispersion of, 47–65, 78–82
  distribution by income groups, 59
  effect of taxes on, 58–59
  employee stock, 58
  interests of, 114–115
  passive character of, 64
  separated from control, xxx, xxxv, 65, 66–111, 358–359

paid-in surplus, 149–157, 158–160
panic, 260
par value shares, 143–145
parasitic stock, 147–149, 175–178
participations, 141–170
  changes in, 192–195
  diluted, 142–163, 179–180
  relative, 160, 187
  unascertained, 163–170
passive property, xxvi, 250–251, 304–305
Pennsylvania, 126, 127, 152, 240
pension trust funds, xx, xxiv
power
  economic, concentration of, 18–46
  of directors, 125–126, 141–185
    automatic check, 163
    limitation on, 146
  reserve power of state, 187
  to acquire stocks of other companies, 232–235
    limitation on, 233–235
  to amend charter, 235–238
  to declare dividends, 135–136, 171–185, 230–232
  to issue stock, 221–230
  to transfer corporate enterprise, 238–242

powers in trust, doctrine of, 219–243
pre-emptive right, 133–136, 142, 147, 160–163, 226–229
  deletion of, 160–163
preferred stock, 168, 172–175, 231–238
  cumulative, 237
  non-cumulative, 172–175, 231–232
  participating, 174–175
private
  control, 67, 86
  enterprise, 8–9, 306
  property, 219, 304–305
production, for use, 45
profit motive, 114–115, 307–308
profits, logic of, 299–302
property, xi–xvi
  active, xxvi, 249–251, 304–305
  law, xvi–xix
  logic of, 293–298
  passive, xix–xxv, xxvi, 250–251, 304–305
  private, 219, 304–305
  rights, 245
proxy, 76–82, 129, 186, 217
  committee, 76, 82
  duty of, 217
  fight, 76–78, 82
  machinery, 129, 186
public markets, see markets
publicity, 259–263, 279–280
  required by law, 279–280
  sources of, 259–260
purchase of own stock, 158–160
pyramiding, 69–71, 108, 183–201

quasi-public corporation, 5–8; see corporation

ratable interest, 221–230
Rathenau, Walther, 4, 309
Real Estate Exchange, 16
reclassification of stock, 138
representation, false, 266–267
rescission, 267, 270–274
reserve power of state, 187

responsibility, owners' lack of, 64, 250–251
revolt
  management, 76–78, 82
  stockholder, 82
revolution
  corporate, 5, 64, 359
  industrial, 5, 112
Rhode Island, 127
rights
  pre-emptive, 133–136, 142, 147, 160–163, 226–229
    deletion of, 160–163
  property, 245
  stockholders', 160, 172, 244–252
  voting, 129–131, 187
risk, changes in, 191–192
Rockefeller, John D., Jr., 76–78

sale of assets, 238
savings, destination of, 62–63
scope of enterprise, 187
  changes in, 190
Securities and Exchange Commission, vii
security markets, see markets
self-perpetuating management, 80, 82, 116
share of stock
  change in concept, 251–252
  position of, 141
short sales, 260–261
Smith, Adam, 303–308
social security funds, xxiv
sovereignty, 66
Soviet Union, xxiv, xxxv–xxxviii
speculation by directors, 286–290
stock
  dividends, 153, 178–179
  holdings, largest, 79–80
  issue of additional, 225–230
  issued for
    cash, 221–222
    property, 221–224
  non-par, 133, 145–146, 153, 156, 225, 229
  non-voting, 71–72, 84, 130–131

stock (Cont.)
  ownership, *see* ownership
  parasitic, 147–149, 175–178
  power of issue, 221–230
  preferred, 168–169, 172–175, 231–238
    cumulative, 237
    non-cumulative, 172–174, 231–232
    participating, 174–175
  purchase rights, 178–179
  purchase warrants, 139, 143, 164–167, 179–182
  reclassification of, 138
  vote-weighted, 72
stockholders
  as fiduciaries, 236
  dependence on markets, 247–248
  discrimination between, 232
  doctrine of dominant, 209–210
  increased number, xxiv, 53–58
  lack of responsibility, 64, 250–251
  number in largest companies, 47–52
  position of, 244–252
  power to vote, 80–82
  preferred, 155
  reason for, xxiii
  relative participations, 160, 187
  revolt by, 82
  rights of, xxvii, 160–161, 172, 244–252

stockholders, rights of (Cont.)
  voting, xix, 160
stockholdings by management, 50–53
surplus, paid-in, 149–157, 159

United States Supreme Court, xvii, xviii, 173, 188, 289
Utah, 191

Van Sweringens, 69–70
Virginia, 127
vote-weighted stock, 72
voting
  by proxy, 80, 82, 129
  cumulative, 188
  rights, 129–131, 187
    absence of, 71–72, 84, 130
  trusts, 72–73, 83, 213

warrants, stock purchase, 139, 143, 164–167, 179–182
wealth
  active, 306
  corporate, 29
  dependent on action of others, 65
  fluctuating value, 65
  liquid, 65, 248–249
  national, 29
  passive, 306
Wisconsin, 229

4760

NORMANDALE COMMUNITY COLLEGE
LIBRARY
9700 FRANCE AVENUE SOUTH
BLOOMINGTON, MN 55431-4399